Bibliographic Displays in the Online Catalog

by Walt Crawford

with Lennie Stovel

and Kathleen Bales

Knowledge Industry Publications, Inc.
White Plains, NY and London

Professional Librarian

Bibliographic Displays in the Online Catalog

Library of Congress Cataloging-in-Publication Data

Crawford, Walt.
    Bibliographic displays in the online catalog.

    (Professional librarian series)
    Bibliography: p.
    Includes index.
    1. Catalogs, On-line.   2. On-line bibliographic
searching.   3. Information display systems—Library
applications.   4. Information display systems—Formatting.
5. Machine-readable bibliographic data.   I. Stovel,
Lennie.   II. Bales, Kathleen.   III. Title.   IV. Series.
Z699.3.C69   1986   025.3′028′5   86-15348
ISBN 0-86729-198-2 (soft)

Printed in the United States of America

10   9   8   7   6   5   4   3   2   1

6/87

Table of Contents

List of Tables

Preface

This book presents the results of a study undertaken by The Research Libraries Group, Inc. (RLG) as a contribution to the library community. The study has its roots in two events: a project and a conference.

In 1984, the J. Paul Getty Trust funded a two-year RLG project with a number of aims. One portion of the overall project was the Patron Access Project. The goal of that project, as stated in one of the final reports from its first phase, was as follows:

> To develop a design for a workstation-based patron access system to work with an online catalog based on RLIN [Research Libraries Information Network] software. The project rests on several assumptions:
>
> - Online catalogs, and particularly patron access, are just beginning to undergo a long process of development, evaluation and improvement.
> - Scholars as information users, and research libraries as information providers, may have special needs that are not likely to be fully addressed by commercial online catalog development.
> - By the end of the decade, scholars will have access to powerful microcomputer-based workstations and can reasonably expect to have access to library catalogs through such workstations.
> - RLIN represents an unusually sophisticated database engine and retrieval methodology, proven in large-scale use, but it is not designed for direct use by scholars or other patrons.
> - RLG should focus on the access needs of scholars as part of its overall goal. Even if no online catalog based on RLIN software ever reaches full production in any library, the development effort should yield useful information and lead to improvements in other online catalogs.[1]

Walt Crawford served as investigator for Phase 1 of the Patron Access Project, studying the literature of online catalogs and public access and preparing an outline of issues for online catalogs. In 1985, Crawford attended the Conference on Online Catalog

Screen Displays, Lakeway Conference Center, Austin, TX, sponsored by the Council on Library Resources (CLR). He came away convinced that the library commmunity could benefit from large-scale tests of bibliographic display designs.

In order to test bibliographic display designs on a large scale, Crawford investigated the possibility of using RLG's large file of contemporary cataloging, which it maintains for use in batch processing. His investigation yielded the Bibliographic Display Testbed program (RBDISP), which was part of the Patron Access Project. The testbed program proved the feasibility of large-scale testing, furnishing a tool that RLG will use to serve its own development needs and those of its members. After the tool was developed, Crawford suggested that a useful project for the wider library community could result. That project would require collaborative effort from RLG's library systems analysts and would require a means of widespread distribution.

C. James Schmidt, executive vice president of RLG and director of RLIN, supported the project and possible commercial publication. With Schmidt's support and the support of other parties within RLG, two RLG library systems analysts were able to join the project. The team prepared a prospectus that was accepted by Knowledge Industry Publications, Inc. This book is the result of that effort.

Many people at RLG have been involved in some phase of this effort; the three names on the title page are those most closely involved. Walt Crawford wrote the programs and the associated documentation for the project, managed the large-scale test runs and wrote most of the text for this book. He provided some possibilities for display design, based on the Patron Access Project study. Lennie Stovel provided much of the display design, investigating different designs for the top and bottom of the screen, different label alternatives and different sets of data elements. Kathleen Bales worked with Stovel to prepare the final sets of data elements and labels and to refine the designs. Both Bales and Stovel reviewed the program design and suggested improvements, keeping the project moving forward and providing professional insight. The results are a true collaborative effort.

Many others were involved in one way or another: David Richards, director of research and development at RLG, selected Walt Crawford for the Patron Access Project; Glee Harrah Cady, assistant director for applications development, agreed to that choice, reviewed the manuscript and provided valuable insights throughout the project; Sarah How, Martha Girard and Susan Robillard of RLG also reviewed the manuscript and provided valuable suggestions, as did Karen Sirabian at Knowledge Industry Publications.

NOTE

1. Crawford, Walt. *Patron Access Project, Phase I; Report to Phase II: Development Issues.* Stanford, CA: The Research Libraries Group, Inc., 1985. (RLG Document Code 85-52) p. 3.

1

Introduction

Any online catalog requires hundreds of design decisions and raises hundreds of questions. Many of these decisions and questions revolve around the way bibliographic records are displayed.

How should bibliographic records be displayed? How many different displays should an online catalog provide? As libraries convert from card catalogs to online catalogs as the primary or only source of bibliographic information, the questions become more crucial and the answers must become more refined. Future online catalog designs should benefit from the successes and failures of the past and present, and such designs should be able to build on a growing body of research into online catalog design. This book is one contribution to that body of research, focusing on the questions above.

Libraries have special needs, and no single display can be equally suitable for all libraries. Libraries may also require differing numbers of displays, depending on local needs and the nature of the collection. Every existing online catalog and circulation system pretending to be an online catalog represents somebody's answer to the two questions above, and almost every online catalog represents different answers. This book offers a number of possibilities, with no attempt at conclusive preferences.

A third question for online displays has rarely been addressed—how often will a design force patrons to view more than one screen to see a complete record? The question is significant because information makes more sense when it can be dealt with at a single glance. A patron can deal with bibliographic and holdings information more rapidly and effectively when the information appears on a single screen than when it is split over two or more screens. Some patrons also may not view additional screens, making the information effectively useless.

The question of single-screen display is important, but it has to date been largely unanswerable. Few libraries or vendors can mount large-scale controlled experiments focusing on particular details of catalog design. Any attempt to answer the question by using an actual online catalog would either be impractical or anecdotal (calling up a few dozen records and seeing how many records go to a second or third screen). If a library attempts to compare different display designs within a real online catalog, patrons will (quite reasonably) become annoyed with contextual shifts as different experiments begin and end.

This book provides some answers to the question of single-screen display, based on large-scale controlled experiments using current bibliographic data. The Research Libraries Group, Inc. (RLG) offers these answers as one of its contributions to the body of knowledge needed to develop better online public access catalogs.

DESIGNING BIBLIOGRAPHIC DISPLAYS

Most online public access catalogs offer flexible display designs, making the librarians partners in the design process. Throughout this discussion, *designer* means *librarian or other professional with a role in the design process.* In practice, design decisions usually involve some combination of systems analysts, librarians and others.

When designing bibliographic displays for an online catalog, a designer must decide the following:

- what fields and subfields to include in each display
- how to arrange and group those fields displayed
- whether to use labeled or cardlike displays
- what labels to use (if any), where to put the labels and where to put fields in relation to labels
- what techniques to use to improve legibility, such as blank lines or narrower text areas
- how many different displays to provide
- what other information to put on the screen, and where to put it

Design does not take place in a vacuum. A librarian must consider the characteristics of the collection, intended uses and users, and the ways in which a library and its catalog relate to other libraries and catalogs in the area. This book deals only with limited aspects of display design. Many other issues are discussed in the related book *Patron Access: Issues for Online Catalogs,* to be published in early 1987 by Knowledge Industry Publications, Inc.[1]

Five major questions appear to determine the success of a particular display:

1. Does the display provide an appropriate amount of information?
2. Will patrons understand the information as it is displayed?
3. Is the display readable and attractive?

4. Will patrons be able to find information rapidly and to find all the information needed?
5. Will patrons be able to view the information on a single screen?

Most work to date has focused on the first question and, to a lesser extent, on the second. Some writers have attempted to deal with the third and fourth questions, but little or no work has been done on the final question.

Figure 1.1 shows the bibliographic record for a book, using a fairly complete labeled display. Figure 1.2 shows the same bibliographic record, using a cardlike display. The labeled display appears superior to the cardlike display. Spacing makes the information easier to read and labeling makes it more understandable. A first reaction would be that the labeled display definitely should be chosen over the cardlike display.

But libraries have more than simple book records in their catalogs. Figures 1.3 and 1.4 show information for a sound recording, using the same labeled display as the one in Figure 1.1. Figures 1.5 and 1.6 show the same bibliographic information using the cardlike display from Figure 1.2. The labeled display is still more open and each item is easier to identify, but it takes significantly more space than the cardlike display. While the cardlike display leaves room for up to 10 lines of holdings and other information on the second screen, the labeled display has only 5 lines available. Still, most analysts would probably prefer the labeled display.

In both cases, the displays use the same number of screens for a given record. A sample of 20, 50, or 100 records picked at random might show the same pattern. Few real tests would involve more than 100 records called up one at a time at a terminal. Such tests could conclude that the cardlike and labeled displays are equally effective in displaying records on a single screen.

The anecdotal evidence is wrong; the records used in the above example do not represent a typical collection. A sample of 14,000 current cataloging records shows significant differences. If we agree that minimal holdings require three lines (a spacing line, labels, and one line of location, call number and status), 30% of the records require a second screen using the cardlike display and 84% require a second screen when using the labeled display. Putting it another way: for items with one copy, more than two thirds can be viewed as a whole on a single cardlike display while only one sixth can be viewed as a whole on a single labeled display. This is a major difference and one that might sway a design decision.

Those numbers show the wide variation in space requirements brought about by a change in display. The labeled display puts most fields on new lines and adds blank lines to improve legibility. Even though both displays use no more than 60 characters of bibliographic text per line, the labeled display requires a substantially higher percentage of split records, when tested on a large sample.

The two displays shown in Figures 1.1 through 1.6 represent two possibilities out of hundreds. If labeling makes sense, several changes in the display used here could reduce the number of second screens needed—for example, eliminating LCCN and ISBN and eliminating some or all of the blank lines. Large-scale test runs can show the effects of each change on screen usage; sample screens will show the effects on legibility and usefulness.

TESTING BIBLIOGRAPHIC DISPLAYS

Large-scale testing of display designs requires a way to generate displays efficiently and to keep track of those displays, and a large database of records suitable for display. Such testing need not be done online, but valid tests require quite large samples. Bibliographic records aren't homogeneous, and a sample of 1000 records for monographs will say little about overall requirements for books or other materials.

RLG developed a computer program to test bibliographic displays on a large scale. That program is described below.

The RLG Bibliographic Display Testbed Program (RBDISP)

The RLG Bibliographic Display Testbed program (RBDISP) was developed to provide a way to generate displays and to produce statistics based on those displays. The program has its basis in RLG's RLIN Reports System (RRS), a generalized set of bibliographic listing programs.

To use the program, a designer creates a control file containing commands to RBDISP. Commands govern the screen layout and the extent, sequence and appearance of bibliographic data on the screen. The designer may control such variables as the contents of the top and bottom of the screen, what portion of the screen is used for bibliographic data, whether there are labels, whether labels are right or left justified, and whether ISBD punctuation is suppressed at the ends of subfields and fields. Additional controls specify actual USMARC fields and subfields to be included and labels to be used.

The program runs against a set of bibliographic records in the Research Libraries Information Network MARC format, RLIN MARC. Three types of input files were used to prepare this book. The largest of the three is the RLIN Monthly Process File. RLIN is an online technical processing system that uses batch procedures to generate products. Those batch procedures involve a file called the Monthly Process File, which contains all RLIN records added or updated using the online RLIN system during the most recent six weeks.

The Monthly Process File covers all material formats (books, serials, maps, scores, sound recordings, machine-readable data files, visual materials, and archival and manuscript control), and generally contains between 700,000 and 900,000 records. This total includes records stored in order to produce printed reports as well as acquisitions records for items not yet received or fully cataloged, and it also includes duplicates, since a record appears once for each day it has been modified. After eliminating acquisitions information, duplicates and records stored to produce reports, the Monthly Process File typically contains between 350,000 and 500,000 cataloged records.

For smaller-scale tests, RBDISP can be run against one day of RLIN input, typically between 19,000 and 25,000 records. For this study, single-day runs were used to refine display designs, and they served to provide sample screens and rough estimates of space requirements.

RBDISP was also run against a specially created file of RLIN MARC records in order to produce the figures in Chapters 2 through 8.

Regardless of the type of input file, a designer can specify simple criteria to select records from the input file for a given test run. The criteria are (1) type of process (so that acquisitions records can be ignored, if desired); and (2) type of material format (so that, for example, a test can be limited to scores and sound recordings only).

RBDISP generates screen images 80 columns wide and 24 lines deep using the display options specified by a control file. The program uses a crude form of widow control—if a field begins within the last two lines of one screen, but does not end on that screen, the field will be moved in its entirety to the next screen.*

The program prints sample screens based on percentage parameters provided for each run. Separate parameters control printing for records that fit on one screen, records that require exactly two, records that require exactly three and records that require four or more screens. All percentages are applied at the beginning of 10,000-record segments. A sampling percentage of .15% for single-screen records will print the first 15 of each 10,000 records that fit on a single screen.

Sampling percentages affect only the number of records printed. RBDISP generates display simulations for all selected records, including proper line breaks and screen breaks, in order to prepare a statistical summary report. This report includes the following information:

- Number of records processed (selected according to criteria of processing type and material format).
- Number and percentage that fit on a single screen with three lines left (for minimal holdings).
- Number and percentage that fit on one screen, without regard to space for holdings.
- For 2 to 10 screens, number and percentage that require that many screens, and a cumulative percentage showing records that fit on that many screens or less.
- Average number of screens per record.
- Overall local density (discussed below).

*The widowing limit is also adjustable, but the default of two lines is used throughout this book.

- Overall global density (discussed below).
- Space available for holdings on the first screen, by lines: that is, for line counts from three to the highest number available, the number and percentage of records with at least that many blank lines left for holdings on the first screen. The number with at least three unused display lines is always the same as the number that fit on one screen with room for minimal holdings.
- Percentage of records within given local density ranges, e.g., 27.98% of records are between 10% and 20% local density.
- The same percentage for global density ranges.

Density is defined as *the percentage of nonblank positions within the display.* A screen image has 24 times 80, or 1920, character positions. If that screen contains 192 characters of text, the display has a 10% density. RBDISP uses a slightly modified definition of density, based on our conviction that single spaces between words constitute information rather than white space, and should be counted as characters. The program tests each position on the screen and looks at the position to the right. If a character appears in a given position *or in the next position,* the position is considered nonblank. (A blank in column 80 is considered white space.)

This modified definition may overstate actual density by as much as 1.25%, since the last blank space in a left-hand margin is considered nonblank. We do not consider that overstatement serious. A more serious overstatement appears in the global density percentages for most test runs, because we found it desirable to separate sections of the screens by rows of dashes rather than by simple blank lines. Those rows of dashes count as characters, thus adding 160 characters, or 8.3%, to every screen.

If readers consider spacing lines to be equivalent to blank space in terms of openness and legibility, then all *global density* figures in this book should be reduced by 8.3%. *Global density* is the density of text within the full screen. *Local density* is the density within that portion of the screen defined for bibliographic display, excluding the lines of dashes and the top and bottom portions of the screen. We came to regard local density as more significant than global density, since patrons quickly tune out the top and bottom of the screen, except when they need information from those portions.

The Definition of Medium Displays

Chapters 2, 3, 4 and 7 use a single definition for fields to be displayed: a medium display level. That display level includes the standard bibliographic description and all access points (not including traced series that do not create notes).

Table 1.1 lists the MARC tags included in the medium level, with brief names. All subfields were used except for numeric subfields and a nonprinting subfield "u" in some entries. Added entries that do not normally appear on printed cards do not appear in these tests.

The related book, *Patron Access: Issues for Online Catalogs,* discusses the pros and cons of including edition, series, place of publication and material description. In

Table 1.1: Fields Included in Medium Displays

```
100-130     Main Entry
245         Title Statement
250         Edition Statement
260-262     Publication, distribution, etc.
300-305     Physical Description
400-490     Series Statements
600-699     Subjects
700-799     Added entries
```

developing a medium-level definition, the authors felt that all access points needed to be included, but also felt that the description should be adequate for most user needs. After some thought and experimentation, the medium level was defined.

We do not assert that this level is ideal, but it does make a good basis for comparison. Other sets of fields appear in Chapters 5, 6 and 8. Early experiments demonstrated that the medium level is a good place to do comparisons, because it shows the most dramatic changes among displays. Almost any display will fit very brief information on a single screen, but very brief information does not seem suitable except to head extensive holdings displays. The need for subject entries has been well documented, and joint authors (and other added entries) surely deserve equal treatment.

Early in the study, we considered the possibility of omitting the statement of responsibility (the $c subfield of field 245) from some or all displays. While statements of responsibility frequently replicate the main entry, adding no information, that is not always the case. For example, presence of illustrators (particularly significant in children's books) isn't always clear without the statement of responsibility. After examining several hundred cases, we determined that medium displays should include all subfields of the title field. The redundant information in most records is less significant than the important information in some records. All three authors feel that, when faced with losing valuable information in order to leave out apparently useless information, the choice should always favor retaining valuable information.

Early Display Tests

An RBDISP test run involves some set of display controls applied against some set of RLIN MARC records. Early work leading to this book involved hundreds of test runs, most of them involving only one day's activity on RLIN (19,000 to 25,000 records). Several dozen early test runs did test the entire Monthly Process File. Early test runs began in November 1985 and ran through December 1985. The authors were testing different arrangements for the top and bottom of a display, different labels for elements and different sets of data, and they were finding remaining defects in RBDISP itself. One major defect—the lack of continuation text for screens other than the first—was not corrected.

Those early runs made several points clear:

- Brief displays can be designed, either labeled or cardlike, to provide basic bibliographic information and leave at least seven lines for holdings information, in at least 90% of records.
- Medium-level displays, with no notes or control numbers, can be designed in labeled or cardlike form, with 90% of records having room on the first screen for minimal holdings, i.e., three lines.
- Complete cardlike displays can include minimal holdings on the first screen in most cases, but complete labeled displays will generally require at least two screens for bibliographic data and minimal holdings.

Early results strongly suggested the need for three levels of single-record display in most systems: (1) a brief bibliographic display to appear with extended holdings information; (2) a medium or standard display expected to fit on one screen at least 9 times out of 10; and (3) a long or complete display that would not be expected to fit on one screen.

We believe that most online catalogs should also include a full MARC tagged display, with visible indicators and subfields, to serve the needs of library staff and a very small percentage of patrons.

Early and later displays were also conditioned by the results of large-scale measurements—shown in Appendix A—of how frequently fields appear. When considering specific fields to be excluded from a given display (in order to make records fit on a single screen), it makes sense to focus on fields that occur frequently.

For all material formats combined, the measurements show that some four dozen fields, identified in Appendix A, require special attention. Other fields occur in 1% of records or less. For any such fields, logic suggests that the fields should be included if they make sense in terms of overall inclusiveness. For example, if a display includes title series statements, then personal name series statements should also be included, even though the statements are quite rare. Rare fields appear in records for specific reasons and since their inclusion in a display will have little effect on overall screen requirements, any close decision should favor inclusion.

Display Tests Represented in This Book

We studied the results of early tests and established a common top and bottom for later tests. We also established a standard set of data elements for medium or standard displays, feeling that medium displays represent the most important (and most difficult) level. Some early displays were refined, and later displays designed, to answer a number of specific questions:

- What should the overall screen look like, and how does use of white space affect legibility and space requirements? Chapter 2 addresses some of those issues, as do later chapters.
- How well will cardlike displays work, and what will seemingly minor variations do

to legibility and space? Chapter 3 discusses and illustrates eight cardlike displays, all for the same medium-level set of data elements.

- How should labeled displays be arranged, and what labels should be used? Chapter 4 discusses and illustrates 12 displays, all using the same medium-level set of data elements; it also shows some alternative labels tested during the project. Chapter 4 continues the attempt, begun in Chapter 3, to show how important small changes are; with few exceptions, each display differs from the preceding display in one, and only one, option.
- How would sets of data elements suggested in library literature work? Chapter 5 discusses and illustrates three cardlike and three labeled displays based on element lists suggested in the literature. The chapter also illustrates two displays based on a simple set of elements developed from the literature, and three displays that label part, but not all, of the data elements.
- While medium-level displays may be most important, most online catalogs also need brief and long displays. Chapter 6 includes a suggested set of data elements for brief displays, along with three display designs using that set. The chapter also includes a suggested set of data elements for long displays and three display designs using that set.
- Nonbook materials may pose display problems different from those of books. Chapter 7 provides more illustrations of mixed formats, using two medium-level displays and two long displays introduced in earlier chapters. Chapter 7 also discusses ISBD punctuation, illustrating two displays that normalize ISBD punctuation.
- Each library may have different needs and draw different conclusions. Each of the three authors considered his or her own preferences, and prepared one or two displays based on those preferences. Chapter 8 illustrates four of those display designs.

All test runs for this book use actual RLIN records as entered and modified by RLG members and RLIN users. Based on sample screens during test runs, a set of 20 records was selected to represent the various material formats. Those records, used for all screen displays in Chapters 2 through 8, have had cataloging errors corrected, but have not been made to conform to current rules. The set is not statistically representative, but does show a mixture of long and short records and a mixture of the various material formats—books, serials, maps, scores, sound recordings, machine-readable data files, visual materials, and archival and manuscript control records. The records were selected to show the appearance of specific fields (for example, a title main entry or an author/title added entry), but they do not show all possible fields. Some of the items represented are current and widely held; others are more obscure. Any online catalog will contain such a mixture and, therefore, any display design must allow for wide variations.

Public Library Cataloging

With between 350,000 and 500,000 records representing current work (new cataloging and retrospective conversion), the Monthly Process File certainly represents a valid sample for research libraries. But does it fairly represent public library cataloging? Some observers would suggest that public library cataloging tends to be simpler than research library cataloging, if only because of the mix of materials cataloged by public libraries.

While RLG is a consortium of research libraries, RLIN does serve quite a few public libraries of all sizes. We established a list of public libraries (excluding the New York Public Research Libraries) using RLIN, and extracted those records from the Monthly Process File. A table of field occurrence and length for public library records appears in Appendix A. As those tables show, public library records are, on average, about 15% shorter than all RLIN records—a significant but not overwhelming difference. The difference was significant enough, however, to encourage us to do two sets of statistical runs, both of which are reflected throughout this book.

Archival and Manuscript Control (AMC) records differ sharply from other records and are less likely to be an integral part of most online catalogs. AMC records may represent large collections of material or single manuscripts. Records for collections may have more than 200 entries and subject headings. Within RLIN, such records average almost 50% larger than other bibliographic records; that extra length shows up distinctly in most display tests. RLIN pioneered use of the AMC format and may have a disproportionate level of AMC records compared with most libraries. Figures 1.7 through 1.9 show an average-length AMC record. In a test run using a long labeled display, half the AMC records took more than two screens to display. Since we felt that AMC records could distort the statistical results, we chose to exclude them from the large-scale test runs. We did run separate tests for AMC records, however; these are illustrated in Chapter 8, and statistical results are given for them in Appendix A.

Limitations and Conditions

No single research project can hope to address all the problems of patron access systems; refinement of these systems will occur over the course of several different research projects. This project was limited in scope, and deliberately excludes some aspects of display testing.

Test runs do not involve actual searches. The search feedback provided in the top portion of each screen is purely an attempt to make the screens somewhat realistic. Neither the search syntax shown nor the constant single-record result should be considered meaningful. The search argument shown repeats the first 18 characters from the first line of the display, with no attempt to create a more realistic search.

Holdings present different display problems for different libraries—problems ranging from few locations and many copies of each title to many locations and different call numbers for the same item, but relatively few copies of each item. We assumed in RBDISP that any display will require at least three lines for holdings. We made no attempt to simulate actual holdings display or to include call numbers within the display. The statistical results for each display show room available for holdings, and they can be used to help evaluate possible bibliographic displays for use with extensive holdings screens.

The project did not attempt to simulate multiple-item displays. Although these displays pose similar design questions, we could not find a satisfactory way to produce meaningful statistical results for such displays because the number of screens required to show a result depends not only on the bibliographic format but also on the average result size.

None of the displays use any form of highlighting except capitalization. Highlighting would not affect the statistical results but could make some display formats look better or worse. We did not try to simulate such effects as reverse video and varied intensities because we did not feel that they would be meaningful in print.

We designed our screens so that they resemble VDT screens as much as possible, but there are certain differences. For example, black ink on white paper does not look the same as green or amber phosphor on a dark background. The character set used in all figures is that used for RLG documentation. While it is a relatively simple character set, it is more detailed than most character sets used for video display terminals, and the characters are substantially smaller than characters on a screen. Finally, the black line surrounding each figure represents a much sharper boundary than a typical video screen, since most such screens surround the 80-by-24 character area with additional dark space.

This study involves a narrow range of possibilities. Special libraries have special needs and, therefore, each library must consider its own collection and its own users when designing a bibliographic display. The tables in Appendix A show field occurrence and display results for each specific material format and should help librarians to use their own professional judgment in designing displays.

ORGANIZATION

The chapters that follow discuss various issues we considered in designing and testing displays, and show some results of those designs. This book consists primarily of sample screens and statistics, and each chapter begins with a brief introduction to the screens that follow.

Chapters 2 through 6 and Chapter 8 use a set of eight sample records for all sample screens. Those displays that illustrate decisions but that we do not consider plausible alternatives for online catalogs usually show two records; the same two records are used for all such displays within a given chapter. Other displays—designs that might be appropriate for online catalogs—are illustrated using all eight sample records, although in some cases the illustrations are split between two chapters. Each of these chapters contains three statistical tables that show the results of large-scale test runs, each run involving between 395,000 and 405,000 records (for all RLIN libraries) or, for public library figures, a constant set of 34,941 records.

Chapter 7 discusses special problems: ISBD punctuation and problems with nonbook formats. The remaining 12 selected test records appear in Chapter 7, illustrating some additional issues. This chapter does not contain any statistical tables.

Appendix A consists almost entirely of two types of tables. The first type shows occurrence and average length for each variably occurring MARC field within the tested files. The second type summarizes the results of all tested displays. The two types of tables appear for all records, for the public library subset, and for each material format except books, because more than 83% of all records are books. Note that the occurrence and average-length tables are based on large samples and can be compared to other studies of MARC field occurrence and length.

Appendix B consists of tagged MARC displays for the 20 records used in Chapters 2 through 8. All bibliographic and control number fields appear, but fields not used in any displays have been omitted from Appendix B.

FURTHER INFORMATION ABOUT THE DISPLAY TESTBED PROGRAM

The RBDISP program may be made available for libraries and other agencies that do not use RLIN but wish to test display designs. The service will be provided for a charge; terms will depend on interest, demand and availability of the staff and computer resources required to prepare and perform the tests. If your library or other agency wishes to test a display using the Display Testbed facility, please contact Walt Crawford at The Research Libraries Group, Inc., Jordan Quadrangle, Stanford, CA 94305.

NOTE

1. Crawford, Walt. *Patron Access: Issues for Online Catalogs.* Forthcoming.

Figure 1.1

```
Search: Dalton, David#
Result: 1 record                    LONG record display -    Screen  1 of  1
------------------------------------------------------------------------------

           AUTHOR(S): Dalton, David.

              TITLE: James Dean, the mutant king; a biography.
   PUBLICATION INFO: [New York, Dell, [1975, c1974]
        DESCRIPTION: 396 p. illus. 18 cm.

           SUBJECTS: Dean, James, 1931-1955.

              NOTES: Bibliography: p. 381-389.
                     ISBN 0-87932-076-1.
                     LCCN: 74-76600




------------------------------------------------------------------------------
Possible NEXT ACTIONs: H for help              + to see the next screen
                       F to see the full record  - to see the previous screen
                       S to begin a new search    D if you are done
            NEXT ACTION?  _                                      EXPER1
```

Figure 1.2

```
Search: Dalton, David#
Result: 1 record                    LONG record display -    Screen  1 of  1
------------------------------------------------------------------------------

       Dalton, David.
         James Dean, the mutant king; a biography. [New York, Dell,
       [1975, c1974]
         396 p. illus. 18 cm.
         Bibliography: p. 381-389.
         ISBN 0-87932-076-1.
         1. Dean, James, 1931-1955.
       LCCN: 74-76600




------------------------------------------------------------------------------
Possible NEXT ACTIONs: H for help              + to see the next screen
                       F to see the full record  - to see the previous screen
                       S to begin a new search    D if you are done
            NEXT ACTION?  _                                      LONCRD1
```

Figure 1.3

```
Search: Rachmaninoff, Ser#
Result: 1 record                    LONG record display -   Screen  1 of  2
-----------------------------------------------------------------------------

          AUTHOR(S): Rachmaninoff, Sergei, 1873-1943.
                     Stokowski, Leopold, 1882-1977.
                     National Philharmonic Orchestra (Great Britain)

              TITLE: [Symphonies, no. 3, op. 44, A minor]
                     Symphony no. 3 in A minor, op. 44; Vocalise, op. 34, no.
                       14 [sound recording], Sergei Rachmaninoff.
  PUBLICATION INFO: New York, N.Y.: Desmar, p1975.
        DESCRIPTION: 1 sound disc: 33 1/3 rpm, stereo.; 12 in.

           SUBJECTS: Symphonies. ** Orchestral music, Arranged.

              NOTES: Desmar : DSM 1007 G.
                     The 2nd work originally for voice and piano.

---------------------------------------------------------------CONTINUED-------
Possible NEXT ACTIONs: H for help              + to see the next screen
                       F to see the full record  - to see the previous screen
                       S to begin a new search  D if you are done
           NEXT ACTION?  _                                         EXPER1
```

Figure 1.4

```
Search: Rachmaninoff, Ser#
Result: 1 record                    LONG record display -   Screen  2 of  2
-----------------------------------------------------------------------------

                     National Philharmonic Orchestra ; Leopold Stokowski,
                       conductor.
                     Recorded May 1975.
                     Durations: 38:42 ; 6:55.
                     Program notes by Francis Crociata and Anthony Hodgson on
                       container.
                     LCCN: 76-762611/R

       OTHER ENTRIES: Rachmaninoff, Sergei, 1873-1943. Romansy, op. 34.
                      Vocalise; arr. 1975.



-----------------------------------------------------------------------------
Possible NEXT ACTIONs: H for help              + to see the next screen
                       F to see the full record  - to see the previous screen
                       S to begin a new search  D if you are done
           NEXT ACTION?  _                                         EXPER1
```

Figure 1.5

```
Search: Rachmaninoff, Ser#
Result: 1 record                    LONG record display -   Screen  1 of  2
--------------------------------------------------------------------------------

        Rachmaninoff, Sergei, 1873-1943.
          [Symphonies, no. 3, op. 44, A minor]
          Symphony no. 3 in A minor, op. 44; Vocalise, op. 34, no. 14
        [sound recording], Sergei Rachmaninoff. -- New York, N.Y.:
        Desmar, p1975.
          1 sound disc: 33 1/3 rpm, stereo.; 12 in.
          Desmar : DSM 1007 G.
          The 2nd work originally for voice and piano.
          National Philharmonic Orchestra ; Leopold Stokowski, conductor.
          Recorded May 1975.
          Durations: 38:42 ; 6:55.
          Program notes by Francis Crociata and Anthony Hodgson on
        container.


-----------------------------------------------------------CONTINUED-------

Possible NEXT ACTIONs: H for help            + to see the next screen
                       F to see the full record   - to see the previous screen
                       S to begin a new search    D if you are done

           NEXT ACTION?   _                             LONCRD1
```

Figure 1.6

```
Search: Rachmaninoff, Ser#
Result: 1 record                    LONG record display -   Screen  2 of  2
--------------------------------------------------------------------------------

          1. Symphonies. 2. Orchestral music, Arranged. I. Stokowski,
        Leopold, 1882-1977. II. Rachmaninoff, Sergei, 1873-1943. Romansy,
        op. 34. Vocalise; arr. 1975. III. National Philharmonic Orchestra
        (Great Britain) IV. Desmar : DSM 1007 G.
        LCCN: 76-762611/R







-----------------------------------------------------------------------------

Possible NEXT ACTIONs: H for help            + to see the next screen
                       F to see the full record   - to see the previous screen
                       S to begin a new search    D if you are done

           NEXT ACTION?   _                             LONCRD1
```

Figure 1.7

```
Search: William, of Conch#
Result: 1 record                    LONG record display -   Screen  1 of  3
----------------------------------------------------------------------------

            AUTHOR(S): William, of Conches, 1080-ca. 1150.
                       Plantagenet, Geoffrey.
                       Henry, II, King of England, 1133-1189.

                TITLE: Dragmaticon.
     PUBLICATION INFO: [Italy, later 15th cent.]
          DESCRIPTION: 1 v. (89 leaves); 21 cm.

             SUBJECTS: William, of Conches, 1080-ca. 1150. ** Cosmology--France--
                       12th century. ** Medicine--15th-18th centuries. **
                       Science--History. ** 15th century--Italy. ** Codices. **
                       Paleography. ** Medieval and Renaissance studies--
                       Italy--15th century. ** Science, technology, and
                       industry--15th century.

------------------------------------------------------------CONTINUED------
Possible NEXT ACTIONs: H for help              + to see the next screen
                       F to see the full record  - to see the previous screen
                       S to begin a new search  D if you are done
          NEXT ACTION?  _                                        EXPER1
```

Figure 1.8

```
Search: William, of Conch#
Result: 1 record                    LONG record display -   Screen  2 of  3
----------------------------------------------------------------------------

            NOTES: William studied in Chartres under leading Aristotelians
                   and was closely connected with St. Bernards' brother,
                   Thierry de Chartres.  After teaching at Chartres for 20
                   years he became tutor in the household of Geoffrey
                   Plantagenet, Duke of Normandy.  The Dragmaticon is
                   dedicated to the Duke and written, in part, to instruct
                   his son Henry, the future King Henry II of England.
          Summary: The Dragmaticon is Williams' revision, made ca.
                   1144-50, of his most important work, De Philosophia
                   Mundi.  Written in dramatic dialogue form, the
                   Dragmaticon touches on all aspects of "The science of
                   the world," i.e. astronomy, geography, meteorology and
                   medicine.  Further, it attempts to reconcile
                   discrepencies between church doctrine and scientific
                   observation.
------------------------------------------------------------CONTINUED------
Possible NEXT ACTIONs: H for help              + to see the next screen
                       F to see the full record  - to see the previous screen
                       S to begin a new search  D if you are done
          NEXT ACTION?  _                                        EXPER1
```

Figure 1.9

```
Search: William, of Conch#
Result: 1 record                         LONG record display -   Screen  3 of  3
-----------------------------------------------------------------------------
                   In Latin, humanistic script which imitates a 12th century
                      hand.
                   Gift of the Associates of Stanford University Libraries,
                      1983.
                   Reported to: Bibliotheque Nationale pre-1600 manuscript
                      census.
                   24 colored drawings and diagrams.




-----------------------------------------------------------------------------
Possible NEXT ACTIONs: H for help          + to see the next screen
                       F to see the full record  - to see the previous screen
                       S to begin a new search   D if you are done
          NEXT ACTION?  _                                        EXPER1
```

2

Overall Screen Design

Patrons can read and comprehend sparse screens (screens with low information density) more rapidly than dense screens. A record displayed on a single screen can be understood more easily than a record split over multiple screens. People don't read very wide lines of text as readily as narrower lines, and spacing helps to clarify information.

All these statements are based on common sense and experience with various online systems. Unfortunately, the statements conflict. For the same amount of information, a record displayed on one screen may have wider lines and will produce a denser screen than the same record split over two screens.

SCREEN CONTEXT: THE TOP AND THE BOTTOM

This project focuses on bibliographic displays, but all displays exist within a context. That context consists of some amount of information that is not part of the bibliographic record and necessarily takes up space that could otherwise be used for bibliographic information.

Existing online systems use as little as 1 or as much as 10 lines of the display to provide a context. Many systems are inadequate for the user because they do not provide any sense of where to go next, once the user has reached a display. Other systems fail by not clarifying how the user got to a certain display.

Early experiments in this project included many different versions of the overall screen. We all found that we much preferred to show context with a three-part screen. The top should show where you are and how you got there; the bottom should show where you can go. Early experiments tested different sizes for the three sections, different ways of separating the sections and different wording for each section.

19

After dozens of different tests, we arrived at the general screen format illustrated in Figure 2.1—two lines at the top and four lines at the bottom, with solid lines of dashes and blank lines separating the top and bottom from the bibliographic display. This format leaves 14 lines for bibliographic information—the area used for every display in this book (with the exception of one display that serves to test the use of more lines).

Is this the right amount of space? Designers must consider their own needs. We find displays that don't show where you can go dismaying, and displays that don't show how you got there equally disturbing. Without the spacing dashes, the eye can't differentiate the three sections quickly. The spacing lines may be most arguable, but our experiments with and without those lines suggest that they help to define the bibliographic display area clearly and make the text easily legible. In practice, we suspect that the best patron access systems will use tops and bottoms that vary in size and content depending on the circumstances, but that most tops and bottoms for single-record displays may well be about the size we have used.

Actual wording for the top and bottom sections is a matter for extended discussion and investigation. It also depends on the design of other portions of the catalog: searching language, error messages and other bibliographic displays. Figure 2.1 shows the wording used in most of this book, not because we felt it was ideal but because it seemed like a good start. Each author has a different sense of how the top and bottom should look: Figures 2.2 and 2.3 show the same item as Figure 2.1, with different tops and bottoms as suggested by individual authors.

SPACING WITHIN THE BIBLIOGRAPHIC DISPLAY

The overall bibliographic display area is whatever is left over after placing the top, bottom and spacing areas. For most of this book, that area is lines 5 through 18 of a 24-line screen. A given display may pack as much information as possible into that space, or it might give up some compactness in the interest of readability.

Four different types of spacing play a role in bibliographic displays:

1. *Horizontal spacing:* A full 80-character line cannot be scanned readily—a narrower line may be more suitable. White space to the left and right of the text makes the text easier to read.
2. *Vertical spacing:* Blank lines between groups of elements make the groups more evident and make items more immediately understandable. Going further, a display could leave blank lines after each field or even between lines of a field. No such displays were tested for this book.
3. *Placement of fields:* Fields may follow one after the other within a paragraph, or each field may begin on a new line.
4. *Placement of labels:* If bibliographic displays contain labels, those labels may be placed in any one of several ways, each having a distinct effect on overall appearance.

We consider all four types of spacing in this book. Some formats illustrating the effects of the first two forms of spacing appear in this chapter, while the next two chapters deal with the remaining forms, among other things.

The authors designed displays with several different spacing patterns, but the widow function of the RBDISP program does remove some of the designer's control. When considering spacing, keep in mind the differences between the printed page and the screen, which we mentioned earlier. Spacing in a printed figure may not have the same appearance as spacing on an actual screen, given the difference between black ink on white paper and light characters on a dark background, as well as the difference between the lines immediately surrounding printed screens and the more open area that usually surrounds the textual portion of a video display.

CMTW—Traditional Cardlike Display

Figures 2.4 and 2.5 show records for a book and a sound recording in display CMTW, a cardlike, medium-level, traditional, wide display. This display uses all 80 columns of the screen for bibliographic text. It is not an *absolutely* traditional cardlike display, for reasons discussed in Chapter 3.

This display places the most information in the smallest space of any display in this book. The portion of the screen used for a record is quite dense, but over a test of 395,082 records, CMTW yields only 26% average local density (that is, percentage of characters in lines 4 through 19 that are not blank). This surprisingly low average density for CMTW can be attributed mainly to its compactness. The portion of the screen actually used for text is quite dense, but that portion is usually only a fraction of the available space. Ninety-eight percent of CMTW records fit on a single screen with room for holdings, and 93% leave at least five lines of the first screen blank.

This first display is the most traditional; similar displays are used in many online catalogs. CMTW has the advantage of compactness and familiarity, but it is less readable than most other displays.

CMTN—Narrow Cardlike Display

Figures 2.6, 2.7 and 2.8 show the same two records in display CMTN, a narrower cardlike display. The only change from the previous display is that text begins in column 10 and is limited to 60 characters, thus leaving balanced left and right margins. CMTN is still wider than the text portion of typed catalog cards or those produced by most computer systems (it has about the same number of characters per line as typeset catalog cards might have). In our judgment, the white space on either side makes the record much easier to read.

As might be expected, there's a price to pay for clarity. The sound recording goes to a second screen in this display, as do quite a few other records. Only 92% of a 395,082-

item test run fit on a single screen with room for holdings, and only 79% had at least five blank lines on the first screen. Local density is essentially the same as for display CMTW.

CMSX—Narrow Cardlike Display with Spacing

Figures 2.9, 2.10 and 2.11 show display CMSX, a narrow cardlike display with some vertical spacing. This display differs from the previous display CMTN by leaving blank lines above physical description, series and tracings.

Once again, the display becomes clearer with added space. Once again, there's a price—and a surprisingly high one. The local density drops slightly, but only 76% of the test run fits on a single screen with room for minimal holdings. The percentage with room for extensive holdings (five lines) drops to only 44%.

Every gain in clarity is accompanied by a loss in compactness. This is a natural balance and one to be considered when evaluating formats.

LMLFT—Labeled Flush-Left

The least legible labeled display in this book appears in Figures 2.12, 2.13 and 2.14. LMLFT is a labeled, medium-level format with flush-left labels and text, with the text immediately following the labels. The results are not attractive, and to some observers may well be less legible than some of the cardlike formats.

LMLFT is probably the least desirable display in this book. Even cruder are those displays using coded abbreviated labels such as ME or CO or IMP and displays combining multiple labeled items on the same lines. The authors decided not to show any such displays in this book since we question their usefulness in general for patron access.

Display LMLFT is almost as efficient as it is ugly. The density is quite high (30% local and 38% global), but 87% of a 404,784-item test run had room on the first screen for minimal holdings and 67% of the items left at least five blank lines on the first screen. While these figures are not as good as the unspaced cardlike displays CMTN and CMTW, they are better than the spaced cardlike display CMSX.

LMLFT combines labels and compactness—but is it easier to understand than CMTW or CMTN, both of which are even more compact?

LMG—Labeled, Gutter-Aligned, Label for Each Group

The best placement for labels and text in a catalog display may be gutter align-ment—right-justified labels and left-justified text, with a gutter of white space between them. Until recently, that design was not used in any online systems. Display LMG, illustrated in Figures 2.15, 2.16 and 2.17, represents a relatively compact example of gutter alignment.

LMG differs from LMLFT in three respects:

1. Bibliographic text begins at a constant position, column 17, and is limited to 60 characters per line.
2. Labels appear immediately to the left of text, right-justified to column 15.
3. Labels appear once for each group of fields, rather than once for each field.

While much more readable than a display with flush-left labels and text, display LMG is not much less efficient. Local density is still high, at 29%, but 81% of a 404,784-item sample had room on the first screen for minimal holdings.

LMGSP—Labeled, Gutter-Aligned, Vertical Spacing

Figures 2.18, 2.19 and 2.20 illustrate the effects of adding spacing lines to the previous display. This display, LMGSP, leaves a blank line between physical description and subjects, and another between subjects and other entries.

The loss of compactness with LMGSP is startling—only 55% of a 404,784-item sample will fit on one screen with room for holdings. Density is reduced to 27%, but at the price of forcing nearly half of all items to a second screen, at least when holdings are displayed.

LMGAT—Labeled, Gutter-Aligned, Author/Title Split

Display LMGAT, illustrated in Figures 2.21, 2.22 and 2.23, adds several refinements to LMGSP. LMGAT begins the display with the title in all cases, groups the main entry with other names, and separates those added entries that include titles, calling them *works*. LMGAT uses spacing that is similar to that of LMGSP, but the addition of new categories increases space requirements. The display appears here primarily because it was used as the basis for the two remaining displays in this chapter.

LMGAT offers excellent clarity and spacing, with local density down to 26%. However, it permits only 41% of a 404,784-item sample to appear on one screen with holdings. The trade-off may be worth it for some libraries because LMGAT is an unusually clear display.

LMGAT17—Labeled, Author/Title Split, More Vertical Lines

Figures 2.24, 2.25 and 2.26 show display LMGAT17, the only tested display that uses more than 14 lines. By eliminating one of the spacing lines between the dashed lines and the bibliographic display, and by compressing prompting to a single line, this display uses 17 lines, but is otherwise identical to LMGAT. The effects are dramatic—85% of items tested have room on the first screen for minimal holdings, and density actually goes down to 22%. Are the relatively cramped vertical spacing and less adequate prompting justified by the fact that LMGAT17 doubles the number of records that can fit on a single screen compared with LMGAT?

LMGAT50—Labeled, Grouped, Narrower

Display LMGAT50, illustrated in Figures 2.27, 2.28 and 2.29, differs from LMGAT only in that it uses a narrower text area. This is the most open of all displays in this project, and in some ways the most legible. Libraries might seriously consider a display this narrow for its advantages in fast reading and clarity.

Predictably, the numbers are not good. Density is quite low at 24%, but only 34% of records tested have room on the first screen for minimal holdings.

SUMMARIZING THE DISPLAYS

The results can be predicted throughout, although the dramatic nature of some changes is less predictable. The more space used for clarity and openness, the more frequently items must go to a second or even a third screen. As noted in Chapters 6 and 7, the effects are much worse for long displays and for some nonbook materials.

Table 2.1 provides an alphabetic list of all displays discussed in this chapter; a similar list appears for each succeeding chapter. Table 2.2 summarizes the screen requirements for the spacing displays illustrated in this chapter. The first number on each line gives the percentage of items that will appear on a single screen leaving three blank lines, enough for minimal holdings; the second number gives the percentage that will appear on a single screen, including those without enough room for any holdings; and the third number lists the percentage that will require two screens, not necessarily including holdings.

Table 2.3 shows some density figures for the same displays. The first number for each line is average local density, within the defined bibliographic display area. The second is average global density. As noted in Chapter 1, these figures may be considered 8.3% high if you regard dashed lines as spacing. The third number is the percentage of items with less than 30% local density, with 30% representing the maximum density for good clarity.

Table 2.4 shows space available for holdings: *4 + lines* is the percentage with at least four blank lines on the first screen; *6 + lines* and *8 + lines* show percentages for lengthy holdings; *8 + lines* allows room for six lines of actual holdings.

Table 2.1: Displays Discussed in Chapter 2

```
Display  Name

CMSX     Cardlike medium display, narrow lines, vertical spacing
CMTN     Cardlike medium display, narrow lines (60 columns)
CMTW     Cardlike medium display, wide lines (80 columns)

LMG      Labeled medium display, gutter aligned with each group labeled
LMGAT    Labeled medium display, gutter aligned, author/title split
LMGAT17  Labeled medium display, like LMGAT but with seventeen display lines

LMGAT50  Labeled medium display, like LMGAT but with 50-column lines
LMGSP    Labeled medium display, gutter aligned, vertical spacing
LMLFT    Labeled medium display with flush-left labels and text
```

Table 2.2: Screen Summary Statistics

Display	Name	One Screen w/Holdings	One Screen: bib. only	Two Screens bib. only
CMTW	Cardlike, Wide	98.45%	99.90%	0.10%
	-- public libraries	99.67%	99.98%	0.02%
CMTN	Cardlike, Narrow	92.47%	99.14%	0.85%
	-- public libraries	97.52%	99.84%	0.16%
CMSX	Cardlike, Spaced	76.16%	97.08%	2.90%
	-- public libraries	88.79%	99.25%	0.75%
LMLFT	Labeled, Flush-Left (both)	87.11%	98.34%	1.63%
	-- public libraries	92.21%	99.42%	0.58%
LMG	Labeled, Gutter, Groups	81.37%	96.67%	3.29%
	-- public libraries	89.05%	98.83%	1.16%
LMGSP	Labeled, Gutter, Spaced	55.31%	90.11%	9.84%
	-- public libraries	67.15%	95.54%	4.46%
LMGAT	Labeled, Author/Title Split	41.23%	85.06%	14.87%
	-- public libraries	51.74%	92.43%	7.56%
LMGAT17	LMGAT with more entry lines	85.06%	97.30%	2.68%
	-- public libraries	92.43%	99.16%	0.84%
LMGAT50	Narrower LMGAT	33.92%	77.84%	21.98%
	-- public libraries	45.34%	88.28%	11.69%

Table 2.3: Density Summary

Display	Name	Local Density	Global Density	L. Density to 30%
CMTW	Cardlike, Wide	26.00%	35.69%	70.69%
	-- public libraries	21.31%	32.93%	85.08%
CMTN	Cardlike, Narrow	26.06%	35.73%	69.86%
	-- public libraries	21.50%	33.04%	84.44%
CMSX	Cardlike, Spaced	25.54%	35.42%	71.41%
	-- public libraries	21.37%	32.96%	84.93%
LMLFT	Labeled, Flush-Left (both)	29.76%	37.97%	57.33%
	-- public libraries	25.25%	35.35%	73.73%
LMG	Labeled, Gutter, Groups	28.98%	37.38%	59.21%
	-- public libraries	24.90%	34.97%	75.44%
LMGSP	Labeled, Gutter, Spaced	27.24%	36.47%	65.65%
	-- public libraries	24.11%	34.61%	78.70%
LMGAT	Labeled, Author/Title Split	25.59%	35.54%	73.06%
	-- public libraries	22.99%	34.03%	83.93%
LMGAT17	LMGAT with more entry lines	22.30%	33.69%	84.83%
	-- public libraries	19.08%	31.28%	93.57%
LMGAT50	Narrower LMGAT	24.06%	34.75%	80.21%
	-- public libraries	22.14%	33.63%	87.89%

Table 2.4: Room for Holdings

Display	Name	Holdings Room on First Screen		
		4+ Lines	6+ Lines	8+ Lines
CMTW	Cardlike, Wide	96.75%	85.74%	47.90%
	-- public libraries	99.07%	93.71%	62.06%
CMTN	Cardlike, Narrow	87.20%	65.26%	26.17%
	-- public libraries	95.10%	79.91%	40.09%
CMSX	Cardlike, Spaced	62.24%	23.85%	2.45%
	-- public libraries	78.13%	36.64%	1.81%
LMLFT	Labeled, Flush-Left (both)	79.01%	51.62%	16.84%
	-- public libraries	85.74%	60.21%	23.86%
LMG	Labeled, Gutter, Groups	72.14%	44.31%	14.10%
	-- public libraries	81.36%	54.43%	21.38%
LMGSP	Labeled, Gutter, Spaced	41.01%	15.24%	4.26%
	-- public libraries	51.52%	22.68%	7.64%
LMGAT	Labeled, Author/Title Split	27.17%	8.35%	1.14%
	-- public libraries	36.34%	14.68%	0.53%
LMGAT17	LMGAT with more entry lines	77.79%	55.35%	27.05%
	-- public libraries	87.37%	67.30%	36.34%
LMGAT50	Narrower LMGAT	21.93%	7.36%	1.06%
	-- public libraries	31.24%	13.57%	0.49%

These numbers demonstrate the effects of given display options over large-scale testing and are the basic significance of this project. You can judge with your eyes how well each display communicates and you can judge from these figures how efficiently each display handles bibliographic information.

Figure 2.1

```
Your search: Tyler, Anne.                          MEDIUM Display
     Finds: 1 record                               Screen  1 of  1
-------------------------------------------------------------------

            Tyler, Anne. THE ACCIDENTAL TOURIST / Anne Tyler. 1st ed.
               New York : Knopf : Distributed by Random House, 1985.
               355 p. ; 22 cm.

       NAMES: Tyler, Anne.




-------------------------------------------------------------------
NEXT ACTIONS    Key: ? for help              + to see the next screen
                     L to see a Longer display   - to see the previous screen
                     F to Find other items   Q to Quit
NEXT ACTION?   _                                              LMCAP
```

Figure 2.2

```
Your search: The accidental to#                    MEDIUM Display
     Finds: 1 record                               Screen  1 of  1
-------------------------------------------------------------------

        TITLE: The accidental tourist / Anne Tyler.

        NAMES: Tyler, Anne.

    PUBLISHED: New York : Knopf : Distributed by Random House, 1985.
     MATERIAL: 355 p. ; 22 cm.




-------------------------------------------------------------------
NEXT ACTIONS    Type: ? for help              + to see the next screen
                      F to Find other items   - to see the previous screen
                      Q to Quit               L to see a Longer display
NEXT ACTION?   _                                              KOBM
```

Figure 2.3

```
Your search: find title The accidental to#              LONG Display
      finds: 1 record                                  Screen  1 of  1
----------------------------------------------------------------------

           TITLE: The accidental tourist / Anne Tyler.

          AUTHOR: Tyler, Anne.

         EDITION: 1st ed.
       PUBLISHED: New York : Knopf : Distributed by Random House, 1985.
        MATERIAL: 355 p. ; 22 cm.




----------------------------------------------------------------------
NEXT ACTIONS:  To get help, type ?       To see the next screen, type +
               To find other items, type F  To see the previous screen, type -
               To quit, type Q           To see a longer display, type L
NEXT ACTION?   _                                                MDSLON
```

Figure 2.4

```
Your search: Anderson, Sparky#                         MEDIUM Display
      Finds: 1 record                                  Screen  1 of  1
----------------------------------------------------------------------
Anderson, Sparky, 1934-
  Bless you boys : diary of the Detroit Tigers' 1984 season / by Sparky
Anderson, with Dan Ewald. -- Chicago : Contemporary Books, c1984.
  231 p. : ill. ; 23 cm.
  1. Detroit Tigers (Baseball team) I. Ewald, Dan.






----------------------------------------------------------------------
NEXT ACTIONS    Key: ? for help              + to see the next screen
                     L to see a Longer display  - to see the previous screen
                     F to Find other items   Q to Quit
NEXT ACTION?   _                                                  CMTW
```

Figure 2.5

```
Your search: Indy, Vincent d'#                    MEDIUM Display
     Finds: 1 record                              Screen  1 of  1
------------------------------------------------------------------

Indy, Vincent d', 1851-1931.
   Suite en re dans le style ancien : op. 24 ; Karadec : op. 34 ; Concert, op. 89
pour piano, flute, violoncello et orchestre a cordes [sound recording] / Vincent
d'Indy. -- France : Erato ; Paris : Distribution en France RCA, p1982.
   1 sound disc : 33 1/3 rpm, stereo. ; 12 in.
   1. Suites (Flutes (2), trumpet with string orchestra) 2. Music, Incidental. 3.
Concertos (Piano, flute, violoncello with string orchestra) I. Rampal, Jean
Pierre. II. Pierlot, Philippe. III. Andre, Maurice. IV. Duchable, Francois. V.
Lodeon, Frederic. VI. Paillard, Jean Francois. VII. Indy, Vincent d', 1851-1931.
Suite dans le style ancien. 1982. VIII. Indy, Vincent d', 1851-1931. Karadec.
1982. IX. Indy, Vincent d', 1851-1931. Concerto, piano, flute, violoncello,
orchestra, op. 89. 1982. X. Orchestre de chambre Jean-Francois Paillard.



------------------------------------------------------------------
NEXT ACTIONS     Key: ? for help              + to see the next screen
                      L to see a Longer display - to see the previous screen
                      F to Find other items    Q to Quit
NEXT ACTION?  _                                           CMTW
```

Figure 2.6

```
Your search: Anderson, Sparky#                    MEDIUM Display
     Finds: 1 record                              Screen  1 of  1
------------------------------------------------------------------

        Anderson, Sparky, 1934-
           Bless you boys : diary of the Detroit Tigers' 1984 season
        / by Sparky Anderson, with Dan Ewald. -- Chicago :
        Contemporary Books, c1984.
           231 p. : ill. ; 23 cm.
           1. Detroit Tigers (Baseball team) I. Ewald, Dan.








------------------------------------------------------------------
NEXT ACTIONS     Key: ? for help              + to see the next screen
                      L to see a Longer display - to see the previous screen
                      F to Find other items    Q to Quit
NEXT ACTION?  _                                           CMTN
```

Figure 2.7

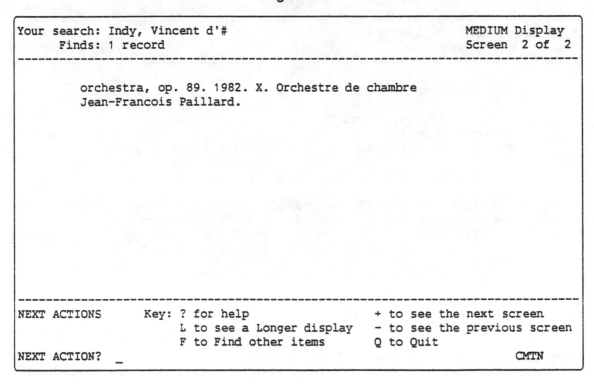

```
Your search: Indy, Vincent d'#                      MEDIUM Display
     Finds: 1 record                                Screen 1 of 2
--------------------------------------------------------------------
       Indy, Vincent d', 1851-1931.
          Suite en re dans le style ancien : op. 24 ; Karadec : op.
       34 ; Concert, op. 89 pour piano, flute, violoncello et
       orchestre a cordes [sound recording] / Vincent d'Indy. --
       France : Erato ; Paris : Distribution en France RCA, p1982.
          1 sound disc : 33 1/3 rpm, stereo. ; 12 in.
          1. Suites (Flutes (2), trumpet with string orchestra) 2.
       Music, Incidental. 3. Concertos (Piano, flute, violoncello
       with string orchestra) I. Rampal, Jean Pierre. II. Pierlot,
       Philippe. III. Andre, Maurice. IV. Duchable, Francois. V.
       Lodeon, Frederic. VI. Paillard, Jean Francois. VII. Indy,
       Vincent d', 1851-1931. Suite dans le style ancien. 1982.
       VIII. Indy, Vincent d', 1851-1931. Karadec. 1982. IX. Indy,
       Vincent d', 1851-1931. Concerto, piano, flute, violoncello,
--------------------------------------------------CONTINUED-------
NEXT ACTIONS      Key: ? for help            + to see the next screen
                       L to see a Longer display  - to see the previous screen
                       F to Find other items      Q to Quit
NEXT ACTION?  _                                          CMTN
```

Figure 2.8

```
Your search: Indy, Vincent d'#                      MEDIUM Display
     Finds: 1 record                                Screen 2 of 2
--------------------------------------------------------------------
       orchestra, op. 89. 1982. X. Orchestre de chambre
       Jean-Francois Paillard.




--------------------------------------------------------------------
NEXT ACTIONS      Key: ? for help            + to see the next screen
                       L to see a Longer display  - to see the previous screen
                       F to Find other items      Q to Quit
NEXT ACTION?  _                                          CMTN
```

Figure 2.9

```
Your search: Anderson, Sparky#                    MEDIUM Display
     Finds: 1 record                              Screen  1 of  1
-----------------------------------------------------------------

        Anderson, Sparky, 1934-
          Bless you boys : diary of the Detroit Tigers' 1984 season
        / by Sparky Anderson, with Dan Ewald. -- Chicago :
        Contemporary Books, c1984.

          231 p. : ill. ; 23 cm.

          1. Detroit Tigers (Baseball team) I. Ewald, Dan.



-----------------------------------------------------------------
NEXT ACTIONS      Key: ? for help          + to see the next screen
                       L to see a Longer display  - to see the previous screen
                       F to Find other items      Q to Quit
NEXT ACTION?  _                                             CMSX
```

Figure 2.10

```
Your search: Indy, Vincent d'#                    MEDIUM Display
     Finds: 1 record                              Screen  1 of  2
-----------------------------------------------------------------

        Indy, Vincent d', 1851-1931.
          Suite en re dans le style ancien : op. 24 ; Karadec : op.
        34 ; Concert, op. 89 pour piano, flute, violoncello et
        orchestre a cordes [sound recording] / Vincent d'Indy. --
        France : Erato ; Paris : Distribution en France RCA, p1982.

          1 sound disc : 33 1/3 rpm, stereo. ; 12 in.

          1. Suites (Flutes (2), trumpet with string orchestra) 2.
        Music, Incidental. 3. Concertos (Piano, flute, violoncello
        with string orchestra) I. Rampal, Jean Pierre. II. Pierlot,
        Philippe. III. Andre, Maurice. IV. Duchable, Francois. V.
        Lodeon, Frederic. VI. Paillard, Jean Francois. VII. Indy,
        Vincent d', 1851-1931. Suite dans le style ancien. 1982.

-------------------------------------------------CONTINUED-------
NEXT ACTIONS      Key: ? for help          + to see the next screen
                       L to see a Longer display  - to see the previous screen
                       F to Find other items      Q to Quit
NEXT ACTION?  _                                             CMSX
```

Figure 2.11

```
┌─────────────────────────────────────────────────────────────────────┐
│ Your search: Indy, Vincent d'#                        MEDIUM Display  │
│       Finds: 1 record                                 Screen  2 of  2 │
│ ─────────────────────────────────────────────────────────────────────│
│                                                                       │
│         VIII. Indy, Vincent d', 1851-1931. Karadec. 1982. IX. Indy,   │
│         Vincent d', 1851-1931. Concerto, piano, flute, violoncello,   │
│         orchestra, op. 89. 1982. X. Orchestre de chambre              │
│         Jean-Francois Paillard.                                       │
│                                                                       │
│                                                                       │
│                                                                       │
│                                                                       │
│                                                                       │
│                                                                       │
│                                                                       │
│                                                                       │
│                                                                       │
│ ─────────────────────────────────────────────────────────────────────│
│ NEXT ACTIONS      Key: ? for help            + to see the next screen │
│                        L to see a Longer display  - to see the previous screen │
│                        F to Find other items  Q to Quit               │
│ NEXT ACTION?   _                                              CMSX     │
└─────────────────────────────────────────────────────────────────────┘
```

Figure 2.12

```
┌─────────────────────────────────────────────────────────────────────┐
│ Your search: AUTHOR: Anderson#                        MEDIUM Display  │
│       Finds: 1 record                                 Screen  1 of  1 │
│ ─────────────────────────────────────────────────────────────────────│
│ AUTHOR: Anderson, Sparky, 1934-                                       │
│ TITLE: Bless you boys : diary of the Detroit Tigers' 1984 season / by Sparky │
│ Anderson, with Dan Ewald.                                             │
│ PUBLISHED: Chicago : Contemporary Books, c1984.                       │
│ MATERIAL: 231 p. : ill. ; 23 cm.                                      │
│ SUBJECT: Detroit Tigers (Baseball team)                               │
│ OTHER ENTRY: Ewald, Dan.                                              │
│                                                                       │
│                                                                       │
│                                                                       │
│                                                                       │
│                                                                       │
│ ─────────────────────────────────────────────────────────────────────│
│ NEXT ACTIONS      Key: ? for help            + to see the next screen │
│                        L to see a Longer display  - to see the previous screen │
│                        F to Find other items  Q to Quit               │
│ NEXT ACTION?   _                                              LMLFT    │
└─────────────────────────────────────────────────────────────────────┘
```

Figure 2.13

```
Your search: AUTHOR: Indy, Vin#                    MEDIUM Display
      Finds: 1 record                              Screen  1 of  2
-----------------------------------------------------------------------

AUTHOR: Indy, Vincent d', 1851-1931.
TITLE: Suite en re dans le style ancien : op. 24 ; Karadec : op. 34 ; Concert,
op. 89 pour piano, flute, violoncello et orchestre a cordes [sound recording] /
Vincent d'Indy.
PUBLISHED: France : Erato ; Paris : Distribution en France RCA, p1982.
MATERIAL: 1 sound disc : 33 1/3 rpm, stereo. ; 12 in.
SUBJECT: Suites (Flutes (2), trumpet with string orchestra)
SUBJECT: Music, Incidental.
SUBJECT: Concertos (Piano, flute, violoncello with string orchestra)
OTHER ENTRY: Rampal, Jean Pierre.
OTHER ENTRY: Pierlot, Philippe.
OTHER ENTRY: Andre, Maurice.
OTHER ENTRY: Duchable, Francois.
OTHER ENTRY: Lodeon, Frederic.


-------------------------------------------------------CONTINUED-------
NEXT ACTIONS     Key: ? for help            + to see the next screen
                      L to see a Longer display  - to see the previous screen
                      F to Find other items   Q to Quit
NEXT ACTION?  _                                           LMLFT
```

Figure 2.14

```
Your search: AUTHOR: Indy, Vin#                    MEDIUM Display
      Finds: 1 record                              Screen  2 of  2
-----------------------------------------------------------------------

OTHER ENTRY: Paillard, Jean Francois.
OTHER ENTRY: Indy, Vincent d', 1851-1931. Suite dans le style ancien. 1982.
OTHER ENTRY: Indy, Vincent d', 1851-1931. Karadec. 1982.
OTHER ENTRY: Indy, Vincent d', 1851-1931. Concerto, piano, flute, violoncello,
orchestra, op. 89. 1982.
OTHER ENTRY: Orchestre de chambre Jean-Francois Paillard.




-------------------------------------------------------------------------
NEXT ACTIONS     Key: ? for help            + to see the next screen
                      L to see a Longer display  - to see the previous screen
                      F to Find other items   Q to Quit
NEXT ACTION?  _                                           LMLFT
```

Figure 2.15

```
Your search: Anderson, Sparky#                           MEDIUM Display
     Finds: 1 record                                     Screen  1 of  1
-----------------------------------------------------------------------

        AUTHOR: Anderson, Sparky, 1934-
         TITLE: Bless you boys : diary of the Detroit Tigers' 1984 season /
                by Sparky Anderson, with Dan Ewald.
     PUBLISHED: Chicago : Contemporary Books, c1984.
      MATERIAL: 231 p. : ill. ; 23 cm.
      SUBJECTS: Detroit Tigers (Baseball team)
 OTHER ENTRIES: Ewald, Dan.




-----------------------------------------------------------------------
NEXT ACTIONS      Key: ? for help          + to see the next screen
                       L to see a Longer display  - to see the previous screen
                       F to Find other items  Q to Quit
NEXT ACTION?  _                                               LMG
```

Figure 2.16

```
Your search: Indy, Vincent d'#                           MEDIUM Display
     Finds: 1 record                                     Screen  1 of  2
-----------------------------------------------------------------------

        AUTHOR: Indy, Vincent d', 1851-1931.
         TITLE: Suite en re dans le style ancien : op. 24 ; Karadec : op. 34
                ; Concert, op. 89 pour piano, flute, violoncello et
                orchestre a cordes [sound recording] / Vincent d'Indy.
     PUBLISHED: France : Erato ; Paris : Distribution en France RCA, p1982.
      MATERIAL: 1 sound disc : 33 1/3 rpm, stereo. ; 12 in.
      SUBJECTS: Suites (Flutes (2), trumpet with string orchestra)
                Music, Incidental.
                Concertos (Piano, flute, violoncello with string orchestra)
 OTHER ENTRIES: Rampal, Jean Pierre.
                Pierlot, Philippe.
                Andre, Maurice.
                Duchable, Francois.
                Lodeon, Frederic.
-----------------------------------------------------CONTINUED-------
NEXT ACTIONS      Key: ? for help          + to see the next screen
                       L to see a Longer display  - to see the previous screen
                       F to Find other items  Q to Quit
NEXT ACTION?  _                                               LMG
```

Figure 2.17

```
Your search: Indy, Vincent d'#                    MEDIUM Display
     Finds: 1 record                              Screen  2 of  2
--------------------------------------------------------------------
                  Paillard, Jean Francois.
                  Indy, Vincent d', 1851-1931. Suite dans le style ancien.
                    1982.
                  Indy, Vincent d', 1851-1931. Karadec. 1982.
                  Indy, Vincent d', 1851-1931. Concerto, piano, flute,
                    violoncello, orchestra, op. 89. 1982.
                  Orchestre de chambre Jean-Francois Paillard.




                  --------------------------------------------------
NEXT ACTIONS      Key: ? for help            + to see the next screen
                       L to see a Longer display  - to see the previous screen
                       F to Find other items   Q to Quit
NEXT ACTION?  _                                              LMG
```

Figure 2.18

```
Your search: Anderson, Sparky#                    MEDIUM Display
     Finds: 1 record                              Screen  1 of  1
--------------------------------------------------------------------
        AUTHOR: Anderson, Sparky, 1934-
         TITLE: Bless you boys : diary of the Detroit Tigers' 1984 season /
                  by Sparky Anderson, with Dan Ewald.
     PUBLISHED: Chicago : Contemporary Books, c1984.
      MATERIAL: 231 p. : ill. ; 23 cm.

      SUBJECTS: Detroit Tigers (Baseball team)

 OTHER ENTRIES: Ewald, Dan.




                  --------------------------------------------------
NEXT ACTIONS      Key: ? for help            + to see the next screen
                       L to see a Longer display  - to see the previous screen
                       F to Find other items   Q to Quit
NEXT ACTION?  _                                              LMGSP
```

Figure 2.19

```
Your search: Indy, Vincent d'#                        MEDIUM Display
       Finds: 1 record                                Screen  1 of  2
-----------------------------------------------------------------------


        AUTHOR: Indy, Vincent d', 1851-1931.
         TITLE: Suite en re dans le style ancien : op. 24 ; Karadec : op. 34
                ; Concert, op. 89 pour piano, flute, violoncello et
                orchestre a cordes [sound recording] / Vincent d'Indy.
     PUBLISHED: France : Erato ; Paris : Distribution en France RCA, p1982.
      MATERIAL: 1 sound disc : 33 1/3 rpm, stereo. ; 12 in.

      SUBJECTS: Suites (Flutes (2), trumpet with string orchestra)
                Music, Incidental.
                Concertos (Piano, flute, violoncello with string orchestra)


 OTHER ENTRIES: Rampal, Jean Pierre.
                Pierlot, Philippe.
                Andre, Maurice.


-----------------------------------------------------CONTINUED-------
NEXT ACTIONS       Key: ? for help            + to see the next screen
                        L to see a Longer display  - to see the previous screen
                        F to Find other items    Q to Quit

NEXT ACTION?   _                                              LMGSP
```

Figure 2.20

```
Your search: Indy, Vincent d'#                        MEDIUM Display
       Finds: 1 record                                Screen  2 of  2
-----------------------------------------------------------------------
                Duchable, Francois.
                Lodeon, Frederic.
                Paillard, Jean Francois.
                Indy, Vincent d', 1851-1931. Suite dans le style ancien.
                  1982.
                Indy, Vincent d', 1851-1931. Karadec. 1982.
                Indy, Vincent d', 1851-1931. Concerto, piano, flute,
                  violoncello, orchestra, op. 89. 1982.
                Orchestre de chambre Jean-Francois Paillard.




-----------------------------------------------------------------------
NEXT ACTIONS       Key: ? for help            + to see the next screen
                        L to see a Longer display  - to see the previous screen
                        F to Find other items    Q to Quit

NEXT ACTION?   _                                              LMGSP
```

Figure 2.21

```
Your search: Bless you boys #                          MEDIUM Display
      Finds: 1 record                                  Screen  1 of  1
----------------------------------------------------------------------

        TITLE: Bless you boys : diary of the Detroit Tigers' 1984 season /
               by Sparky Anderson, with Dan Ewald.
    PUBLISHED: Chicago : Contemporary Books, c1984.
     MATERIAL: 231 p. : ill. ; 23 cm.

        NAMES: Anderson, Sparky, 1934-
               Ewald, Dan.

     SUBJECTS: Detroit Tigers (Baseball team)




----------------------------------------------------------------------
NEXT ACTIONS      Key: ? for help              + to see the next screen
                       L to see a Longer display  - to see the previous screen
                       F to Find other items    Q to Quit
NEXT ACTION?   _                                          LMGAT
```

Figure 2.22

```
Your search: Suite en re dans #                        MEDIUM Display
      Finds: 1 record                                  Screen  1 of  2
----------------------------------------------------------------------

        TITLE: Suite en re dans le style ancien : op. 24 ; Karadec : op. 34
               ; Concert, op. 89 pour piano, flute, violoncello et
               orchestre a cordes [sound recording] / Vincent d'Indy.
    PUBLISHED: France : Erato ; Paris : Distribution en France RCA, p1982.
     MATERIAL: 1 sound disc : 33 1/3 rpm, stereo. ; 12 in.

        NAMES: Indy, Vincent d', 1851-1931.
               Rampal, Jean Pierre.
               Pierlot, Philippe.
               Andre, Maurice.
               Duchable, Francois.
               Lodeon, Frederic.
               Paillard, Jean Francois.


-------------------------------------------------------CONTINUED-------
NEXT ACTIONS      Key: ? for help              + to see the next screen
                       L to see a Longer display  - to see the previous screen
                       F to Find other items    Q to Quit
NEXT ACTION?   _                                          LMGAT
```

Figure 2.23

```
Your search: Suite en re dans #                          MEDIUM Display
     Finds: 1 record                                     Screen  2 of  2
------------------------------------------------------------------------

               Orchestre de chambre Jean-Francois Paillard.

     SUBJECTS: Suites (Flutes (2), trumpet with string orchestra)
               Music, Incidental.
               Concertos (Piano, flute, violoncello with string orchestra)

        WORKS: Indy, Vincent d', 1851-1931. Suite dans le style ancien.
                  1982.
               Indy, Vincent d', 1851-1931. Karadec. 1982.
               Indy, Vincent d', 1851-1931. Concerto, piano, flute,
                  violoncello, orchestra, op. 89. 1982.



------------------------------------------------------------------------
NEXT ACTIONS     Key: ? for help               + to see the next screen
                      L to see a Longer display - to see the previous screen
                      F to Find other items    Q to Quit
NEXT ACTION?   _                                              LMGAT
```

Figure 2.24

```
Your search: Bless you boys #                            MEDIUM Display
     Finds: 1 record                                     Screen  1 of  1
------------------------------------------------------------------------
       TITLE: Bless you boys : diary of the Detroit Tigers' 1984 season /
                 by Sparky Anderson, with Dan Ewald.
   PUBLISHED: Chicago : Contemporary Books, c1984.
    MATERIAL: 231 p. : ill. ; 23 cm.

       NAMES: Anderson, Sparky, 1934-
              Ewald, Dan.

    SUBJECTS: Detroit Tigers (Baseball team)




------------------------------------------------------------------------
Key: + for next screen, - for previous screen, ? for Help, Q to Quit
NEXT ACTION?   _                                             LMGAT17
```

Figure 2.25

```
Your search: Suite en re dans #                    MEDIUM Display
      Finds: 1 record                              Screen  1 of  2
-----------------------------------------------------------------------
          TITLE: Suite en re dans le style ancien : op. 24 ; Karadec : op. 34
                 ; Concert, op. 89 pour piano, flute, violoncello et
                 orchestre a cordes [sound recording] / Vincent d'Indy.
      PUBLISHED: France : Erato ; Paris : Distribution en France RCA, p1982.
       MATERIAL: 1 sound disc : 33 1/3 rpm, stereo. ; 12 in.

          NAMES: Indy, Vincent d', 1851-1931.
                 Rampal, Jean Pierre.
                 Pierlot, Philippe.
                 Andre, Maurice.
                 Duchable, Francois.
                 Lodeon, Frederic.
                 Paillard, Jean Francois.
                 Orchestre de chambre Jean-Francois Paillard.

       SUBJECTS: Suites (Flutes (2), trumpet with string orchestra)
                 Music, Incidental.

-------------------------------------------------------CONTINUED-------
Key: + for next screen, - for previous screen, ? for Help, Q to Quit
NEXT ACTION?  _                                           LMGAT17
```

Figure 2.26

```
Your search: Suite en re dans #                    MEDIUM Display
      Finds: 1 record                              Screen  2 of  2
-----------------------------------------------------------------------
                 Concertos (Piano, flute, violoncello with string orchestra)

          WORKS: Indy, Vincent d', 1851-1931. Suite dans le style ancien.
                 1982.
                 Indy, Vincent d', 1851-1931. Karadec. 1982.
                 Indy, Vincent d', 1851-1931. Concerto, piano, flute,
                 violoncello, orchestra, op. 89. 1982.




-----------------------------------------------------------------------
Key: + for next screen, - for previous screen, ? for Help, Q to Quit
NEXT ACTION?  _                                           LMGAT17
```

Figure 2.27

```
Your search: Bless you boys #                          MEDIUM Display
    Finds: 1 record                                    Screen  1 of  1
----------------------------------------------------------------------

           TITLE: Bless you boys : diary of the Detroit Tigers' 1984
                  season / by Sparky Anderson, with Dan Ewald.
       PUBLISHED: Chicago : Contemporary Books, c1984.
        MATERIAL: 231 p. : ill. ; 23 cm.

           NAMES: Anderson, Sparky, 1934-
                  Ewald, Dan.


        SUBJECTS: Detroit Tigers (Baseball team)




----------------------------------------------------------------------
NEXT ACTIONS     Key: ? for help              + to see the next screen
                      L to see a Longer display  - to see the previous screen
                      F to Find other items   Q to Quit
NEXT ACTION?  _                                            LMGAT50
```

Figure 2.28

```
Your search: Suite en re dans #                        MEDIUM Display
    Finds: 1 record                                    Screen  1 of  2
----------------------------------------------------------------------

           TITLE: Suite en re dans le style ancien : op. 24 ;
                  Karadec : op. 34 ; Concert, op. 89 pour piano,
                  flute, violoncello et orchestre a cordes [sound
                  recording] / Vincent d'Indy.
       PUBLISHED: France : Erato ; Paris : Distribution en France
                  RCA, p1982.
        MATERIAL: 1 sound disc : 33 1/3 rpm, stereo. ; 12 in.

           NAMES: Indy, Vincent d', 1851-1931.
                  Rampal, Jean Pierre.
                  Pierlot, Philippe.
                  Andre, Maurice.
                  Duchable, Francois.
                  Lodeon, Frederic.

-----------------------------------------------------CONTINUED-------
NEXT ACTIONS     Key: ? for help              + to see the next screen
                      L to see a Longer display  - to see the previous screen
                      F to Find other items   Q to Quit
NEXT ACTION?  _                                            LMGAT50
```

Figure 2.29

```
Your search: Suite en re dans #                         MEDIUM Display
     Finds: 1 record                                    Screen  2 of  2
--------------------------------------------------------------------------
                   Paillard, Jean Francois.
                   Orchestre de chambre Jean-Francois Paillard.

         SUBJECTS: Suites (Flutes (2), trumpet with string orchestra)
                   Music, Incidental.
                   Concertos (Piano, flute, violoncello with string
                     orchestra)

            WORKS: Indy, Vincent d', 1851-1931. Suite dans le style
                     ancien. 1982.
                   Indy, Vincent d', 1851-1931. Karadec. 1982.
                   Indy, Vincent d', 1851-1931. Concerto, piano,
                     flute, violoncello, orchestra, op. 89. 1982.


--------------------------------------------------------------------------
NEXT ACTIONS      Key: ? for help              + to see the next screen
                       L to see a Longer display  - to see the previous screen
                       F to Find other items   Q to Quit

NEXT ACTION?  _                                            LMGAT50
```

3

Cardlike Displays

Do cardlike displays have any place in contemporary online catalogs?

Librarians find catalog cards familiar, as do many library patrons, but it's reasonable to assume that patrons cannot use a cardlike display as effectively as they can use a labeled display. Studies on patron understanding of card elements demonstrate that patrons generally don't articulate the elements very well. The studies fail to clarify whether the problem is the cardlike arrangement, or whether patrons simply don't pay attention to elements for which they have no use.

The question of whether patrons will find *useful* information in a labeled display that they would not find in a cardlike display is an important one, and has not yet been answered. It seems clear that labeled displays clarify information for librarians and patrons alike.

We believe that well-designed labeled displays, such as the title-first, spaced and grouped display LMGAT (Figures 2.21–2.23, 4.34–4.41 and 7.17–7.36), make elements clearer than do cardlike displays, even those with spacing, such as CMSX (Figures 2.9– 2.11, 3.9–3.14 and 7.1–7.16). Our own experiences and responses from those who viewed early samples indicate that labeled displays make information easier to identify and understand. All else being equal, each author would recommend in favor of labeled displays, and might even eliminate most cardlike displays from the study.

But all else is not equal. Cardlike displays pack large amounts of information into a small amount of space. As demonstrated by the statistics in Chapter 2 for all RLIN cataloging, the spaced narrow cardlike display CMTN is significantly more efficient than the labeled display, LMGAT. Even for somewhat simpler public library cataloging, LMGAT (Figures 2.21–2.23, 4.34–4.41 and 7.17–7.36) had space for minimal holdings on the first screen for only 52% of items tested, while CMTN (Figures 2.6–2.8 and 3.3–3.8) had that much space for 98% of the same items. Libraries must balance the gain in clarity of having nearly all items displayed on one screen against the loss in clarity of not having labels.

Cardlike displays present a familiar context for those patrons accustomed to card catalogs, who may otherwise be nervous about online catalogs. That may not be a good thing, as cardlike displays also help patrons to think of an online access system as being merely an "online card catalog."

We do not argue in favor of cardlike displays, but we do feel that the evidence makes it premature to rule them out. This book studies a greater variety of labeled displays but includes some cardlike displays at every appropriate level. Designers and librarians should study the direct comparisons (samples and statistics alike) and draw their own conclusions.

MODIFYING CARDLIKE DISPLAYS

Cardlike displays need not carry all the baggage of catalog cards. Since we see no plausible reason to carry uninformative tracings such as *I. Title* or *II. Series* within an online catalog, we have eliminated those tracings from all displays.

Most cardlike displays in online catalogs differ from catalog cards in one significant respect—number of characters per line. The typical online cardlike display uses all 80 characters of a line, while typical catalog cards use from 35 to 60 characters per line. As illustrated in Chapter 2, reducing the line width from 80 characters to 60 characters makes the screen more open and the text more readable. Except for the wide display CMTW (Figures 2.4–2.5 and 3.1–3.2), all cardlike displays in this book use a 60-character line. Chapter 2 also introduced vertical spacing as a way of improving clarity; most cardlike displays in this book include some vertical spacing, as do most printed catalog cards.

Modifications in the traditional unit record catalog card may make cardlike displays more readable. One possible change abandons the tracings paragraph and instead starts each subject, series and added entry on a new line. Another places the title first, adding the main entry to the set of added entries, thus eliminating the controversial differentiation between one entry and others.

Another possible cardlike variation uses a citation-style bibliographic description, placing more information in a single paragraph. Several citation styles exist, most of them fairly similar to one another. A citation style will certainly be familiar to researchers and students, and will serve those who must prepare bibliographies, as the information on the display can be downloaded, printed or copied almost verbatim. A citation-style display based on cataloging records won't exactly match any normal citation style, for several reasons having to do with punctuation and the contents of the title field.

Should a citation-style display begin with a title or with a main entry? Most citation styles place authors' names first, except in cases that would normally be cataloged as title main entries. For many music items, citations beginning with titles seem peculiar and somewhat meaningless.

Another variation used frequently in libraries (though usually not in citations) presents the short title in all capital letters. That variation, when used in a citation display or in a traditional unit record display, helps call attention to the title.

This chapter illustrates the variations mentioned above. Other designers might arrive at more radical departures from catalog cards while retaining unlabeled displays. We are probably conditioned by familiarity with printed cards and by the admittedly close relationship between USMARC and traditional catalog cards.

THE EXAMPLES AND STATISTICS

All eight displays illustrated in this chapter use the medium-level fields described in Chapter 2 and listed in Table 2.1. Three of the eight were introduced in Chapter 2; five more variations appear for the first time in this chapter. Table 3.1 lists the displays discussed and illustrated in this chapter.

Two bibliographic records are used to illustrate all eight displays in this chapter. The first represents a printed musical score; the second represents conference proceedings, with a conference main entry. Four more bibliographic records are introduced in this chapter, to round out the set of eight used to allow comparisons of more interesting displays. In addition to the two records noted above and the two introduced in Chapter 2, the remaining records represent a collection of plays with a title main entry; a map

Table 3.1: Displays Discussed in Chapter 3

Display	Name
CMCAP	Cardlike medium display (citation-style) with capitalized title
CMCIT	Cardlike medium display with citation-style description
CMSL	Cardlike medium display, narrow lines, new line for each entry
CMSX	Cardlike medium display, narrow lines, vertical spacing
CMTCIT	Cardlike medium display with title-citation description
CMTL	Cardlike medium display, title first, new line for each entry
CMTN	Cardlike medium display, narrow lines (60 columns)
CMTW	Cardlike medium display, wide lines (80 columns)
LMGAT	Labeled medium display, gutter aligned, author/title split

with a personal name main entry; a periodical likely to be found in almost every library; and the record for a videocassette version of a classic film.

CMTW—Cardlike, Traditional, Wide Lines

This display was introduced in Chapter 2 (Figures 2.4 and 2.5). Two additional examples appear in Figures 3.1 and 3.2.

CMTN—Cardlike, Traditional, Narrow

This display was also introduced in Chapter 2 (Figures 2.6–2.8). It differs from the previous display by reducing the width of the bibliographic display. Because it is compact yet readable, display CMTN may be the most useful display option for libraries that choose to use cardlike displays. Six new examples appear in Figures 3.3 through 3.8 to complete the set of eight examples.

CMSX—Cardlike, Traditional, Spaced

The third cardlike display illustrated in Chapter 2 (Figures 2.9–2.11) also seems to be a reasonable alternative for some online catalogs. Display CMSX is the most open of the traditional cardlike forms. Figures 3.9 through 3.14 illustrate the remaining six examples.

CMSL—Cardlike, Spaced, New Line for Each Entry

Tracings make sense to most librarians, but short subject headings and other brief entries may be lost within a tracings paragraph. Display CMSL, illustrated in Figures 3.15 through 3.24, starts each added entry and subject heading on a new line. The display uses the same line width and spacing lines that CMSX uses.

This display requires significantly more space than CMSX requires. Since the most common added entries and subjects average about half a line in length (see Table A.4 in Appendix A), that result should not be surprising. Figures 2.10, 2.11, 3.32 and 3.33 show the results for a record with 13 subjects and added entries. The spaced traditional display CMSX requires 10 lines for tracings. CMSL requires 15 lines to show the same information, but makes the entries more prominent. The statistical results show the overall effect. CMSX has room for holdings on the first screen in 76% of cases tested; CMSL, in only 60%. Public library results are almost directly comparable: 88% for CMSX, 74% for CMSL—meaning that twice as many records require a second screen.

A library considering a display that is similar to CMSL might wish to number each entry to ease extended searching (i.e., to allow patrons to ask for all items with "entry

#3"). This book does not illustrate such numbering, for cardlike or for labeled formats, largely because of program limitations.

CMTL—Cardlike, Title-First, New Line for Each Entry

Should the title appear first? Display CMTL differs from CMSL, above, by moving the main entry from the top of the display to the top of the added entries and subjects. Figures 3.25 through 3.27 show two illustrations.

This display provides clear information for many monographs and for other materials with distinctive titles. Both examples in this chapter show effective use of the display. Without a label for the author or other entries, however, this display was unclear for many sound recordings and scores, whose titles are frequently less distinctive. A full set of illustrations for a title-first display appears later, for display CMTCIT (Figures 3.37–3.45).

CMTL and CMSL are essentially very similar; the only difference lies in the placement of the main entry. Statistics for CMSL also apply to CMTL.

CMCIT—Citation-Style, New Line for Each Entry

Display CMCIT shows one possible citation arrangement, illustrated in Figures 3.28 through 3.36. The descriptive paragraphs are combined into a single paragraph that roughly resembles a standard citation. The citation styles called for by both *The Chicago Manual of Style* and American National Standard Z39.29 place joint authors at the beginning of a citation, and neither style uses the punctuation used in cataloging. We made no attempt to translate cataloging conventions to a more exact Chicago or ANSI citation style, and we retained some data elements that would not normally appear in a citation.

Some libraries may find a display similar to CMCIT worthwhile. The display provides information in a fairly compact space. The first screen has room for holdings in 84% of items tested, 92% for public libraries. While those numbers are not as high as the ones for the two unspaced cardlike displays, they are significantly better than the numbers for displays with blank spaces or displays with new lines for each entry.

CMTCIT—Title Citation, New Line for Each Entry

Another variation on citation-style displays places the title first. This display, CMTCIT, has some of the same problems as CMTL. A full set of illustrations in Figures 3.37 through 3.45 shows the effects.

Table 3.2: Screen Summary Statistics

Display	Name	One Screen w/Holdings	One Screen: bib. only	Two Screens bib. only
CMTW	Cardlike, Wide	98.45%	99.90%	0.10%
	-- public libraries	99.67%	99.98%	0.02%
CMTN	Cardlike, Narrow	92.47%	99.14%	0.85%
	-- public libraries	97.52%	99.84%	0.16%
CMSX	Cardlike, Spaced	76.16%	97.08%	2.90%
	-- public libraries	88.79%	99.25%	0.75%
CMSL	Cardlike, Spaced, Line/Entry	60.85%	91.68%	8.27%
	-- public libraries	74.10%	96.73%	3.26%
CMCIT	Citation-style Unlabeled	84.45%	97.07%	2.90%
	-- public libraries	92.35%	99.14%	0.85%
CMTCIT	Title citation, Unlabeled	81.94%	96.66%	3.30%
	-- public libraries	90.31%	98.94%	1.05%

Since the main entry receives a separate line in this display, it is slightly less compact than CMCIT above. 82% of items tested (90% for public libraries) have room for holdings on the first screen.

CMCAP—Citation-Style, Capitalized Short Title

Display option CMCAP differs from the earlier CMCIT only in that the short title (subfield a of field 245) appears in capital letters. This method of highlighting title information makes the title stand out within a citation and has no effect on space requirements. Figures 3.46 and 3.47 illustrate the display. Statistics for CMCIT also apply to CMCAP.

SUMMARY

Cardlike displays provide compact information, but they may not provide it as clearly as do labeled displays. Tables 3.2, 3.3 and 3.4 show the summary statistics for most of the cardlike displays tested at the medium level.

When compared with the statistics in Chapter 4, those statistics make the strongest case for cardlike displays. The most compact labeled display required two screens for 13% of items tested, eight times as many as the 1.6% for the most compact cardlike display. A citation-like unlabeled display giving each entry a new line, CMCIT, forced only slightly more items to a second screen than the least legible labeled display did. Some 16% of items, one out of six, require a second screen using CMCIT; almost 59%, or roughly three out of five, require a second screen using the very legible LMGAT. The situation for public library cataloging is even clearer. CMCIT requires a second screen

Table 3.3: Density Summary

Display	Name	Local Density	Global Density	L. Density to 30%
CMTW	Cardlike, Wide	26.00%	35.69%	70.69%
	-- public libraries	21.31%	32.93%	85.08%
CMTN	Cardlike, Narrow	26.06%	35.73%	69.86%
	-- public libraries	21.50%	33.04%	84.44%
CMSX	Cardlike, Spaced	25.54%	35.42%	71.41%
	-- public libraries	21.37%	32.96%	84.93%
CMSL	Cardlike, Spaced, Line/Entry	23.57%	34.28%	79.50%
	-- public libraries	20.23%	32.29%	89.54%
CMCIT	Citation-style Unlabeled	24.53%	35.03%	75.07%
	-- public libraries	20.36%	32.59%	87.83%
CMTCIT	Title citation, Unlabeled	24.43%	35.02%	75.47%
	-- public libraries	20.32%	32.62%	88.03%

Table 3.4: Room for Holdings

Display	Name	Holdings Room on First Screen 4+ Lines	6+ Lines	8+ Lines
CMTW	Cardlike, Wide	96.75%	85.74%	47.90%
	-- public libraries	99.07%	93.71%	62.06%
CMTN	Cardlike, Narrow	87.20%	65.26%	26.17%
	-- public libraries	95.10%	79.91%	40.09%
CMSX	Cardlike, Spaced	62.24%	23.85%	2.45%
	-- public libraries	78.13%	36.64%	1.81%
CMSL	Cardlike, Spaced, Line/Entry	46.95%	18.11%	2.30%
	-- public libraries	59.99%	27.23%	1.72%
CMCIT	Citation-style Unlabeled	76.88%	52.86%	21.25%
	-- public libraries	86.94%	65.79%	33.14%
CMTCIT	Title citation, Unlabeled	73.06%	45.95%	15.18%
	-- public libraries	83.20%	57.57%	24.85%

for less than 8% of items tested, one out of twelve; LMGAT requires a second screen for more than 48%, or nearly half.

The statistical case is clear. Is that case sufficient? No designer used a cardlike display as his or her "designer's choice," but the case is strong enough to bear consideration.

Figure 3.1

```
Your search: Brubeck, Dave#                           MEDIUM Display
     Finds: 1 record                                  Screen  1 of  1
------------------------------------------------------------------------

Brubeck, Dave.
  Bossa nova U.S.A. / [as performed by] the Dave Brubeck Quartet ; piano solo
transcriptions by Howard Brubeck. -- San Francisco, Calif. : Derry Music Co. ;
New York, N.Y. : C. Hansen, distributor, c1963.
  49 p. of music ; 28 cm.
  1. Piano music (Jazz), Arranged. 2. Jazz quartets--Piano scores. I. Brubeck,
Howard R. II. Brubeck, Howard R. Theme for June; arr. III. Macero, Teo, 1925-
Coracao sensivel; arr. IV. Dave Brubeck Quartet.




------------------------------------------------------------------------
NEXT ACTIONS      Key: ? for help              + to see the next screen
                       L to see a Longer display  - to see the previous screen
                       F to Find other items   Q to Quit
NEXT ACTION?  _                                            CMTW
```

Figure 3.2

```
Your search: Bureau of Mines T#                       MEDIUM Display
     Finds: 1 record                                  Screen  1 of  1
------------------------------------------------------------------------

Bureau of Mines Technology Transfer Seminars (1982 : Pittsburgh, Pa.)
  Postdisaster survival and rescue research : proceedings, Bureau of Mines
Technology Transfer Seminar, Pittsburgh, Pa., November 16, 1982 / compiled by
staff, Bureau of Mines. -- [Avondale, Md.] : U.S. Dept. of the Interior, Bureau
of Mines, 1982.
  iii, 91 p. : ill. ; 28 cm. -- (Bureau of Mines information circular ; 8907)
  1. Mine accidents--Congresses. 2. Mine rescue work--Congresses. I. United
States. Bureau of Mines.




------------------------------------------------------------------------
NEXT ACTIONS      Key: ? for help              + to see the next screen
                       L to see a Longer display  - to see the previous screen
                       F to Find other items   Q to Quit
NEXT ACTION?  _                                            CMTW
```

Figure 3.3

```
Your search: Best American pla#                    MEDIUM Display
     Finds: 1 record                               Screen  1 of  1
-------------------------------------------------------------------

        Best American plays : sixth series, 1963-1967 / edited by
           John Gassner and Clive Barnes, with an introduction and
           prefaces to the plays by Clive Barnes. -- New York :
           Crown, c1971.
           xii, 594 p. ; 24 cm.
           1. American drama--20th century. 2. American drama--
        Collected works. I. Gassner, John, 1903-1967. II. Barnes,
        Clive, 1927-




-------------------------------------------------------------------
NEXT ACTIONS       Key: ? for help           + to see the next screen
                        L to see a Longer display  - to see the previous screen
                        F to Find other items      Q to Quit
NEXT ACTION?   _                                             CMTN
```

Figure 3.4

```
Your search: Brubeck, Dave#                        MEDIUM Display
     Finds: 1 record                               Screen  1 of  1
-------------------------------------------------------------------

        Brubeck, Dave.
          Bossa nova U.S.A. / [as performed by] the Dave Brubeck
        Quartet ; piano solo transcriptions by Howard Brubeck. --
        San Francisco, Calif. : Derry Music Co. ;  New York, N.Y. :
        C. Hansen, distributor, c1963.
          49 p. of music ; 28 cm.
          1. Piano music (Jazz), Arranged. 2. Jazz quartets--Piano
        scores. I. Brubeck, Howard R. II. Brubeck, Howard R. Theme
        for June; arr. III. Macero, Teo, 1925- Coracao sensivel;
        arr. IV. Dave Brubeck Quartet.




-------------------------------------------------------------------
NEXT ACTIONS       Key: ? for help           + to see the next screen
                        L to see a Longer display  - to see the previous screen
                        F to Find other items      Q to Quit
NEXT ACTION?   _                                             CMTN
```

Figure 3.5

```
Your search: Stewart, William #                    MEDIUM Display
       Finds: 1 record                              Screen  1 of  1
---------------------------------------------------------------------

         Stewart, William Herman, 1932-
           The explorer's historical tourist map of Alaska, with maps
         of Anchorage, Fairbanks & Juneau : with notes on the Arctic,
         wildlife, hunting, fishing, camping, exploring &
         prospecting, festivals & events / cartography by William H.
         Stewart. -- Charleston, W.Va. : Economic Service Council,
         1983.
           1 map : col. ; 65 x 71 cm., folded to 23 x 11 cm.
           1. Alaska--Maps, Tourist. 2. Alaska--Maps, Pictorial. I.
         Economic Service Council.




---------------------------------------------------------------------
NEXT ACTIONS      Key: ? for help          + to see the next screen
                       L to see a Longer display  - to see the previous screen
                       F to Find other items      Q to Quit
NEXT ACTION?  _                                              CMTN
```

Figure 3.6

```
Your search: Time.                                 MEDIUM Display
       Finds: 1 record                              Screen  1 of  1
---------------------------------------------------------------------

         Time. [Chicago, etc., Time Inc.]
           v. ill. (incl. ports.) 28 cm.
           I. Hadden, Briton, ed. II. Luce, Henry Robinson, 1898- ed.






---------------------------------------------------------------------
NEXT ACTIONS      Key: ? for help          + to see the next screen
                       L to see a Longer display  - to see the previous screen
                       F to Find other items      Q to Quit
NEXT ACTION?  _                                              CMTN
```

Figure 3.7

```
Your search: Bureau of Mines T#                    MEDIUM Display
      Finds: 1 record                              Screen 1 of 1
-------------------------------------------------------------------

         Bureau of Mines Technology Transfer Seminars (1982 :
           Pittsburgh, Pa.)
         Postdisaster survival and rescue research : proceedings,
       Bureau of Mines Technology Transfer Seminar, Pittsburgh,
       Pa., November 16, 1982 / compiled by staff, Bureau of Mines.
       -- [Avondale, Md.] : U.S. Dept. of the Interior, Bureau of
       Mines, 1982.
         iii, 91 p. : ill. ; 28 cm. -- (Bureau of Mines information
       circular ; 8907)
         1. Mine accidents--Congresses. 2. Mine rescue work--
       Congresses. I. United States. Bureau of Mines.




-------------------------------------------------------------------
NEXT ACTIONS       Key: ? for help             + to see the next screen
                        L to see a Longer display  - to see the previous screen
                        F to Find other items   Q to Quit
NEXT ACTION?  _                                           CMTN
```

Figure 3.8

```
Your search: Citizen Kane                          MEDIUM Display
      Finds: 1 record                              Screen 1 of 1
-------------------------------------------------------------------

         Citizen Kane [videorecording] / an RKO Radio Picture ; a
           Mercury production ; Orson Welles, direction, production.
           -- New York, N.Y. : VidAmerica, c1982.
           1 videocassette (119 min.) : sd., b&w ; 1/2 in. --
         (Classic series)
           1. Feature films. I. Welles, Orson, 1915- II. VidAmerica
         (Firm) III. RKO Radio Pictures, inc. IV. Mercury
         Productions.




-------------------------------------------------------------------
NEXT ACTIONS       Key: ? for help             + to see the next screen
                        L to see a Longer display  - to see the previous screen
                        F to Find other items   Q to Quit
NEXT ACTION?  _                                           CMTN
```

Figure 3.9

```
Your search: Best American pla#                    MEDIUM Display
     Finds: 1 record                              Screen  1 of  1
-----------------------------------------------------------------------

        Best American plays : sixth series, 1963-1967 / edited by
           John Gassner and Clive Barnes, with an introduction and
           prefaces to the plays by Clive Barnes. -- New York :
           Crown, c1971.

        xii, 594 p. ; 24 cm.

        1. American drama--20th century. 2. American drama--
        Collected works. I. Gassner, John, 1903-1967. II. Barnes,
        Clive, 1927-




-----------------------------------------------------------------------
NEXT ACTIONS     Key: ? for help          + to see the next screen
                      L to see a Longer display  - to see the previous screen
                      F to Find other items      Q to Quit
NEXT ACTION?  _                                            CMSX
```

Figure 3.10

```
Your search: Brubeck, Dave#                        MEDIUM Display
     Finds: 1 record                              Screen  1 of  1
-----------------------------------------------------------------------

        Brubeck, Dave.
          Bossa nova U.S.A. / [as performed by] the Dave Brubeck
        Quartet ; piano solo transcriptions by Howard Brubeck. --
        San Francisco, Calif. : Derry Music Co. ;  New York, N.Y. :
        C. Hansen, distributor, c1963.

        49 p. of music ; 28 cm.

        1. Piano music (Jazz), Arranged. 2. Jazz quartets--Piano
        scores. I. Brubeck, Howard R. II. Brubeck, Howard R. Theme
        for June; arr. III. Macero, Teo, 1925- Coracao sensivel;
        arr. IV. Dave Brubeck Quartet.



-----------------------------------------------------------------------
NEXT ACTIONS     Key: ? for help          + to see the next screen
                      L to see a Longer display  - to see the previous screen
                      F to Find other items      Q to Quit
NEXT ACTION?  _                                            CMSX
```

Figure 3.11

```
Your search: Stewart, William #                    MEDIUM Display
       Finds: 1 record                             Screen  1 of  1
---------------------------------------------------------------------

        Stewart, William Herman, 1932-
          The explorer's historical tourist map of Alaska, with maps
        of Anchorage, Fairbanks & Juneau : with notes on the Arctic,
        wildlife, hunting, fishing, camping, exploring &
        prospecting, festivals & events / cartography by William H.
        Stewart. -- Charleston, W.Va. : Economic Service Council,
        1983.

          1 map : col. ; 65 x 71 cm., folded to 23 x 11 cm.

          1. Alaska--Maps, Tourist. 2. Alaska--Maps, Pictorial. I.
        Economic Service Council.




        ------------------------------------------------------------
NEXT ACTIONS      Key: ? for help           + to see the next screen
                       L to see a Longer display  - to see the previous screen
                       F to Find other items  Q to Quit
NEXT ACTION?   _                                            CMSX
```

Figure 3.12

```
Your search: Time.                                 MEDIUM Display
       Finds: 1 record                             Screen  1 of  1
---------------------------------------------------------------------

        Time. [Chicago, etc., Time Inc.]

          v. ill. (incl. ports.) 28 cm.

          I. Hadden, Briton, ed. II. Luce, Henry Robinson, 1898- ed.








        ------------------------------------------------------------
NEXT ACTIONS      Key: ? for help           + to see the next screen
                       L to see a Longer display  - to see the previous screen
                       F to Find other items  Q to Quit
NEXT ACTION?   _                                            CMSX
```

Figure 3.13

```
Your search: Bureau of Mines T#                    MEDIUM Display
       Finds: 1 record                             Screen  1 of  1
-----------------------------------------------------------------------

        Bureau of Mines Technology Transfer Seminars (1982 :
          Pittsburgh, Pa.)
          Postdisaster survival and rescue research : proceedings,
        Bureau of Mines Technology Transfer Seminar, Pittsburgh,
        Pa., November 16, 1982 / compiled by staff, Bureau of Mines.
        -- [Avondale, Md.] : U.S. Dept. of the Interior, Bureau of
        Mines, 1982.

          iii, 91 p. : ill. ; 28 cm.
          (Bureau of Mines information circular ; 8907)

          1. Mine accidents--Congresses. 2. Mine rescue work--
        Congresses. I. United States. Bureau of Mines.


-----------------------------------------------------------------------
NEXT ACTIONS      Key: ? for help            + to see the next screen
                       L to see a Longer display  - to see the previous screen
                       F to Find other items  Q to Quit
NEXT ACTION?  _                                            CMSX
```

Figure 3.14

```
Your search: Citizen Kane                          MEDIUM Display
       Finds: 1 record                             Screen  1 of  1
-----------------------------------------------------------------------

        Citizen Kane [videorecording] / an RKO Radio Picture ; a
          Mercury production ; Orson Welles, direction, production.
          -- New York, N.Y. : VidAmerica, c1982.

          1 videocassette (119 min.) : sd., b&w ; 1/2 in.
          (Classic series)

          1. Feature films. I. Welles, Orson, 1915- II. VidAmerica
        (Firm) III. RKO Radio Pictures, inc. IV. Mercury
        Productions.




-----------------------------------------------------------------------
NEXT ACTIONS      Key: ? for help            + to see the next screen
                       L to see a Longer display  - to see the previous screen
                       F to Find other items  Q to Quit
NEXT ACTION? _                                             CMSX
```

Figure 3.15

```
Your search: Anderson, Sparky#                    MEDIUM Display
      Finds: 1 record                             Screen  1 of  1
-----------------------------------------------------------------

        Anderson, Sparky, 1934-
          Bless you boys : diary of the Detroit Tigers' 1984 season
        / by Sparky Anderson, with Dan Ewald. -- Chicago :
        Contemporary Books, c1984.


          231 p. : ill. ; 23 cm.


        Detroit Tigers (Baseball team)
        Ewald, Dan.




        -----------------------------------------------------------
NEXT ACTIONS        Key: ? for help              + to see the next screen
                        L to see a Longer display  - to see the previous screen
                        F to Find other items    Q to Quit
NEXT ACTION?  _                                            CMSL
```

Figure 3.16

```
Your search: Best American play#                  MEDIUM Display
      Finds: 1 record                             Screen  1 of  1
-----------------------------------------------------------------

        Best American plays : sixth series, 1963-1967 / edited by
          John Gassner and Clive Barnes, with an introduction and
          prefaces to the plays by Clive Barnes. -- New York :
          Crown, c1971.

          xii, 594 p. ; 24 cm.

        American drama--20th century.
        American drama--Collected works.
        Gassner, John, 1903-1967.
        Barnes, Clive, 1927-



        -----------------------------------------------------------
NEXT ACTIONS        Key: ? for help              + to see the next screen
                        L to see a Longer display  - to see the previous screen
                        F to Find other items    Q to Quit
NEXT ACTION?  _                                            .CMSL
```

Figure 3.17

```
Your search: Brubeck, Dave#                         MEDIUM Display
      Finds: 1 record                               Screen 1 of 1
------------------------------------------------------------------------

        Brubeck, Dave.
          Bossa nova U.S.A. / [as performed by] the Dave Brubeck
        Quartet ; piano solo transcriptions by Howard Brubeck. --
        San Francisco, Calif. : Derry Music Co. ;  New York, N.Y. :
        C. Hansen, distributor, c1963.

          49 p. of music ; 28 cm.

        Piano music (Jazz), Arranged.
        Jazz quartets--Piano scores.
        Brubeck, Howard R.
        Brubeck, Howard R. Theme for June; arr.
        Macero, Teo, 1925- Coracao sensivel; arr.
        Dave Brubeck Quartet.

------------------------------------------------------------------------
NEXT ACTIONS      Key: ? for help            + to see the next screen
                       L to see a Longer display  - to see the previous screen
                       F to Find other items   Q to Quit
NEXT ACTION?  _                                             CMSL
```

Figure 3.18

```
Your search: Stewart, William #                     MEDIUM Display
      Finds: 1 record                               Screen 1 of 1
------------------------------------------------------------------------

        Stewart, William Herman, 1932-
          The explorer's historical tourist map of Alaska, with maps
        of Anchorage, Fairbanks & Juneau : with notes on the Arctic,
        wildlife, hunting, fishing, camping, exploring &
        prospecting, festivals & events / cartography by William H.
        Stewart. -- Charleston, W.Va. : Economic Service Council,
        1983.

          1 map : col. ; 65 x 71 cm., folded to 23 x 11 cm.

        Alaska--Maps, Tourist.
        Alaska--Maps, Pictorial.
        Economic Service Council.

------------------------------------------------------------------------
NEXT ACTIONS      Key: ? for help            + to see the next screen
                       L to see a Longer display  - to see the previous screen
                       F to Find other items   Q to Quit
NEXT ACTION?  _                                             CMSL
```

Figure 3.19

```
+-------------------------------------------------------------------+
| Your search: Indy, Vincent d'#                      MEDIUM Display |
|       Finds: 1 record                               Screen  1 of  2|
| ------------------------------------------------------------------|
|                                                                   |
|           Indy, Vincent d', 1851-1931.                            |
|              Suite en re dans le style ancien : op. 24 ; Karadec : op.|
|           34 ; Concert, op. 89 pour piano, flute, violoncello et  |
|           orchestre a cordes [sound recording] / Vincent d'Indy. --|
|           France : Erato ; Paris : Distribution en France RCA, p1982.|
|                                                                   |
|              1 sound disc : 33 1/3 rpm, stereo. ; 12 in.          |
|                                                                   |
|           Suites (Flutes (2), trumpet with string orchestra)      |
|           Music, Incidental.                                      |
|           Concertos (Piano, flute, violoncello with string orchestra)|
|           Rampal, Jean Pierre.                                    |
|           Pierlot, Philippe.                                      |
|           Andre, Maurice.                                        |
|                                                                   |
| ------------------------------------------------CONTINUED-------  |
| NEXT ACTIONS      Key: ? for help            + to see the next screen |
|                        L to see a Longer display  - to see the previous screen|
|                        F to Find other items   Q to Quit          |
| NEXT ACTION?  _                                            CMSL    |
+-------------------------------------------------------------------+
```

Figure 3.20

```
+-------------------------------------------------------------------+
| Your search: Indy, Vincent d'#                      MEDIUM Display |
|       Finds: 1 record                               Screen  2 of  2|
| ------------------------------------------------------------------|
|                                                                   |
|           Duchable, Francois.                                     |
|           Lodeon, Frederic.                                       |
|           Paillard, Jean Francois.                                |
|           Indy, Vincent d', 1851-1931. Suite dans le style ancien.|
|             1982.                                                 |
|           Indy, Vincent d', 1851-1931. Karadec. 1982.             |
|           Indy, Vincent d', 1851-1931. Concerto, piano, flute,    |
|             violoncello, orchestra, op. 89. 1982.                 |
|           Orchestre de chambre Jean-Francois Paillard.            |
|                                                                   |
|                                                                   |
|                                                                   |
|                                                                   |
|                                                                   |
| ------------------------------------------------------------------|
| NEXT ACTIONS      Key: ? for help            + to see the next screen |
|                        L to see a Longer display  - to see the previous screen|
|                        F to Find other items   Q to Quit          |
| NEXT ACTION?  _                                            CMSL    |
+-------------------------------------------------------------------+
```

Figure 3.21

```
Your search: Time.                                MEDIUM Display
     Finds: 1 record                              Screen  1 of  1
-------------------------------------------------------------------

        Time. [Chicago, etc., Time Inc.]

          v. ill. (incl. ports.) 28 cm.

        Hadden, Briton, ed.
        Luce, Henry Robinson, 1898- ed.




-------------------------------------------------------------------
NEXT ACTIONS      Key: ? for help          + to see the next screen
                       L to see a Longer display  - to see the previous screen
                       F to Find other items      Q to Quit
NEXT ACTION?  _                                              CMSL
```

Figure 3.22

```
Your search: Bureau of Mines T#                   MEDIUM Display
     Finds: 1 record                              Screen  1 of  2
-------------------------------------------------------------------

        Bureau of Mines Technology Transfer Seminars (1982 :
          Pittsburgh, Pa.)
          Postdisaster survival and rescue research : proceedings,
        Bureau of Mines Technology Transfer Seminar, Pittsburgh,
        Pa., November 16, 1982 / compiled by staff, Bureau of Mines.
        -- [Avondale, Md.] : U.S. Dept. of the Interior, Bureau of
        Mines, 1982.

          iii, 91 p. : ill. ; 28 cm.

          (Bureau of Mines information circular ; 8907)

        Mine accidents--Congresses.
        Mine rescue work--Congresses.
-------------------------------------------------------CONTINUED-------
NEXT ACTIONS      Key: ? for help          + to see the next screen
                       L to see a Longer display  - to see the previous screen
                       F to Find other items      Q to Quit
NEXT ACTION?  _                                              CMSL
```

Figure 3.23

```
Your search: Bureau of Mines T#                       MEDIUM Display
       Finds: 1 record                                Screen  2 of  2
----------------------------------------------------------------------

        United States. Bureau of Mines.




















----------------------------------------------------------------------
NEXT ACTIONS       Key: ? for help            + to see the next screen
                        L to see a Longer display  - to see the previous screen
                        F to Find other items  Q to Quit
NEXT ACTION?  _                                              CMSL
```

Figure 3.24

```
Your search: Citizen Kane                             MEDIUM Display
       Finds: 1 record                                Screen  1 of  1
----------------------------------------------------------------------

        Citizen Kane [videorecording] / an RKO Radio Picture ; a
          Mercury production ; Orson Welles, direction, production.
          -- New York, N.Y. : VidAmerica, c1982.

          1 videocassette (119 min.) : sd., b&w ; 1/2 in.

        (Classic series)

        Feature films.
        Welles, Orson, 1915-
        VidAmerica (Firm)
        RKO Radio Pictures, inc.
        Mercury Productions.


----------------------------------------------------------------------
NEXT ACTIONS       Key: ? for help            + to see the next screen
                        L to see a Longer display  - to see the previous screen
                        F to Find other items  Q to Quit
NEXT ACTION?  _                                              CMSL
```

Figure 3.25

```
Your search: Bossa nova U.S.A#                      MEDIUM Display
      Finds: 1 record                               Screen  1 of  1
----------------------------------------------------------------------

        Bossa nova U.S.A. / [as performed by] the Dave Brubeck
          Quartet ; piano solo transcriptions by Howard Brubeck. San
          Francisco, Calif. : Derry Music Co. ;  New York, N.Y. : C.
          Hansen, distributor, c1963.


        49 p. of music ; 28 cm.


        Brubeck, Dave.
        Brubeck, Howard R.
        Brubeck, Howard R. Theme for June; arr.
        Macero, Teo, 1925- Coracao sensivel; arr.
        Dave Brubeck Quartet.
        Piano music (Jazz), Arranged.
        Jazz quartets--Piano scores.


----------------------------------------------------------------------
NEXT ACTIONS     Key: ? for help              + to see the next screen
                      L to see a Longer display  - to see the previous screen
                      F to Find other items   Q to Quit
NEXT ACTION?  _                                              CMTL
```

Figure 3.26

```
Your search: Postdisaster surv#                     MEDIUM Display
      Finds: 1 record                               Screen  1 of  2
----------------------------------------------------------------------

        Postdisaster survival and rescue research : proceedings,
          Bureau of Mines Technology Transfer Seminar, Pittsburgh,
          Pa., November 16, 1982 / compiled by staff, Bureau of
          Mines. [Avondale, Md.] : U.S. Dept. of the Interior,
          Bureau of Mines, 1982.

        iii, 91 p. : ill. ; 28 cm.

        (Bureau of Mines information circular ; 8907)

        Bureau of Mines Technology Transfer Seminars (1982 :
          Pittsburgh, Pa.)
        United States. Bureau of Mines.
        Mine accidents--Congresses.

-------------------------------------------------------CONTINUED-------
NEXT ACTIONS     Key: ? for help              + to see the next screen
                      L to see a Longer display  - to see the previous screen
                      F to Find other items   Q to Quit
NEXT ACTION?  _                                              CMTL
```

Figure 3.27

```
Your search: Postdisaster surv#                    MEDIUM Display
      Finds: 1 record                              Screen  2 of  2
------------------------------------------------------------------------

      Mine rescue work--Congresses.









------------------------------------------------------------------------
NEXT ACTIONS       Key: ? for help            + to see the next screen
                        L to see a Longer display  - to see the previous screen
                        F to Find other items  Q to Quit

NEXT ACTION?   _                                            CMTL
```

Figure 3.28

```
Your search: Anderson, Sparky#                     CITATION Display
      Finds: 1 record                              Screen  1 of  1
------------------------------------------------------------------------

      Anderson, Sparky, 1934- Bless you boys : diary of the
          Detroit Tigers' 1984 season / by Sparky Anderson, with
          Dan Ewald. Chicago : Contemporary Books, c1984. 231 p. :
          ill. ; 23 cm.

      Detroit Tigers (Baseball team)
      Ewald, Dan.






------------------------------------------------------------------------
NEXT ACTIONS       Key: ? for help            + to see the next screen
                        L to see a Longer display  - to see the previous screen
                        F to Find other items  Q to Quit

NEXT ACTION?   _                                            CMCIT
```

Figure 3.29

```
Your search: Best American pla#                    CITATION Display
     Finds: 1 record                               Screen  1 of  1
-------------------------------------------------------------------

        Best American plays : sixth series, 1963-1967 / edited by
            John Gassner and Clive Barnes, with an introduction and
            prefaces to the plays by Clive Barnes. New York : Crown,
            c1971. xii, 594 p. ; 24 cm.

        American drama--20th century.
        American drama--Collected works.
        Gassner, John, 1903-1967.
        Barnes, Clive, 1927-




        -----------------------------------------------------------
NEXT ACTIONS        Key: ? for help            + to see the next screen
                         L to see a Longer display   - to see the previous screen
                         F to Find other items    Q to Quit
NEXT ACTION?  _                                           CMCIT
```

Figure 3.30

```
Your search: Brubeck, Dave. Bo#                    CITATION Display
     Finds: 1 record                               Screen  1 of  1
-------------------------------------------------------------------

        Brubeck, Dave. Bossa nova U.S.A. / [as performed by] the
            Dave Brubeck Quartet ; piano solo transcriptions by
            Howard Brubeck. San Francisco, Calif. : Derry Music Co.
            ; New York, N.Y. : C. Hansen, distributor, c1963. 49 p.
            of music ; 28 cm.

        Piano music (Jazz), Arranged.
        Jazz quartets--Piano scores.
        Brubeck, Howard R.
        Brubeck, Howard R. Theme for June; arr.
        Macero, Teo, 1925- Coracao sensivel; arr.
        Dave Brubeck Quartet.



        -----------------------------------------------------------
NEXT ACTIONS        Key: ? for help            + to see the next screen
                         L to see a Longer display   - to see the previous screen
                         F to Find other items    Q to Quit
NEXT ACTION?  _                                           CMCIT
```

Figure 3.31

```
Your search: Stewart, William #                    CITATION Display
     Finds: 1 record                               Screen  1 of  1
---------------------------------------------------------------------

        Stewart, William Herman, 1932- The explorer's historical
            tourist map of Alaska, with maps of Anchorage, Fairbanks
            & Juneau : with notes on the Arctic, wildlife, hunting,
            fishing, camping, exploring & prospecting, festivals &
            events / cartography by William H. Stewart. Charleston,
            W.Va. : Economic Service Council, 1983. 1 map : col. ;
            65 x 71 cm., folded to 23 x 11 cm.

        Alaska--Maps, Tourist.
        Alaska--Maps, Pictorial.
        Economic Service Council.




    ----------------------------------------------------------------
NEXT ACTIONS      Key: ? for help              + to see the next screen
                       L to see a Longer display  - to see the previous screen
                       F to Find other items   Q to Quit
NEXT ACTION?   _                                             CMCIT
```

Figure 3.32

```
Your search: Indy, Vincent d'#                    CITATION Display
     Finds: 1 record                               Screen  1 of  2
---------------------------------------------------------------------

        Indy, Vincent d', 1851-1931. Suite en re dans le style
            ancien : op. 24 ; Karadec : op. 34 ; Concert, op. 89
            pour piano, flute, violoncello et orchestre a cordes
            [sound recording] / Vincent d'Indy. France : Erato ;
            Paris : Distribution en France RCA, p1982. 1 sound disc
            : 33 1/3 rpm, stereo. ; 12 in.

        Suites (Flutes (2), trumpet with string orchestra)
        Music, Incidental.
        Concertos (Piano, flute, violoncello with string orchestra)
        Rampal, Jean Pierre.
        Pierlot, Philippe.
        Andre, Maurice.
        Duchable, Francois.

    ------------------------------------------------------CONTINUED-------
NEXT ACTIONS      Key: ? for help              + to see the next screen
                       L to see a Longer display  - to see the previous screen
                       F to Find other items   Q to Quit
NEXT ACTION?   _                                             CMCIT
```

Figure 3.33

```
Your search: Indy, Vincent d'#                      CITATION Display
     Finds: 1 record                                Screen  2 of  2
-----------------------------------------------------------------------

        Lodeon, Frederic.
        Paillard, Jean Francois.
        Indy, Vincent d', 1851-1931. Suite dans le style ancien.
           1982.
        Indy, Vincent d', 1851-1931. Karadec. 1982.
        Indy, Vincent d', 1851-1931. Concerto, piano, flute,
           violoncello, orchestra, op. 89. 1982.
        Orchestre de chambre Jean-Francois Paillard.




-----------------------------------------------------------------------
NEXT ACTIONS     Key: ? for help              + to see the next screen
                      L to see a Longer display  - to see the previous screen
                      F to Find other items   Q to Quit
NEXT ACTION?  _                                            CMCIT
```

Figure 3.34

```
Your search: Time.                                  CITATION Display
     Finds: 1 record                                Screen  1 of  1
-----------------------------------------------------------------------

        Time. [Chicago, etc., Time Inc.] v. ill. (incl. ports.) 28
           cm.

        Hadden, Briton, ed.
        Luce, Henry Robinson, 1898- ed.






-----------------------------------------------------------------------
NEXT ACTIONS     Key: ? for help              + to see the next screen
                      L to see a Longer display  - to see the previous screen
                      F to Find other items   Q to Quit
NEXT ACTION?  _                                            CMCIT
```

Figure 3.35

```
Your search: Bureau of Mines T#                   CITATION Display
     Finds: 1 record                              Screen  1 of  1
------------------------------------------------------------------------


        Bureau of Mines Technology Transfer Seminars (1982 :
            Pittsburgh, Pa.) Postdisaster survival and rescue
            research : proceedings, Bureau of Mines Technology
            Transfer Seminar, Pittsburgh, Pa., November 16, 1982 /
            compiled by staff, Bureau of Mines. [Avondale, Md.] :
            U.S. Dept. of the Interior, Bureau of Mines, 1982. iii,
            91 p. : ill. ; 28 cm. (Bureau of Mines information
            circular ; 8907)


        Mine accidents--Congresses.
        Mine rescue work--Congresses.
        United States. Bureau of Mines.




------------------------------------------------------------------------
NEXT ACTIONS       Key: ? for help            + to see the next screen
                        L to see a Longer display  - to see the previous screen
                        F to Find other items   Q to Quit

NEXT ACTION?   _                                            CMCIT
```

Figure 3.36

```
Your search: Citizen Kane                         CITATION Display
     Finds: 1 record                              Screen  1 of  1
------------------------------------------------------------------------


        Citizen Kane [videorecording] / an RKO Radio Picture ; a
            Mercury production ; Orson Welles, direction,
            production. New York, N.Y. : VidAmerica, c1982. 1
            videocassette (119 min.) : sd., b&w ; 1/2 in. (Classic
            series)

        Feature films.
        Welles, Orson, 1915-
        VidAmerica (Firm)
        RKO Radio Pictures, inc.
        Mercury Productions.




------------------------------------------------------------------------
NEXT ACTIONS       Key: ? for help            + to see the next screen
                        L to see a Longer display  - to see the previous screen
                        F to Find other items   Q to Quit

NEXT ACTION?   _                                            CMCIT
```

Figure 3.37

```
Your search: Bless you boys #                          CITATION Display
     Finds: 1 record                                   Screen  1 of  1
-----------------------------------------------------------------------

        Bless you boys : diary of the Detroit Tigers' 1984 season /
           by Sparky Anderson, with Dan Ewald. Chicago :
           Contemporary Books, c1984. 231 p. : ill. ; 23 cm.

        Anderson, Sparky, 1934-
        Ewald, Dan.
        Detroit Tigers (Baseball team)




-----------------------------------------------------------------------

NEXT ACTIONS      Key: ? for help              + to see the next screen
                       L to see a Longer display  - to see the previous screen
                       F to Find other items   Q to Quit

NEXT ACTION?   _                                           CMTCIT
```

Figure 3.38

```
Your search: Best American pla#                        CITATION Display
     Finds: 1 record                                   Screen  1 of  1
-----------------------------------------------------------------------

        Best American plays : sixth series, 1963-1967 / edited by
           John Gassner and Clive Barnes, with an introduction and
           prefaces to the plays by Clive Barnes. New York : Crown,
           c1971. xii, 594 p. ; 24 cm.

        Gassner, John, 1903-1967.
        Barnes, Clive, 1927-
        American drama--20th century.
        American drama--Collected works.




-----------------------------------------------------------------------

NEXT ACTIONS      Key: ? for help              + to see the next screen
                       L to see a Longer display  - to see the previous screen
                       F to Find other items   Q to Quit

NEXT ACTION?   _                                           CMTCIT
```

Figure 3.39

```
Your search: Bossa nova U.S.A#                        CITATION Display
     Finds: 1 record                                  Screen  1 of  1
-------------------------------------------------------------------------


        Bossa nova U.S.A. / [as performed by] the Dave Brubeck
            Quartet ; piano solo transcriptions by Howard Brubeck.
            San Francisco, Calif. : Derry Music Co. ;  New York,
            N.Y. : C. Hansen, distributor, c1963. 49 p. of music ;
            28 cm.


        Brubeck, Dave.
        Brubeck, Howard R.
        Brubeck, Howard R. Theme for June; arr.
        Macero, Teo, 1925- Coracao sensivel; arr.
        Dave Brubeck Quartet.
        Piano music (Jazz), Arranged.
        Jazz quartets--Piano scores.



-------------------------------------------------------------------------
NEXT ACTIONS      Key: ? for help              + to see the next screen
                       L to see a Longer display  - to see the previous screen
                       F to Find other items    Q to Quit

NEXT ACTION?   _                                          CMTCIT
```

Figure 3.40

```
Your search: The explorer's hi#                       CITATION Display
     Finds: 1 record                                  Screen  1 of  1
-------------------------------------------------------------------------


        The explorer's historical tourist map of Alaska, with maps
            of Anchorage, Fairbanks & Juneau : with notes on the
            Arctic, wildlife, hunting, fishing, camping, exploring &
            prospecting, festivals & events / cartography by William
            H. Stewart. Charleston, W.Va. : Economic Service
            Council, 1983. 1 map : col. ; 65 x 71 cm., folded to 23
            x 11 cm.

        Stewart, William Herman, 1932-
        Economic Service Council.
        Alaska--Maps, Tourist.
        Alaska--Maps, Pictorial.



-------------------------------------------------------------------------
NEXT ACTIONS      Key: ? for help              + to see the next screen
                       L to see a Longer display  - to see the previous screen
                       F to Find other items    Q to Quit

NEXT ACTION?   _                                          CMTCIT
```

Figure 3.41

```
Your search: Suite en re dans #                      CITATION Display
     Finds: 1 record                                 Screen  1 of  2
--------------------------------------------------------------------------


          Suite en re dans le style ancien : op. 24 ; Karadec : op. 34
             ; Concert, op. 89 pour piano, flute, violoncello et
             orchestre a cordes [sound recording] / Vincent d'Indy.
             France : Erato ; Paris : Distribution en France RCA,
             p1982. 1 sound disc : 33 1/3 rpm, stereo. ; 12 in.

          Indy, Vincent d', 1851-1931.
          Rampal, Jean Pierre.
          Pierlot, Philippe.
          Andre, Maurice.
          Duchable, Francois.
          Lodeon, Frederic.
          Paillard, Jean Francois.



     --------------------------------------------------------CONTINUED-------
NEXT ACTIONS      Key: ? for help              + to see the next screen
                       L to see a Longer display   - to see the previous screen
                       F to Find other items       Q to Quit

NEXT ACTION?   _                                              CMTCIT
```

Figure 3.42

```
Your search: Suite en re dans #                      CITATION Display
     Finds: 1 record                                 Screen  2 of  2
--------------------------------------------------------------------------

          Indy, Vincent d', 1851-1931. Suite dans le style ancien.
             1982.
          Indy, Vincent d', 1851-1931. Karadec. 1982.
          Indy, Vincent d', 1851-1931. Concerto, piano, flute,
             violoncello, orchestra, op. 89. 1982.
          Orchestre de chambre Jean-Francois Paillard.
          Suites (Flutes (2), trumpet with string orchestra)
          Music, Incidental.
          Concertos (Piano, flute, violoncello with string orchestra)




     --------------------------------------------------------------------
NEXT ACTIONS      Key: ? for help              + to see the next screen
                       L to see a Longer display   - to see the previous screen
                       F to Find other items       Q to Quit
NEXT ACTION?   _                                              CMTCIT
```

Figure 3.43

```
Your search: Time.                                   CITATION Display
     Finds: 1 record                                 Screen 1 of 1
---------------------------------------------------------------------

        Time. [Chicago, etc., Time Inc.] v. ill. (incl. ports.) 28
           cm.

        Hadden, Briton, ed.
        Luce, Henry Robinson, 1898- ed.




---------------------------------------------------------------------
NEXT ACTIONS      Key: ? for help            + to see the next screen
                       L to see a Longer display  - to see the previous screen
                       F to Find other items  Q to Quit
NEXT ACTION?  _                                              CMTCIT
```

Figure 3.44

```
Your search: Postdisaster surv#                      CITATION Display
     Finds: 1 record                                 Screen 1 of 1
---------------------------------------------------------------------

        Postdisaster survival and rescue research : proceedings,
           Bureau of Mines Technology Transfer Seminar, Pittsburgh,
           Pa., November 16, 1982 / compiled by staff, Bureau of
           Mines. [Avondale, Md.] : U.S. Dept. of the Interior,
           Bureau of Mines, 1982. iii, 91 p. : ill. ; 28 cm.
           (Bureau of Mines information circular ; 8907)

        Bureau of Mines Technology Transfer Seminars (1982 :
           Pittsburgh, Pa.)
        United States. Bureau of Mines.
        Mine accidents--Congresses.
        Mine rescue work--Congresses.


---------------------------------------------------------------------
NEXT ACTIONS      Key: ? for help            + to see the next screen
                       L to see a Longer display  - to see the previous screen
                       F to Find other items  Q to Quit
NEXT ACTION?  _                                              CMTCIT
```

Figure 3.45

```
Your search: Citizen Kane                          CITATION Display
      Finds: 1 record                              Screen  1 of  1
--------------------------------------------------------------------

        Citizen Kane [videorecording] / an RKO Radio Picture ; a
           Mercury production ; Orson Welles, direction,
           production. New York, N.Y. : VidAmerica, c1982. 1
           videocassette (119 min.) : sd., b&w ; 1/2 in. (Classic
           series)

        Welles, Orson, 1915-
        VidAmerica (Firm)
        RKO Radio Pictures, inc.
        Mercury Productions.
        Feature films.



--------------------------------------------------------------------
NEXT ACTIONS      Key: ? for help            + to see the next screen
                       L to see a Longer display  - to see the previous screen
                       F to Find other items  Q to Quit
NEXT ACTION?  _                                            CMTCIT
```

Figure 3.46

```
Your search: Brubeck, Dave. Bo#                    CITATION Display
      Finds: 1 record                              Screen  1 of  1
--------------------------------------------------------------------

        Brubeck, Dave. BOSSA NOVA U.S.A. / [as performed by] the
           Dave Brubeck Quartet ; piano solo transcriptions by
           Howard Brubeck. San Francisco, Calif. : Derry Music Co.
           ; New York, N.Y. : C. Hansen, distributor, c1963. 49 p.
           of music ; 28 cm.

        Piano music (Jazz), Arranged.
        Jazz quartets--Piano scores.
        Brubeck, Howard R.
        Brubeck, Howard R. Theme for June; arr.
        Macero, Teo, 1925- Coracao sensivel; arr.
        Dave Brubeck Quartet.



--------------------------------------------------------------------
NEXT ACTIONS      Key: ? for help            + to see the next screen
                       L to see a Longer display  - to see the previous screen
                       F to Find other items  Q to Quit
NEXT ACTION?  _                                            CMCAP
```

Figure 3.47

```
Your search: Bureau of Mines T#                          CITATION Display
        Finds: 1 record                                  Screen  1 of  1
----------------------------------------------------------------------------

        Bureau of Mines Technology Transfer Seminars (1982 :
            Pittsburgh, Pa.) POSTDISASTER SURVIVAL AND RESCUE
            RESEARCH : proceedings, Bureau of Mines Technology
            Transfer Seminar, Pittsburgh, Pa., November 16, 1982 /
            compiled by staff, Bureau of Mines. [Avondale, Md.] :
            U.S. Dept. of the Interior, Bureau of Mines, 1982. iii,
            91 p. : ill. ; 28 cm. (Bureau of Mines information
            circular ; 8907)

        Mine accidents--Congresses.
        Mine rescue work--Congresses.
        United States. Bureau of Mines.



----------------------------------------------------------------------------
NEXT ACTIONS      Key: ? for help            + to see the next screen
                       L to see a Longer display   - to see the previous screen
                       F to Find other items  Q to Quit
NEXT ACTION?   _                                            CMCAP
```

4

Labeled Displays

Labels can clarify bibliographic information, but only if the labels are clear themselves. A display with understandable, appropriately placed labels, good margins and good use of spacing should communicate more rapidly and effectively than a simple cardlike display. The labeled display will inevitably require more space, meaning that more items will require second and third screens.

Many libraries will accept that penalty in the interest of clear communication; designers should at least consider labeled displays for some or all bibliographic displays. Most people reviewing the early displays used in this project were library professionals, quite familiar with cardlike displays, since RLIN offers a pure cardlike display and has no labeled display. Nearly all of those reviewers preferred the labeled alternatives.

The space problem with labeled displays is not simply that more screens must be transmitted and that users can't view all the information at once. Some users will fail to display the second or third screen, making the information on that screen useless. Clear labels don't help if information isn't displayed at all.

CHOOSING THE RIGHT LABELS

Labeled displays clarify information only if the labels are clear. In order to make sense to patrons, labels should meet certain requirements:

- Labels should be words or phrases, not abbreviations or codes.
- Labels should be in common English, not library jargon.
- Labels should identify the fields properly.
- Labels should be highlighted to stand out from the text.

Some existing online systems fail to meet those seemingly obvious standards. Some labeled displays use AU, SO, IM, CO, IMPRT, AAUTH and other arcane codes, which certainly don't communicate to typical patrons (or, in some cases, even to librarians—SO is an actual label, and its meaning is still cloudy). A strong case can be made that a traditional cardlike display is preferable to a labeled display that uses codes and unintelligible abbreviations.

Current systems using words for labels don't seem to do much better. The terms MAIN ENTRY, IMPRINT, TRACINGS and COLLATION appear in one form or another as labels within online catalogs. Some systems compound the problem by including other unlabeled fields below labeled fields. One system includes physical description under IMPRINT, one includes both publication information and physical description under TITLE, another includes physical description under EDITION and another includes it under PUBLISHER. In each of these cases, the attempt to communicate is clouded by labels and placement that fail to clarify.

What constitutes library jargon is a matter for discussion. IMPRINT, COLLATION, MAIN ENTRY and TRACINGS are clearly library (and, in some cases, publishing) jargon. ADDED ENTRY is probably library jargon. The terms SERIES, SUBJECT, UNIFORM TITLE and PAGINATION all raise some questions, and other names may be jargon. CORPORATE AUTHOR is probably a jargon term, partly because of the unfortunate word *corporate*. Most patrons can understand that The Beatles aren't a person but are capable of authorship, but most patrons don't think of The Beatles as a corporation.

Designers and librarians must consider labels carefully. We do not feel that the labels used in displays in this chapter constitute the final word nor, for that matter, did we settle on a single set of labels. Note that different labels appear in different displays, and that still more choices appear in later chapters, especially in Chapter 8.

The labels used in this chapter represent the results of many experiments, but also represent a certain degree of compromise. Displays discussed and illustrated in this chapter are listed in Table 4.1; those displays include a number of different choices for labels. In the end, we found OTHER ENTRY to be a way of avoiding problems, though none of us is delighted with the choice. Table 4.2 shows the labels that we tried for various fields during testing.

Labels can be highlighted in several ways: all capital letters, reverse video, half intensity or double intensity. Reverse printing is not a fair representation of reverse video, and neither that nor half intensity nor double intensity was possible within our testing system. We found that capitalized labels worked quite well; one display in this chapter provides upper and lower case labels for comparison.

LABELED DISPLAY OPTIONS

We found it easy to generate dozens of labeled displays, even retaining the same set of data elements. We also found that we could not easily evaluate the effects of any given change, because each display had several things that were different from any other display. Given the almost endless number of possible labeled displays and the difficulties of comparisons, this chapter takes a deliberately narrow set of possibilities. We were surprised that this narrow set of possibilities encompasses such a wide range of appearances.

An independent observer might suggest that all the displays in this chapter show signs of catalog-card orientation in the way fields are grouped, the order of elements and other aspects. That's a fair observation, here as for cardlike displays. While many of the labeled displays do break away from main entry, all of the displays in this chapter group descriptive elements in the same traditional order. That order—title, publisher, date and pagination—can be found in most standard citation styles as well as in catalog cards. We did not look for radical departures. We did conclude that added entries should appear before notes, but none of the medium-level displays includes notes.

Displays in this chapter appear in a specific order for a reason. Each display differs from the previous display, or from another baseline display, by one, *and only one,* characteristic (with the possible exception of labels used). When comparing the sometimes sharply different appearance of two different displays for the same record, consider that those differences arise from changing only one of the many design elements of the display.

LMLFT—Flush-Left Labels and Text

Display LMLFT is the most elementary labeled display in this book, and was introduced in Chapter 2 (Figures 2.12–2.14). We do not regard it as particularly readable,

Table 4.1: Displays Discussed in Chapter 4

Display	Name
LMBL	Labeled medium display, flush-left labels, block-indented text
LMG	Labeled medium display, gutter aligned with each group labeled
LMGAT	Labeled medium display, gutter aligned, author/title split
LMGCON	Labeled medium display, gutter aligned, concatenated entries
LMGLC	Labeled medium display, gutter aligned, upper & lower case labels
LMGNI	Labeled medium display, gutter aligned, no indentation
LMGSP	Labeled medium display, gutter aligned, vertical spacing
LMGT	Labeled medium display, gutter aligned, title first
LMGWI	Labeled medium display, like LMGAT but with wide indentation
LMLFI	Labeled medium display, flush-left labels and text, indentation
LMLFT	Labeled medium display, flush-left labels and text
LMRI	Labeled medium display, gutter aligned with each field labeled

Table 4.2: Labels Used in Various Tests

TAGS	LABELS USED
100	AUTHOR
100-111	AUTHOR, Author, NAME, NAMES
100-130	AUTHOR, AUTHOR(S)
100-130*	WORKS
110	CORPORATE AUTHOR
110-130	OTHER ENTRIES
111	CONFERENCE
130	OTHER ENTRIES, TITLE, Title, WORK, WORKS
240	TITLE, OTHER ENTRIES, WORKS
245	TITLE, Title
250-255	EDITION, Edition
260-262	PUBLISHED, Published, PUBLICATION INFO, DATE, ETC.
260-262@	DATE
300-305	MATERIAL, Material, CONTAINS, DESCRIPTION, SIZE, ETC.
310-351	NOTES
362	TITLE, EDITION
400-490	SERIES, Series
500-590	NOTES
600-657	SUBJECTS, Subjects, TOPICS
700-711	AUTHOR(S), NAMES
700-711*	WORKS, RELATED WORKS
700-711#	OTHER ENTRIES
700-730	OTHER ENTRIES
700-730*	WORKS
700-740	OTHER ENTRIES, Other Entries
700-740#	NAMES
730	WORKS
752	NAMES, SUBJECTS
752-755	SUBJECTS
760-787	NOTES, OTHER ENTRIES
773	NOTES, OTHER ENTRIES
800-830	SERIES
Qualifiers	* Fields containing subfield ‡t (Title)
	@ Date subfields only
	# Fields not containing subfield ‡t (Title)

and it is probably worse than a good cardlike display. It appears here as a starting point for other designs, to show how appearance changes (and, in most cases, improves) as elements are modified. Figures 4.1 and 4.2 also illustrate LMLFT. This display and the next use the full width of the screen for text.

Labels used in this and the next three displays, all of which label each field, are as follows:

- AUTHOR for the main entry (100–130)
- TITLE for the title statement (245)
- EDITION for the edition statement (250)
- PUBLISHED for publication, distribution, etc. (imprint) (260–262)
- MATERIAL for the physical description (300–305)
- SERIES for each series statement (400–490)
- SUBJECT for each subject added entry (600–699)
- OTHER ENTRY for each added entry (700–740, 796–798)

LMLFI—Flush-Left Labels and Text with Indentation

The second display, LMLFI, differs from the first only in that any additional lines of a field are indented two spaces, making the fields slightly more readable. Figures 4.3 and 4.4 illustrate the effects of that change. While LMLFI is still difficult to read, it is somewhat more legible than LMLFT.

LMBL—Flush-Left Labels, Block-Indented Text

Display LMBL moves all text over to column 17 and narrows the maximum line length to 60 characters, but leaves the labels at the far left. This display, or a variant with one label for each group of fields, represents a fairly common variety of labeled display. It is certainly far more legible than either LMLFT or LMLFI, as can be seen in Figures 4.5 and 4.6.

Naturally, the blocked text takes up somewhat more space. LMBL and LMRI, below, require exactly the same amount of space, so statistics for LMBL are given in the next section.

LMRI—Gutter-Aligned, Each Field Labeled

Joseph Matthews deserves credit for suggesting (in a paper given at the 1985 Lakeway Conference) this alternative, used for the remaining displays in this chapter. Gutter alignment combines blocked, left-adjusted text and right-adjusted labels, lining up the information around a blank gutter. Only recently have online systems using gutter alignment appeared (other than those using abbreviated fixed-length labels).

When Walt Crawford first heard Matthews suggest this alternative, his reaction was the same as that of most others at the 1985 Lakeway Conference—it sounded awful. But, as Figures 4.7 and 4.8 show, it doesn't look awful; as Matthews suggested, it works quite well. Matthews did *not* suggest this rather cramped format with its label per field; his key suggestion was the gutter alignment.

The effect of moving text to column 17 is to narrow the text column, which means that more space is required to display records. Where LMLFT has room for minimal holdings on the first screen 87% of the time, LMRI and LMBL have that room only 81% of the time. That loss is almost certainly tolerable, given the much better legibility of LMRI.

LMG—Gutter-Aligned, Each Group Labeled

While display LMRI (above) provides good legibility, the display itself is quite dense. Individual labels tend to blur into the column of labels, particularly when displaying a series of one-line fields such as subjects. Display LMG, first introduced in Chapter 2 (Figures 2.15–2.17), uses one label for each group of fields, reducing the number of labels and the display density.

Two labels change in LMG. SUBJECT becomes SUBJECTS, and OTHER ENTRY becomes OTHER ENTRIES. This display is the first labeled option that we feel might be a reasonable choice for a library. The remaining six items from the set of comparisons appear as Figures 4.9 through 4.14. The amount of space required is exactly the same as for LMRI, but the display density is slightly lower—28.9% for LMG compared with 29.9% for LMRI.

One limitation in RBDISP first appears in Figure 2.17, an earlier illustration of LMG. When an item goes to a second screen, the first field on that screen may not be labeled, and none of the bibliographic entry repeats on the second screen. We do *not* recommend that practice for actual online catalogs. Any such systems should repeat the label for the first field of the new screen, and should provide some repetitive bibliographic data to relate the second screen back to the first.

LMGLC—Gutter-Aligned, Upper and Lower Case Labels

Display LMGLC, illustrated in Figures 4.15 and 4.16, differs from LMG only in that labels appear in upper and lower case, rather than as all capitals. The authors feel that capitalized labels work better, but some systems do use upper and lower case labels.

LMGCON—Gutter-Aligned, Concatenated Entries

This display illustrates a technique actually used in some online systems. Subjects (and, for display LMGCON, series entries and other entries) appear as a paragraph, separated by some constant text.

We selected a single asterisk as the separating text for these samples. Other possibilities include two asterisks, a slash, a back slash or Roman and Arabic numerals as in traditional tracings. Of those possibilities, the slash seems an unfortunate choice, because it can appear in text and is used as ISBD punctuation.

Does LMGCON represent a useful alternative? Figures 4.17 through 4.25 show the eight test items for your consideration. Note particularly the items for Dave Brubeck, Vincent d'Indy and *Citizen Kane,* where several entries appear together.

LMGCON offers greater compactness than other gutter-aligned labeled displays: 88% of tested items had room on the first screen for minimal holdings, a slightly better figure than for the crude LMLFT (87%) and significantly better than for LMG (81%). For public libraries, LMGCON does even better—95%, as compared with LMG's 89% and LMLFT's 92%.

LMGSP—Gutter-Aligned, Vertical Spacing

Display LMGSP goes back to LMG, the first display with group labels, as a baseline. This display adds blank lines above series, subjects and other entries. The six items not illustrated in Chapter 2 (Figures 2.18–2.20) appear in Figures 4.26 through 4.31. As noted in Chapter 2, LMGSP adds greater clarity at the expense of using more space. Adding those few vertical spaces produces a surprising jump in the number of items that go to a second screen. In order to show minimal holdings, an extra 93,000 items out of a 400,000-item sample require at least a second screen. Without room for holdings, the differences are still startling: 13,322 items require two screens using LMG, while 39,815—three times as many—require two screens using LMGSP. Only 5704 require two screens using LMGCON (concatenated subjects and added entries), without considering space for holdings.

We did not illustrate use of even more spacing, such as adding blank lines above publication information and physical description, or even adding a blank line after each field, because the results are predictable: fewer and fewer items can be accommodated on a single screen.

LMGT—Gutter-Aligned, Title First

Display LMGT differs from LMGSP in two ways: instead of appearing as AUTHOR, main entries other than titles appear as the first OTHER ENTRY, and the title always appears first. Figures 4.32 and 4.33 show two items using this display. The display requires exactly the same amount of space as LMGSP, though with very slightly lower density.

We found that title-first labeled displays work better than title-first cardlike displays, but the labels used for LMGT do not seem particularly good. We could not arrive at a suitable label for the mix of fields included in OTHER ENTRIES; after studying the problem, we arrived at the next display.

LMGAT—Gutter-Aligned, Author/Title Split

This display, and the two that follow, differ from LMGT in a fundamental way. LMGAT splits OTHER ENTRIES into two groups: those that have titles within the entry and those that do not. The former group, NAMES, appears above SERIES; the latter, WORKS, appears where OTHER ENTRIES formerly appeared.

LMGAT is an unusually readable and clear display, though the label used for entries with title subfields is certainly open to challenge. We arrived at NAMES for entries without titles; WORKS seems to be a good possibility for entries with titles, and directly describes most of the fields in that category. This display was introduced in Chapter 2 (Figures 2.21–2.23) and six more records are illustrated in Figures 4.34 through 4.41. LMGAT is also used in Chapter 7 (Figures 7.17–7.36).

Many items do not have name entries other than the main entry, but most items have main entries. As a result, LMGAT adds an additional blank line in quite a few cases, and it requires even more space than LMGSP. Only 41% of items tested leave room for holdings on the first screen. Public libraries fare a little better, with just over one-half the items tested having holdings room on the first screen.

Indentation Experiments

The last two displays show variations in field indentation. Both have the same spacing, labels and arrangement as LMGAT.

Display LMGNI has no indentation, with additional lines of each field listing flush with the first line. Figures 4.42 and 4.43 show two items using that format. The difference between LMGAT and LMGNI is largely a matter of taste. Most existing online systems do not indent additional lines, but LMGAT should make it easier to distinguish between long added entries.

Display LMGWI (shown in Figures 4.44–4.46) uses a wider indentation of four spaces compared with LMGAT's two spaces. The wide indentation requires slightly more display space than the narrow indentation in LMGAT, but the difference is almost negligible. As with LMGNI, the difference is largely a matter of taste, and LMGWI might be a suitable display for some libraries.

SUMMARY

Labeled displays almost always require more space than cardlike displays. Tables 4.3, 4.4 and 4.5 show the summary statistics for labeled displays at the medium level.

Well-designed labeled displays should provide clearer information. Vertical spacing helps to group elements but can cause many more records to go to a second screen. The possibilities for labeled displays seem endless. We deliberately chose a narrow section of

Table 4.3: Screen Summary Statistics

Display	Name	One Screen w/Holdings	One Screen: bib. only	Two Screens bib. only
LMLFT	Labeled, Flush-Left (both)	87.11%	98.34%	1.63%
	-- public libraries	92.21%	99.42%	0.58%
LMRI	Labeled, Gutter, Each Field	81.37%	96.67%	3.29%
	-- public libraries	89.05%	98.83%	1.16%
LMG	Labeled, Gutter, Groups	81.37%	96.67%	3.29%
	-- public libraries	89.05%	98.83%	1.16%
LMGCON	Labeled, Gutter, Concat.	88.27%	98.58%	1.41%
	-- public libraries	95.14%	99.68%	0.32%
LMGSP	Labeled, Gutter, Spaced	55.31%	90.11%	9.84%
	-- public libraries	67.15%	95.54%	4.46%
LMGAT	Labeled, Author/Title Split	41.23%	85.06%	14.87%
	-- public libraries	51.74%	92.43%	7.56%
LMGWI	Labeled, A/T Split, Wide Ind.	41.05%	84.77%	15.15%
	-- public libraries	51.60%	92.30%	7.69%

Table 4.4: Density Summary

Display	Name	Local Density	Global Density	L. Density to 30%
LMLFT	Labeled, Flush-Left (both)	29.76%	37.97%	57.33%
	-- public libraries	25.25%	35.35%	73.73%
LMRI	Labeled, Gutter, Each Field	29.94%	37.99%	55.57%
	-- public libraries	25.74%	35.51%	71.66%
LMG	Labeled, Gutter, Groups	28.98%	37.38%	59.21%
	-- public libraries	24.90%	34.97%	75.44%
LMGCON	Labeled, Gutter, Concat.	29.78%	38.00%	56.84%
	-- public libraries	25.33%	35.37%	73.81%
LMGSP	Labeled, Gutter, Spaced	27.24%	36.47%	65.65%
	-- public libraries	24.11%	34.61%	78.70%
LMGAT	Labeled, Author/Title Split	25.59%	35.54%	73.06%
	-- public libraries	22.99%	34.03%	83.93%
LMGWI	Labeled, A/T Split, Wide Ind.	25.52%	35.50%	73.35%
	-- public libraries	22.97%	34.01%	84.05%

Table 4.5: Room for Holdings

Display	Name	Holdings Room on First Screen 4+ Lines	6+ Lines	8+ Lines
LMLFT	Labeled, Flush-Left (both)	79.01%	51.62%	16.84%
	-- public libraries	85.74%	60.21%	23.86%
LMRI	Labeled, Gutter, Each Field	72.14%	44.31%	14.10%
	-- public libraries	81.36%	54.43%	21.38%
LMG	Labeled, Gutter, Groups	72.14%	44.31%	14.10%
	-- public libraries	81.36%	54.43%	21.38%
LMGCON	Labeled, Gutter, Concat.	80.66%	52.75%	16.29%
	-- public libraries	90.34%	66.28%	24.84%
LMGSP	Labeled, Gutter, Spaced	41.01%	15.24%	4.26%
	-- public libraries	51.52%	22.68%	7.64%
LMGAT	Labeled, Author/Title Split	27.17%	8.35%	1.14%
	-- public libraries	36.34%	14.68%	0.53%
LMGWI	Labeled, A/T Split, Wide Ind.	27.08%	8.33%	1.14%
	-- public libraries	36.28%	14.67%	0.53%

possibilities. We also avoided abbreviations and codes for labels, and we wonder whether such labels are preferable to good unlabeled designs.

The preparation of clear, unambiguous labels requires careful thought—to determine the appropriate order of elements; to determine suitable groups; and to strike a balance between openness and number of screens required for display. As these examples show, even the smallest details can make a substantial difference in clarity and space requirements.

Labeled Displays 85

Figure 4.1

```
Your search: AUTHOR: Anderson#                          MEDIUM Display
     Finds: 1 record                                    Screen  1 of  1
---------------------------------------------------------------------

AUTHOR: Anderson, Sparky, 1934-
TITLE: Bless you boys : diary of the Detroit Tigers' 1984 season / by Sparky
Anderson, with Dan Ewald.
PUBLISHED: Chicago : Contemporary Books, c1984.
MATERIAL: 231 p. : ill. ; 23 cm.
SUBJECT: Detroit Tigers (Baseball team)
OTHER ENTRY: Ewald, Dan.




---------------------------------------------------------------------
NEXT ACTIONS      Key: ? for help             + to see the next screen
                       L to see a Longer display  - to see the previous screen
                       F to Find other items   Q to Quit
NEXT ACTION?   _                                              LMLFT
```

Figure 4.2

```
Your search: TITLE: Citizen Ka#                         MEDIUM Display
     Finds: 1 record                                    Screen  1 of  1
---------------------------------------------------------------------

TITLE: Citizen Kane [videorecording] / an RKO Radio Picture ; a Mercury
production ; Orson Welles, direction, production.
PUBLISHED: New York, N.Y. : VidAmerica, c1982.
MATERIAL: 1 videocassette (119 min.) : sd., b&w ; 1/2 in.
SERIES: Classic series.
SUBJECT: Feature films.
OTHER ENTRY: Welles, Orson, 1915-
OTHER ENTRY: VidAmerica (Firm)
OTHER ENTRY: RKO Radio Pictures, inc.
OTHER ENTRY: Mercury Productions.



---------------------------------------------------------------------
NEXT ACTIONS      Key: ? for help             + to see the next screen
                       L to see a Longer display  - to see the previous screen
                       F to Find other items   Q to Quit
NEXT ACTION?  _                                               LMLFT
```

Figure 4.3

```
Your search: AUTHOR: Anderson#                    MEDIUM Display
       Finds: 1 record                           Screen  1 of  1
-----------------------------------------------------------------------

AUTHOR: Anderson, Sparky, 1934-
TITLE: Bless you boys : diary of the Detroit Tigers' 1984 season / by Sparky
  Anderson, with Dan Ewald.
PUBLISHED: Chicago : Contemporary Books, c1984.
MATERIAL: 231 p. : ill. ; 23 cm.
SUBJECT: Detroit Tigers (Baseball team)
OTHER ENTRY: Ewald, Dan.




                    -----------------------------------------------------
NEXT ACTIONS       Key: ? for help              + to see the next screen
                        L to see a Longer display  - to see the previous screen
                        F to Find other items   Q to Quit
NEXT ACTION?  _                                             LMLFI
```

Figure 4.4

```
Your search: TITLE: Citizen Ka#                   MEDIUM Display
       Finds: 1 record                           Screen  1 of  1
-----------------------------------------------------------------------

TITLE: Citizen Kane [videorecording] / an RKO Radio Picture ; a Mercury
  production ; Orson Welles, direction, production.
PUBLISHED: New York, N.Y. : VidAmerica, c1982.
MATERIAL: 1 videocassette (119 min.) : sd., b&w ; 1/2 in.
SERIES: Classic series.
SUBJECT: Feature films.
OTHER ENTRY: Welles, Orson, 1915-
OTHER ENTRY: VidAmerica (Firm)
OTHER ENTRY: RKO Radio Pictures, inc.
OTHER ENTRY: Mercury Productions.



                    -----------------------------------------------------
NEXT ACTIONS       Key: ? for help              + to see the next screen
                        L to see a Longer display  - to see the previous screen
                        F to Find other items   Q to Quit
NEXT ACTION?  _                                             LMLFI
```

Figure 4.5

```
┌──────────────────────────────────────────────────────────────────────┐
│ Your search: Anderson, Sparky#                       MEDIUM Display    │
│       Finds: 1 record                                Screen  1 of  1   │
│ ---------------------------------------------------------------------- │
│                                                                        │
│                                                                        │
│ AUTHOR:          Anderson, Sparky, 1934-                               │
│ TITLE:           Bless you boys : diary of the Detroit Tigers' 1984 season / │
│                     by Sparky Anderson, with Dan Ewald.                 │
│ PUBLISHED:       Chicago : Contemporary Books, c1984.                  │
│ MATERIAL:        231 p. : ill. ; 23 cm.                                │
│ SUBJECT:         Detroit Tigers (Baseball team)                        │
│ OTHER ENTRY:     Ewald, Dan.                                           │
│                                                                        │
│                                                                        │
│                                                                        │
│                                                                        │
│                                                                        │
│                                                                        │
│                                                                        │
│ -------------------------------------------------------------------    │
│                                                                        │
│ NEXT ACTIONS      Key: ? for help            + to see the next screen  │
│                        L to see a Longer display  - to see the previous screen │
│                        F to Find other items    Q to Quit              │
│ NEXT ACTION?   _                                             LMBL      │
└──────────────────────────────────────────────────────────────────────┘
```

Figure 4.6

```
┌──────────────────────────────────────────────────────────────────────┐
│ Your search: Citizen Kane                            MEDIUM Display    │
│       Finds: 1 record                                Screen  1 of  1   │
│ ---------------------------------------------------------------------- │
│                                                                        │
│                                                                        │
│ TITLE:           Citizen Kane [videorecording] / an RKO Radio Picture ; a │
│                     Mercury production ; Orson Welles, direction, production. │
│ PUBLISHED:       New York, N.Y. : VidAmerica, c1982.                   │
│ MATERIAL:        1 videocassette (119 min.) : sd., b&w ; 1/2 in.       │
│ SERIES:          Classic series.                                       │
│ SUBJECT:         Feature films.                                        │
│ OTHER ENTRY:     Welles, Orson, 1915-                                  │
│ OTHER ENTRY:     VidAmerica (Firm)                                     │
│ OTHER ENTRY:     RKO Radio Pictures, inc.                              │
│ OTHER ENTRY:     Mercury Productions.                                  │
│                                                                        │
│                                                                        │
│                                                                        │
│ -------------------------------------------------------------------    │
│                                                                        │
│ NEXT ACTIONS      Key: ? for help            + to see the next screen  │
│                        L to see a Longer display  - to see the previous screen │
│                        F to Find other items    Q to Quit              │
│ NEXT ACTION?   _                                             LMBL      │
└──────────────────────────────────────────────────────────────────────┘
```

Figure 4.7

```
Your search: Anderson, Sparky#                        MEDIUM Display
     Finds: 1 record                                  Screen  1 of  1
------------------------------------------------------------------------


        AUTHOR: Anderson, Sparky, 1934-
         TITLE: Bless you boys : diary of the Detroit Tigers' 1984 season /
                by Sparky Anderson, with Dan Ewald.
     PUBLISHED: Chicago : Contemporary Books, c1984.
      MATERIAL: 231 p. : ill. ; 23 cm.
       SUBJECT: Detroit Tigers (Baseball team)
   OTHER ENTRY: Ewald, Dan.




------------------------------------------------------------------------
NEXT ACTIONS       Key: ? for help             + to see the next screen
                        L to see a Longer display  - to see the previous screen
                        F to Find other items   Q to Quit
NEXT ACTION?   _                                             LMRI
```

Figure 4.8

```
Your search: Citizen Kane                             MEDIUM Display
     Finds: 1 record                                  Screen  1 of  1
------------------------------------------------------------------------


         TITLE: Citizen Kane [videorecording] / an RKO Radio Picture ; a
                Mercury production ; Orson Welles, direction, production.
     PUBLISHED: New York, N.Y. : VidAmerica, c1982.
      MATERIAL: 1 videocassette (119 min.) : sd., b&w ; 1/2 in.
        SERIES: Classic series.
       SUBJECT: Feature films.
   OTHER ENTRY: Welles, Orson, 1915-
   OTHER ENTRY: VidAmerica (Firm)
   OTHER ENTRY: RKO Radio Pictures, inc.
   OTHER ENTRY: Mercury Productions.



------------------------------------------------------------------------
NEXT ACTIONS       Key: ? for help             + to see the next screen
                        L to see a Longer display  - to see the previous screen
                        F to Find other items   Q to Quit
NEXT ACTION?   _                                             LMRI
```

Figure 4.9

```
Your search: Best American pla#                        MEDIUM Display
     Finds: 1 record                                   Screen  1 of  1
-------------------------------------------------------------------------


        TITLE: Best American plays : sixth series, 1963-1967 / edited by
               John Gassner and Clive Barnes, with an introduction and
               prefaces to the plays by Clive Barnes.
    PUBLISHED: New York : Crown, c1971.
     MATERIAL: xii, 594 p. ; 24 cm.
     SUBJECTS: American drama--20th century.
               American drama--Collected works.
OTHER ENTRIES: Gassner, John, 1903-1967.
               Barnes, Clive, 1927-




-------------------------------------------------------------------------
NEXT ACTIONS      Key: ? for help            + to see the next screen
                       L to see a Longer display  - to see the previous screen
                       F to Find other items  Q to Quit

NEXT ACTION?  _                                                  LMG
```

Figure 4.10

```
Your search: Brubeck, Dave#                            MEDIUM Display
     Finds: 1 record                                   Screen  1 of  1
-------------------------------------------------------------------------


       AUTHOR: Brubeck, Dave.
        TITLE: Bossa nova U.S.A. / [as performed by] the Dave Brubeck
               Quartet ; piano solo transcriptions by Howard Brubeck.
    PUBLISHED: San Francisco, Calif. : Derry Music Co. ;  New York, N.Y. :
               C. Hansen, distributor, c1963.
     MATERIAL: 49 p. of music ; 28 cm.
     SUBJECTS: Piano music (Jazz), Arranged.
               Jazz quartets--Piano scores.
OTHER ENTRIES: Brubeck, Howard R.
               Brubeck, Howard R. Theme for June; arr.
               Macero, Teo, 1925- Coracao sensivel; arr.
               Dave Brubeck Quartet.


-------------------------------------------------------------------------
NEXT ACTIONS      Key: ? for help            + to see the next screen
                       L to see a Longer display  - to see the previous screen
                       F to Find other items  Q to Quit

NEXT ACTION?  _                                                  LMG
```

Figure 4.11

```
Your search: Stewart, William #                    MEDIUM Display
     Finds: 1 record                               Screen  1 of  1
-----------------------------------------------------------------------

        AUTHOR: Stewart, William Herman, 1932-      i
         TITLE: The explorer's historical tourist map of Alaska, with maps
                of Anchorage, Fairbanks & Juneau : with notes on the
                Arctic, wildlife, hunting, fishing, camping, exploring &
                prospecting, festivals & events / cartography by William
                H. Stewart.
     PUBLISHED: Charleston, W.Va. : Economic Service Council, 1983.
      MATERIAL: 1 map : col. ; 65 x 71 cm., folded to 23 x 11 cm.
      SUBJECTS: Alaska--Maps, Tourist.
                Alaska--Maps, Pictorial.
  OTHER ENTRIES: Economic Service Council.




-----------------------------------------------------------------------
NEXT ACTIONS      Key: ? for help          + to see the next screen
                       L to see a Longer display  - to see the previous screen
                       F to Find other items   Q to Quit
NEXT ACTION?  _                                             LMG
```

Figure 4.12

```
Your search: Time.                                 MEDIUM Display
     Finds: 1 record                               Screen  1 of  1
-----------------------------------------------------------------------

         TITLE: Time.
     PUBLISHED: [Chicago, etc., Time Inc.]
      MATERIAL: v. ill. (incl. ports.) 28 cm.
  OTHER ENTRIES: Hadden, Briton, ed.
                Luce, Henry Robinson, 1898- ed.






-----------------------------------------------------------------------
NEXT ACTIONS      Key: ? for help          + to see the next screen
                       L to see a Longer display  - to see the previous screen
                       F to Find other items   Q to Quit
NEXT ACTION?  _                                             LMG
```

Figure 4.13

```
Your search: Bureau of Mines T#                    MEDIUM Display
      Finds: 1 record                             Screen  1 of  1
-------------------------------------------------------------------

         AUTHOR: Bureau of Mines Technology Transfer Seminars (1982 :
                 Pittsburgh, Pa.)
          TITLE: Postdisaster survival and rescue research : proceedings,
                 Bureau of Mines Technology Transfer Seminar, Pittsburgh,
                 Pa., November 16, 1982 / compiled by staff, Bureau of
                 Mines.
      PUBLISHED: [Avondale, Md.] : U.S. Dept. of the Interior, Bureau of
                 Mines, 1982.
       MATERIAL: iii, 91 p. : ill. ; 28 cm.
         SERIES: Bureau of Mines information circular ; 8907.
       SUBJECTS: Mine accidents--Congresses.
                 Mine rescue work--Congresses.
  OTHER ENTRIES: United States. Bureau of Mines.


  -----------------------------------------------------------------
NEXT ACTIONS      Key: ? for help              + to see the next screen
                       L to see a Longer display   - to see the previous screen
                       F to Find other items   Q to Quit

NEXT ACTION?  _                                                  LMG
```

Figure 4.14

```
Your search: Citizen Kane                          MEDIUM Display
      Finds: 1 record                             Screen  1 of  1
-------------------------------------------------------------------

          TITLE: Citizen Kane [videorecording] / an RKO Radio Picture ; a
                 Mercury production ; Orson Welles, direction, production.
      PUBLISHED: New York, N.Y. : VidAmerica, c1982.
       MATERIAL: 1 videocassette (119 min.) : sd., b&w ; 1/2 in.
         SERIES: Classic series.
       SUBJECTS: Feature films.
  OTHER ENTRIES: Welles, Orson, 1915-
                 VidAmerica (Firm)
                 RKO Radio Pictures, inc.
                 Mercury Productions.



  -----------------------------------------------------------------
NEXT ACTIONS      Key: ? for help              + to see the next screen
                       L to see a Longer display   - to see the previous screen
                       F to Find other items   Q to Quit

NEXT ACTION?  _                                                  LMG
```

Figure 4.15

```
Your search: Anderson, Sparky#                        MEDIUM Display
     Finds: 1 record                                  Screen  1 of  1
-----------------------------------------------------------------------

        Author: Anderson, Sparky, 1934-
         Title: Bless you boys : diary of the Detroit Tigers' 1984 season /
                by Sparky Anderson, with Dan Ewald.
     Published: Chicago : Contemporary Books, c1984.
      Material: 231 p. : ill. ; 23 cm.
      Subjects: Detroit Tigers (Baseball team)
  Other Entries: Ewald, Dan.




-----------------------------------------------------------------------
NEXT ACTIONS     Key: ? for help              + to see the next screen
                      L to see a Longer display - to see the previous screen
                      F to Find other items   Q to Quit
NEXT ACTION?  _                                            LMGLC
```

Figure 4.16

```
Your search: Citizen Kane                            MEDIUM Display
     Finds: 1 record                                  Screen  1 of  1
-----------------------------------------------------------------------

         Title: Citizen Kane [videorecording] / an RKO Radio Picture ; a
                Mercury production ; Orson Welles, direction, production.
     Published: New York, N.Y. : VidAmerica, c1982.
      Material: 1 videocassette (119 min.) : sd., b&w ; 1/2 in.
        Series: Classic series.
      Subjects: Feature films.
  Other Entries: Welles, Orson, 1915-
                VidAmerica (Firm)
                RKO Radio Pictures, inc.
                Mercury Productions.



-----------------------------------------------------------------------
NEXT ACTIONS     Key: ? for help              + to see the next screen
                      L to see a Longer display - to see the previous screen
                      F to Find other items   Q to Quit
NEXT ACTION?  _                                            LMGLC
```

Figure 4.17

```
Your search: Anderson, Sparky#                      MEDIUM Display
     Finds: 1 record                                Screen  1 of  1
------------------------------------------------------------------------

        AUTHOR: Anderson, Sparky, 1934-
         TITLE: Bless you boys : diary of the Detroit Tigers' 1984 season /
                by Sparky Anderson, with Dan Ewald.
     PUBLISHED: Chicago : Contemporary Books, c1984.
      MATERIAL: 231 p. : ill. ; 23 cm.
      SUBJECTS: Detroit Tigers (Baseball team)
 OTHER ENTRIES: Ewald, Dan.




------------------------------------------------------------------------

NEXT ACTIONS      Key: ? for help              + to see the next screen
                       L to see a Longer display  - to see the previous screen
                       F to Find other items   Q to Quit

NEXT ACTION?  _                                             LMGCON
```

Figure 4.18

```
Your search: Best American pla#                     MEDIUM Display
     Finds: 1 record                                Screen  1 of  1
------------------------------------------------------------------------

         TITLE: Best American plays : sixth series, 1963-1967 / edited by
                John Gassner and Clive Barnes, with an introduction and
                prefaces to the plays by Clive Barnes.
     PUBLISHED: New York : Crown, c1971.
      MATERIAL: xii, 594 p. ; 24 cm.
      SUBJECTS: American drama--20th century. * American drama--Collected
                works.
 OTHER ENTRIES: Gassner, John, 1903-1967. * Barnes, Clive, 1927-




------------------------------------------------------------------------

NEXT ACTIONS      Key: ? for help              + to see the next screen
                       L to see a Longer display  - to see the previous screen
                       F to Find other items   Q to Quit

NEXT ACTION?  _                                             LMGCON
```

Figure 4.19

```
Your search: Brubeck, Dave#                    MEDIUM Display
     Finds: 1 record                           Screen  1 of  1
-----------------------------------------------------------------------

         AUTHOR: Brubeck, Dave.
          TITLE: Bossa nova U.S.A. / [as performed by] the Dave Brubeck
                 Quartet ; piano solo transcriptions by Howard Brubeck.
      PUBLISHED: San Francisco, Calif. : Derry Music Co. ;  New York, N.Y. :
                 C. Hansen, distributor, c1963.
       MATERIAL: 49 p. of music ; 28 cm.
       SUBJECTS: Piano music (Jazz), Arranged. * Jazz quartets--Piano scores.
  OTHER ENTRIES: Brubeck, Howard R. * Brubeck, Howard R. Theme for June; arr.
                 * Macero, Teo, 1925- Coracao sensivel; arr. * Dave Brubeck
                 Quartet.




      --------------------------------------------------------------
NEXT ACTIONS     Key: ? for help              + to see the next screen
                      L to see a Longer display  - to see the previous screen
                      F to Find other items    Q to Quit
NEXT ACTION?  _                                           LMGCON
```

Figure 4.20

```
Your search: Stewart, William #                MEDIUM Display
     Finds: 1 record                           Screen  1 of  1
-----------------------------------------------------------------------

         AUTHOR: Stewart, William Herman, 1932-
          TITLE: The explorer's historical tourist map of Alaska, with maps
                 of Anchorage, Fairbanks & Juneau : with notes on the
                 Arctic, wildlife, hunting, fishing, camping, exploring &
                 prospecting, festivals & events / cartography by William
                 H. Stewart.
      PUBLISHED: Charleston, W.Va. : Economic Service Council, 1983.
       MATERIAL: 1 map : col. ; 65 x 71 cm., folded to 23 x 11 cm.
       SUBJECTS: Alaska--Maps, Tourist. * Alaska--Maps, Pictorial.
  OTHER ENTRIES: Economic Service Council.




      --------------------------------------------------------------
NEXT ACTIONS     Key: ? for help              + to see the next screen
                      L to see a Longer display  - to see the previous screen
                      F to Find other items    Q to Quit
NEXT ACTION?  _                                           LMGCON
```

Figure 4.21

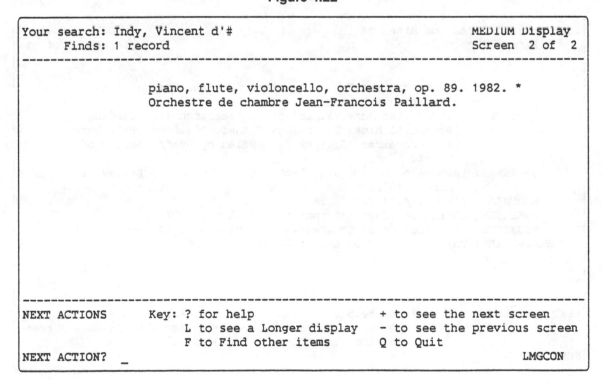

```
Your search: Indy, Vincent d'#                      MEDIUM Display
     Finds: 1 record                                Screen  1 of  2
---------------------------------------------------------------------------

        AUTHOR: Indy, Vincent d', 1851-1931.
         TITLE: Suite en re dans le style ancien : op. 24 ; Karadec : op. 34
                ; Concert, op. 89 pour piano, flute, violoncello et
                orchestre a cordes [sound recording] / Vincent d'Indy.
     PUBLISHED: France : Erato ; Paris : Distribution en France RCA, p1982.
      MATERIAL: 1 sound disc : 33 1/3 rpm, stereo. ; 12 in.
      SUBJECTS: Suites (Flutes (2), trumpet with string orchestra) * Music,
                Incidental. * Concertos (Piano, flute, violoncello with
                string orchestra)
  OTHER ENTRIES: Rampal, Jean Pierre. * Pierlot, Philippe. * Andre, Maurice.
                * Duchable, Francois. * Lodeon, Frederic. * Paillard, Jean
                Francois. * Indy, Vincent d', 1851-1931. Suite dans le
                style ancien. 1982. * Indy, Vincent d', 1851-1931.
                Karadec. 1982. * Indy, Vincent d', 1851-1931. Concerto,

-----------------------------------------------------------CONTINUED-------
NEXT ACTIONS      Key: ? for help                + to see the next screen
                       L to see a Longer display  - to see the previous screen
                       F to Find other items      Q to Quit
NEXT ACTION?  _                                              LMGCON
```

Figure 4.22

```
Your search: Indy, Vincent d'#                      MEDIUM Display
     Finds: 1 record                                Screen  2 of  2
---------------------------------------------------------------------------

                piano, flute, violoncello, orchestra, op. 89. 1982. *
                Orchestre de chambre Jean-Francois Paillard.












---------------------------------------------------------------------------
NEXT ACTIONS      Key: ? for help                + to see the next screen
                       L to see a Longer display  - to see the previous screen
                       F to Find other items      Q to Quit
NEXT ACTION?  _                                              LMGCON
```

Figure 4.23

```
Your search: Time.                                    MEDIUM Display
      Finds: 1 record                                 Screen  1 of  1
----------------------------------------------------------------------

        TITLE: Time.
    PUBLISHED: [Chicago, etc., Time Inc.]
     MATERIAL: v. ill. (incl. ports.) 28 cm.
 OTHER ENTRIES: Hadden, Briton, ed. * Luce, Henry Robinson, 1898- ed.








      ----------------------------------------------------------------
NEXT ACTIONS      Key: ? for help              + to see the next screen
                       L to see a Longer display  - to see the previous screen
                       F to Find other items    Q to Quit
NEXT ACTION?  _                                          LMGCON
```

Figure 4.24

```
Your search: Bureau of Mines T#                       MEDIUM Display
      Finds: 1 record                                 Screen  1 of  1
----------------------------------------------------------------------

       AUTHOR: Bureau of Mines Technology Transfer Seminars (1982 :
               Pittsburgh, Pa.)
        TITLE: Postdisaster survival and rescue research : proceedings,
               Bureau of Mines Technology Transfer Seminar, Pittsburgh,
               Pa., November 16, 1982 / compiled by staff, Bureau of
               Mines.
    PUBLISHED: [Avondale, Md.] : U.S. Dept. of the Interior, Bureau of
               Mines, 1982.
     MATERIAL: iii, 91 p. : ill. ; 28 cm.
       SERIES: Bureau of Mines information circular ; 8907.
     SUBJECTS: Mine accidents--Congresses. * Mine rescue work--Congresses.
 OTHER ENTRIES: United States. Bureau of Mines.



      ----------------------------------------------------------------
NEXT ACTIONS      Key: ? for help              + to see the next screen
                       L to see a Longer display  - to see the previous screen
                       F to Find other items    Q to Quit
NEXT ACTION?  _                                          LMGCON
```

Figure 4.25

```
Your search: Citizen Kane                            MEDIUM Display
      Finds: 1 record                                Screen  1 of  1
--------------------------------------------------------------------


         TITLE: Citizen Kane [videorecording] / an RKO Radio Picture ; a
                Mercury production ; Orson Welles, direction, production.
     PUBLISHED: New York, N.Y. : VidAmerica, c1982.
      MATERIAL: 1 videocassette (119 min.) : sd., b&w ; 1/2 in.
        SERIES: Classic series.
      SUBJECTS: Feature films.
 OTHER ENTRIES: Welles, Orson, 1915- * VidAmerica (Firm) * RKO Radio
                Pictures, inc. * Mercury Productions.




--------------------------------------------------------------------
NEXT ACTIONS      Key: ? for help            + to see the next screen
                       L to see a Longer display  - to see the previous screen
                       F to Find other items  Q to Quit
NEXT ACTION?   _                                          LMGCON
```

Figure 4.26

```
Your search: Best American pla#                      MEDIUM Display
      Finds: 1 record                                Screen  1 of  1
--------------------------------------------------------------------


         TITLE: Best American plays : sixth series, 1963-1967 / edited by
                John Gassner and Clive Barnes, with an introduction and
                prefaces to the plays by Clive Barnes.
     PUBLISHED: New York : Crown, c1971.
      MATERIAL: xii, 594 p. ; 24 cm.

      SUBJECTS: American drama--20th century.
                American drama--Collected works.

 OTHER ENTRIES: Gassner, John, 1903-1967.
                Barnes, Clive, 1927-



--------------------------------------------------------------------
NEXT ACTIONS      Key: ? for help            + to see the next screen
                       L to see a Longer display  - to see the previous screen
                       F to Find other items  Q to Quit
NEXT ACTION?   _                                          LMGSP
```

Figure 4.27

```
Your search: Brubeck, Dave#                          MEDIUM Display
      Finds: 1 record                               Screen  1 of  1
----------------------------------------------------------------------

         AUTHOR: Brubeck, Dave.
          TITLE: Bossa nova U.S.A. / [as performed by] the Dave Brubeck
                 Quartet ; piano solo transcriptions by Howard Brubeck.
      PUBLISHED: San Francisco, Calif. : Derry Music Co. ;  New York, N.Y. :
                 C. Hansen, distributor, c1963.
       MATERIAL: 49 p. of music ; 28 cm.

       SUBJECTS: Piano music (Jazz), Arranged.
                 Jazz quartets--Piano scores.

  OTHER ENTRIES: Brubeck, Howard R.
                 Brubeck, Howard R. Theme for June; arr.
                 Macero, Teo, 1925- Coracao sensivel; arr.
                 Dave Brubeck Quartet.

----------------------------------------------------------------------
NEXT ACTIONS      Key: ? for help             + to see the next screen
                       L to see a Longer display - to see the previous screen
                       F to Find other items   Q to Quit
NEXT ACTION?  _                                          LMGSP
```

Figure 4.28

```
Your search: Stewart, William #                      MEDIUM Display
      Finds: 1 record                               Screen  1 of  1
----------------------------------------------------------------------

         AUTHOR: Stewart, William Herman, 1932-
          TITLE: The explorer's historical tourist map of Alaska, with maps
                 of Anchorage, Fairbanks & Juneau : with notes on the
                 Arctic, wildlife, hunting, fishing, camping, exploring &
                 prospecting, festivals & events / cartography by William
                 H. Stewart.
      PUBLISHED: Charleston, W.Va. : Economic Service Council, 1983.
       MATERIAL: 1 map : col. ; 65 x 71 cm., folded to 23 x 11 cm.

       SUBJECTS: Alaska--Maps, Tourist.
                 Alaska--Maps, Pictorial.

  OTHER ENTRIES: Economic Service Council.

----------------------------------------------------------------------
NEXT ACTIONS      Key: ? for help             + to see the next screen
                       L to see a Longer display - to see the previous screen
                       F to Find other items   Q to Quit
NEXT ACTION?  _                                          LMGSP
```

Figure 4.29

```
Your search: Time.                                    MEDIUM Display
     Finds: 1 record                                  Screen  1 of  1
-------------------------------------------------------------------------

         TITLE: Time.
     PUBLISHED: [Chicago, etc., Time Inc.]
      MATERIAL: v. ill. (incl. ports.) 28 cm.

 OTHER ENTRIES: Hadden, Briton, ed.
                Luce, Henry Robinson, 1898- ed.




-------------------------------------------------------------------------
NEXT ACTIONS       Key: ? for help            + to see the next screen
                        L to see a Longer display  - to see the previous screen
                        F to Find other items  Q to Quit
NEXT ACTION?   _                                            LMGSP
```

Figure 4.30

```
Your search: Bureau of Mines T#                       MEDIUM Display
     Finds: 1 record                                  Screen  2 of  2
-------------------------------------------------------------------------

          Mine rescue work--Congresses.

 OTHER ENTRIES: United States. Bureau of Mines.





-------------------------------------------------------------------------
NEXT ACTIONS       Key: ? for help            + to see the next screen
                        L to see a Longer display  - to see the previous screen
                        F to Find other items  Q to Quit
NEXT ACTION?   _                                            LMGSP
```

Figure 4.31

```
Your search: Citizen Kane                          MEDIUM Display
      Finds: 1 record                              Screen  1 of  1
------------------------------------------------------------------------


        TITLE: Citizen Kane [videorecording] / an RKO Radio Picture ; a
               Mercury production ; Orson Welles, direction, production.
    PUBLISHED: New York, N.Y. : VidAmerica, c1982.
     MATERIAL: 1 videocassette (119 min.) : sd., b&w ; 1/2 in.


       SERIES: Classic series.


     SUBJECTS: Feature films.


 OTHER ENTRIES: Welles, Orson, 1915-
               VidAmerica (Firm)
               RKO Radio Pictures, inc.
               Mercury Productions.



------------------------------------------------------------------------
NEXT ACTIONS      Key: ? for help              + to see the next screen
                       L to see a Longer display   - to see the previous screen
                       F to Find other items   Q to Quit
NEXT ACTION?  _                                             LMGSP
```

Figure 4.32

```
Your search: Bless you boys #                      MEDIUM Display
      Finds: 1 record                              Screen  1 of  1
------------------------------------------------------------------------


        TITLE: Bless you boys : diary of the Detroit Tigers' 1984 season /
               by Sparky Anderson, with Dan Ewald.
    PUBLISHED: Chicago : Contemporary Books, c1984.
     MATERIAL: 231 p. : ill. ; 23 cm.


     SUBJECTS: Detroit Tigers (Baseball team)


 OTHER ENTRIES: Anderson, Sparky, 1934-
               Ewald, Dan.




------------------------------------------------------------------------
NEXT ACTIONS      Key: ? for help              + to see the next screen
                       L to see a Longer display   - to see the previous screen
                       F to Find other items   Q to Quit
NEXT ACTION?  _                                             LMGT
```

Figure 4.33

```
Your search: Citizen Kane                        MEDIUM Display
     Finds: 1 record                             Screen  1 of  1
------------------------------------------------------------------

        TITLE: Citizen Kane [videorecording] / an RKO Radio Picture ; a
               Mercury production ; Orson Welles, direction, production.
    PUBLISHED: New York, N.Y. : VidAmerica, c1982.
     MATERIAL: 1 videocassette (119 min.) : sd., b&w ; 1/2 in.

       SERIES: Classic series.

     SUBJECTS: Feature films.

 OTHER ENTRIES: Welles, Orson, 1915-
               VidAmerica (Firm)
               RKO Radio Pictures, inc.
               Mercury Productions.


------------------------------------------------------------------
NEXT ACTIONS      Key: ? for help          + to see the next screen
                       L to see a Longer display   - to see the previous screen
                       F to Find other items   Q to Quit
NEXT ACTION?  _                                          LMGT
```

Figure 4.34

```
Your search: Best American pla#                  MEDIUM Display
     Finds: 1 record                             Screen  1 of  1
------------------------------------------------------------------

        TITLE: Best American plays : sixth series, 1963-1967 / edited by
               John Gassner and Clive Barnes, with an introduction and
               prefaces to the plays by Clive Barnes.
    PUBLISHED: New York : Crown, c1971.
     MATERIAL: xii, 594 p. ; 24 cm.

        NAMES: Gassner, John, 1903-1967.
               Barnes, Clive, 1927-

     SUBJECTS: American drama--20th century.
               American drama--Collected works.



------------------------------------------------------------------
NEXT ACTIONS      Key: ? for help          + to see the next screen
                       L to see a Longer display   - to see the previous screen
                       F to Find other items   Q to Quit
NEXT ACTION?  _                                          LMGAT
```

Figure 4.35

```
Your search: Bossa nova U.S.A#                        MEDIUM Display
     Finds: 1 record                                  Screen  1 of  2
----------------------------------------------------------------------

         TITLE: Bossa nova U.S.A. / [as performed by] the Dave Brubeck
                Quartet ; piano solo transcriptions by Howard Brubeck.
     PUBLISHED: San Francisco, Calif. : Derry Music Co. ;  New York, N.Y. :
                C. Hansen, distributor, c1963.
      MATERIAL: 49 p. of music ; 28 cm.

         NAMES: Brubeck, Dave.
                Brubeck, Howard R.
                Dave Brubeck Quartet.

      SUBJECTS: Piano music (Jazz), Arranged.
                Jazz quartets--Piano scores.

         WORKS: Brubeck, Howard R. Theme for June; arr.

-------------------------------------------------------CONTINUED-------

NEXT ACTIONS      Key: ? for help            + to see the next screen
                       L to see a Longer display  - to see the previous screen
                       F to Find other items  Q to Quit
NEXT ACTION?  _                                               LMGAT
```

Figure 4.36

```
Your search: Bossa nova U.S.A#                        MEDIUM Display
     Finds: 1 record                                  Screen  2 of  2
----------------------------------------------------------------------

         Macero, Teo, 1925- Coracao sensivel; arr.



----------------------------------------------------------------------
NEXT ACTIONS      Key: ? for help            + to see the next screen
                       L to see a Longer display  - to see the previous screen
                       F to Find other items  Q to Quit
NEXT ACTION?  _                                               LMGAT
```

Figure 4.37

```
Your search: The explorer's hi#                    MEDIUM Display
     Finds: 1 record                               Screen 1 of 1
----------------------------------------------------------------------

       TITLE: The explorer's historical tourist map of Alaska, with maps
              of Anchorage, Fairbanks & Juneau : with notes on the
              Arctic, wildlife, hunting, fishing, camping, exploring &
              prospecting, festivals & events / cartography by William
              H. Stewart.
   PUBLISHED: Charleston, W.Va. : Economic Service Council, 1983.
    MATERIAL: 1 map : col. ; 65 x 71 cm., folded to 23 x 11 cm.

       NAMES: Stewart, William Herman, 1932-
              Economic Service Council.

    SUBJECTS: Alaska--Maps, Tourist.
              Alaska--Maps, Pictorial.


----------------------------------------------------------------------

NEXT ACTIONS     Key: ? for help            + to see the next screen
                      L to see a Longer display  - to see the previous screen
                      F to Find other items  Q to Quit

NEXT ACTION?  _                                            LMGAT
```

Figure 4.38

```
Your search: Time.                                 MEDIUM Display
     Finds: 1 record                               Screen 1 of 1
----------------------------------------------------------------------

       TITLE: Time.
   PUBLISHED: [Chicago, etc., Time Inc.]
    MATERIAL: v. ill. (incl. ports.) 28 cm.

       NAMES: Hadden, Briton, ed.
              Luce, Henry Robinson, 1898- ed.




----------------------------------------------------------------------

NEXT ACTIONS     Key: ? for help            + to see the next screen
                      L to see a Longer display  - to see the previous screen
                      F to Find other items  Q to Quit

NEXT ACTION?  _                                            LMGAT
```

Figure 4.39

```
Your search: Postdisaster surv#                          MEDIUM Display
      Finds: 1 record                                     Screen  1 of  2
---------------------------------------------------------------------------


          TITLE: Postdisaster survival and rescue research : proceedings,
                 Bureau of Mines Technology Transfer Seminar, Pittsburgh,
                 Pa., November 16, 1982 / compiled by staff, Bureau of
                 Mines.
      PUBLISHED: [Avondale, Md.] : U.S. Dept. of the Interior, Bureau of
                 Mines, 1982.
       MATERIAL: iii, 91 p. : ill. ; 28 cm.

          NAMES: Bureau of Mines Technology Transfer Seminars (1982 :
                 Pittsburgh, Pa.)
                 United States. Bureau of Mines.

         SERIES: Bureau of Mines information circular ; 8907.


------------------------------------------------------------CONTINUED-------
NEXT ACTIONS       Key: ? for help            + to see the next screen
                        L to see a Longer display  - to see the previous screen
                        F to Find other items   Q to Quit
NEXT ACTION?   _                                              LMGAT
```

Figure 4.40

```
Your search: Postdisaster surv#                          MEDIUM Display
      Finds: 1 record                                     Screen  2 of  2
---------------------------------------------------------------------------

       SUBJECTS: Mine accidents--Congresses.
                 Mine rescue work--Congresses.









----------------------------------------------------------------------------
NEXT ACTIONS       Key: ? for help            + to see the next screen
                        L to see a Longer display  - to see the previous screen
                        F to Find other items   Q to Quit
NEXT ACTION?   _                                              LMGAT
```

Figure 4.41

```
Your search: Citizen Kane                          MEDIUM Display
      Finds: 1 record                              Screen  1 of  1
-----------------------------------------------------------------------

        TITLE: Citizen Kane [videorecording] / an RKO Radio Picture ; a
               Mercury production ; Orson Welles, direction, production.
    PUBLISHED: New York, N.Y. : VidAmerica, c1982.
     MATERIAL: 1 videocassette (119 min.) : sd., b&w ; 1/2 in.

        NAMES: Welles, Orson, 1915-
               VidAmerica (Firm)
               RKO Radio Pictures, inc.
               Mercury Productions.

       SERIES: Classic series.

     SUBJECTS: Feature films.


-----------------------------------------------------------------------
NEXT ACTIONS      Key: ? for help              + to see the next screen
                       L to see a Longer display  - to see the previous screen
                       F to Find other items   Q to Quit
NEXT ACTION?   _                                           LMGAT
```

Figure 4.42

```
Your search: Bless you boys #                      MEDIUM Display
      Finds: 1 record                              Screen  1 of  1
-----------------------------------------------------------------------

        TITLE: Bless you boys : diary of the Detroit Tigers' 1984 season /
               by Sparky Anderson, with Dan Ewald.
    PUBLISHED: Chicago : Contemporary Books, c1984.
     MATERIAL: 231 p. : ill. ; 23 cm.

        NAMES: Anderson, Sparky, 1934-
               Ewald, Dan.

     SUBJECTS: Detroit Tigers (Baseball team)



-----------------------------------------------------------------------
NEXT ACTIONS      Key: ? for help              + to see the next screen
                       L to see a Longer display  - to see the previous screen
                       F to Find other items   Q to Quit
NEXT ACTION?   _                                           LMGNI
```

Figure 4.43

```
Your search: Citizen Kane                          MEDIUM Display
     Finds: 1 record                               Screen  1 of  1
----------------------------------------------------------------------


        TITLE: Citizen Kane [videorecording] / an RKO Radio Picture ; a
               Mercury production ; Orson Welles, direction, production.
    PUBLISHED: New York, N.Y. : VidAmerica, c1982.
     MATERIAL: 1 videocassette (119 min.) : sd., b&w ; 1/2 in.

        NAMES: Welles, Orson, 1915-
               VidAmerica (Firm)
               RKO Radio Pictures, inc.
               Mercury Productions.

       SERIES: Classic series.

     SUBJECTS: Feature films.


----------------------------------------------------------------------
NEXT ACTIONS     Key: ? for help            + to see the next screen
                      L to see a Longer display  - to see the previous screen
                      F to Find other items  Q to Quit
NEXT ACTION?  _                                              LMGNI
```

Figure 4.44

```
Your search: Bless you boys #                      MEDIUM Display
     Finds: 1 record                               Screen  1 of  1
----------------------------------------------------------------------

        TITLE: Bless you boys : diary of the Detroit Tigers' 1984 season /
               by Sparky Anderson, with Dan Ewald.
    PUBLISHED: Chicago : Contemporary Books, c1984.
     MATERIAL: 231 p. : ill. ; 23 cm.

        NAMES: Anderson, Sparky, 1934-
               Ewald, Dan.

     SUBJECTS: Detroit Tigers (Baseball team)




----------------------------------------------------------------------
NEXT ACTIONS     Key: ? for help            + to see the next screen
                      L to see a Longer display  - to see the previous screen
                      F to Find other items  Q to Quit
NEXT ACTION?  _                                              LMGWI
```

Figure 4.45

```
Your search: Citizen Kane                         MEDIUM Display
      Finds: 1 record                             Screen  1 of  2
------------------------------------------------------------------------


           TITLE: Citizen Kane [videorecording] / an RKO Radio Picture ; a
                  Mercury production ; Orson Welles, direction,
                  production.
       PUBLISHED: New York, N.Y. : VidAmerica, c1982.
        MATERIAL: 1 videocassette (119 min.) : sd., b&w ; 1/2 in.

           NAMES: Welles, Orson, 1915-
                  VidAmerica (Firm)
                  RKO Radio Pictures, inc.
                  Mercury Productions.

          SERIES: Classic series.


    ---------------------------------------------------------CONTINUED-------
NEXT ACTIONS      Key: ? for help            + to see the next screen
                       L to see a Longer display   - to see the previous screen
                       F to Find other items   Q to Quit
NEXT ACTION?  _                                             LMGWI
```

Figure 4.46

```
Your search: Citizen Kane                         MEDIUM Display
      Finds: 1 record                             Screen  2 of  2
------------------------------------------------------------------------

        SUBJECTS: Feature films.










    ------------------------------------------------------------------
NEXT ACTIONS      Key: ? for help            + to see the next screen
                       L to see a Longer display   - to see the previous screen
                       F to Find other items   Q to Quit
NEXT ACTION?  _                                             LMGWI
```

5

Mixed and Special Displays

All the displays in the previous chapters use the same data elements, and are either consistently cardlike or consistently labeled. This chapter illustrates some other possibilities for medium-level displays, namely, three mixed displays and eight displays showing other sets of data elements. Table 5.1 lists the displays discussed and illustrated in this chapter.

MIXED DISPLAYS

Most discussions of labeled displays assume that every field will be labeled, singly or within groups. Not all existing displays provide labels for each group or field, however; as noted in Chapter 4, some omissions may cause confusion as to what fields actually mean.

At least one current system uses a hybrid display, with a cardlike or citation-style entry followed by labeled access points. Such a display apparently assumes that patrons can recognize author, title, edition, publication information and physical description, but that labels help to clarify series, subjects and other entry points.

LMPART—Partially Labeled Medium Display

Display LMPART retains the field order of LMGAT (Figures 2.21–2.23, 4.34–4.41 and 7.17–7.36), and differs from that display only in that no labels appear for title, edition, publication information or physical description. Figures 5.1 through 5.3 illustrate display LMPART.

Table 5.1: Displays Discussed in Chapter 5

Display	Name
CMSX	Cardlike medium display, narrow lines, vertical spacing
CXMATT	Cardlike display based on Joseph Matthews' list of fields
CXPLM1	Cardlike display based on Richard Palmer's short list of fields
CXPLM2	Cardlike display based on Richard Palmer's long list of fields
CXSIMPL	Simple cardlike display
LMCAP	Walt Crawford's medium display
LMCIT	Partially labeled medium display with citation-style description
LMGAT	Labeled medium display, gutter aligned, author/title split
LMGT	Labeled medium display, gutter aligned, title first
LMPART	Partially labeled medium display
LMGSP	Labeled medium display, gutter aligned, vertical spacing
LMTCIT	Partially labeled medium display with title-citation description
LXMATT	Labeled display based on Joseph Matthews' list of fields
LXPLM1	Labeled display based on Richard Palmer's short list of fields
LXPLM2	Labeled display based on Richard Palmer's long list of fields
LXSIMPL	Simple labeled display

LMCIT—Partially Labeled, Citation-Style Description

LMCIT differs from LMPART in that the unlabeled elements appear as a single paragraph, and include the main entry (which appears twice in the display). Figures 5.4 through 5.6 illustrate LMCIT; more extensive illustrations, with the short title capitalized, appear in Chapter 8 as display LMCAP (Figures 8.20–8.30).

LMTCIT—Partially Labeled, Title-Citation Description

LMTCIT differs from LMCIT by dropping the main entry from the bibliographic description. It differs from LMPART (Figures 5.1–5.3) by grouping unlabeled elements into a block-intended paragraph. Figures 5.7 through 5.16 illustrate LMTCIT. Both this display and LMCIT appear to be possible candidates for online catalogs.

LMTCIT presents understandable information in a moderately compact form: 60% of items tested leave room on the first screen for minimal holdings, a significantly higher number than LMGAT at 41%. Another possible advantage of LMTCIT is that it includes edition, publication information and physical description, but reduces the space required for these elements and the apparent importance assigned to them. Some writers have suggested that patrons have no use for edition, publication information and physical description. We disagree, and point out that physical description represents vital information for many nonbook items.

OTHER SETS OF DATA ELEMENTS

The remaining displays in this chapter illustrate four possible sets of "satisfactory" data elements. The first represents an assertion by one of the authors as to the simplest single-record display that presents sufficient information. The others are taken from the literature. In each case, the set of data elements is presented as a cardlike display similar to CMSX (Figures 2.9–2.11, 3.9–3.14 and 7.1–7.16) and as a labeled display similar to LMGAT (Figures 2.21–2.23, 4.34–4.41 and 7.17–7.36). Each display shows the full set of eight items.

CXSIMPL and LXSIMPL—Simplest Displays

Displays CXSIMPL and LXSIMPL are based on the assertion that: ". . . every single-record display should include: authors (1xx and 7xx); title (including subtitle); date; series; subjects . . ."[1] The cardlike display CXSIMPL, illustrated in Figures 5.17 through 5.25, differs from CMSX, the traditional spaced cardlike format, by omitting several elements:

- edition (250)
- physical description (300–305)
- place of publication and name of publisher (260 subfields a and b)
- statement of responsibility (245 subfield c)

The labeled display LXSIMPL, illustrated in Figures 5.26 through 5.34, is based on LMGT (Figures 4.32 and 4.33), with the same elements omitted.

As the figures demonstrate, useful information disappears when the fields listed above are dropped. Crawford feels that these displays are overly simplistic, although they do save quite a bit of space.

CXSIMPL has room for holdings on the first screen for 96% of items tested, compared with 76% for CMSX. LXSIMPL has such room for 90% of the items, compared with 55% for the nearly comparable LMGSP. The savings are real, but the price is probably too high.

CXMATT and LXMATT—Matthews' Displays

Joseph Matthews presented a list of suggested data elements for a completely satisfactory display during a 1984 Council on Library Resources conference on online catalog design issues:

A display providing the following data elements would satisfy over 97% of reader and staff needs:
- Names;
- Title, subtitle;
- Uniform title;
- Subject headings;
- Added entries;
- Volume number, volume title;
- Edition statement;
- Date of publication;
- Edition and history note;
- References;
- ISBN or control number.[2]

We interpreted that list to call for the following changes from our normal medium list:

- Add uniform title (field 240).
- Eliminate statement of responsibility (245 subfield c).
- Eliminate place of publication and name of publisher (260 subfields a, b).
- Eliminate physical description (fields 300–305).
- Add control numbers such as ISBN (ISBN, ISSN, SRN, STRN and publisher's number for music).

We doubt that Matthews would favor a cardlike display, but we did define such a display. CXMATT is illustrated in Figures 5.35 through 5.43. Although not quite as compact as CXSIMPL, CXMATT provides very compact displays—92% of items leave room for minimal holdings on the first screen.

The labeled version of Matthews' list, LXMATT, is illustrated in Figures 5.44 through 5.53. This display is based directly on LMGAT (Figures 2.21–2.23, 4.34–4.41 and 7.17–7.36) and is slightly more compact, with 51% of items showing holdings on the first screen, compared with 41% for LMGAT.

Matthews has offered a number of guidelines for displays. We believe that LXMATT follows almost all of his suggestions, including gutter alignment, capitalized full words or phrases for labels, extensive use of white space and low density. Average local density for LXMATT is only 19%, substantially lower than the 26% for LMGAT.

CXPLM1 and LXPLM1—Palmer's Shorter Displays

Richard P. Palmer reported on card catalog use in a 1972 monograph, *Computerizing the Card Catalog in the University Library;* his findings (and summary of earlier studies) have been widely interpreted since that date. The displays CXPLM1 and LXPLM1 are derived from an indirect report on Palmer's findings:

Palmer explored the potential of computer catalogs and found that a successful search could be accomplished 84% of the time with only author, title, call number (reflecting location), date, publication and subject heading information. If contents notes were included, the success rate would increase to more than 90%.[3]

We took the standard medium format and made the following changes:

- eliminating the edition (field 250)
- eliminating the physical description (fields 300–305)
- eliminating added entries (fields 700–740)
- adding the contents note (field 505)

While there is a difference between searching for something successfully and seeing all needed information in the resulting display, the examples may be interesting. CXPLM1, illustrated in Figures 5.54 through 5.63, leaves room for holdings on the first screen 95% of the time. LXPLM1, illustrated in Figures 5.64 through 5.73, leaves such room 79% of the time. Note that this display does not include authors other than the main entry; among other unfortunate results, that may mean that items are retrieved based on information that does not display.

CXPLM2 and LXPLM2—Palmer's Longer Displays

We prepared another pair of displays based on a direct citation from Palmer:

Over three-fourths of the catalog's patrons used the title, author, and call number (including location). Slightly over half . . . made use of the subject headings. A little over one-third used the date of publication. Just over 20 percent used the contents note. Fifteen percent used the edition statement. About 13 percent used the number of volumes. Ten percent used the place of publication, joint author, and publisher. All other items were used by fewer than 10 percent.[4]

"Number of volumes" could be interpreted to require inclusion of material description; we did not do so for these displays. Thus, the displays differ from CXPLM1 and LXPLM1, above, in two ways: the edition statement (field 250) is restored and added entries (fields 700–740) are restored.

CXPLM2, illustrated in Figures 5.74 through 5.84, has room for holdings on the first screen in 92% of items tested. LXPLM2, illustrated in Figures 5.85 through 5.95, has similar room 75% of the time.

SUMMARY

Different approaches to display design can yield good results. The authors could not reach a consensus on the desirability of citation-like displays, but we do agree that they represent one interesting approach. Tables 5.2, 5.3 and 5.4 show the summary statistics for displays illustrated in this chapter.

When we prepare displays based on published notes about required data elements, we may be doing the writers a disservice. A distinction must be made between what it

Table 5.2: Screen Summary Statistics

Display	Name	One Screen w/Holdings	One Screen: bib. only	Two Screens bib. only
LMTCIT	Title-citation, labeled	60.33%	91.77%	8.17%
	-- public libraries	71.94%	96.46%	3.53%
CXSIMPL	"Simple" Cardlike	95.77%	99.64%	0.35%
	-- public libraries	99.04%	99.93%	0.07%
LXSIMPL	"Simple" Labeled	89.72%	98.58%	1.39%
	-- public libraries	95.39%	99.63%	0.37%
CXMATT	Matthews Cardlike	92.21%	99.34%	0.65%
	-- public libraries	96.90%	99.85%	0.15%
LXMATT	Matthews Labeled	50.58%	90.45%	9.49%
	-- public libraries	49.29%	93.73%	6.25%
CXPLM1	Palmer 1 Cardlike	94.92%	98.91%	1.04%
	-- public libraries	98.15%	99.76%	0.23%
LXPLM1	Palmer 1 Labeled	79.26%	97.04%	2.87%
	-- public libraries	85.31%	98.77%	1.21%
CXPLM2	Palmer 2 Cardlike	91.70%	98.24%	1.67%
	-- public libraries	97.12%	99.59%	0.40%
LXPLM2	Palmer 2 Labeled	75.26%	94.85%	4.98%
	-- public libraries	82.81%	97.98%	1.98%

takes to identify an item, and how much information a patron can use effectively. The first Palmer list was concerned only with information required to identify an item; the second list was based on what patrons say they use. Neither list takes into account nonbook materials. Bibliographic displays for such materials suffer more than displays for books when the physical description and the name of the publisher are omitted.

Are any of the displays in the second part of this chapter suitable as the most complete displays for public access? We do not believe so. Physical description can be important; pagination can help any patron in choosing a book on a subject. Series statements can be quite useful, though they are not usually used heavily.

Palmer goes on to report that bibliography notes, pagination and translator notes were used by more than 5% of patrons. We would expect a library to choose to serve the information needs of all its patrons, not just 90%, particularly when those needs can be served using information already available in the bibliographic records. While displays illustrated in this chapter might be useful as medium-level displays, they omit too much useful information to be suitable as long displays.

NOTES

1. Crawford, Walt. *Patron Access Project, Phase I; Report to Phase II: Development Issues.* Stanford, CA: The Research Libraries Group, Inc.; 1985. (RLG Document Code 85-52.) p. 114.

Table 5.3: Density Summary

Display	Name	Local Density	Global Density	L. Density to 30%
LMTCIT	Title-citation, labeled	24.77%	35.12%	75.34%
	-- public libraries	21.23%	33.05%	87.22%
CXSIMPL	"Simple" Cardlike	17.49%	30.94%	90.16%
	-- public libraries	13.14%	28.37%	96.72%
LXSIMPL	"Simple" Labeled	19.14%	31.91%	89.31%
	-- public libraries	14.94%	29.44%	96.34%
CXMATT	Matthews Cardlike	18.96%	31.69%	88.07%
	-- public libraries	15.59%	29.69%	95.09%
LXMATT	Matthews Labeled	19.12%	31.80%	93.37%
	-- public libraries	16.51%	30.25%	97.88%
CXPLM1	Palmer 1 Cardlike	21.03%	32.90%	84.98%
	-- public libraries	17.53%	30.83%	92.89%
LXPLM1	Palmer 1 Labeled	22.80%	33.96%	82.73%
	-- public libraries	19.54%	32.06%	91.61%
CXPLM2	Palmer 2 Cardlike	23.32%	34.24%	78.12%
	-- public libraries	19.10%	31.74%	89.41%
LXPLM2	Palmer 2 Labeled	24.76%	35.10%	76.05%
	-- public libraries	21.16%	33.01%	87.43%

Table 5.4: Room for Holdings

| Display | Name | Holdings Room on First Screen | | |
		4+ Lines	6+ Lines	8+ Lines
LMTCIT	Title-citation, labeled	45.62%	17.13%	5.94%
	-- public libraries	57.38%	26.10%	12.34%
CXSIMPL	"Simple" Cardlike	92.31%	76.47%	43.67%
	-- public libraries	97.99%	90.46%	61.76%
LXSIMPL	"Simple" Labeled	83.61%	60.15%	23.18%
	-- public libraries	91.49%	71.45%	33.09%
CXMATT	Matthews Cardlike	85.99%	60.39%	25.38%
	-- public libraries	93.03%	68.68%	22.03%
LXMATT	Matthews Labeled	36.17%	14.40%	4.13%
	-- public libraries	32.83%	12.34%	1.83%
CXPLM1	Palmer 1 Cardlike	91.55%	75.23%	35.19%
	-- public libraries	96.49%	85.88%	47.00%
LXPLM1	Palmer 1 Labeled	66.53%	29.99%	9.18%
	-- public libraries	73.67%	37.27%	16.22%
CXPLM2	Palmer 2 Cardlike	86.94%	67.07%	28.05%
	-- public libraries	94.68%	80.42%	41.03%
LXPLM2	Palmer 2 Labeled	63.86%	31.96%	5.50%
	-- public libraries	72.13%	40.68%	8.92%

2. Matthews, Joseph S. "Screen Layouts and Displays." Aveney, Brian, ed. *Online Catalog Design Issues: A Series of Discussions.* Washington: Council on Library Resources; 1984 July. p. 114.

3. *Command Language and Screen Displays for Public Online Systems: Report of a Meeting Sponsored by the Council on Library Resources, March 29–30, 1984, Dublin, Ohio.* Peters, Paul Evan, ed. Washington: CLR; 1985. p. 40–41.

4. Palmer, Richard P. *Computerizing the Card Catalog in the University Library.* Littleton, CO: Libraries Unlimited; 1972. p. 81.

Figure 5.1

```
Your search: The explorer's hi#                    MEDIUM Display
      Finds: 1 record                              Screen  1 of  1
-----------------------------------------------------------------------

        The explorer's historical tourist map of Alaska, with maps
           of Anchorage, Fairbanks & Juneau : with notes on the
           Arctic, wildlife, hunting, fishing, camping, exploring &
           prospecting, festivals & events / cartography by William
           H. Stewart.
        Charleston, W.Va. : Economic Service Council, 1983.
        1 map : col. ; 65 x 71 cm., folded to 23 x 11 cm.

        NAMES: Stewart, William Herman, 1932-
               Economic Service Council.

     SUBJECTS: Alaska--Maps, Tourist.
               Alaska--Maps, Pictorial.


     --------------------------------------------------------------
NEXT ACTIONS      Key: ? for help             + to see the next screen
                       L to see a Longer display  - to see the previous screen
                       F to Find other items   Q to Quit
NEXT ACTION?  _                                          LMPART
```

Figure 5.2

```
Your search: Suite en re dans #                    MEDIUM Display
      Finds: 1 record                              Screen  1 of  2
-----------------------------------------------------------------------

        Suite en re dans le style ancien : op. 24 ; Karadec : op. 34
           ; Concert, op. 89 pour piano, flute, violoncello et
           orchestre a cordes [sound recording] / Vincent d'Indy.
        France : Erato ; Paris : Distribution en France RCA, p1982.
        1 sound disc : 33 1/3 rpm, stereo. ; 12 in.

        NAMES: Indy, Vincent d', 1851-1931.
               Rampal, Jean Pierre.
               Pierlot, Philippe.
               Andre, Maurice.
               Duchable, Francois.
               Lodeon, Frederic.
               Paillard, Jean Francois.


     -----------------------------------------------CONTINUED-------
NEXT ACTIONS      Key: ? for help             + to see the next screen
                       L to see a Longer display  - to see the previous screen
                       F to Find other items   Q to Quit
NEXT ACTION?  _                                          LMPART
```

Figure 5.3

```
Your search: Suite en re dans #                    MEDIUM Display
     Finds: 1 record                               Screen  2 of  2
-------------------------------------------------------------------

            Orchestre de chambre Jean-Francois Paillard.

   SUBJECTS: Suites (Flutes (2), trumpet with string orchestra)
             Music, Incidental.
             Concertos (Piano, flute, violoncello with string orchestra)

      WORKS: Indy, Vincent d', 1851-1931. Suite dans le style ancien.
                1982.
             Indy, Vincent d', 1851-1931. Karadec. 1982.
             Indy, Vincent d', 1851-1931. Concerto, piano, flute,
                violoncello, orchestra, op. 89. 1982.



-------------------------------------------------------------------
NEXT ACTIONS     Key: ? for help              + to see the next screen
                      L to see a Longer display - to see the previous screen
                      F to Find other items    Q to Quit
NEXT ACTION?  _                                            LMPART
```

Figure 5.4

```
Your search: Stewart, William #                    MEDIUM Display
     Finds: 1 record                               Screen  1 of  1
-------------------------------------------------------------------

       Stewart, William Herman, 1932- The explorer's historical
          tourist map of Alaska, with maps of Anchorage, Fairbanks
          & Juneau : with notes on the Arctic, wildlife, hunting,
          fishing, camping, exploring & prospecting, festivals &
          events / cartography by William H. Stewart. Charleston,
          W.Va. : Economic Service Council, 1983. 1 map : col. ;
          65 x 71 cm., folded to 23 x 11 cm.

      NAMES: Stewart, William Herman, 1932-
             Economic Service Council.

   SUBJECTS: Alaska--Maps, Tourist.
             Alaska--Maps, Pictorial.


-------------------------------------------------------------------
NEXT ACTIONS     Key: ? for help              + to see the next screen
                      L to see a Longer display - to see the previous screen
                      F to Find other items    Q to Quit
NEXT ACTION?  _                                            LMCIT
```

Figure 5.5

```
Your search: Indy, Vincent d'#                    MEDIUM Display
       Finds: 1 record                            Screen  1 of  2
-------------------------------------------------------------------

          Indy, Vincent d', 1851-1931. Suite en re dans le style
                ancien : op. 24 ; Karadec : op. 34 ; Concert, op. 89
                pour piano, flute, violoncello et orchestre a cordes
                [sound recording] / Vincent d'Indy. France : Erato ;
                Paris : Distribution en France RCA, p1982. 1 sound disc
                : 33 1/3 rpm, stereo. ; 12 in.

          NAMES: Indy, Vincent d', 1851-1931.
                 Rampal, Jean Pierre.
                 Pierlot, Philippe.
                 Andre, Maurice.
                 Duchable, Francois.
                 Lodeon, Frederic.
                 Paillard, Jean Francois.

     -------------------------------------------------CONTINUED-------
NEXT ACTIONS      Key: ? for help           + to see the next screen
                       L to see a Longer display   - to see the previous screen
                       F to Find other items  Q to Quit
NEXT ACTION?   _                                          LMCIT
```

Figure 5.6

```
Your search: Indy, Vincent d'#                    MEDIUM Display
       Finds: 1 record                            Screen  2 of  2
-------------------------------------------------------------------

             Orchestre de chambre Jean-Francois Paillard.

        SUBJECTS: Suites (Flutes (2), trumpet with string orchestra)
                  Music, Incidental.
                  Concertos (Piano, flute, violoncello with string orchestra)

          WORKS: Indy, Vincent d', 1851-1931. Suite dans le style ancien.
                 1982.
                 Indy, Vincent d', 1851-1931. Karadec. 1982.
                 Indy, Vincent d', 1851-1931. Concerto, piano, flute,
                 violoncello, orchestra, op. 89. 1982.



     --------------------------------------------------------------
NEXT ACTIONS      Key: ? for help           + to see the next screen
                       L to see a Longer display   - to see the previous screen
                       F to Find other items  Q to Quit
NEXT ACTION?   _                                          LMCIT
```

Figure 5.7

```
Your search: Bless you boys #                          MEDIUM Display
     Finds: 1 record                                   Screen  1 of  1
------------------------------------------------------------------------

        Bless you boys : diary of the Detroit Tigers' 1984 season /
           by Sparky Anderson, with Dan Ewald. Chicago : Contemporary
           Books, c1984. 231 p. : ill. ; 23 cm.

        NAMES: Anderson, Sparky, 1934-
               Ewald, Dan.

        SUBJECTS: Detroit Tigers (Baseball team)




        ------------------------------------------------------------------
NEXT ACTIONS      Key: ? for help              + to see the next screen
                       L to see a Longer display  - to see the previous screen
                       F to Find other items    Q to Quit
NEXT ACTION?   _                                          LMTCIT
```

Figure 5.8

```
Your search: Best American pla#                        MEDIUM Display
     Finds: 1 record                                   Screen  1 of  1
------------------------------------------------------------------------

        Best American plays : sixth series, 1963-1967 / edited by
           John Gassner and Clive Barnes, with an introduction and
           prefaces to the plays by Clive Barnes. New York : Crown,
           c1971. xii, 594 p. ; 24 cm.

        NAMES: Gassner, John, 1903-1967.
               Barnes, Clive, 1927-

        SUBJECTS: American drama--20th century.
                  American drama--Collected works.




        ------------------------------------------------------------------
NEXT ACTIONS      Key: ? for help              + to see the next screen
                       L to see a Longer display  - to see the previous screen
                       F to Find other items    Q to Quit
NEXT ACTION?   _                                          LMTCIT
```

Figure 5.9

```
Your search: Bossa nova U.S.A#                         MEDIUM Display
      Finds: 1 record                                  Screen  1 of  2
--------------------------------------------------------------------------

           Bossa nova U.S.A. / [as performed by] the Dave Brubeck
             Quartet ; piano solo transcriptions by Howard Brubeck. San
             Francisco, Calif. : Derry Music Co. ;  New York, N.Y. : C.
             Hansen, distributor, c1963. 49 p. of music ; 28 cm.

           NAMES: Brubeck, Dave.
                  Brubeck, Howard R.
                  Dave Brubeck Quartet.

        SUBJECTS: Piano music (Jazz), Arranged.
                  Jazz quartets--Piano scores.

           WORKS: Brubeck, Howard R. Theme for June; arr.


-------------------------------------------------------CONTINUED-------
NEXT ACTIONS      Key: ? for help           + to see the next screen
                       L to see a Longer display  - to see the previous screen
                       F to Find other items  Q to Quit
NEXT ACTION?   _                                             LMTCIT
```

Figure 5.10

```
Your search: Bossa nova U.S.A#                         MEDIUM Display
      Finds: 1 record                                  Screen  2 of  2
--------------------------------------------------------------------------

           Macero, Teo, 1925- Coracao sensivel; arr.








-------------------------------------------------------
NEXT ACTIONS      Key: ? for help           + to see the next screen
                       L to see a Longer display  - to see the previous screen
                       F to Find other items  Q to Quit
NEXT ACTION?   _                                             LMTCIT
```

Figure 5.11

```
Your search: The explorer's hi#                        MEDIUM Display
     Finds: 1 record                                   Screen  1 of  1
-----------------------------------------------------------------------

         The explorer's historical tourist map of Alaska, with maps
            of Anchorage, Fairbanks & Juneau : with notes on the
            Arctic, wildlife, hunting, fishing, camping, exploring &
            prospecting, festivals & events / cartography by William
            H. Stewart. Charleston, W.Va. : Economic Service Council,
            1983. 1 map : col. ; 65 x 71 cm., folded to 23 x 11 cm.

         NAMES: Stewart, William Herman, 1932-
                Economic Service Council.

       SUBJECTS: Alaska--Maps, Tourist.
                 Alaska--Maps, Pictorial.


     ------------------------------------------------------------------
NEXT ACTIONS      Key: ? for help               + to see the next screen
                       L to see a Longer display - to see the previous screen
                       F to Find other items    Q to Quit
NEXT ACTION?   _                                            LMTCIT
```

Figure 5.12

```
Your search: Suite en re dans #                        MEDIUM Display
     Finds: 1 record                                   Screen  1 of  2
-----------------------------------------------------------------------

         Suite en re dans le style ancien : op. 24 ; Karadec : op. 34
            ; Concert, op. 89 pour piano, flute, violoncello et
            orchestre a cordes [sound recording] / Vincent d'Indy.
            France : Erato ; Paris : Distribution en France RCA,
            p1982. 1 sound disc : 33 1/3 rpm, stereo. ; 12 in.

         NAMES: Indy, Vincent d', 1851-1931.
                Rampal, Jean Pierre.
                Pierlot, Philippe.
                Andre, Maurice.
                Duchable, Francois.
                Lodeon, Frederic.
                Paillard, Jean Francois.


     ---------------------------------------------------CONTINUED-------
NEXT ACTIONS      Key: ? for help               + to see the next screen
                       L to see a Longer display - to see the previous screen
                       F to Find other items    Q to Quit
NEXT ACTION?   _                                            LMTCIT
```

Figure 5.13

```
Your search: Suite en re dans #                    MEDIUM Display
     Finds: 1 record                               Screen  2 of  2
---------------------------------------------------------------

              Orchestre de chambre Jean-Francois Paillard.

     SUBJECTS: Suites (Flutes (2), trumpet with string orchestra)
               Music, Incidental.
               Concertos (Piano, flute, violoncello with string orchestra)

        WORKS: Indy, Vincent d', 1851-1931. Suite dans le style ancien.
                 1982.
               Indy, Vincent d', 1851-1931. Karadec. 1982.
               Indy, Vincent d', 1851-1931. Concerto, piano, flute,
                 violoncello, orchestra, op. 89. 1982.



---------------------------------------------------------------
NEXT ACTIONS     Key: ? for help            + to see the next screen
                      L to see a Longer display  - to see the previous screen
                      F to Find other items   Q to Quit
NEXT ACTION?  _                                        LMTCIT
```

Figure 5.14

```
Your search: Time.                                 MEDIUM Display
     Finds: 1 record                               Screen  1 of  1
---------------------------------------------------------------

        Time. [Chicago, etc., Time Inc.] v. ill. (incl. ports.) 28
          cm.

        NAMES: Hadden, Briton, ed.
               Luce, Henry Robinson, 1898- ed.






---------------------------------------------------------------
NEXT ACTIONS     Key: ? for help            + to see the next screen
                      L to see a Longer display  - to see the previous screen
                      F to Find other items   Q to Quit
NEXT ACTION?  _                                        LMTCIT
```

Figure 5.15

```
Your search: Postdisaster surv#                      MEDIUM Display
      Finds: 1 record                                Screen  1 of  1
---------------------------------------------------------------------


        Postdisaster survival and rescue research : proceedings,
          Bureau of Mines Technology Transfer Seminar, Pittsburgh,
          Pa., November 16, 1982 / compiled by staff, Bureau of
          Mines. [Avondale, Md.] : U.S. Dept. of the Interior,
          Bureau of Mines, 1982. iii, 91 p. : ill. ; 28 cm.

        NAMES: Bureau of Mines Technology Transfer Seminars (1982 :
                 Pittsburgh, Pa.)
               United States. Bureau of Mines.

     SUBJECTS: Mine accidents--Congresses.
               Mine rescue work--Congresses.

       SERIES: Bureau of Mines information circular ; 8907.


---------------------------------------------------------------------
NEXT ACTIONS      Key: ? for help              + to see the next screen
                       L to see a Longer display  - to see the previous screen
                       F to Find other items    Q to Quit
NEXT ACTION?   _                                            LMTCIT
```

Figure 5.16

```
Your search: Citizen Kane                            MEDIUM Display
      Finds: 1 record                                Screen  1 of  1
---------------------------------------------------------------------


        Citizen Kane [videorecording] / an RKO Radio Picture ; a
          Mercury production ; Orson Welles, direction, production.
          New York, N.Y. : VidAmerica, c1982. 1 videocassette (119
          min.) : sd., b&w ; 1/2 in.

        NAMES: Welles, Orson, 1915-
               VidAmerica (Firm)
               RKO Radio Pictures, inc.
               Mercury Productions.

     SUBJECTS: Feature films.

       SERIES: Classic series.



---------------------------------------------------------------------
NEXT ACTIONS      Key: ? for help              + to see the next screen
                       L to see a Longer display  - to see the previous screen
                       F to Find other items    Q to Quit
NEXT ACTION?   _                                            LMTCIT
```

Figure 5.17

```
Your search: Anderson, Sparky#                    MEDIUM Display
       Finds: 1 record                            Screen  1 of  1
---------------------------------------------------------------

        Anderson, Sparky, 1934-
          Bless you boys : diary of the Detroit Tigers' 1984 season.
        -- c1984.

          1. Detroit Tigers (Baseball team) I. Ewald, Dan.




        ---------------------------------------------------------
NEXT ACTIONS       Key: ? for help           + to see the next screen
                        L to see a Longer display  - to see the previous screen
                        F to Find other items  Q to Quit
NEXT ACTION?  _                                    CXSIMPL
```

Figure 5.18

```
Your search: Best American pla#                   MEDIUM Display
       Finds: 1 record                            Screen  1 of  1
---------------------------------------------------------------

        Best American plays : sixth series, 1963-1967. -- c1971.

          1. American drama--20th century. 2. American drama--
        Collected works. I. Gassner, John, 1903-1967. II. Barnes,
        Clive, 1927-




        ---------------------------------------------------------
NEXT ACTIONS       Key: ? for help           + to see the next screen
                        L to see a Longer display  - to see the previous screen
                        F to Find other items  Q to Quit
NEXT ACTION?  _                                    CXSIMPL
```

Figure 5.19

```
Your search: Brubeck, Dave#                        MEDIUM Display
     Finds: 1 record                               Screen  1 of  1
------------------------------------------------------------------------

          Brubeck, Dave.
            Bossa nova U.S.A. -- c1963.

            1. Piano music (Jazz), Arranged. 2. Jazz quartets--Piano
          scores. I. Brubeck, Howard R. II. Brubeck, Howard R. Theme
          for June; arr. III. Macero, Teo, 1925- Coracao sensivel;
          arr. IV. Dave Brubeck Quartet.




          --------------------------------------------------------------
NEXT ACTIONS      Key: ? for help              + to see the next screen
                       L to see a Longer display - to see the previous screen
                       F to Find other items     Q to Quit
NEXT ACTION?   _                                          CXSIMPL
```

Figure 5.20

```
Your search: Stewart, William #                    MEDIUM Display
     Finds: 1 record                               Screen  1 of  1
------------------------------------------------------------------------

          Stewart, William Herman, 1932-
            The explorer's historical tourist map of Alaska, with maps
          of Anchorage, Fairbanks & Juneau : with notes on the Arctic,
          wildlife, hunting, fishing, camping, exploring &
          prospecting, festivals & events. -- 1983.

            1. Alaska--Maps, Tourist. 2. Alaska--Maps, Pictorial. I.
          Economic Service Council.




          --------------------------------------------------------------
NEXT ACTIONS      Key: ? for help              + to see the next screen
                       L to see a Longer display - to see the previous screen
                       F to Find other items     Q to Quit
NEXT ACTION?   _                                          CXSIMPL
```

Figure 5.21

```
Your search: Indy, Vincent d'#                          MEDIUM Display
       Finds: 1 record                                  Screen  1 of  2
-----------------------------------------------------------------------

        Indy, Vincent d', 1851-1931.
           Suite en re dans le style ancien : op. 24 ; Karadec : op.
        34 ; Concert, op. 89 pour piano, flute, violoncello et
        orchestre a cordes [sound recording] -- p1982.

           1. Suites (Flutes (2), trumpet with string orchestra) 2.
        Music, Incidental. 3. Concertos (Piano, flute, violoncello
        with string orchestra) I. Rampal, Jean Pierre. II. Pierlot,
        Philippe. III. Andre, Maurice. IV. Duchable, Francois. V.
        Lodeon, Frederic. VI. Paillard, Jean Francois. VII. Indy,
        Vincent d', 1851-1931. Suite dans le style ancien. 1982.
        VIII. Indy, Vincent d', 1851-1931. Karadec. 1982. IX. Indy,
        Vincent d', 1851-1931. Concerto, piano, flute, violoncello,
        orchestra, op. 89. 1982. X. Orchestre de chambre

--------------------------------------------------------CONTINUED-------
NEXT ACTIONS      Key: ? for help          + to see the next screen
                       L to see a Longer display  - to see the previous screen
                       F to Find other items      Q to Quit
NEXT ACTION?   _                                          CXSIMPL
```

Figure 5.22

```
Your search: Indy, Vincent d'#                          MEDIUM Display
       Finds: 1 record                                  Screen  2 of  2
-----------------------------------------------------------------------

        Jean-Francois Paillard.







-----------------------------------------------------------------------
NEXT ACTIONS      Key: ? for help          + to see the next screen
                       L to see a Longer display  - to see the previous screen
                       F to Find other items      Q to Quit
NEXT ACTION?   _                                          CXSIMPL
```

Figure 5.23

```
Your search: Time.                              MEDIUM Display
     Finds: 1 record                            Screen  1 of  1
---------------------------------------------------------------

        Time.

           I. Hadden, Briton, ed. II. Luce, Henry Robinson, 1898- ed.




---------------------------------------------------------------
NEXT ACTIONS      Key: ? for help              + to see the next screen
                       L to see a Longer display  - to see the previous screen
                       F to Find other items   Q to Quit
NEXT ACTION?  _                                           CXSIMPL
```

Figure 5.24

```
Your search: Bureau of Mines T#                MEDIUM Display
     Finds: 1 record                            Screen  1 of  1
---------------------------------------------------------------

        Bureau of Mines Technology Transfer Seminars (1982 :
          Pittsburgh, Pa.)
          Postdisaster survival and rescue research : proceedings,
        Bureau of Mines Technology Transfer Seminar, Pittsburgh,
        Pa., November 16, 1982. -- 1982.

        (Bureau of Mines information circular ; 8907)

          1. Mine accidents--Congresses. 2. Mine rescue work--
        Congresses. I. United States. Bureau of Mines.



---------------------------------------------------------------
NEXT ACTIONS      Key: ? for help              + to see the next screen
                       L to see a Longer display  - to see the previous screen
                       F to Find other items   Q to Quit
NEXT ACTION?  _                                           CXSIMPL
```

Figure 5.25

```
Your search: Citizen Kane                          MEDIUM Display
      Finds: 1 record                              Screen  1 of  1
-------------------------------------------------------------------

          Citizen Kane [videorecording] -- c1982.

          (Classic series)

           1. Feature films. I. Welles, Orson, 1915- II. VidAmerica
          (Firm) III. RKO Radio Pictures, inc. IV. Mercury
          Productions.




          ----------------------------------------------------------
NEXT ACTIONS       Key: ? for help            + to see the next screen
                        L to see a Longer display  - to see the previous screen
                        F to Find other items      Q to Quit
NEXT ACTION?  _                                              CXSIMPL
```

Figure 5.26

```
Your search: Bless you boys #                      MEDIUM Display
      Finds: 1 record                              Screen  1 of  1
-------------------------------------------------------------------

        TITLE: Bless you boys : diary of the Detroit Tigers' 1984 season.

      AUTHORS: Anderson, Sparky, 1934-
               Ewald, Dan.
         DATE: c1984.
     SUBJECTS: Detroit Tigers (Baseball team)





          ----------------------------------------------------------
NEXT ACTIONS       Key: ? for help            + to see the next screen
                        L to see a Longer display  - to see the previous screen
                        F to Find other items      Q to Quit
NEXT ACTION?  _                                              LXSIMPL
```

Figure 5.27

```
Your search: Best American pla#                    MEDIUM Display
     Finds: 1 record                               Screen  1 of  1
------------------------------------------------------------------------

         TITLE: Best American plays : sixth series, 1963-1967.

       AUTHORS: Gassner, John, 1903-1967.
                Barnes, Clive, 1927-
          DATE: c1971.
      SUBJECTS: American drama--20th century.
                American drama--Collected works.




------------------------------------------------------------------------
NEXT ACTIONS       Key: ? for help            + to see the next screen
                        L to see a Longer display  - to see the previous screen
                        F to Find other items   Q to Quit
NEXT ACTION?  _                                            LXSIMPL
```

Figure 5.28

```
Your search: Bossa nova U.S.A#                     MEDIUM Display
     Finds: 1 record                               Screen  1 of  1
------------------------------------------------------------------------

         TITLE: Bossa nova U.S.A.

       AUTHORS: Brubeck, Dave.
                Brubeck, Howard R.
                Brubeck, Howard R. Theme for June; arr.
                Macero, Teo, 1925- Coracao sensivel; arr.
                Dave Brubeck Quartet.
          DATE: c1963.
      SUBJECTS: Piano music (Jazz), Arranged.
                Jazz quartets--Piano scores.



------------------------------------------------------------------------
NEXT ACTIONS       Key: ? for help            + to see the next screen
                        L to see a Longer display  - to see the previous screen
                        F to Find other items   Q to Quit
NEXT ACTION?  _                                            LXSIMPL
```

Figure 5.29

```
Your search: The explorer's hi#                    MEDIUM Display
      Finds: 1 record                              Screen 1 of  1
-----------------------------------------------------------------------

          TITLE: The explorer's historical tourist map of Alaska, with maps
                 of Anchorage, Fairbanks & Juneau : with notes on the
                 Arctic, wildlife, hunting, fishing, camping, exploring &
                 prospecting, festivals & events.

        AUTHORS: Stewart, William Herman, 1932-
                 Economic Service Council.
           DATE: 1983.
       SUBJECTS: Alaska--Maps, Tourist.
                 Alaska--Maps, Pictorial.




-----------------------------------------------------------------------
NEXT ACTIONS     Key: ? for help            + to see the next screen
                      L to see a Longer display  - to see the previous screen
                      F to Find other items  Q to Quit
NEXT ACTION?  _                                            LXSIMPL
```

Figure 5.30

```
Your search: Suite en re dans #                    MEDIUM Display
      Finds: 1 record                              Screen  1 of  2
-----------------------------------------------------------------------

          TITLE: Suite en re dans le style ancien : op. 24 ; Karadec : op. 34
                 ; Concert, op. 89 pour piano, flute, violoncello et
                 orchestre a cordes [sound recording]

        AUTHORS: Indy, Vincent d', 1851-1931.
                 Rampal, Jean Pierre.
                 Pierlot, Philippe.
                 Andre, Maurice.
                 Duchable, Francois.
                 Lodeon, Frederic.
                 Paillard, Jean Francois.
                 Indy, Vincent d', 1851-1931. Suite dans le style ancien.
                    1982.
                 Indy, Vincent d', 1851-1931. Karadec. 1982.

---------------------------------------------------------CONTINUED-------
NEXT ACTIONS     Key: ? for help            + to see the next screen
                      L to see a Longer display  - to see the previous screen
                      F to Find other items  Q to Quit
NEXT ACTION?  _                                            LXSIMPL
```

Figure 5.31

```
Your search: Suite en re dans #                    MEDIUM Display
     Finds: 1 record                               Screen  2 of  2
----------------------------------------------------------------------

               Indy, Vincent d', 1851-1931. Concerto, piano, flute,
                  violoncello, orchestra, op. 89. 1982.
               Orchestre de chambre Jean-Francois Paillard.
       DATE: p1982.
   SUBJECTS: Suites (Flutes (2), trumpet with string orchestra)
             Music, Incidental.
             Concertos (Piano, flute, violoncello with string orchestra)




----------------------------------------------------------------------
NEXT ACTIONS      Key: ? for help            + to see the next screen
                       L to see a Longer display  - to see the previous screen
                       F to Find other items  Q to Quit
NEXT ACTION?  _                                          LXSIMPL
```

Figure 5.32

```
Your search: Time.                                 MEDIUM Display
     Finds: 1 record                               Screen  1 of  1
----------------------------------------------------------------------

      TITLE: Time.

    AUTHORS: Hadden, Briton, ed.
             Luce, Henry Robinson, 1898- ed.






----------------------------------------------------------------------
NEXT ACTIONS      Key: ? for help            + to see the next screen
                       L to see a Longer display  - to see the previous screen
                       F to Find other items  Q to Quit
NEXT ACTION?  _                                          LXSIMPL
```

Figure 5.33

```
Your search: Postdisaster surv#                          MEDIUM Display
       Finds: 1 record                                   Screen  1 of  1
-------------------------------------------------------------------------

         TITLE: Postdisaster survival and rescue research : proceedings,
                Bureau of Mines Technology Transfer Seminar, Pittsburgh,
                Pa., November 16, 1982.

       AUTHORS: Bureau of Mines Technology Transfer Seminars (1982 :
                Pittsburgh, Pa.)
                United States. Bureau of Mines.
          DATE: 1982.
        SERIES: Bureau of Mines information circular ; 8907.
      SUBJECTS: Mine accidents--Congresses.
                Mine rescue work--Congresses.




-------------------------------------------------------------------------
NEXT ACTIONS       Key: ? for help            + to see the next screen
                        L to see a Longer display  - to see the previous screen
                        F to Find other items  Q to Quit
NEXT ACTION?  _                                             LXSIMPL
```

Figure 5.34

```
Your search: Citizen Kane                                MEDIUM Display
       Finds: 1 record                                   Screen  1 of  1
-------------------------------------------------------------------------

         TITLE: Citizen Kane [videorecording]

       AUTHORS: Welles, Orson, 1915-
                VidAmerica (Firm)
                RKO Radio Pictures, inc.
                Mercury Productions.
          DATE: c1982.
        SERIES: Classic series.
      SUBJECTS: Feature films.




-------------------------------------------------------------------------
NEXT ACTIONS       Key: ? for help            + to see the next screen
                        L to see a Longer display  - to see the previous screen
                        F to Find other items  Q to Quit
NEXT ACTION?  _                                             LXSIMPL
```

Figure 5.35

```
Your search: Anderson, Sparky#                    MEDIUM Display
     Finds: 1 record                              Screen 1 of 1
------------------------------------------------------------------------

          Anderson, Sparky, 1934-
            Bless you boys : diary of the Detroit Tigers' 1984 season.
          -- c1984.

            ISBN 0-8092-5307-0 (pbk.)

            1. Detroit Tigers (Baseball team) I. Ewald, Dan.




------------------------------------------------------------------------
NEXT ACTIONS     Key: ? for help           + to see the next screen
                      L to see a Longer display  - to see the previous screen
                      F to Find other items    Q to Quit
NEXT ACTION?  _                                          CXMATT
```

Figure 5.36

```
Your search: Best American pla#                   MEDIUM Display
     Finds: 1 record                              Screen 1 of 1
------------------------------------------------------------------------

          Best American plays : sixth series, 1963-1967. -- c1971.

            ISBN 0-517-50951-2

            1. American drama--20th century. 2. American drama--
          Collected works. I. Gassner, John, 1903-1967. II. Barnes,
          Clive, 1927-




------------------------------------------------------------------------
NEXT ACTIONS     Key: ? for help           + to see the next screen
                      L to see a Longer display  - to see the previous screen
                      F to Find other items    Q to Quit
NEXT ACTION?  _                                          CXMATT
```

Figure 5.37

```
Your search: Brubeck, Dave#                          MEDIUM Display
      Finds: 1 record                                Screen 1 of 1
--------------------------------------------------------------------

        Brubeck, Dave.
          [Bossa nova U.S.A. Selections; arr.]
          Bossa nova U.S.A. -- c1963.

          Publisher's no. : Derry Music Co. : D233.

          1. Piano music (Jazz), Arranged. 2. Jazz quartets--Piano
        scores. I. Brubeck, Howard R. II. Brubeck, Howard R. Theme
        for June; arr. III. Macero, Teo, 1925- Coracao sensivel;
        arr. IV. Dave Brubeck Quartet.




--------------------------------------------------------------------
NEXT ACTIONS      Key: ? for help            + to see the next screen
                       L to see a Longer display - to see the previous screen
                       F to Find other items  Q to Quit

NEXT ACTION?  _                                           CXMATT
```

Figure 5.38

```
Your search: Stewart, William #                      MEDIUM Display
      Finds: 1 record                                Screen 1 of 1
--------------------------------------------------------------------

        Stewart, William Herman, 1932-
          The explorer's historical tourist map of Alaska, with maps
        of Anchorage, Fairbanks & Juneau : with notes on the Arctic,
        wildlife, hunting, fishing, camping, exploring &
        prospecting, festivals & events. -- 1983.

          1. Alaska--Maps, Tourist. 2. Alaska--Maps, Pictorial. I.
        Economic Service Council.





--------------------------------------------------------------------
NEXT ACTIONS      Key: ? for help            + to see the next screen
                       L to see a Longer display - to see the previous screen
                       F to Find other items  Q to Quit

NEXT ACTION?  _                                           CXMATT
```

Figure 5.39

```
Your search: Indy, Vincent d'#                      MEDIUM Display
       Finds: 1 record                              Screen  1 of  2
-----------------------------------------------------------------------

         Indy, Vincent d', 1851-1931.
           [Instrumental music. Selections]
           Suite en re dans le style ancien : op. 24 ; Karadec : op.
         34 ; Concert, op. 89 pour piano, flute, violoncello et
         orchestre a cordes [sound recording] -- p1982.

           Erato : STU 71423.

           1. Suites (Flutes (2), trumpet with string orchestra) 2.
         Music, Incidental. 3. Concertos (Piano, flute, violoncello
         with string orchestra) I. Rampal, Jean Pierre. II. Pierlot,
         Philippe. III. Andre, Maurice. IV. Duchable, Francois. V.
         Lodeon, Frederic. VI. Paillard, Jean Francois. VII. Indy,
         Vincent d', 1851-1931. Suite dans le style ancien. 1982.

-------------------------------------------------------CONTINUED-------
NEXT ACTIONS      Key: ? for help             + to see the next screen
                       L to see a Longer display  - to see the previous screen
                       F to Find other items   Q to Quit
NEXT ACTION?  _                                            CXMATT
```

Figure 5.40

```
Your search: Indy, Vincent d'#                      MEDIUM Display
       Finds: 1 record                              Screen  2 of  2
-----------------------------------------------------------------------

         VIII. Indy, Vincent d', 1851-1931. Karadec. 1982. IX. Indy,
         Vincent d', 1851-1931. Concerto, piano, flute, violoncello,
         orchestra, op. 89. 1982. X. Orchestre de chambre
         Jean-Francois Paillard.




-----------------------------------------------------------------------
NEXT ACTIONS      Key: ? for help             + to see the next screen
                       L to see a Longer display  - to see the previous screen
                       F to Find other items   Q to Quit
NEXT ACTION?  _                                            CXMATT
```

Figure 5.41

```
Your search: Time.                              MEDIUM Display
     Finds: 1 record                            Screen  1 of  1
------------------------------------------------------------------

      Time.

        ISSN 0040-781X.

        I. Hadden, Briton, ed. II. Luce, Henry Robinson, 1898- ed.




------------------------------------------------------------------
NEXT ACTIONS      Key: ? for help          + to see the next screen
                       L to see a Longer display  - to see the previous screen
                       F to Find other items   Q to Quit
NEXT ACTION?  _                                      CXMATT
```

Figure 5.42

```
Your search: Bureau of Mines T#                 MEDIUM Display
     Finds: 1 record                            Screen  1 of  1
------------------------------------------------------------------
        Bureau of Mines Technology Transfer Seminars (1982 :
          Pittsburgh, Pa.)
          Postdisaster survival and rescue research : proceedings,
        Bureau of Mines Technology Transfer Seminar, Pittsburgh,
        Pa., November 16, 1982. -- 1982.

        (Bureau of Mines information circular ; 8907)

          1. Mine accidents--Congresses. 2. Mine rescue work--
        Congresses. I. United States. Bureau of Mines.



------------------------------------------------------------------
NEXT ACTIONS      Key: ? for help          + to see the next screen
                       L to see a Longer display  - to see the previous screen
                       F to Find other items   Q to Quit
NEXT ACTION?  _                                      CXMATT
```

Figure 5.43

```
Your search: Citizen Kane                        MEDIUM Display
     Finds: 1 record                             Screen  1 of  1
--------------------------------------------------------------------

          Citizen Kane [videorecording] -- c1982.

           (Classic series)

            1. Feature films. I. Welles, Orson, 1915- II. VidAmerica
          (Firm) III. RKO Radio Pictures, inc. IV. Mercury
          Productions.




        ------------------------------------------------------------
NEXT ACTIONS      Key: ? for help            + to see the next screen
                       L to see a Longer display  - to see the previous screen
                       F to Find other items  Q to Quit
NEXT ACTION?   _                                          CXMATT
```

Figure 5.44

```
Your search: Bless you boys #                    MEDIUM Display
     Finds: 1 record                             Screen  1 of  1
--------------------------------------------------------------------

        TITLE: Bless you boys : diary of the Detroit Tigers' 1984 season.
         DATE: c1984.

        NAMES: Anderson, Sparky, 1934-
               Ewald, Dan.

         ISBN: 0-8092-5307-0 (pbk.)

     SUBJECTS: Detroit Tigers (Baseball team)




        ------------------------------------------------------------
NEXT ACTIONS      Key: ? for help            + to see the next screen
                       L to see a Longer display  - to see the previous screen
                       F to Find other items  Q to Quit
NEXT ACTION?   _                                          LXMATT
```

Figure 5.45

```
Your search: Best American pla#                      MEDIUM Display
      Finds: 1 record                                Screen  1 of  1
-----------------------------------------------------------------------

         TITLE: Best American plays : sixth series, 1963-1967.
          DATE: c1971.

         NAMES: Gassner, John, 1903-1967.
                Barnes, Clive, 1927-

          ISBN: 0-517-50951-2

      SUBJECTS: American drama--20th century.
                American drama--Collected works.



-----------------------------------------------------------------------
NEXT ACTIONS      Key: ? for help          + to see the next screen
                       L to see a Longer display  - to see the previous screen
                       F to Find other items  Q to Quit
NEXT ACTION?  _                                      LXMATT
```

Figure 5.46

```
Your search: Bossa nova U.S.A#                       MEDIUM Display
      Finds: 1 record                                Screen  1 of  2
-----------------------------------------------------------------------

         TITLE: Bossa nova U.S.A.
                (Bossa nova U.S.A. Selections; arr.)
          DATE: c1963.

         NAMES: Brubeck, Dave.
                Brubeck, Howard R.
                Dave Brubeck Quartet.

       PUB. NO.: Derry Music Co. : D233.

      SUBJECTS: Piano music (Jazz), Arranged.
                Jazz quartets--Piano scores.

         WORKS: Brubeck, Howard R. Theme for June; arr.
--------------------------------------------------CONTINUED-------
NEXT ACTIONS      Key: ? for help          + to see the next screen
                       L to see a Longer display  - to see the previous screen
                       F to Find other items  Q to Quit
NEXT ACTION?  _                                      LXMATT
```

Figure 5.47

```
┌─────────────────────────────────────────────────────────────────────┐
│Your search: Bossa nova U.S.A#                      MEDIUM Display     │
│      Finds: 1 record                               Screen  2 of  2    │
│-----------------------------------------------------------------------│
│                                                                       │
│          Macero, Teo, 1925- Coracao sensivel; arr.                    │
│                                                                       │
│                                                                       │
│                                                                       │
│                                                                       │
│                                                                       │
│                                                                       │
│                                                                       │
│                                                                       │
│                                                                       │
│                                                                       │
│-----------------------------------------------------------------------│
│NEXT ACTIONS      Key: ? for help           + to see the next screen   │
│                       L to see a Longer display  - to see the previous screen│
│                       F to Find other items      Q to Quit            │
│NEXT ACTION?   _                                          LXMATT       │
└─────────────────────────────────────────────────────────────────────┘
```

Figure 5.48

```
┌─────────────────────────────────────────────────────────────────────┐
│Your search: The explorer's hi#                     MEDIUM Display     │
│      Finds: 1 record                               Screen  1 of  1    │
│-----------------------------------------------------------------------│
│        TITLE: The explorer's historical tourist map of Alaska, with maps│
│               of Anchorage, Fairbanks & Juneau : with notes on the    │
│               Arctic, wildlife, hunting, fishing, camping, exploring &│
│               prospecting, festivals & events.                        │
│         DATE: 1983.                                                   │
│                                                                       │
│        NAMES: Stewart, William Herman, 1932-                          │
│               Economic Service Council.                               │
│                                                                       │
│     SUBJECTS: Alaska--Maps, Tourist.                                  │
│               Alaska--Maps, Pictorial.                                │
│                                                                       │
│                                                                       │
│-----------------------------------------------------------------------│
│NEXT ACTIONS      Key: ? for help           + to see the next screen   │
│                       L to see a Longer display  - to see the previous screen│
│                       F to Find other items      Q to Quit            │
│NEXT ACTION?   _                                          LXMATT       │
└─────────────────────────────────────────────────────────────────────┘
```

Figure 5.49

```
Your search: Suite en re dans #                          MEDIUM Display
      Finds: 1 record                                    Screen  1 of  2
----------------------------------------------------------------------------

         TITLE: Suite en re dans le style ancien : op. 24 ; Karadec : op. 34
                  ; Concert, op. 89 pour piano, flute, violoncello et
                  orchestre a cordes [sound recording]
                (Instrumental music. Selections)
          DATE: p1982.

         NAMES: Indy, Vincent d', 1851-1931.
                Rampal, Jean Pierre.
                Pierlot, Philippe.
                Andre, Maurice.
                Duchable, Francois.
                Lodeon, Frederic.
                Paillard, Jean Francois.


    --------------------------------------------------------CONTINUED-------
NEXT ACTIONS      Key: ? for help           + to see the next screen
                       L to see a Longer display  - to see the previous screen
                       F to Find other items  Q to Quit
NEXT ACTION?   _                                            LXMATT
```

Figure 5.50

```
Your search: Suite en re dans #                          MEDIUM Display
      Finds: 1 record                                    Screen  2 of  2
----------------------------------------------------------------------------

                Orchestre de chambre Jean-Francois Paillard.

      PUB. NO.: Erato : MCE 71423.
                Erato : STU 71423.

      SUBJECTS: Suites (Flutes (2), trumpet with string orchestra)
                Music, Incidental.
                Concertos (Piano, flute, violoncello with string orchestra)

         WORKS: Indy, Vincent d', 1851-1931. Suite dans le style ancien.
                  1982.
                Indy, Vincent d', 1851-1931. Karadec. 1982.
                Indy, Vincent d', 1851-1931. Concerto, piano, flute,
                  violoncello, orchestra, op. 89. 1982.

    ----------------------------------------------------------------------
NEXT ACTIONS      Key: ? for help           + to see the next screen
                       L to see a Longer display  - to see the previous screen
                       F to Find other items  Q to Quit
NEXT ACTION?   _                                            LXMATT
```

Figure 5.51

```
Your search: Time.                              MEDIUM Display
      Finds: 1 record                           Screen  1 of  1
-----------------------------------------------------------------------

        TITLE: Time.

        NAMES: Hadden, Briton, ed.
               Luce, Henry Robinson, 1898- ed.

         ISSN: 0040-781X.




-----------------------------------------------------------------------
NEXT ACTIONS      Key: ? for help              + to see the next screen
                       L to see a Longer display  - to see the previous screen
                       F to Find other items    Q to Quit
NEXT ACTION?   _                                          LXMATT
```

Figure 5.52

```
Your search: Postdisaster surv#                 MEDIUM Display
      Finds: 1 record                           Screen  1 of  1
-----------------------------------------------------------------------

        TITLE: Postdisaster survival and rescue research : proceedings,
               Bureau of Mines Technology Transfer Seminar, Pittsburgh,
               Pa., November 16, 1982.
         DATE: 1982.

        NAMES: Bureau of Mines Technology Transfer Seminars (1982 :
               Pittsburgh, Pa.)
               United States. Bureau of Mines.

       SERIES: Bureau of Mines information circular ; 8907.

     SUBJECTS: Mine accidents--Congresses.
               Mine rescue work--Congresses.

-----------------------------------------------------------------------
NEXT ACTIONS      Key: ? for help              + to see the next screen
                       L to see a Longer display  - to see the previous screen
                       F to Find other items    Q to Quit
NEXT ACTION?   _                                          LXMATT
```

Figure 5.53

```
Your search: Citizen Kane                        MEDIUM Display
       Finds: 1 record                           Screen  1 of  1
-----------------------------------------------------------------------

          TITLE: Citizen Kane [videorecording]
           DATE: c1982.

          NAMES: Welles, Orson, 1915-
                 VidAmerica (Firm)
                 RKO Radio Pictures, inc.
                 Mercury Productions.

         SERIES: Classic series.

       SUBJECTS: Feature films.




     ------------------------------------------------------------------
NEXT ACTIONS      Key: ? for help          + to see the next screen
                       L to see a Longer display  - to see the previous screen
                       F to Find other items  Q to Quit
NEXT ACTION?  _                                           LXMATT
```

Figure 5.54

```
Your search: Anderson, Sparky#                   MEDIUM Display
       Finds: 1 record                           Screen  1 of  1
-----------------------------------------------------------------------

        Anderson, Sparky, 1934-
          Bless you boys : diary of the Detroit Tigers' 1984 season
   · / by Sparky Anderson, with Dan Ewald. -- Chicago :
        Contemporary Books, c1984.

          1. Detroit Tigers (Baseball team)






     ------------------------------------------------------------------
NEXT ACTIONS      Key: ? for help          + to see the next screen
                       L to see a Longer display  - to see the previous screen
                       F to Find other items  Q to Quit
NEXT ACTION?  _                                           CXPLM1
```

Figure 5.55

```
Your search: Best American pla#                    MEDIUM Display
      Finds: 1 record                              Screen  1 of  2
------------------------------------------------------------------------

        Best American plays : sixth series, 1963-1967 / edited by
          John Gassner and Clive Barnes, with an introduction and
          prefaces to the plays by Clive Barnes. -- New York :
          Crown, c1971.

          Contents: Tiny Alice / E. Albee -- Blues for Mister
        Charlie / J. Baldwin -- The last analysis / S. Bellow --
        Hogan's goat / W. Alfred -- The fantasticks / T. Jones --
        The sign in Sidney Brustein's window / L. Hansberry -- The
        lion in winter / J. Goldman -- Hughie / E. O'Neill -- The
        toilet / L. Jones -- You know I can't hear you when the
        water is running / R. Anderson -- Benito Cereno / R. Lowell
        -- Fiddler on the roof / J. Stein -- Slow dance on the
        killing ground / W. Hanley -- In white America / M.B.

----------------------------------------------------------CONTINUED-------
NEXT ACTIONS      Key: ? for help            + to see the next screen
                       L to see a Longer display  - to see the previous screen
                       F to Find other items  Q to Quit

NEXT ACTION?   _                                        CXPLM1
```

Figure 5.56

```
Your search: Best American pla#                    MEDIUM Display
      Finds: 1 record                              Screen  2 of  2
------------------------------------------------------------------------

        Duberman -- The owl and the pussycat / B. Manhoff -- The odd
        couple / W. Simon -- The subject was roses / F.D. Gilroy.

          1. American drama--20th century. 2. American drama--
        Collected works.




------------------------------------------------------------------------
NEXT ACTIONS      Key: ? for help            + to see the next screen
                       L to see a Longer display  - to see the previous screen
                       F to Find other items  Q to Quit

NEXT ACTION?   _                                        CXPLM1
```

Figure 5.57

```
Your search: Brubeck, Dave#                      MEDIUM Display
      Finds: 1 record                            Screen  1 of  2
-----------------------------------------------------------------

        Brubeck, Dave.
          Bossa nova U.S.A. / [as performed by] the Dave Brubeck
        Quartet ; piano solo transcriptions by Howard Brubeck. --
        San Francisco, Calif. : Derry Music Co. ;  New York, N.Y. :
        C. Hansen, distributor, c1963.

          Contents: Bossa nova U.S. A. / Dave Brubeck -- Vento
        fresco = Cool wind / Dave Brubeck -- Theme for June / Howard
        R. Brubeck -- Coracao sensivel = Tender heart / Teo Macero
        -- Irmao amigo = Brother friend / Dave Brubeck -- There'll
        be no tomorrow / Dave Brubeck -- Cantiga nov swing = Swing a
        new song / Dave Brubeck -- Lamento = Lament / Dave Brubeck.



------------------------------------------------------CONTINUED-------
NEXT ACTIONS      Key: ? for help          + to see the next screen
                       L to see a Longer display  - to see the previous screen
                       F to Find other items  Q to Quit
NEXT ACTION?  _                                         CXPLM1
```

Figure 5.58

```
Your search: Brubeck, Dave#                      MEDIUM Display
      Finds: 1 record                            Screen  2 of  2
-----------------------------------------------------------------

          1. Piano music (Jazz), Arranged. 2. Jazz quartets--Piano
        scores.










------------------------------------------------------------------
NEXT ACTIONS      Key: ? for help          + to see the next screen
                       L to see a Longer display  - to see the previous screen
                       F to Find other items  Q to Quit
NEXT ACTION?  _                                         CXPLM1
```

Figure 5.59

```
Your search: Stewart, William #                      MEDIUM Display
     Finds: 1 record                                 Screen  1 of  1
-----------------------------------------------------------------------

        Stewart, William Herman, 1932-
          The explorer's historical tourist map of Alaska, with maps
        of Anchorage, Fairbanks & Juneau : with notes on the Arctic,
        wildlife, hunting, fishing, camping, exploring &
        prospecting, festivals & events / cartography by William H.
        Stewart. -- Charleston, W.Va. : Economic Service Council,
        1983.

          1. Alaska--Maps, Tourist. 2. Alaska--Maps, Pictorial.




        -----------------------------------------------------------
NEXT ACTIONS     Key: ? for help          + to see the next screen
                      L to see a Longer display  - to see the previous screen
                      F to Find other items  Q to Quit
NEXT ACTION?  _                                          CXPLM1
```

Figure 5.60

```
Your search: Indy, Vincent d'#                       MEDIUM Display
     Finds: 1 record                                 Screen  1 of  1
-----------------------------------------------------------------------

        Indy, Vincent d', 1851-1931.
          Suite en re dans le style ancien : op. 24 ; Karadec : op.
        34 ; Concert, op. 89 pour piano, flute, violoncello et
        orchestre a cordes [sound recording] / Vincent d'Indy. --
        France : Erato ; Paris : Distribution en France RCA, p1982.

          1. Suites (Flutes (2), trumpet with string orchestra) 2.
        Music, Incidental. 3. Concertos (Piano, flute, violoncello
        with string orchestra)




        -----------------------------------------------------------
NEXT ACTIONS     Key: ? for help          + to see the next screen
                      L to see a Longer display  - to see the previous screen
                      F to Find other items  Q to Quit
NEXT ACTION?  _                                          CXPLM1
```

Figure 5.61

```
Your search: Time.                               MEDIUM Display
       Finds: 1 record                           Screen  1 of  1
-------------------------------------------------------------------

         Time. [Chicago, etc., Time Inc.]




















-------------------------------------------------------------------
NEXT ACTIONS       Key: ? for help          + to see the next screen
                        L to see a Longer display  - to see the previous screen
                        F to Find other items  Q to Quit
NEXT ACTION?    _                                         CXPLM1
```

Figure 5.62

```
Your search: Bureau of Mines T#                  MEDIUM Display
       Finds: 1 record                           Screen  1 of  1
-------------------------------------------------------------------

         Bureau of Mines Technology Transfer Seminars (1982 :
           Pittsburgh, Pa.)
           Postdisaster survival and rescue research : proceedings,
         Bureau of Mines Technology Transfer Seminar, Pittsburgh,
         Pa., November 16, 1982 / compiled by staff, Bureau of Mines.
         -- [Avondale, Md.] : U.S. Dept. of the Interior, Bureau of
         Mines, 1982.

           1. Mine accidents--Congresses. 2. Mine rescue work--
         Congresses.





-------------------------------------------------------------------
NEXT ACTIONS       Key: ? for help          + to see the next screen
                        L to see a Longer display  - to see the previous screen
                        F to Find other items  Q to Quit
NEXT ACTION?    _                                         CXPLM1
```

Figure 5.63

```
Your search: Citizen Kane                        MEDIUM Display
      Finds: 1 record                            Screen 1 of  1
--------------------------------------------------------------------

        Citizen Kane [videorecording] / an RKO Radio Picture ; a
          Mercury production ; Orson Welles, direction, production.
          -- New York, N.Y. : VidAmerica, c1982.

        1. Feature films.




--------------------------------------------------------------------
NEXT ACTIONS      Key: ? for help            + to see the next screen
                       L to see a Longer display  - to see the previous screen
                       F to Find other items  Q to Quit
NEXT ACTION?   _                                          CXPLM1
```

Figure 5.64

```
Your search: Bless you boys #                    MEDIUM Display
      Finds: 1 record                            Screen 1 of  1
--------------------------------------------------------------------

        TITLE: Bless you boys : diary of the Detroit Tigers' 1984 season /
                 by Sparky Anderson, with Dan Ewald.
    PUBLISHED: Chicago : Contemporary Books, c1984.

       AUTHOR: Anderson, Sparky, 1934-

     SUBJECTS: Detroit Tigers (Baseball team)




--------------------------------------------------------------------
NEXT ACTIONS      Key: ? for help            + to see the next screen
                       L to see a Longer display  - to see the previous screen
                       F to Find other items  Q to Quit
NEXT ACTION?   _                                          LXPLM1
```

Figure 5.65

```
Your search: Best American pla#                      MEDIUM Display
     Finds: 1 record                                 Screen  1 of  2
-------------------------------------------------------------------

        TITLE: Best American plays : sixth series, 1963-1967 / edited by
               John Gassner and Clive Barnes, with an introduction and
               prefaces to the plays by Clive Barnes.
    PUBLISHED: New York : Crown, c1971.

     SUBJECTS: American drama--20th century.
               American drama--Collected works.

     CONTENTS: Tiny Alice / E. Albee -- Blues for Mister Charlie / J.
               Baldwin -- The last analysis / S. Bellow -- Hogan's goat /
               W. Alfred -- The fantasticks / T. Jones -- The sign in
               Sidney Brustein's window / L. Hansberry -- The lion in
               winter / J. Goldman -- Hughie / E. O'Neill -- The toilet /
               L. Jones -- You know I can't hear you when the water is

-------------------------------------------------------CONTINUED-------
NEXT ACTIONS      Key: ? for help            + to see the next screen
                       L to see a Longer display  - to see the previous screen
                       F to Find other items    Q to Quit
NEXT ACTION?  _                                          LXPLM1
```

Figure 5.66

```
Your search: Best American pla#                      MEDIUM Display
     Finds: 1 record                                 Screen  2 of  2
-------------------------------------------------------------------

               running / R. Anderson -- Benito Cereno / R. Lowell --
               Fiddler on the roof / J. Stein -- Slow dance on the
               killing ground / W. Hanley -- In white America / M.B.
               Duberman -- The owl and the pussycat / B. Manhoff -- The
               odd couple / W. Simon -- The subject was roses / F.D.
               Gilroy.




-------------------------------------------------------------------
NEXT ACTIONS      Key: ? for help            + to see the next screen
                       L to see a Longer display  - to see the previous screen
                       F to Find other items    Q to Quit
NEXT ACTION?  _                                          LXPLM1
```

Figure 5.67

```
Your search: Bossa nova U.S.A#                    MEDIUM Display
     Finds: 1 record                              Screen  1 of  2
---------------------------------------------------------------------

         TITLE: Bossa nova U.S.A. / [as performed by] the Dave Brubeck
                Quartet ; piano solo transcriptions by Howard Brubeck.
     PUBLISHED: San Francisco, Calif. : Derry Music Co. ;  New York, N.Y. :
                C. Hansen, distributor, c1963.

        AUTHOR: Brubeck, Dave.

      SUBJECTS: Piano music (Jazz), Arranged.
                Jazz quartets--Piano scores.

      CONTENTS: Bossa nova U.S. A. / Dave Brubeck -- Vento fresco = Cool
                wind / Dave Brubeck -- Theme for June / Howard R. Brubeck
                -- Coracao sensivel = Tender heart / Teo Macero -- Irmao
                amigo = Brother friend / Dave Brubeck -- There'll be no

---------------------------------------------------------CONTINUED-------
NEXT ACTIONS      Key: ? for help            + to see the next screen
                       L to see a Longer display  - to see the previous screen
                       F to Find other items   Q to Quit
NEXT ACTION?  _                                          LXPLM1
```

Figure 5.68

```
Your search: Bossa nova U.S.A#                    MEDIUM Display
     Finds: 1 record                              Screen  2 of  2
---------------------------------------------------------------------

                tomorrow / Dave Brubeck -- Cantiga nov swing = Swing a new
                song / Dave Brubeck -- Lamento = Lament / Dave Brubeck.

























---------------------------------------------------------------------
NEXT ACTIONS      Key: ? for help            + to see the next screen
                       L to see a Longer display  - to see the previous screen
                       F to Find other items   Q to Quit
NEXT ACTION?  _                                          LXPLM1
```

Figure 5.69

```
Your search: The explorer's hi#                      MEDIUM Display
     Finds: 1 record                                 Screen  1 of  1
-----------------------------------------------------------------------

          TITLE: The explorer's historical tourist map of Alaska, with maps
                 of Anchorage, Fairbanks & Juneau : with notes on the
                 Arctic, wildlife, hunting, fishing, camping, exploring &
                 prospecting, festivals & events / cartography by William
                 H. Stewart.
      PUBLISHED: Charleston, W.Va. : Economic Service Council, 1983.

         AUTHOR: Stewart, William Herman, 1932-

       SUBJECTS: Alaska--Maps, Tourist.
                 Alaska--Maps, Pictorial.




-----------------------------------------------------------------------
NEXT ACTIONS      Key: ? for help              + to see the next screen
                      L to see a Longer display  - to see the previous screen
                      F to Find other items    Q to Quit
NEXT ACTION?  _                                          LXPLM1
```

Figure 5.70

```
Your search: Suite en re dans #                      MEDIUM Display
     Finds: 1 record                                 Screen  1 of  1
-----------------------------------------------------------------------

          TITLE: Suite en re dans le style ancien : op. 24 ; Karadec : op. 34
                 ; Concert, op. 89 pour piano, flute, violoncello et
                 orchestre a cordes [sound recording] / Vincent d'Indy.
      PUBLISHED: France : Erato ; Paris : Distribution en France RCA, p1982.

         AUTHOR: Indy, Vincent d', 1851-1931.

       SUBJECTS: Suites (Flutes (2), trumpet with string orchestra)
                 Music, Incidental.
                 Concertos (Piano, flute, violoncello with string orchestra)




-----------------------------------------------------------------------
NEXT ACTIONS      Key: ? for help              + to see the next screen
                      L to see a Longer display  - to see the previous screen
                      F to Find other items    Q to Quit
NEXT ACTION?  _                                          LXPLM1
```

Figure 5.71

```
Your search: Time.                                MEDIUM Display
     Finds: 1 record                              Screen  1 of  1
--------------------------------------------------------------------------

        TITLE: Time.
    PUBLISHED: [Chicago, etc., Time Inc.]




--------------------------------------------------------------------------
NEXT ACTIONS      Key: ? for help          + to see the next screen
                       L to see a Longer display  - to see the previous screen
                       F to Find other items   Q to Quit
NEXT ACTION?   _                                            LXPLM1
```

Figure 5.72

```
Your search: Postdisaster surv#                   MEDIUM Display
     Finds: 1 record                              Screen  1 of  1
--------------------------------------------------------------------------

        TITLE: Postdisaster survival and rescue research : proceedings,
               Bureau of Mines Technology Transfer Seminar, Pittsburgh,
               Pa., November 16, 1982 / compiled by staff, Bureau of
               Mines.
    PUBLISHED: [Avondale, Md.] : U.S. Dept. of the Interior, Bureau of
               Mines, 1982.

       AUTHOR: Bureau of Mines Technology Transfer Seminars (1982 :
               Pittsburgh, Pa.)

     SUBJECTS: Mine accidents--Congresses.
               Mine rescue work--Congresses.


--------------------------------------------------------------------------
NEXT ACTIONS      Key: ? for help          + to see the next screen
                       L to see a Longer display  - to see the previous screen
                       F to Find other items   Q to Quit
NEXT ACTION?   _                                            LXPLM1
```

Figure 5.73

```
Your search: Citizen Kane                           MEDIUM Display
     Finds: 1 record                                Screen  1 of  1
-----------------------------------------------------------------------


        TITLE: Citizen Kane [videorecording] / an RKO Radio Picture ; a
               Mercury production ; Orson Welles, direction, production.
    PUBLISHED: New York, N.Y. : VidAmerica, c1982.

     SUBJECTS: Feature films.








-----------------------------------------------------------------------
NEXT ACTIONS      Key: ? for help          + to see the next screen
                       L to see a Longer display  - to see the previous screen
                       F to Find other items  Q to Quit

NEXT ACTION?   _                                            LXPLM1
```

Figure 5.74

```
Your search: Anderson, Sparky#                      MEDIUM Display
     Finds: 1 record                                Screen  1 of  1
-----------------------------------------------------------------------

        Anderson, Sparky, 1934-
          Bless you boys : diary of the Detroit Tigers' 1984 season
        / by Sparky Anderson, with Dan Ewald. -- Chicago :
        Contemporary Books, c1984.

           1. Detroit Tigers (Baseball team) I. Ewald, Dan.






-----------------------------------------------------------------------
NEXT ACTIONS      Key: ? for help          + to see the next screen
                       L to see a Longer display  - to see the previous screen
                       F to Find other items  Q to Quit

NEXT ACTION?   _                                            CXPLM2
```

Figure 5.75

```
Your search: Best American pla#                         MEDIUM Display
       Finds: 1 record                                  Screen  1 of  2
-----------------------------------------------------------------------

          Best American plays : sixth series, 1963-1967 / edited by
            John Gassner and Clive Barnes, with an introduction and
            prefaces to the plays by Clive Barnes. -- New York :
            Crown, c1971.

          Contents: Tiny Alice / E. Albee -- Blues for Mister
          Charlie / J. Baldwin -- The last analysis / S. Bellow --
          Hogan's goat / W. Alfred -- The fantasticks / T. Jones --
          The sign in Sidney Brustein's window / L. Hansberry -- The
          lion in winter / J. Goldman -- Hughie / E. O'Neill -- The
          toilet / L. Jones -- You know I can't hear you when the
          water is running / R. Anderson -- Benito Cereno / R. Lowell
          -- Fiddler on the roof / J. Stein -- Slow dance on the
          killing ground / W. Hanley -- In white America / M.B.

------------------------------------------------------------CONTINUED-------
NEXT ACTIONS      Key: ? for help            + to see the next screen
                       L to see a Longer display  - to see the previous screen
                       F to Find other items  Q to Quit
NEXT ACTION?   _                                             CXPLM2
```

Figure 5.76

```
Your search: Best American pla#                         MEDIUM Display
       Finds: 1 record                                  Screen  2 of  2
-----------------------------------------------------------------------

          Duberman -- The owl and the pussycat / B. Manhoff -- The odd
          couple / W. Simon -- The subject was roses / F.D. Gilroy.

           1. American drama--20th century. 2. American drama--
          Collected works. I. Gassner, John, 1903-1967. II. Barnes,
          Clive, 1927-






-----------------------------------------------------------------------
NEXT ACTIONS      Key: ? for help            + to see the next screen
                       L to see a Longer display  - to see the previous screen
                       F to Find other items  Q to Quit
NEXT ACTION?   _                                             CXPLM2
```

Figure 5.77

```
Your search: Brubeck, Dave#                          MEDIUM Display
      Finds: 1 record                                Screen  1 of  2
-----------------------------------------------------------------------

        Brubeck, Dave.
          Bossa nova U.S.A. / [as performed by] the Dave Brubeck
        Quartet ; piano solo transcriptions by Howard Brubeck. --
        San Francisco, Calif. : Derry Music Co. ;  New York, N.Y. :
        C. Hansen, distributor, c1963.

          Contents: Bossa nova U.S. A. / Dave Brubeck -- Vento
        fresco = Cool wind / Dave Brubeck -- Theme for June / Howard
        R. Brubeck -- Coracao sensivel = Tender heart / Teo Macero
        -- Irmao amigo = Brother friend / Dave Brubeck -- There'll
        be no tomorrow / Dave Brubeck -- Cantiga nov swing = Swing a
        new song / Dave Brubeck -- Lamento = Lament / Dave Brubeck.



-------------------------------------------------------CONTINUED-------
NEXT ACTIONS      Key: ? for help          + to see the next screen
                       L to see a Longer display  - to see the previous screen
                       F to Find other items   Q to Quit
NEXT ACTION?    _                                         CXPLM2
```

Figure 5.78

```
Your search: Brubeck, Dave#                          MEDIUM Display
      Finds: 1 record                                Screen  2 of  2
-----------------------------------------------------------------------

          1. Piano music (Jazz), Arranged. 2. Jazz quartets--Piano
        scores. I. Brubeck, Howard R. II. Brubeck, Howard R. Theme
        for June; arr. III. Macero, Teo, 1925- Coracao sensivel;
        arr. IV. Dave Brubeck Quartet.








-----------------------------------------------------------------------
NEXT ACTIONS      Key: ? for help          + to see the next screen
                       L to see a Longer display  - to see the previous screen
                       F to Find other items   Q to Quit
NEXT ACTION?    _                                         CXPLM2
```

Figure 5.79

```
Your search: Stewart, William #                      MEDIUM Display
       Finds: 1 record                               Screen  1 of  1
------------------------------------------------------------------------

        Stewart, William Herman, 1932-
          The explorer's historical tourist map of Alaska, with maps
        of Anchorage, Fairbanks & Juneau : with notes on the Arctic,
        wildlife, hunting, fishing, camping, exploring &
        prospecting, festivals & events / cartography by William H.
        Stewart. -- Charleston, W.Va. : Economic Service Council,
        1983.

          1. Alaska--Maps, Tourist. 2. Alaska--Maps, Pictorial. I.
        Economic Service Council.




------------------------------------------------------------------------
NEXT ACTIONS     Key: ? for help              + to see the next screen
                      L to see a Longer display  - to see the previous screen
                      F to Find other items    Q to Quit
NEXT ACTION?   _                                        CXPLM2
```

Figure 5.80

```
Your search: Indy, Vincent d'#                       MEDIUM Display
       Finds: 1 record                               Screen  1 of  2
------------------------------------------------------------------------

          Indy, Vincent d', 1851-1931.
            Suite en re dans le style ancien : op. 24 ; Karadec : op.
          34 ; Concert, op. 89 pour piano, flute, violoncello et
          orchestre a cordes [sound recording] / Vincent d'Indy. --
          France : Erato ; Paris : Distribution en France RCA, p1982.

            1. Suites (Flutes (2), trumpet with string orchestra) 2.
          Music, Incidental. 3. Concertos (Piano, flute, violoncello
          with string orchestra) I. Rampal, Jean Pierre. II. Pierlot,
          Philippe. III. Andre, Maurice. IV. Duchable, Francois. V.
          Lodeon, Frederic. VI. Paillard, Jean Francois. VII. Indy,
          Vincent d', 1851-1931. Suite dans le style ancien. 1982.
          VIII. Indy, Vincent d', 1851-1931. Karadec. 1982. IX. Indy,
          Vincent d', 1851-1931. Concerto, piano, flute, violoncello,

-----------------------------------------------------------CONTINUED-------
NEXT ACTIONS     Key: ? for help              + to see the next screen
                      L to see a Longer display  - to see the previous screen
                      F to Find other items    Q to Quit
NEXT ACTION?   _                                        CXPLM2
```

Figure 5.81

```
Your search: Indy, Vincent d'#                    MEDIUM Display
      Finds: 1 record                             Screen  2 of  2
-----------------------------------------------------------------
            orchestra, op. 89. 1982. X. Orchestre de chambre
            Jean-Francois Paillard.




            
            
            
            
            
            
            
-----------------------------------------------------------------
NEXT ACTIONS      Key: ? for help          + to see the next screen
                       L to see a Longer display  - to see the previous screen
                       F to Find other items  Q to Quit
NEXT ACTION?   _                                          CXPLM2
```

Figure 5.82

```
Your search: Time.                                MEDIUM Display
      Finds: 1 record                             Screen  1 of  1
-----------------------------------------------------------------
        Time. [Chicago, etc., Time Inc.]

         I. Hadden, Briton, ed. II. Luce, Henry Robinson, 1898- ed.




            
            
            
            
            
-----------------------------------------------------------------
NEXT ACTIONS      Key: ? for help          + to see the next screen
                       L to see a Longer display  - to see the previous screen
                       F to Find other items  Q to Quit
NEXT ACTION?   _                                          CXPLM2
```

Figure 5.83

```
Your search: Bureau of Mines T#                      MEDIUM Display
        Finds: 1 record                              Screen  1 of  1
------------------------------------------------------------------------


            Bureau of Mines Technology Transfer Seminars (1982 :
              Pittsburgh, Pa.)
             Postdisaster survival and rescue research : proceedings,
            Bureau of Mines Technology Transfer Seminar, Pittsburgh,
            Pa., November 16, 1982 / compiled by staff, Bureau of Mines.
            -- [Avondale, Md.] : U.S. Dept. of the Interior, Bureau of
            Mines, 1982.

             1. Mine accidents--Congresses. 2. Mine rescue work--
            Congresses. I. United States. Bureau of Mines.




------------------------------------------------------------------------
NEXT ACTIONS      Key: ? for help            + to see the next screen
                       L to see a Longer display  - to see the previous screen
                       F to Find other items  Q to Quit

NEXT ACTION?   _                                          CXPLM2
```

Figure 5.84

```
Your search: Citizen Kane                            MEDIUM Display
        Finds: 1 record                              Screen  1 of  1
------------------------------------------------------------------------

            Citizen Kane [videorecording] / an RKO Radio Picture ; a
              Mercury production ; Orson Welles, direction, production.
              -- New York, N.Y. : VidAmerica, c1982.

             1. Feature films. I. Welles, Orson, 1915- II. VidAmerica
            (Firm) III. RKO Radio Pictures, inc. IV. Mercury
            Productions.




------------------------------------------------------------------------
NEXT ACTIONS      Key: ? for help            + to see the next screen
                       L to see a Longer display  - to see the previous screen
                       F to Find other items  Q to Quit

NEXT ACTION?   _                                          CXPLM2
```

Figure 5.85

```
Your search: Bless you boys #                         MEDIUM Display
      Finds: 1 record                                 Screen  1 of  1
----------------------------------------------------------------------

        TITLE: Bless you boys : diary of the Detroit Tigers' 1984 season /
               by Sparky Anderson, with Dan Ewald.

      AUTHORS: Anderson, Sparky, 1934-
               Ewald, Dan.
    PUBLISHED: Chicago : Contemporary Books, c1984.
     SUBJECTS: Detroit Tigers (Baseball team)




----------------------------------------------------------------------
NEXT ACTIONS      Key: ? for help              + to see the next screen
                       L to see a Longer display  - to see the previous screen
                       F to Find other items    Q to Quit
NEXT ACTION?   _                                          LXPLM2
```

Figure 5.86

```
Your search: Best American pla#                       MEDIUM Display
      Finds: 1 record                                 Screen  1 of  2
----------------------------------------------------------------------

        TITLE: Best American plays : sixth series, 1963-1967 / edited by
               John Gassner and Clive Barnes, with an introduction and
               prefaces to the plays by Clive Barnes.

      AUTHORS: Gassner, John, 1903-1967.
               Barnes, Clive, 1927-
    PUBLISHED: New York : Crown, c1971.
     SUBJECTS: American drama--20th century.
               American drama--Collected works.

     CONTENTS: Tiny Alice / E. Albee -- Blues for Mister Charlie / J.
               Baldwin -- The last analysis / S. Bellow -- Hogan's goat /
               W. Alfred -- The fantasticks / T. Jones -- The sign in
               Sidney Brustein's window / L. Hansberry -- The lion in
------------------------------------------------------CONTINUED-------
NEXT ACTIONS      Key: ? for help              + to see the next screen
                       L to see a Longer display  - to see the previous screen
                       F to Find other items    Q to Quit
NEXT ACTION?   _                                          LXPLM2
```

Figure 5.87

```
Your search: Best American pla#                      MEDIUM Display
      Finds: 1 record                                Screen  2 of  2
------------------------------------------------------------------------

                   winter / J. Goldman -- Hughie / E. O'Neill -- The toilet /
                   L. Jones -- You know I can't hear you when the water is
                   running / R. Anderson -- Benito Cereno / R. Lowell --
                   Fiddler on the roof / J. Stein -- Slow dance on the
                   killing ground / W. Hanley -- In white America / M.B.
                   Duberman -- The owl and the pussycat / B. Manhoff -- The
                   odd couple / W. Simon -- The subject was roses / F.D.
                   Gilroy.




------------------------------------------------------------------------
NEXT ACTIONS      Key: ? for help              + to see the next screen
                       L to see a Longer display - to see the previous screen
                       F to Find other items    Q to Quit
NEXT ACTION?   _                                           LXPLM2
```

Figure 5.88

```
Your search: Bossa nova U.S.A#                       MEDIUM Display
      Finds: 1 record                                Screen  1 of  2
------------------------------------------------------------------------

         TITLE: Bossa nova U.S.A. / [as performed by] the Dave Brubeck
                Quartet ; piano solo transcriptions by Howard Brubeck.

       AUTHORS: Brubeck, Dave.
                Brubeck, Howard R.
                Brubeck, Howard R. Theme for June; arr.
                Macero, Teo, 1925- Coracao sensivel; arr.
                Dave Brubeck Quartet.
     PUBLISHED: San Francisco, Calif. : Derry Music Co. ;  New York, N.Y. :
                C. Hansen, distributor, c1963.
      SUBJECTS: Piano music (Jazz), Arranged.
                Jazz quartets--Piano scores.



-----------------------------------------------------------CONTINUED-------
NEXT ACTIONS      Key: ? for help              + to see the next screen
                       L to see a Longer display - to see the previous screen
                       F to Find other items    Q to Quit
NEXT ACTION?   _                                           LXPLM2
```

Figure 5.89

```
Your search: Bossa nova U.S.A#                        MEDIUM Display
         Finds: 1 record                               Screen  2 of  2
-------------------------------------------------------------------------

      CONTENTS: Bossa nova U.S. A. / Dave Brubeck -- Vento fresco = Cool
                wind / Dave Brubeck -- Theme for June / Howard R. Brubeck
                -- Coracao sensivel = Tender heart / Teo Macero -- Irmao
                amigo = Brother friend / Dave Brubeck -- There'll be no
                tomorrow / Dave Brubeck -- Cantiga nov swing = Swing a new
                song / Dave Brubeck -- Lamento = Lament / Dave Brubeck.





    ----------------------------------------------------------------------
NEXT ACTIONS      Key: ? for help              + to see the next screen
                       L to see a Longer display  - to see the previous screen
                       F to Find other items    Q to Quit
NEXT ACTION?   _                                            LXPLM2
```

Figure 5.90

```
Your search: The explorer's hi#                       MEDIUM Display
         Finds: 1 record                               Screen  1 of  1
-------------------------------------------------------------------------

         TITLE: The explorer's historical tourist map of Alaska, with maps
                of Anchorage, Fairbanks & Juneau : with notes on the
                Arctic, wildlife, hunting, fishing, camping, exploring &
                prospecting, festivals & events / cartography by William
                H. Stewart.

       AUTHORS: Stewart, William Herman, 1932-
                Economic Service Council.
     PUBLISHED: Charleston, W.Va. : Economic Service Council, 1983.
      SUBJECTS: Alaska--Maps, Tourist.
                Alaska--Maps, Pictorial.



    ----------------------------------------------------------------------
NEXT ACTIONS      Key: ? for help              + to see the next screen
                       L to see a Longer display  - to see the previous screen
                       F to Find other items    Q to Quit
NEXT ACTION?   _                                            LXPLM2
```

Figure 5.91

```
Your search: Suite en re dans #                        MEDIUM Display
      Finds: 1 record                                  Screen  1 of  2
-----------------------------------------------------------------------

        TITLE: Suite en re dans le style ancien : op. 24 ; Karadec : op. 34
               ; Concert, op. 89 pour piano, flute, violoncello et
               orchestre a cordes [sound recording] / Vincent d'Indy.

      AUTHORS: Indy, Vincent d', 1851-1931.
               Rampal, Jean Pierre.
               Pierlot, Philippe.
               Andre, Maurice.
               Duchable, Francois.
               Lodeon, Frederic.
               Paillard, Jean Francois.
               Indy, Vincent d', 1851-1931. Suite dans le style ancien.
               1982.
               Indy, Vincent d', 1851-1931. Karadec. 1982.

----------------------------------------------------------CONTINUED-------
NEXT ACTIONS    Key: ? for help            + to see the next screen
                     L to see a Longer display  - to see the previous screen
                     F to Find other items      Q to Quit
NEXT ACTION?  _                                           LXPLM2
```

Figure 5.92

```
Your search: Suite en re dans #                        MEDIUM Display
      Finds: 1 record                                  Screen  2 of  2
-----------------------------------------------------------------------

               Indy, Vincent d', 1851-1931. Concerto, piano, flute,
                  violoncello, orchestra, op. 89. 1982.
               Orchestre de chambre Jean-Francois Paillard.
    PUBLISHED: France : Erato ; Paris : Distribution en France RCA, p1982.
     SUBJECTS: Suites (Flutes (2), trumpet with string orchestra)
               Music, Incidental.
               Concertos (Piano, flute, violoncello with string orchestra)




-----------------------------------------------------------------------
NEXT ACTIONS    Key: ? for help            + to see the next screen
                     L to see a Longer display  - to see the previous screen
                     F to Find other items      Q to Quit
NEXT ACTION?  _                                           LXPLM2
```

Figure 5.93

```
Your search: Time.                              MEDIUM Display
     Finds: 1 record                            Screen  1 of  1
------------------------------------------------------------------

        TITLE: Time.

      AUTHORS: Hadden, Briton, ed.
               Luce, Henry Robinson, 1898- ed.
    PUBLISHED: [Chicago, etc., Time Inc.]




------------------------------------------------------------------
NEXT ACTIONS      Key: ? for help           + to see the next screen
                       L to see a Longer display  - to see the previous screen
                       F to Find other items    Q to Quit
NEXT ACTION?  _                                       LXPLM2
```

Figure 5.94

```
Your search: Postdisaster surv#                 MEDIUM Display
     Finds: 1 record                            Screen  1 of  1
------------------------------------------------------------------

        TITLE: Postdisaster survival and rescue research : proceedings,
               Bureau of Mines Technology Transfer Seminar, Pittsburgh,
               Pa., November 16, 1982 / compiled by staff, Bureau of
               Mines.

      AUTHORS: Bureau of Mines Technology Transfer Seminars (1982 :
               Pittsburgh, Pa.)
               United States. Bureau of Mines.
    PUBLISHED: [Avondale, Md.] : U.S. Dept. of the Interior, Bureau of
               Mines, 1982.
     SUBJECTS: Mine accidents--Congresses.
               Mine rescue work--Congresses.


------------------------------------------------------------------
NEXT ACTIONS      Key: ? for help           + to see the next screen
                       L to see a Longer display  - to see the previous screen
                       F to Find other items    Q to Quit
NEXT ACTION?  _                                       LXPLM2
```

Figure 5.95

```
Your search: Citizen Kane                              MEDIUM Display
      Finds: 1 record                                  Screen  1 of  1
----------------------------------------------------------------------

        TITLE: Citizen Kane [videorecording] / an RKO Radio Picture ; a
               Mercury production ; Orson Welles, direction, production.

      AUTHORS: Welles, Orson, 1915-
               VidAmerica (Firm)
               RKO Radio Pictures, inc.
               Mercury Productions.
    PUBLISHED: New York, N.Y. : VidAmerica, c1982.
     SUBJECTS: Feature films.




----------------------------------------------------------------------

NEXT ACTIONS      Key: ? for help          + to see the next screen
                       L to see a Longer display  - to see the previous screen
                       F to Find other items  Q to Quit
NEXT ACTION?  _                                          LXPLM2
```

6

Brief and Long Displays

Medium-level displays will meet the needs of most patrons in most libraries. For some patrons, however, two more levels are necessary, depending on the design of the catalog. This chapter considers a few possible brief and long displays, identified in Table 6.1.

Table 6.1: Displays Discussed in Chapter 6

Display	Name
CBCAP	Citation-style brief display with capitalized short title
CBRF1	Cardlike brief display
CLCIT1	Cardlike long display with citation-style description
CLON1	Cardlike long display
LBRF1	Labeled brief display
LLON1	Labeled long display
LMGAT	Labeled medium display, gutter aligned, author/title split

BRIEF DISPLAYS

A brief display does not provide complete information on an item's authors, access points or subjects. We see such displays as useful for headings on extensive holdings displays and as possible displays for multiple-item screens (though most multiple-item displays are much briefer).

Our minimum definition for a brief entry is that it should provide sufficient information to identify an item. After considering the role of nonprint materials in modern libraries, we are convinced that even a brief display should include physical description. Fortunately, as the tables in Appendix A show, the average physical description fits on a single labeled line, or on one-half a line, in a citation-style or cardlike display.

We feel that both the name of the publisher and the publication date are needed to identify an item; place of publication is less important. After much consideration, we concluded that the complete title statement should be included in the brief display, particularly since this format does not include added entries.

Table 6.2 shows the MARC fields and subfields in the first two brief displays, CBRF1 and LBRF1. The third display, CBCAP, includes a slight modification—the edition and place of publication also appear, making a relatively complete citation form.

Table 6.2: Fields Included in Brief Displays

Fields	Description	Subfields
100–130	Main entry	all but u
245	Title statement	all
260,262	Publisher, date of publication	b,c
261	Imprint for films, pre-AACR1 Rev. (exc. location)	a,b,d
300–301	Physical description	all
305,308	Physical description	all

CBRF1—Cardlike Brief

CBRF1 is a brief cardlike display, illustrated in Figures 6.1 through 6.8. This display leaves room for minimal holdings on 99.7% of all items tested, and room for holdings on 99.98% of all public library items. More significant for brief displays is how many lines of holdings will show on the first screen. The statistics for CBRF1 are as follows:

- 99% have room for at least five lines
- 97% have room for at least six lines
- 94% have room for at least seven lines
- 86% have room for at least eight lines

In other words, the entry itself requires six lines or less in 86% of items tested. For public libraries, the display is even more effective: 94% of the items tested have room for at least eight lines of holdings, and 76% leave room for nine or more lines.

LBRF1—Labeled Brief

Do very brief displays require labels? Display LBRF1 presents a labeled equivalent to CBRF1, without any spacing lines. This display places title first, with the author (labeled NAME) directly below it. Figures 6.9 through 6.16 show the quality of the display. While almost everything still fits on one screen with room for holdings—99.5% of all items tested, 99.96% of public library items—the space available for holdings is not as good as for CBRF1. CBRF1 yields the following results:

- 98% have room for at least five lines
- 96% have room for at least six lines
- 91% have room for at least seven lines
- 78% have room for at least eight lines

That's still good, but LBRF1 has less room available for multiple locations and copies. Tested against public library cataloging, 89% have room for at least eight lines of holdings and 53% have room for nine or more lines.

CBCAP—Citation, Capitalized Short Title

Display CBCAP provides a third alternative, with somewhat more information included. It restores the edition and place of publication, as illustrated in Figures 6.17 through 6.24. By including all information within a single paragraph, this display allows even more room for holdings. Even though CBCAP presents more information than CBRF1 and LBRF1, the overall figures are as good as for CBRF1: 99.7% of all items, and 99.97% of public library items, left room for minimal holdings. Space available for holdings is even better, as evidenced by the following statistics:

- 99% have room for at least five lines
- 98% have room for at least six lines
- 96% have room for at least seven lines
- 91% have room for at least eight lines
- 79% have room for at least nine lines

A majority of items—50.3%—require 4 lines or less to display, leaving room for 10 lines of holdings. That figure rises to 67% for public library items, with 90% having room for nine lines or more.

How does CBCAP compare with LBRF1 AND CBRF1 for clarity and appearance? That's a matter of taste and judgment, but what's clear is that CBCAP provides a more complete brief entry in very little space.

LONG DISPLAYS

Brief displays provide minimal identification. Medium displays should place an item in context and identify all alternative access routes. For those patrons who want to know as much about an item as possible before going to look at it, a longer display is necessary. Therefore, the long display should contain as much information as seems to be of any possible use to library patrons.

Some online catalogs use a tagged MARC display as the only long display. We agree that a tagged display should be available for that tiny minority of patrons who can make use of it, if only because most online systems must have such a display for staff use. We do not feel that a tagged display provides a reasonable substitute for a longer display arranged more suitably for patron use.

Lennie Stovel and Kathleen Bales, the two primary library analysts for this project, developed a two-level list of elements for long displays. Table 6.3 shows the MARC fields included in the first of those levels, illustrated in the three displays that follow. This list adds uniform title, additional serials volume and publication information, series tracings, publication patterns, linking entries and notes to the set of fields included in the medium level. Excluded from the list are local entries, control numbers, standard numbers and standard number subfields of subject entries and linking entries.

Table 6.3: Fields in Long Displays

```
100-130   Main entry
240       Uniform title
245       Title statement
250-254   Edition statement, Musical presentation
362       Dates of publication / volumes
255       Mathematical data area
260-262   Publication, distribution, etc. (imprint)
300-305   Physical description
340       Medium
400-490   Series statements
800-830   Series added entries
315       Frequency
321       Former frequency
310       Current frequency
351       File structure / sort sequence
500-589   Notes
760-787   Linking entries
600-657   Subject entries
700-730   Added entries
752       Place of Publication or Production (Access point)
```

The second level of inclusion for long displays involves a number of local options: local added entries and notes, standard numbers, and standard number subfields. Except for standard numbers, most fields that would appear in these even longer displays are defined within RLIN MARC rather than USMARC; that list does not appear here. Both levels omit a number of other fields, such as coded elements, control numbers, certain alternative title fields and some other fields of no apparent use to any patron.

The list in Table 6.3 can be considered a sound basis for a complete display. A library may add to that list in order to meet local needs but should be cautious about deleting items from the list. We assume that catalogers do not add fields to bibliographic records without some reason, and we would be reluctant to second-guess them by assuming that notes and entries do not serve any purpose.

CLON1—Cardlike Long

Display CLON1 shows the first level of long elements in a traditional narrow cardlike display. The arrangement is similar to CMSX (Figures 2.9–2.11, 3.9–3.14 and 7.1–7.16), with notes added before tracings, as they would be on catalog cards.

CLON1, illustrated in Figures 6.25 through 6.41, does differ from traditional catalog cards in a few respects. "Series traced differently" do not appear, and all series appear together, rather than including some within the tracings paragraph. Additional examples using CLON1 appear in Figures 7.37 through 7.60.

One of the most startling changes in a long display appears in the record for *Time*. That record, so brief in all medium displays, suddenly grows to three screens, thanks to a wealth of notes on indexing. Many serials have a similar wealth of information in notes and linking entries.

CLON1 provides more information and takes much more space than other cardlike displays, which is to be expected. While 78% of items tested using CLON1 will fit on a single screen without holdings, only 34% have room for minimal holdings. An important question for long displays is how frequently items require three or more screens. For a long format, CLON1 is reasonably compact: 99.4% of all items can be displayed using one or two screens. Even for this most compact long format, some items seem to go on forever. Even though archival records were not included, five items could not be completely displayed within the program's 10-screen limit.

Should notes appear before subjects and added entries? CLON1 is deliberately traditional, including the way it is ordered. We would suggest that the traditional ordering is not a good one for online catalogs, as it de-emphasizes joint authors and subjects in favor of less important information. On the other hand, notes for sound recordings and films may be more important than some subjects and added entries. Here, as elsewhere, professional judgment and the character of a library's collection should enter into the decision.

CLCIT1—Cardlike Long with Citation-Style Description

Display CLCIT1 begins with a citation-like display, adds notes and finishes by listing each entry and subject on a separate line. Figures 6.42 through 6.57 illustrate this display. As with CLON1, above, a reasonable alternative would place notes at the end of the display.

The statistical results of CLCIT1 may be surprising. A majority of items tested (54%) can be displayed on a single screen with room for minimal holdings, and 84% of the items tested will fit on one screen without holdings. For public library items, the comparable figures are 70% and 93%.

LLON1—Labeled Long

Display LLON1 is similar to LMGAT, the gutter-aligned display with names and works separated, with notes added at the end. LLON1 also adds field 362 (dates of publication/volumes) and field 255 (mathematical data area) to the EDITION group. Field 130 moves to WORKS, where it seems to belong, and other uniform title fields (240 and 730) move there also. The only other change from LMGAT is the set of fields included as the NOTES group. Figures 6.58 through 6.75 illustrate LLON1, as do Figures 7.61 through 7.88. (For comparison, display LMGAT is illustrated in Figures 2.21–2.23, 4.34–4.41 and 7.17–7.36.)

Predictably, display LLON1 takes more space than the others. Only 22% of items tested could fit on one screen with minimal holdings, and only 63% fit on a single screen without holdings. Most items (99%) can still be displayed on 1 or 2 screens; out of a 423,000-item sample, the number that will not fit on 10 screens rises to 7.

SUMMARY

Tables 6.4, 6.5 and 6.6 show the summary statistics for displays illustrated in this chapter. A brief display (either cardlike or labeled) that is sufficient to identify an item can include the full title statement and still have room for six or more lines of holdings in 78% or more of items tested, 88% for public libraries.

Table 6.4: Screen Summary Statistics

Display	Name	One Screen w/Holdings	One Screen: bib. only	Two Screens bib. only
CBRF1	Cardlike Brief	99.70%	99.97%	0.03%
	-- public libraries	99.98%	100.00%	--
LBRF1	Labeled Brief	99.55%	99.96%	0.04%
	-- public libraries	99.96%	100.00%	--
CBCAP	Citation, capitalized title	99.70%	99.96%	0.04%
	-- public libraries	99.97%	100.00%	--
CLON1	Cardlike Long	33.81%	77.89%	21.53%
	-- public libraries	51.81%	90.82%	9.11%
CLCIT1	Citation Long	54.33%	84.41%	15.06%
	-- public libraries	69.61%	93.28%	6.65%
LLON1	Labeled Long	21.54%	63.61%	35.33%
	-- public libraries	34.74%	77.55%	22.33%

Table 6.5: Density Summary

Display	Name	Local Density	Global Density	L. Density to 30%
CBRF1	Cardlike Brief	14.85%	29.19%	96.97%
	-- public libraries	12.67%	27.89%	99.32%
LBRF1	Labeled Brief	17.54%	30.79%	95.46%
	-- public libraries	15.39%	29.54%	98.78%
CBCAP	Citation, capitalized title	16.18%	30.00%	96.21%
	-- public libraries	14.02%	28.74%	99.04%
CLON1	Cardlike Long	27.21%	36.30%	65.93%
	-- public libraries	23.77%	34.26%	76.01%
CLCIT1	Citation Long	27.69%	36.87%	63.85%
	-- public libraries	23.31%	34.32%	77.36%
LLON1	Labeled Long	27.05%	36.23%	65.56%
	-- public libraries	24.17%	34.56%	76.72%

Table 6.6: Room for Holdings (Brief Displays Only)

Display	Name	Holdings Room on First Screen 4+ Lines	6+ Lines	8+ Lines
CBRF1	Cardlike Brief	99.38%	97.32%	86.12%
	-- public libraries	99.95%	99.44%	94.32%
LBRF1	Labeled Brief	99.08%	96.05%	77.99%
	-- public libraries	99.88%	99.02%	88.48%
CBCAP	Citation, capitalized title	99.43%	97.83%	90.79%
	-- public libraries	99.95%	99.61%	96.83%

Although long displays will require multiple screens, they must be made available for those patrons who need them. A citation-style long display will fit on a single screen for almost 70% of public library records, with room for minimal holdings, but it may not be very legible. A more legible display may require two screens (even without holdings) for one out of four public library items and more than one out of three academic library items. Very few records for monographs will ever require more than two screens, but some records, particularly those for sound recordings, scores and serials, may require quite a few.

Libraries should consider designing long displays that constitute extensions of medium displays. Such displays will keep patrons well oriented, and make the process of acquiring more information a natural one. Two of the formats in Chapter 8 specifically raise the possibility of designing displays in this way, as does display LLON1 in this chapter.

Figure 6.1

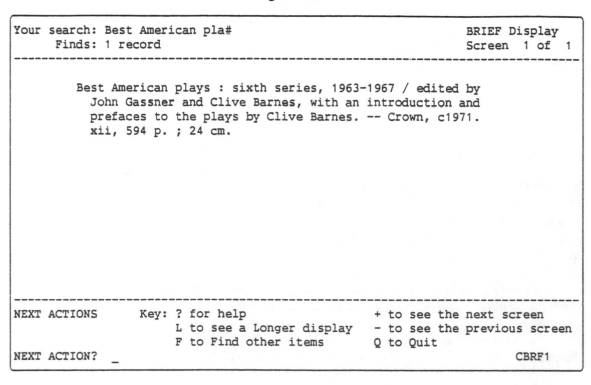

```
Your search: Anderson, Sparky#                       BRIEF Display
      Finds: 1 record                                 Screen  1 of  1
-----------------------------------------------------------------------

        Anderson, Sparky, 1934-
          Bless you boys : diary of the Detroit Tigers' 1984 season
        / by Sparky Anderson, with Dan Ewald. -- Contemporary Books,
        c1984.
          231 p. : ill. ; 23 cm.




        -------------------------------------------------------------
NEXT ACTIONS       Key: ? for help            + to see the next screen
                        L to see a Longer display  - to see the previous screen
                        F to Find other items  Q to Quit
NEXT ACTION?   _                                           CBRF1
```

Figure 6.2

```
Your search: Best American pla#                       BRIEF Display
      Finds: 1 record                                 Screen  1 of  1
-----------------------------------------------------------------------

        Best American plays : sixth series, 1963-1967 / edited by
          John Gassner and Clive Barnes, with an introduction and
          prefaces to the plays by Clive Barnes. -- Crown, c1971.
          xii, 594 p. ; 24 cm.




        -------------------------------------------------------------
NEXT ACTIONS       Key: ? for help            + to see the next screen
                        L to see a Longer display  - to see the previous screen
                        F to Find other items  Q to Quit
NEXT ACTION?   _                                           CBRF1
```

Figure 6.3

```
Your search: Brubeck, Dave#                          BRIEF Display
      Finds: 1 record                                Screen  1 of  1
---------------------------------------------------------------------

        Brubeck, Dave.
          Bossa nova U.S.A. / [as performed by] the Dave Brubeck
        Quartet ; piano solo transcriptions by Howard Brubeck. --
        Derry Music Co. ; C. Hansen, distributor, c1963.
          49 p. of music ; 28 cm.




---------------------------------------------------------------------
NEXT ACTIONS      Key: ? for help              + to see the next screen
                       L to see a Longer display  - to see the previous screen
                       F to Find other items      Q to Quit
NEXT ACTION?  _                                            CBRF1
```

Figure 6.4

```
Your search: Stewart, William #                      BRIEF Display
      Finds: 1 record                                Screen  1 of  1
---------------------------------------------------------------------

        Stewart, William Herman, 1932-
          The explorer's historical tourist map of Alaska, with maps
        of Anchorage, Fairbanks & Juneau : with notes on the Arctic,
        wildlife, hunting, fishing, camping, exploring &
        prospecting, festivals & events / cartography by William H.
        Stewart. -- Economic Service Council, 1983.
          1 map : col. ; 65 x 71 cm., folded to 23 x 11 cm.




---------------------------------------------------------------------
NEXT ACTIONS      Key: ? for help              + to see the next screen
                       L to see a Longer display  - to see the previous screen
                       F to Find other items      Q to Quit
NEXT ACTION?  _                                            CBRF1
```

Figure 6.5

```
Your search: Indy, Vincent d'#                      BRIEF Display
     Finds: 1 record                                Screen  1 of  1
------------------------------------------------------------------------

        Indy, Vincent d', 1851-1931.
          Suite en re dans le style ancien : op. 24 ; Karadec : op.
        34 ; Concert, op. 89 pour piano, flute, violoncello et
        orchestre a cordes [sound recording] / Vincent d'Indy. --
        Erato ; Distribution en France RCA, p1982.
          1 sound disc : 33 1/3 rpm, stereo. ; 12 in.




------------------------------------------------------------------------
NEXT ACTIONS      Key: ? for help            + to see the next screen
                       L to see a Longer display  - to see the previous screen
                       F to Find other items  Q to Quit
NEXT ACTION?   _                                         CBRF1
```

Figure 6.6

```
Your search: Time.                                  BRIEF Display
     Finds: 1 record                                Screen  1 of  1
------------------------------------------------------------------------

        Time. Time Inc.]
          v. ill. (incl. ports.) 28 cm.







------------------------------------------------------------------------
NEXT ACTIONS      Key: ? for help            + to see the next screen
                       L to see a Longer display  - to see the previous screen
                       F to Find other items  Q to Quit
NEXT ACTION?   _                                         CBRF1
```

Figure 6.7

```
Your search: Bureau of Mines T#                    BRIEF Display
        Finds: 1 record                            Screen  1 of  1
-------------------------------------------------------------------

          Bureau of Mines Technology Transfer Seminars (1982 :
             Pittsburgh, Pa.)
             Postdisaster survival and rescue research : proceedings,
          Bureau of Mines Technology Transfer Seminar, Pittsburgh,
          Pa., November 16, 1982 / compiled by staff, Bureau of Mines.
          -- U.S. Dept. of the Interior, Bureau of Mines, 1982.
             iii, 91 p. : ill. ; 28 cm.




-------------------------------------------------------------------
NEXT ACTIONS      Key: ? for help            + to see the next screen
                       L to see a Longer display  - to see the previous screen
                       F to Find other items    Q to Quit
NEXT ACTION?   _                                        CBRF1
```

Figure 6.8

```
Your search: Citizen Kane                          BRIEF Display
        Finds: 1 record                            Screen  1 of  1
-------------------------------------------------------------------

          Citizen Kane [videorecording] / an RKO Radio Picture ; a
             Mercury production ; Orson Welles, direction, production.
             -- VidAmerica, c1982.
             1 videocassette (119 min.) : sd., b&w ; 1/2 in.







-------------------------------------------------------------------
NEXT ACTIONS      Key: ? for help            + to see the next screen
                       L to see a Longer display  - to see the previous screen
                       F to Find other items    Q to Quit
NEXT ACTION?   _                                        CBRF1
```

Figure 6.9

```
Your search: Bless you boys #                        BRIEF Display
      Finds: 1 record                                Screen  1 of  1
----------------------------------------------------------------------

         TITLE: Bless you boys : diary of the Detroit Tigers' 1984 season /
                by Sparky Anderson, with Dan Ewald.
          NAME: Anderson, Sparky, 1934-
     PUBLISHED: Contemporary Books, c1984.
      MATERIAL: 231 p. : ill. ; 23 cm.




----------------------------------------------------------------------
NEXT ACTIONS      Key: ? for help            + to see the next screen
                       L to see a Longer display  - to see the previous screen
                       F to Find other items  Q to Quit
NEXT ACTION?  _                                            LBRF1
```

Figure 6.10

```
Your search: Best American pla#                      BRIEF Display
      Finds: 1 record                                Screen  1 of  1
----------------------------------------------------------------------

         TITLE: Best American plays : sixth series, 1963-1967 / edited by
                John Gassner and Clive Barnes, with an introduction and
                prefaces to the plays by Clive Barnes.
     PUBLISHED: Crown, c1971.
      MATERIAL: xii, 594 p. ; 24 cm.




----------------------------------------------------------------------
NEXT ACTIONS      Key: ? for help            + to see the next screen
                       L to see a Longer display  - to see the previous screen
                       F to Find other items  Q to Quit
NEXT ACTION?  _                                            LBRF1
```

Figure 6.11

```
Your search: Bossa nova U.S.A#                     BRIEF Display
      Finds: 1 record                              Screen  1 of  1
-------------------------------------------------------------------

        TITLE: Bossa nova U.S.A. / [as performed by] the Dave Brubeck
               Quartet ; piano solo transcriptions by Howard Brubeck.
         NAME: Brubeck, Dave.
    PUBLISHED: Derry Music Co. ; C. Hansen, distributor, c1963.
     MATERIAL: 49 p. of music ; 28 cm.




-------------------------------------------------------------------
NEXT ACTIONS      Key: ? for help             + to see the next screen
                       L to see a Longer display  - to see the previous screen
                       F to Find other items   Q to Quit
NEXT ACTION?  _                                            LBRF1
```

Figure 6.12

```
Your search: The explorer's hi#                    BRIEF Display
      Finds: 1 record                              Screen  1 of  1
-------------------------------------------------------------------

        TITLE: The explorer's historical tourist map of Alaska, with maps
               of Anchorage, Fairbanks & Juneau : with notes on the
               Arctic, wildlife, hunting, fishing, camping, exploring &
               prospecting, festivals & events / cartography by William
               H. Stewart.
         NAME: Stewart, William Herman, 1932-
    PUBLISHED: Economic Service Council, 1983.
     MATERIAL: 1 map : col. ; 65 x 71 cm., folded to 23 x 11 cm.




-------------------------------------------------------------------
NEXT ACTIONS      Key: ? for help             + to see the next screen
                       L to see a Longer display  - to see the previous screen
                       F to Find other items   Q to Quit
NEXT ACTION?  _                                            LBRF1
```

Figure 6.13

```
Your search: Suite en re dans #                      BRIEF Display
      Finds: 1 record                                Screen  1 of  1
------------------------------------------------------------------------

          TITLE: Suite en re dans le style ancien : op. 24 ; Karadec : op. 34
                 ; Concert, op. 89 pour piano, flute, violoncello et
                 orchestre a cordes [sound recording] / Vincent d'Indy.
           NAME: Indy, Vincent d', 1851-1931.
      PUBLISHED: Erato ; Distribution en France RCA, p1982.
       MATERIAL: 1 sound disc : 33 1/3 rpm, stereo. ; 12 in.




------------------------------------------------------------------------
NEXT ACTIONS      Key: ? for help              + to see the next screen
                       L to see a Longer display - to see the previous screen
                       F to Find other items     Q to Quit
NEXT ACTION?   _                                              LBRF1
```

Figure 6.14

```
Your search: Time.                                   BRIEF Display
       Finds: 1 record                               Screen  1 of  1
------------------------------------------------------------------------

         TITLE: Time.
     PUBLISHED: Time Inc.]
      MATERIAL: v. ill. (incl. ports.) 28 cm.






------------------------------------------------------------------------
NEXT ACTIONS      Key: ? for help              + to see the next screen
                       L to see a Longer display - to see the previous screen
                       F to Find other items     Q to Quit
NEXT ACTION?   _                                              LBRF1
```

Figure 6.15

```
Your search: Postdisaster surv#                      BRIEF Display
    Finds: 1 record                                  Screen  1 of  1
--------------------------------------------------------------------

        TITLE: Postdisaster survival and rescue research : proceedings,
               Bureau of Mines Technology Transfer Seminar, Pittsburgh,
               Pa., November 16, 1982 / compiled by staff, Bureau of
               Mines.
         NAME: Bureau of Mines Technology Transfer Seminars (1982 :
               Pittsburgh, Pa.)
    PUBLISHED: U.S. Dept. of the Interior, Bureau of Mines, 1982.
     MATERIAL: iii, 91 p. : ill. ; 28 cm.




                  --------------------------------------------------
NEXT ACTIONS      Key: ? for help              + to see the next screen
                       L to see a Longer display  - to see the previous screen
                       F to Find other items    Q to Quit
NEXT ACTION?   _                                            LBRF1
```

Figure 6.16

```
Your search: Citizen Kane                            BRIEF Display
    Finds: 1 record                                  Screen  1 of  1
--------------------------------------------------------------------

        TITLE: Citizen Kane [videorecording] / an RKO Radio Picture ; a
               Mercury production ; Orson Welles, direction, production.
    PUBLISHED: VidAmerica, c1982.
     MATERIAL: 1 videocassette (119 min.) : sd., b&w ; 1/2 in.






                  --------------------------------------------------
NEXT ACTIONS      Key: ? for help              + to see the next screen
                       L to see a Longer display  - to see the previous screen
                       F to Find other items    Q to Quit
NEXT ACTION?   _                                            LBRF1
```

Figure 6.17

```
Your search: Anderson, Sparky#                        BRIEF Display
     Finds: 1 record·                                 Screen  1 of  1
------------------------------------------------------------------------

        Anderson, Sparky, 1934- BLESS YOU BOYS : diary of the
            Detroit Tigers' 1984 season / by Sparky Anderson, with
            Dan Ewald. Chicago : Contemporary Books, c1984. 231 p. :
            ill. ; 23 cm.




------------------------------------------------------------------------
NEXT ACTIONS      Key: ? for help            + to see the next screen
                       L to see a Longer display  - to see the previous screen
                       F to Find other items    Q to Quit
NEXT ACTION?   _                                           CBCAP
```

Figure 6.18

```
Your search: BEST AMERICAN PLA#                       BRIEF Display
     Finds: 1 record                                  Screen  1 of  1
------------------------------------------------------------------------

        BEST AMERICAN PLAYS : sixth series, 1963-1967 / edited by
            John Gassner and Clive Barnes, with an introduction and
            prefaces to the plays by Clive Barnes. New York : Crown,
            c1971. xii, 594 p. ; 24 cm.




------------------------------------------------------------------------
NEXT ACTIONS      Key: ? for help            + to see the next screen
                       L to see a Longer display  - to see the previous screen
                       F to Find other items    Q to Quit
NEXT ACTION?   _                                           CBCAP
```

Figure 6.19

```
Your search: Brubeck, Dave. BO#                    BRIEF Display
     Finds: 1 record                               Screen  1 of  1
----------------------------------------------------------------------

        Brubeck, Dave. BOSSA NOVA U.S.A. / [as performed by] the
            Dave Brubeck Quartet ; piano solo transcriptions by
            Howard Brubeck. San Francisco, Calif. : Derry Music Co.
            ; New York, N.Y. : C. Hansen, distributor, c1963. 49 p.
            of music ; 28 cm.






----------------------------------------------------------------------

NEXT ACTIONS        Key: ? for help             + to see the next screen
                         L to see a Longer display  - to see the previous screen
                         F to Find other items    Q to Quit
NEXT ACTION?   _                                    CBCAP
```

Figure 6.20

```
Your search: Stewart, William #                    BRIEF Display
     Finds: 1 record                               Screen  1 of  1
----------------------------------------------------------------------

        Stewart, William Herman, 1932- THE EXPLORER'S HISTORICAL
            TOURIST MAP OF ALASKA, WITH MAPS OF ANCHORAGE, FAIRBANKS
            & JUNEAU : with notes on the Arctic, wildlife, hunting,
            fishing, camping, exploring & prospecting, festivals &
            events / cartography by William H. Stewart. Charleston,
            W.Va. : Economic Service Council, 1983. 1 map : col. ;
            65 x 71 cm., folded to 23 x 11 cm.




----------------------------------------------------------------------

NEXT ACTIONS        Key: ? for help             + to see the next screen
                         L to see a Longer display  - to see the previous screen
                         F to Find other items    Q to Quit
NEXT ACTION?   _                                    CBCAP
```

Figure 6.21

```
Your search: Indy, Vincent d'#                          BRIEF Display
     Finds: 1 record                                    Screen  1 of  1
------------------------------------------------------------------------

         Indy, Vincent d', 1851-1931. SUITE EN RE DANS LE STYLE
             ANCIEN : op. 24 ; Karadec : op. 34 ; Concert, op. 89
             pour piano, flute, violoncello et orchestre a cordes
             [sound recording] / Vincent d'Indy. France : Erato ;
             Paris : Distribution en France RCA, p1982. 1 sound disc
             : 33 1/3 rpm, stereo. ; 12 in.









------------------------------------------------------------------------
NEXT ACTIONS      Key: ? for help             + to see the next screen
                       L to see a Longer display  - to see the previous screen
                       F to Find other items   Q to Quit
NEXT ACTION?   _                                            CBCAP
```

Figure 6.22

```
Your search: TIME.                                      BRIEF Display
     Finds: 1 record                                    Screen  1 of  1
------------------------------------------------------------------------

          TIME. [Chicago, etc., Time Inc.] v. ill. (incl. ports.) 28
              cm.










------------------------------------------------------------------------
NEXT ACTIONS      Key: ? for help             + to see the next screen
                       L to see a Longer display  - to see the previous screen
                       F to Find other items   Q to Quit
NEXT ACTION?   _                                            CBCAP
```

Figure 6.23

```
Your search: Bureau of Mines T#                    BRIEF Display
      Finds: 1 record                              Screen  1 of  1
-----------------------------------------------------------------

        Bureau of Mines Technology Transfer Seminars (1982 :
            Pittsburgh, Pa.) POSTDISASTER SURVIVAL AND RESCUE
            RESEARCH : proceedings, Bureau of Mines Technology
            Transfer Seminar, Pittsburgh, Pa., November 16, 1982 /
            compiled by staff, Bureau of Mines. [Avondale, Md.] :
            U.S. Dept. of the Interior, Bureau of Mines, 1982. iii,
            91 p. : ill. ; 28 cm.




-----------------------------------------------------------------
NEXT ACTIONS      Key: ? for help           + to see the next screen
                       L to see a Longer display  - to see the previous screen
                       F to Find other items      Q to Quit
NEXT ACTION?  _                                            CBCAP
```

Figure 6.24

```
Your search: CITIZEN KANE                          BRIEF Display
      Finds: 1 record                              Screen  1 of  1
-----------------------------------------------------------------

        CITIZEN KANE [videorecording] / an RKO Radio Picture ; a
            Mercury production ; Orson Welles, direction,
            production. New York, N.Y. : VidAmerica, c1982. 1
            videocassette (119 min.) : sd., b&w ; 1/2 in.






-----------------------------------------------------------------
NEXT ACTIONS      Key: ? for help           + to see the next screen
                       L to see a Longer display  - to see the previous screen
                       F to Find other items      Q to Quit
NEXT ACTION?  _                                            CBCAP
```

Figure 6.25

```
Your search: Anderson, Sparky#                        LONG Display
      Finds: 1 record                                 Screen  1 of  1
---------------------------------------------------------------------

        Anderson, Sparky, 1934-
          Bless you boys : diary of the Detroit Tigers' 1984 season
        / by Sparky Anderson, with Dan Ewald. -- Chicago :
        Contemporary Books, c1984.

          231 p. : ill. ; 23 cm.

          1. Detroit Tigers (Baseball team) I. Ewald, Dan.




---------------------------------------------------------------------
NEXT ACTIONS      Key: ? for help              + to see the next screen
                       B to see a Brief display - to see the previous screen
                       F to Find other items   Q to Quit
NEXT ACTION?   _                                          CLON1
```

Figure 6.26

```
Your search: Best American pla#                       LONG Display
      Finds: 1 record                                 Screen  1 of  2
---------------------------------------------------------------------

        Best American plays : sixth series, 1963-1967 / edited by
          John Gassner and Clive Barnes, with an introduction and
          prefaces to the plays by Clive Barnes. -- New York :
          Crown, c1971.

          xii, 594 p. ; 24 cm.

        Contents: Tiny Alice / E. Albee -- Blues for Mister
        Charlie / J. Baldwin -- The last analysis / S. Bellow --
        Hogan's goat / W. Alfred -- The fantasticks / T. Jones --
        The sign in Sidney Brustein's window / L. Hansberry -- The
        lion in winter / J. Goldman -- Hughie / E. O'Neill -- The
        toilet / L. Jones -- You know I can't hear you when the
        water is running / R. Anderson -- Benito Cereno / R. Lowell

-----------------------------------------------------CONTINUED-------
NEXT ACTIONS      Key: ? for help              + to see the next screen
                       B to see a Brief display - to see the previous screen
                       F to Find other items   Q to Quit
NEXT ACTION?   _                                          CLON1
```

Figure 6.27

```
Your search: Best American pla#                      LONG Display
       Finds: 1 record                               Screen  2 of  2
-------------------------------------------------------------------

        -- Fiddler on the roof / J. Stein -- Slow dance on the
        killing ground / W. Hanley -- In white America / M.B.
        Duberman -- The owl and the pussycat / B. Manhoff -- The odd
        couple / W. Simon -- The subject was roses / F.D. Gilroy.

          1. American drama--20th century. 2. American drama--
        Collected works. I. Gassner, John, 1903-1967. II. Barnes,
        Clive, 1927-




-------------------------------------------------------------------
NEXT ACTIONS       Key: ? for help           + to see the next screen
                        B to see a Brief display   - to see the previous screen
                        F to Find other items      Q to Quit
NEXT ACTION?  _                                            CLON1
```

Figure 6.28

```
Your search: Brubeck, Dave#                          LONG Display
       Finds: 1 record                               Screen  1 of  2
-------------------------------------------------------------------

        Brubeck, Dave.
          [Bossa nova U.S.A. Selections; arr.]
          Bossa nova U.S.A. / [as performed by] the Dave Brubeck
        Quartet ; piano solo transcriptions by Howard Brubeck. --
        San Francisco, Calif. : Derry Music Co. ;  New York, N.Y. :
        C. Hansen, distributor, c1963.

          49 p. of music ; 28 cm.

          Jazz quartets arr. for piano solo; chord symbols and
        fingerings included.
          "Trolley song and This can't be love do not appear in this
        collection due to copyright restrictions."

-----------------------------------------------------CONTINUED-------
NEXT ACTIONS       Key: ? for help           + to see the next screen
                        B to see a Brief display   - to see the previous screen
                        F to Find other items      Q to Quit
NEXT ACTION?  _                                            CLON1
```

Figure 6.29

```
Your search: Brubeck, Dave#                        LONG Display
     Finds: 1 record                               Screen  2 of  2
------------------------------------------------------------------------

        Notes on the music by Dave Brubeck, principal composer, on
     covers.
        Contents: Bossa nova U.S. A. / Dave Brubeck -- Vento
     fresco = Cool wind / Dave Brubeck -- Theme for June / Howard
     R. Brubeck -- Coracao sensivel = Tender heart / Teo Macero
     -- Irmao amigo = Brother friend / Dave Brubeck -- There'll
     be no tomorrow / Dave Brubeck -- Cantiga nov swing = Swing a
     new song / Dave Brubeck -- Lamento = Lament / Dave Brubeck.

        1. Piano music (Jazz), Arranged. 2. Jazz quartets--Piano
     scores. I. Brubeck, Howard R. II. Brubeck, Howard R. Theme
     for June; arr. III. Macero, Teo, 1925- Coracao sensivel;
     arr. IV. Dave Brubeck Quartet.


------------------------------------------------------------------------
NEXT ACTIONS     Key: ? for help              + to see the next screen
                      B to see a Brief display - to see the previous screen
                      F to Find other items   Q to Quit
NEXT ACTION?   _                                          CLON1
```

Figure 6.30

```
Your search: Stewart, William #                    LONG Display
     Finds: 1 record                               Screen  1 of  2
------------------------------------------------------------------------

     Stewart, William Herman, 1932-
        The explorer's historical tourist map of Alaska, with maps
     of Anchorage, Fairbanks & Juneau : with notes on the Arctic,
     wildlife, hunting, fishing, camping, exploring &
     prospecting, festivals & events / cartography by William H.
     Stewart. -- Scale [ca. 1:3,200,000] (E 1720--W 1300/N 700--N
     520). -- Charleston, W.Va. : Economic Service Council, 1983.

        1 map : col. ; 65 x 71 cm., folded to 23 x 11 cm.

        Panel title.
        Pictorial map.
        Includes inset of the Aleutian Islands, notes, 3 diagrams,
     and ill.

--------------------------------------------------------CONTINUED-------
NEXT ACTIONS     Key: ? for help              + to see the next screen
                      B to see a Brief display - to see the previous screen
                      F to Find other items   Q to Quit
NEXT ACTION?   _                                          CLON1
```

Figure 6.31

```
Your search: Stewart, William #                    LONG Display
      Finds: 1 record                              Screen  2 of  2
----------------------------------------------------------------

        Ancillary maps: Comparative size of Alaska -- Top of the
     world -- Juneau -- Fairbanks -- Anchorage.

        1. Alaska--Maps, Tourist. 2. Alaska--Maps, Pictorial. I.
     Economic Service Council.




----------------------------------------------------------------
NEXT ACTIONS      Key: ? for help           + to see the next screen
                       B to see a Brief display  - to see the previous screen
                       F to Find other items      Q to Quit
NEXT ACTION?  _                                        CLON1
```

Figure 6.32

```
Your search: Indy, Vincent d'#                     LONG Display
      Finds: 1 record                              Screen  1 of  3
----------------------------------------------------------------

        Indy, Vincent d', 1851-1931.
          [Instrumental music. Selections]
          Suite en re dans le style ancien : op. 24 ; Karadec : op.
     34 ; Concert, op. 89 pour piano, flute, violoncello et
     orchestre a cordes [sound recording] / Vincent d'Indy. --
     France : Erato ; Paris : Distribution en France RCA, p1982.

        1 sound disc : 33 1/3 rpm, stereo. ; 12 in.

        The 2nd work incidental music.
        Jean-Pierre Rampal, Philippe Pierlot, flutes, Maurice
     Andre, trumpet (in the 1st work) ; Francois-Rene Duchable,
     piano, Jean-Pierre Rampal, flute, Frederic Lodeon,
     violoncello (in the 3rd) ; Orchestre de chambre
------------------------------------------------CONTINUED------
NEXT ACTIONS      Key: ? for help           + to see the next screen
                       B to see a Brief display  - to see the previous screen
                       F to Find other items      Q to Quit
NEXT ACTION?  _                                        CLON1
```

Figure 6.33

```
Your search: Indy, Vincent d'#                        LONG Display
      Finds: 1 record                                 Screen  2 of  3
----------------------------------------------------------------------


        Jean-Francois Paillard ; Jean-Francois Paillard, conductor.
          Recorded Jan. and Apr., 1981, l'IRCAM-Espace de
        Projection, Paris.
          Eds. recorded: Heugel.
          Issued also as cassette: MCE 71423.

        1. Suites (Flutes (2), trumpet with string orchestra) 2.
        Music, Incidental. 3. Concertos (Piano, flute, violoncello
        with string orchestra) I. Rampal, Jean Pierre. II. Pierlot,
        Philippe. III. Andre, Maurice. IV. Duchable, Francois. V.
        Lodeon, Frederic. VI. Paillard, Jean Francois. VII. Indy,
        Vincent d', 1851-1931. Suite dans le style ancien. 1982.
        VIII. Indy, Vincent d', 1851-1931. Karadec. 1982. IX. Indy,
        Vincent d', 1851-1931. Concerto, piano, flute, violoncello,

----------------------------------------------------------CONTINUED-------
NEXT ACTIONS      Key: ? for help            + to see the next screen
                       B to see a Brief display  - to see the previous screen
                       F to Find other items     Q to Quit
NEXT ACTION?  _                                              CLON1
```

Figure 6.34

```
Your search: Indy, Vincent d'#                        LONG Display
      Finds: 1 record                                 Screen  3 of  3
----------------------------------------------------------------------

        orchestra, op. 89. 1982. X. Orchestre de chambre
        Jean-Francois Paillard.








----------------------------------------------------------------------
NEXT ACTIONS      Key: ? for help            + to see the next screen
                       B to see a Brief display  - to see the previous screen
                       F to Find other items     Q to Quit
NEXT ACTION?  _                                              CLON1
```

Figure 6.35

```
Your search: Time.                              LONG Display
      Finds: 1 record                           Screen  1 of  3
---------------------------------------------------------------------

        Time.
          v. 1-  Mar. 3, 1923-
          [Chicago, etc., Time Inc.]

          v. ill. (incl. ports.) 28 cm.

          Weekly (except one week a year) <, Dec. 26, 1977->
          Weekly <, April 15, 1985->
          Indexed selectively by: ABI/INFORM March 1975-Jan. 1978.
          Indexed in its entirety by: Abridged readers' guide to
        periodical literature.
          Indexed selectively by: Book review index.
          Indexed selectively by: Cumulative index to nursing &
        allied health literature.

      -------------------------------------------------CONTINUED-------
NEXT ACTIONS      Key: ? for help             + to see the next screen
                       B to see a Brief display  - to see the previous screen
                       F to Find other items   Q to Quit

NEXT ACTION?   _                                          CLON1
```

Figure 6.36

```
Your search: Time.                              LONG Display
      Finds: 1 record                           Screen  2 of  3
---------------------------------------------------------------------

          Indexed selectively by: Film literature index.
          Indexed selectively by: Hospital literature index.
          Indexed selectively by: Infobank Jan. 1969-
          Indexed selectively by: Popular magazine review 1984-
          Indexed selectively by: Predicasts.
          Indexed by: Biography index.
          Indexed in its entirety by: Readers' guide to periodical
        literature.
          Indexed selectively by: Media review digest.
          Indexed selectively by: Energy information abstracts.
          Indexed selectively by: Environment abstracts.
          Indexes: Individual indexes cumulated in one volume, v.
        35-44.
          Indexes: Vols. 45-60, 1945-52. 1 v.

      -------------------------------------------------CONTINUED-------
NEXT ACTIONS      Key: ? for help             + to see the next screen
                       B to see a Brief display  - to see the previous screen
                       F to Find other items   Q to Quit

NEXT ACTION?   _                                          CLON1
```

Figure 6.37

```
Your search: Time.                              LONG Display
     Finds: 1 record                            Screen  3 of  3
-----------------------------------------------------------------


        Editors: 1923-<24> B. Hadden, H. R. Luce.
        Absorbed: Literary digest (New York, N.Y. : 1937)

        I. Hadden, Briton, ed. II. Luce, Henry Robinson, 1898- ed.




-----------------------------------------------------------------
NEXT ACTIONS      Key: ? for help            + to see the next screen
                       B to see a Brief display  - to see the previous screen
                       F to Find other items  Q to Quit
NEXT ACTION?   _                                CLON1
```

Figure 6.38

```
Your search: Bureau of Mines T#                 LONG Display
     Finds: 1 record                            Screen  1 of  2
-----------------------------------------------------------------

     Bureau of Mines Technology Transfer Seminars (1982 :
       Pittsburgh, Pa.)
       Postdisaster survival and rescue research : proceedings,
     Bureau of Mines Technology Transfer Seminar, Pittsburgh,
     Pa., November 16, 1982 / compiled by staff, Bureau of Mines.
     -- [Avondale, Md.] : U.S. Dept. of the Interior, Bureau of
     Mines, 1982.

       iii, 91 p. : ill. ; 28 cm.
       (Information circular (United States. Bureau of Mines) ;
     8907.)

       Includes bibliographies.


------------------------------------------------CONTINUED-------
NEXT ACTIONS      Key: ? for help            + to see the next screen
                       B to see a Brief display  - to see the previous screen
                       F to Find other items  Q to Quit
NEXT ACTION?   _                                CLON1
```

Figure 6.39

```
Your search: Bureau of Mines T#                      LONG Display
       Finds: 1 record                               Screen  2 of  2
-------------------------------------------------------------------------

        1. Mine accidents--Congresses. 2. Mine rescue work--
     Congresses. I. United States. Bureau of Mines.




-------------------------------------------------------------------------
NEXT ACTIONS      Key: ? for help            + to see the next screen
                       B to see a Brief display   - to see the previous screen
                       F to Find other items       Q to Quit
NEXT ACTION?   _                                            CLON1
```

Figure 6.40

```
Your search: Citizen Kane                            LONG Display
       Finds: 1 record                               Screen  1 of  2
-------------------------------------------------------------------------

     Citizen Kane [videorecording] / an RKO Radio Picture ; a
        Mercury production ; Orson Welles, direction, production.
        -- New York, N.Y. : VidAmerica, c1982.

        1 videocassette (119 min.) : sd., b&w ; 1/2 in.
         -- (Classic series)

        Cast: Orson Welles, Joseph Cotton, Agnes Moorehead,
     Everett Sloane.
        Credits: Photography, Gregg Toland ; music, Bernard
     Herrmann ; screenplay, Orson Welles, Herman J. Mankiewicz.
        Originally produced as motion picture in 1941.
        VHS.
        1941 Academy Award for best screenplay.
----------------------------------------------------------CONTINUED-------
NEXT ACTIONS      Key: ? for help            + to see the next screen
                       B to see a Brief display   - to see the previous screen
                       F to Find other items       Q to Quit
NEXT ACTION?   _                                            CLON1
```

Figure 6.41

```
Your search: Citizen Kane                          LONG Display
       Finds: 1 record                             Screen  2 of  2
----------------------------------------------------------------------

       Summary: A story of the rise and fall of a great man as
    the result of his accumulation of wealth and subsequent
    isolation from the world. Based on the life of newspaper
    tycoon William Randolph Hearst, this is classic American
    cinema.
       VidAmerica: #903.

       1. Feature films. I. Welles, Orson, 1915- II. VidAmerica
    (Firm) III. RKO Radio Pictures, inc. IV. Mercury
    Productions.




    -------------------------------------------------------------------
NEXT ACTIONS     Key: ? for help            + to see the next screen
                      B to see a Brief display  - to see the previous screen
                      F to Find other items  Q to Quit
NEXT ACTION?  _                                         CLON1
```

Figure 6.42

```
Your search: Anderson, Sparky#                     CITATION Display
       Finds: 1 record                             Screen  1 of  1
----------------------------------------------------------------------

       Anderson, Sparky, 1934- Bless you boys : diary of the
           Detroit Tigers' 1984 season / by Sparky Anderson, with
           Dan Ewald. Chicago : Contemporary Books, c1984. 231 p. :
           ill. ; 23 cm.

       Detroit Tigers (Baseball team)
       Ewald, Dan.






    -------------------------------------------------------------------
NEXT ACTIONS     Key: ? for help            + to see the next screen
                      B to see a Brief display  - to see the previous screen
                      F to Find other items  Q to Quit
NEXT ACTION?  _                                         CLCIT1
```

Figure 6.43

```
Your search: Best American pla#                    CITATION Display
      Finds: 1 record                              Screen  1 of  2
--------------------------------------------------------------------

        Best American plays : sixth series, 1963-1967 / edited by
            John Gassner and Clive Barnes, with an introduction and
            prefaces to the plays by Clive Barnes. New York : Crown,
            c1971. xii, 594 p. ; 24 cm.

           Contents: Tiny Alice / E. Albee -- Blues for Mister
        Charlie / J. Baldwin -- The last analysis / S. Bellow --
        Hogan's goat / W. Alfred -- The fantasticks / T. Jones --
        The sign in Sidney Brustein's window / L. Hansberry -- The
        lion in winter / J. Goldman -- Hughie / E. O'Neill -- The
        toilet / L. Jones -- You know I can't hear you when the
        water is running / R. Anderson -- Benito Cereno / R. Lowell
        -- Fiddler on the roof / J. Stein -- Slow dance on the
        killing ground / W. Hanley -- In white America / M.B.

-------------------------------------------------------CONTINUED-------
NEXT ACTIONS      Key: ? for help            + to see the next screen
                       B to see a Brief display   - to see the previous screen
                       F to Find other items     Q to Quit
NEXT ACTION?  _                                           CLCIT1
```

Figure 6.44

```
Your search: Best American pla#                    CITATION Display
      Finds: 1 record                              Screen  2 of  2
--------------------------------------------------------------------

        Duberman -- The owl and the pussycat / B. Manhoff -- The odd
        couple / W. Simon -- The subject was roses / F.D. Gilroy.

        American drama--20th century.
        American drama--Collected works.
        Gassner, John, 1903-1967.
        Barnes, Clive, 1927-




--------------------------------------------------------------------
NEXT ACTIONS      Key: ? for help            + to see the next screen
                       B to see a Brief display   - to see the previous screen
                       F to Find other items     Q to Quit
NEXT ACTION?  _                                           CLCIT1
```

Figure 6.45

```
Your search: Brubeck, Dave. Bo#                    CITATION Display
      Finds: 1 record                              Screen  1 of  2
------------------------------------------------------------------------

        Brubeck, Dave. Bossa nova U.S.A. / [as performed by] the
           Dave Brubeck Quartet ; piano solo transcriptions by
           Howard Brubeck. San Francisco, Calif. : Derry Music Co.
           ; New York, N.Y. : C. Hansen, distributor, c1963. 49 p.
           of music ; 28 cm.

        Jazz quartets arr. for piano solo; chord symbols and
        fingerings included.
        "Trolley song and This can't be love do not appear in this
        collection due to copyright restrictions."
        Notes on the music by Dave Brubeck, principal composer, on
        covers.


------------------------------------------------------------CONTINUED-------
NEXT ACTIONS      Key: ? for help             + to see the next screen
                       B to see a Brief display  - to see the previous screen
                       F to Find other items    Q to Quit
NEXT ACTION?  _                                           CLCIT1
```

Figure 6.46

```
Your search: Brubeck, Dave. Bo#                    CITATION Display
      Finds: 1 record                              Screen  2 of  2
------------------------------------------------------------------------

        Contents: Bossa nova U.S. A. / Dave Brubeck -- Vento
        fresco = Cool wind / Dave Brubeck -- Theme for June / Howard
        R. Brubeck -- Coracao sensivel = Tender heart / Teo Macero
        -- Irmao amigo = Brother friend / Dave Brubeck -- There'll
        be no tomorrow / Dave Brubeck -- Cantiga nov swing = Swing a
        new song / Dave Brubeck -- Lamento = Lament / Dave Brubeck.

        Piano music (Jazz), Arranged.
        Jazz quartets--Piano scores.
        Brubeck, Howard R.
        Brubeck, Howard R. Theme for June; arr.
        Macero, Teo, 1925- Coracao sensivel; arr.
        Dave Brubeck Quartet.


------------------------------------------------------------------------
NEXT ACTIONS      Key: ? for help             + to see the next screen
                       B to see a Brief display  - to see the previous screen
                       F to Find other items    Q to Quit
NEXT ACTION?  _                                           CLCIT1
```

Figure 6.47

```
Your search: Stewart, William #                    CITATION Display
       Finds: 1 record                             Screen  1 of  2
------------------------------------------------------------------------


            Stewart, William Herman, 1932- The explorer's historical
                tourist map of Alaska, with maps of Anchorage, Fairbanks
                & Juneau : with notes on the Arctic, wildlife, hunting,
                fishing, camping, exploring & prospecting, festivals &
                events / cartography by William H. Stewart. Charleston,
                W.Va. : Economic Service Council, 1983. 1 map : col. ;
                65 x 71 cm., folded to 23 x 11 cm.

            Panel title.
            Pictorial map.
            Includes inset of the Aleutian Islands, notes, 3 diagrams,
         and ill.




-----------------------------------------------------------------CONTINUED-------
NEXT ACTIONS        Key: ? for help              + to see the next screen
                         B to see a Brief display   - to see the previous screen
                         F to Find other items      Q to Quit
NEXT ACTION?  _                                                  CLCIT1
```

Figure 6.48

```
Your search: Stewart, William #                    CITATION Display
       Finds: 1 record                             Screen  2 of  2
------------------------------------------------------------------------


            Ancillary maps: Comparative size of Alaska -- Top of the
         world -- Juneau -- Fairbanks -- Anchorage.

         Alaska--Maps, Tourist.
         Alaska--Maps, Pictorial.
         Economic Service Council.







-----------------------------------------------------------------
NEXT ACTIONS        Key: ? for help              + to see the next screen
                         B to see a Brief display   - to see the previous screen
                         F to Find other items      Q to Quit
NEXT ACTION?  _                                                  CLCIT1
```

Figure 6.49

```
Your search: Indy, Vincent d'#                    CITATION Display
        Finds: 1 record                          Screen  1 of  3
-------------------------------------------------------------------

        Indy, Vincent d', 1851-1931. Suite en re dans le style
            ancien : op. 24 ; Karadec : op. 34 ; Concert, op. 89
            pour piano, flute, violoncello et orchestre a cordes
            [sound recording] / Vincent d'Indy. France : Erato ;
            Paris : Distribution en France RCA, p1982. 1 sound disc
            : 33 1/3 rpm, stereo. ; 12 in.

        The 2nd work incidental music.
         Jean-Pierre Rampal, Philippe Pierlot, flutes, Maurice
        Andre, trumpet (in the 1st work) ; Francois-Rene Duchable,
        piano, Jean-Pierre Rampal, flute, Frederic Lodeon,
        violoncello (in the 3rd) ; Orchestre de chambre
        Jean-Francois Paillard ; Jean-Francois Paillard, conductor.


-----------------------------------------------------CONTINUED-------
NEXT ACTIONS     Key: ? for help          + to see the next screen
                      B to see a Brief display   - to see the previous screen
                      F to Find other items      Q to Quit
NEXT ACTION?  _                                        CLCIT1
```

Figure 6.50

```
Your search: Indy, Vincent d'#                    CITATION Display
        Finds: 1 record                          Screen  2 of  3
-------------------------------------------------------------------

        Recorded Jan. and Apr., 1981, l'IRCAM-Espace de
        Projection, Paris.
         Eds. recorded: Heugel.
         Issued also as cassette: MCE 71423.

        Suites (Flutes (2), trumpet with string orchestra)
        Music, Incidental.
        Concertos (Piano, flute, violoncello with string orchestra)
        Rampal, Jean Pierre.
        Pierlot, Philippe.
        Andre, Maurice.
        Duchable, Francois.
        Lodeon, Frederic.
        Paillard, Jean Francois.


-----------------------------------------------------CONTINUED-------
NEXT ACTIONS     Key: ? for help          + to see the next screen
                      B to see a Brief display   - to see the previous screen
                      F to Find other items      Q to Quit
NEXT ACTION?  _                                        CLCIT1
```

Figure 6.51

```
Your search: Indy, Vincent d'#                    CITATION Display
     Finds: 1 record                               Screen  3 of  3
--------------------------------------------------------------------

        Indy, Vincent d', 1851-1931. Suite dans le style ancien.
           1982.
        Indy, Vincent d', 1851-1931. Karadec. 1982.
        Indy, Vincent d', 1851-1931. Concerto, piano, flute,
           violoncello, orchestra, op. 89. 1982.
        Orchestre de chambre Jean-Francois Paillard.




--------------------------------------------------------------------
NEXT ACTIONS     Key: ? for help           + to see the next screen
                      B to see a Brief display   - to see the previous screen
                      F to Find other items  Q to Quit
NEXT ACTION?  _                                          CLCIT1
```

Figure 6.52

```
Your search: Time.                                CITATION Display
     Finds: 1 record                               Screen  1 of  3
--------------------------------------------------------------------

        Time. [Chicago, etc., Time Inc.] v. ill. (incl. ports.) 28
           cm.

        Weekly (except one week a year) <, Dec. 26, 1977->
        Weekly <, April 15, 1985->
        Indexed selectively by: ABI/INFORM March 1975-Jan. 1978.
        Indexed in its entirety by: Abridged readers' guide to
        periodical literature.
        Indexed selectively by: Book review index.
        Indexed selectively by: Cumulative index to nursing &
        allied health literature.
        Indexed selectively by: Film literature index.
        Indexed selectively by: Hospital literature index.
        Indexed selectively by: Infobank Jan. 1969-

-------------------------------------------------CONTINUED-------
NEXT ACTIONS     Key: ? for help           + to see the next screen
                      B to see a Brief display   - to see the previous screen
                      F to Find other items  Q to Quit
NEXT ACTION?  _                                          CLCIT1
```

Figure 6.53

```
Your search: Time.                                      CITATION Display
       Finds: 1 record                                  Screen  2 of  3
---------------------------------------------------------------------------

        Indexed selectively by: Popular magazine review 1984-
        Indexed selectively by: Predicasts.
        Indexed by: Biography index.
        Indexed in its entirety by: Readers' guide to periodical
    literature.
        Indexed selectively by: Media review digest.
        Indexed selectively by: Energy information abstracts.
        Indexed selectively by: Environment abstracts.
        Indexes: Individual indexes cumulated in one volume, v.
    35-44.
        Indexes: Vols. 45-60, 1945-52. 1 v.
        Editors: 1923-<24> B. Hadden, H. R. Luce.
        Absorbed: Literary digest (New York, N.Y. : 1937)


------------------------------------------------------------CONTINUED-------
NEXT ACTIONS      Key: ? for help            + to see the next screen
                       B to see a Brief display   - to see the previous screen
                       F to Find other items   Q to Quit
NEXT ACTION?   _                                            CLCIT1
```

Figure 6.54

```
Your search: Time.                                      CITATION Display
       Finds: 1 record                                  Screen  3 of  3
---------------------------------------------------------------------------

        Hadden, Briton, ed.
        Luce, Henry Robinson, 1898- ed.







------------------------------------------------------------------
NEXT ACTIONS      Key: ? for help            + to see the next screen
                       B to see a Brief display   - to see the previous screen
                       F to Find other items   Q to Quit
NEXT ACTION?   _                                            CLCIT1
```
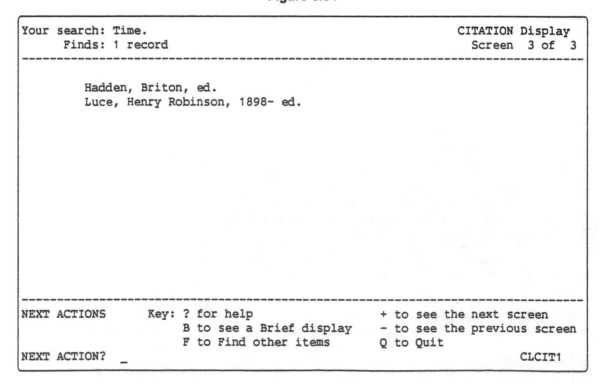

Figure 6.55

```
Your search: Bureau of Mines T#                    CITATION Display
      Finds: 1 record                               Screen  1 of  1
---------------------------------------------------------------------

        Bureau of Mines Technology Transfer Seminars (1982 :
           Pittsburgh, Pa.) Postdisaster survival and rescue
           research : proceedings, Bureau of Mines Technology
           Transfer Seminar, Pittsburgh, Pa., November 16, 1982 /
           compiled by staff, Bureau of Mines. [Avondale, Md.] :
           U.S. Dept. of the Interior, Bureau of Mines, 1982. iii,
           91 p. : ill. ; 28 cm. (Information circular (United
           States. Bureau of Mines) ; 8907.)

        Includes bibliographies.

        Mine accidents--Congresses.
        Mine rescue work--Congresses.
        United States. Bureau of Mines.


---------------------------------------------------------------------
NEXT ACTIONS      Key: ? for help            + to see the next screen
                       B to see a Brief display  - to see the previous screen
                       F to Find other items     Q to Quit
NEXT ACTION?   _                                          CLCIT1
```

Figure 6.56

```
Your search: Citizen Kane                          CITATION Display
      Finds: 1 record                               Screen  1 of  2
---------------------------------------------------------------------

        Citizen Kane [videorecording] / an RKO Radio Picture ; a
           Mercury production ; Orson Welles, direction,
           production. New York, N.Y. : VidAmerica, c1982. 1
           videocassette (119 min.) : sd., b&w ; 1/2 in. --
           (Classic series)

         Cast: Orson Welles, Joseph Cotton, Agnes Moorehead,
        Everett Sloane.
         Credits: Photography, Gregg Toland ; music, Bernard
        Herrmann ; screenplay, Orson Welles, Herman J. Mankiewicz.
         Originally produced as motion picture in 1941.
         VHS.
         1941 Academy Award for best screenplay.


-------------------------------------------------------CONTINUED-------
NEXT ACTIONS      Key: ? for help            + to see the next screen
                       B to see a Brief display  - to see the previous screen
                       F to Find other items     Q to Quit
NEXT ACTION?   _                                          CLCIT1
```

Figure 6.57

```
Your search: Citizen Kane                            CITATION Display
       Finds: 1 record                               Screen  2 of  2
-------------------------------------------------------------------------

        Summary: A story of the rise and fall of a great man as
     the result of his accumulation of wealth and subsequent
     isolation from the world. Based on the life of newspaper
     tycoon William Randolph Hearst, this is classic American
     cinema.
        VidAmerica: #903.

     Feature films.
     Welles, Orson, 1915-
     VidAmerica (Firm)
     RKO Radio Pictures, inc.
     Mercury Productions.


-------------------------------------------------------------------------
NEXT ACTIONS      Key: ? for help            + to see the next screen
                       B to see a Brief display  - to see the previous screen
                       F to Find other items  Q to Quit
NEXT ACTION?   _                                            CLCIT1
```

Figure 6.58

```
Your search: Bless you boys #                        LONG Display
       Finds: 1 record                               Screen  1 of  1
-------------------------------------------------------------------------

        TITLE: Bless you boys : diary of the Detroit Tigers' 1984 season /
               by Sparky Anderson, with Dan Ewald.
     PUBLISHED: Chicago : Contemporary Books, c1984.
     MATERIAL: 231 p. : ill. ; 23 cm.

        NAMES: Anderson, Sparky, 1934-
               Ewald, Dan.

     SUBJECTS: Detroit Tigers (Baseball team)



-------------------------------------------------------------------------
NEXT ACTIONS      Key: ? for help            + to see the next screen
                       B to see a Brief display  - to see the previous screen
                       F to Find other items  Q to Quit
NEXT ACTION?   _                                            LLON1
```

Figure 6.59

```
Your search: Best American pla#                    LONG Display
      Finds: 1 record                              Screen  1 of  2
------------------------------------------------------------------

        TITLE: Best American plays : sixth series, 1963-1967 / edited by
               John Gassner and Clive Barnes, with an introduction and
               prefaces to the plays by Clive Barnes.
    PUBLISHED: New York : Crown, c1971.
     MATERIAL: xii, 594 p. ; 24 cm.

        NAMES: Gassner, John, 1903-1967.
               Barnes, Clive, 1927-

     SUBJECTS: American drama--20th century.
               American drama--Collected works.


------------------------------------------------------CONTINUED-------
NEXT ACTIONS     Key: ? for help           + to see the next screen
                      B to see a Brief display   - to see the previous screen
                      F to Find other items  Q to Quit
NEXT ACTION?  _                                         LLON1
```

Figure 6.60

```
Your search: Best American pla#                    LONG Display
      Finds: 1 record                              Screen  2 of  2
------------------------------------------------------------------

        NOTES: Contents: Tiny Alice / E. Albee -- Blues for Mister Charlie
               / J. Baldwin -- The last analysis / S. Bellow -- Hogan's
               goat / W. Alfred -- The fantasticks / T. Jones -- The sign
               in Sidney Brustein's window / L. Hansberry -- The lion in
               winter / J. Goldman -- Hughie / E. O'Neill -- The toilet /
               L. Jones -- You know I can't hear you when the water is
               running / R. Anderson -- Benito Cereno / R. Lowell --
               Fiddler on the roof / J. Stein -- Slow dance on the
               killing ground / W. Hanley -- In white America / M.B.
               Duberman -- The owl and the pussycat / B. Manhoff -- The
               odd couple / W. Simon -- The subject was roses / F.D.
               Gilroy.


-------------------------------------------------------------------
NEXT ACTIONS     Key: ? for help           + to see the next screen
                      B to see a Brief display   - to see the previous screen
                      F to Find other items  Q to Quit
NEXT ACTION?  _                                         LLON1
```

Figure 6.61

```
Your search: Bossa nova U.S.A#                        LONG Display
     Finds: 1 record                                  Screen  1 of  3
-----------------------------------------------------------------------


        TITLE: Bossa nova U.S.A. / [as performed by] the Dave Brubeck
               Quartet ; piano solo transcriptions by Howard Brubeck.
    PUBLISHED: San Francisco, Calif. : Derry Music Co. ;  New York, N.Y. :
               C. Hansen, distributor, c1963.
     MATERIAL: 49 p. of music ; 28 cm.

        NAMES: Brubeck, Dave.
               Brubeck, Howard R.
               Dave Brubeck Quartet.

     SUBJECTS: Piano music (Jazz), Arranged.
               Jazz quartets--Piano scores.

        WORKS: Bossa nova U.S.A. Selections; arr.


-----------------------------------------------------CONTINUED-------
NEXT ACTIONS      Key: ? for help          + to see the next screen
                       B to see a Brief display   - to see the previous screen
                       F to Find other items      Q to Quit

NEXT ACTION?  _                                            LLON1
```

Figure 6.62

```
Your search: Bossa nova U.S.A#                        LONG Display
     Finds: 1 record                                  Screen  2 of  3
-----------------------------------------------------------------------

               Brubeck, Howard R. Theme for June; arr.
               Macero, Teo, 1925- Coracao sensivel; arr.

        NOTES: Jazz quartets arr. for piano solo; chord ·symbols and
               fingerings included.
               "Trolley song and This can't be love do not appear in this
               collection due to copyright restrictions."
               Notes on the music by Dave Brubeck, principal composer, on
               covers.
               Contents: Bossa nova U.S. A. / Dave Brubeck -- Vento fresco
               = Cool wind / Dave Brubeck -- Theme for June / Howard R.
               Brubeck -- Coracao sensivel = Tender heart / Teo Macero --
               Irmao amigo = Brother friend / Dave Brubeck -- There'll be
               no tomorrow / Dave Brubeck -- Cantiga nov swing = Swing a

-----------------------------------------------------CONTINUED-------
NEXT ACTIONS      Key: ? for help          + to see the next screen
                       B to see a Brief display   - to see the previous screen
                       F to Find other items      Q to Quit

NEXT ACTION?  _                                            LLON1
```

Figure 6.63

```
Your search: Bossa nova U.S.A#                      LONG Display
     Finds: 1 record                                Screen  3 of  3
-----------------------------------------------------------------------

               new song / Dave Brubeck -- Lamento = Lament / Dave
               Brubeck.









-----------------------------------------------------------------------
NEXT ACTIONS       Key: ? for help           + to see the next screen
                        B to see a Brief display   - to see the previous screen
                        F to Find other items      Q to Quit
NEXT ACTION?  _                                            LLON1
```

Figure 6.64

```
Your search: The explorer's hi#                     LONG Display
     Finds: 1 record                                Screen  1 of  2
-----------------------------------------------------------------------

        TITLE: The explorer's historical tourist map of Alaska, with maps
               of Anchorage, Fairbanks & Juneau : with notes on the
               Arctic, wildlife, hunting, fishing, camping, exploring &
               prospecting, festivals & events / cartography by William
               H. Stewart.
      EDITION: Scale [ca. 1:3,200,000] (E 1720--W 1300/N 700--N 520).
    PUBLISHED: Charleston, W.Va. : Economic Service Council, 1983.
     MATERIAL: 1 map : col. ; 65 x 71 cm., folded to 23 x 11 cm.

        NAMES: Stewart, William Herman, 1932-
               Economic Service Council.

     SUBJECTS: Alaska--Maps, Tourist.


---------------------------------------------------------CONTINUED-------
NEXT ACTIONS       Key: ? for help           + to see the next screen
                        B to see a Brief display   - to see the previous screen
                        F to Find other items      Q to Quit
NEXT ACTION?  _                                            LLON1
```

Figure 6.65

```
Your search: The explorer's hi#                      LONG Display
      Finds: 1 record                                Screen  2 of  2
-----------------------------------------------------------------------
              Alaska--Maps, Pictorial.

        NOTES: Panel title.
               Pictorial map.
               Includes inset of the Aleutian Islands, notes, 3 diagrams,
                 and ill.
               Ancillary maps: Comparative size of Alaska -- Top of the
                 world -- Juneau -- Fairbanks -- Anchorage.




      -----------------------------------------------------------------
NEXT ACTIONS     Key: ? for help              + to see the next screen
                      B to see a Brief display  - to see the previous screen
                      F to Find other items    Q to Quit
NEXT ACTION?  _                                         LLON1
```

Figure 6.66

```
Your search: Suite en re dans #                      LONG Display
      Finds: 1 record                                Screen  1 of  3
-----------------------------------------------------------------------
        TITLE: Suite en re dans le style ancien : op. 24 ; Karadec : op. 34
               ; Concert, op. 89 pour piano, flute, violoncello et
               orchestre a cordes [sound recording] / Vincent d'Indy.
    PUBLISHED: France : Erato ; Paris : Distribution en France RCA, p1982.
     MATERIAL: 1 sound disc : 33 1/3 rpm, stereo. ; 12 in.

        NAMES: Indy, Vincent d', 1851-1931.
               Rampal, Jean Pierre.
               Pierlot, Philippe.
               Andre, Maurice.
               Duchable, Francois.
               Lodeon, Frederic.
               Paillard, Jean Francois.


      ---------------------------------------------------CONTINUED-------
NEXT ACTIONS     Key: ? for help              + to see the next screen
                      B to see a Brief display  - to see the previous screen
                      F to Find other items    Q to Quit
NEXT ACTION?  _                                         LLON1
```

Figure 6.67

```
Your search: Suite en re dans #                      LONG Display
     Finds: 1 record                                 Screen  2 of  3
-----------------------------------------------------------------------

             Orchestre de chambre Jean-Francois Paillard.

    SUBJECTS: Suites (Flutes (2), trumpet with string orchestra)
              Music, Incidental.
              Concertos (Piano, flute, violoncello with string orchestra)

       WORKS: Instrumental music. Selections.
              Indy, Vincent d', 1851-1931. Suite dans le style ancien.
                1982.
              Indy, Vincent d', 1851-1931. Karadec. 1982.
              Indy, Vincent d', 1851-1931. Concerto, piano, flute,
                violoncello, orchestra, op. 89. 1982.

       NOTES: The 2nd work incidental music.

    -------------------------------------------------------CONTINUED-------
NEXT ACTIONS      Key: ? for help              + to see the next screen
                       B to see a Brief display  - to see the previous screen
                       F to Find other items     Q to Quit
NEXT ACTION?   _                                            LLON1
```

Figure 6.68

```
Your search: Suite en re dans #                      LONG Display
     Finds: 1 record                                 Screen  3 of  3
-----------------------------------------------------------------------

          Jean-Pierre Rampal, Philippe Pierlot, flutes, Maurice Andre,
             trumpet (in the 1st work) ; Francois-Rene Duchable, piano,
             Jean-Pierre Rampal, flute, Frederic Lodeon, violoncello
             (in the 3rd) ; Orchestre de chambre Jean-Francois Paillard
             ; Jean-Francois Paillard, conductor.
          Recorded Jan. and Apr., 1981, l'IRCAM-Espace de Projection,
             Paris.
          Eds. recorded: Heugel.
          Issued also as cassette: MCE 71423.




    -------------------------------------------------------------------
NEXT ACTIONS      Key: ? for help              + to see the next screen
                       B to see a Brief display  - to see the previous screen
                       F to Find other items     Q to Quit
NEXT ACTION?   _                                            LLON1
```

Figure 6.69

```
Your search: Time.                                 LONG Display
      Finds: 1 record                              Screen  1 of  3
-------------------------------------------------------------------------


         TITLE: Time.
       EDITION: v. 1-   Mar. 3, 1923-
     PUBLISHED: [Chicago, etc., Time Inc.]
      MATERIAL: v. ill. (incl. ports.) 28 cm.

         NAMES: Hadden, Briton, ed.
                Luce, Henry Robinson, 1898- ed.

         NOTES: Weekly (except one week a year) <, Dec. 26, 1977->
                Weekly <, April 15, 1985->
                Indexed selectively by: ABI/INFORM March 1975-Jan. 1978.
                Indexed in its entirety by: Abridged readers' guide to
                   periodical literature.
                Indexed selectively by: Book review index.

---------------------------------------------------------CONTINUED-------
NEXT ACTIONS      Key: ? for help              + to see the next screen
                       B to see a Brief display - to see the previous screen
                       F to Find other items    Q to Quit
NEXT ACTION?   _                                            LLON1
```

Figure 6.70

```
Your search: Time.                                 LONG Display
      Finds: 1 record                              Screen  2 of  3
-------------------------------------------------------------------------

                Indexed selectively by: Cumulative index to nursing & allied
                   health literature.
                Indexed selectively by: Film literature index.
                Indexed selectively by: Hospital literature index.
                Indexed selectively by: Infobank Jan. 1969-
                Indexed selectively by: Popular magazine review 1984-
                Indexed selectively by: Predicasts.
                Indexed by: Biography index.
                Indexed in its entirety by: Readers' guide to periodical
                   literature.
                Indexed selectively by: Media review digest.
                Indexed selectively by: Energy information abstracts.
                Indexed selectively by: Environment abstracts.


---------------------------------------------------------CONTINUED-------
NEXT ACTIONS      Key: ? for help              + to see the next screen
                       B to see a Brief display - to see the previous screen
                       F to Find other items    Q to Quit
NEXT ACTION?   _                                            LLON1
```

Figure 6.71

```
Your search: Time.                                    LONG Display
      Finds: 1 record                                 Screen  3 of  3
------------------------------------------------------------------------

            Indexes: Individual indexes cumulated in one volume, v.
               35-44.
            Indexes: Vols. 45-60, 1945-52. 1 v.
            Editors: 1923-<24> B. Hadden, H. R. Luce.
            Absorbed: Literary digest (New York, N.Y. : 1937)





------------------------------------------------------------------------
NEXT ACTIONS      Key: ? for help             + to see the next screen
                       B to see a Brief display  - to see the previous screen
                       F to Find other items   Q to Quit
NEXT ACTION?   _                                           LLON1
```

Figure 6.72

```
Your search: Postdisaster surv#                       LONG Display
      Finds: 1 record                                 Screen  1 of  2
------------------------------------------------------------------------

        TITLE: Postdisaster survival and rescue research : proceedings,
               Bureau of Mines Technology Transfer Seminar, Pittsburgh,
               Pa., November 16, 1982 / compiled by staff, Bureau of
               Mines.
    PUBLISHED: [Avondale, Md.] : U.S. Dept. of the Interior, Bureau of
               Mines, 1982.
     MATERIAL: iii, 91 p. : ill. ; 28 cm.

        NAMES: Bureau of Mines Technology Transfer Seminars (1982 :
               Pittsburgh, Pa.)
               United States. Bureau of Mines.



------------------------------------------------------------CONTINUED-------
NEXT ACTIONS      Key: ? for help             + to see the next screen
                       B to see a Brief display  - to see the previous screen
                       F to Find other items   Q to Quit
NEXT ACTION?   _                                           LLON1
```

Figure 6.73

```
Your search: Postdisaster surv#                        LONG Display
      Finds: 1 record                                  Screen  2 of  2
---------------------------------------------------------------------------

         SERIES: Information circular (United States. Bureau of Mines) ;
                 8907.

       SUBJECTS: Mine accidents--Congresses.
                 Mine rescue work--Congresses.

          NOTES: Includes bibliographies.




---------------------------------------------------------------------------
NEXT ACTIONS      Key: ? for help            + to see the next screen
                       B to see a Brief display  - to see the previous screen
                       F to Find other items  Q to Quit
NEXT ACTION?  _                                           LLON1
```

Figure 6.74

```
Your search: Citizen Kane                              LONG Display
      Finds: 1 record                                  Screen  1 of  2
---------------------------------------------------------------------------

          TITLE: Citizen Kane [videorecording] / an RKO Radio Picture ; a
                 Mercury production ; Orson Welles, direction, production.
      PUBLISHED: New York, N.Y. : VidAmerica, c1982.
       MATERIAL: 1 videocassette (119 min.) : sd., b&w ; 1/2 in.

          NAMES: Welles, Orson, 1915-
                 VidAmerica (Firm)
                 RKO Radio Pictures, inc.
                 Mercury Productions.

         SERIES: Classic series.

       SUBJECTS: Feature films.


-------------------------------------------------------------CONTINUED-------
NEXT ACTIONS      Key: ? for help            + to see the next screen
                       B to see a Brief display  - to see the previous screen
                       F to Find other items  Q to Quit
NEXT ACTION?  _                                           LLON1
```

Figure 6.75

```
Your search: Citizen Kane                          LONG Display
      Finds: 1 record                              Screen  2 of  2
----------------------------------------------------------------------

      NOTES: Cast: Orson Welles, Joseph Cotton, Agnes Moorehead, Everett
             Sloane.
             Credits: Photography, Gregg Toland ; music, Bernard Herrmann
              ; screenplay, Orson Welles, Herman J. Mankiewicz.
             Originally produced as motion picture in 1941.
             VHS.
             1941 Academy Award for best screenplay.
             Summary: A story of the rise and fall of a great man as the
              result of his accumulation of wealth and subsequent
              isolation from the world. Based on the life of newspaper
              tycoon William Randolph Hearst, this is classic American
              cinema.
             VidAmerica: #903.


----------------------------------------------------------------------
NEXT ACTIONS      Key: ? for help            + to see the next screen
                       B to see a Brief display  - to see the previous screen
                       F to Find other items  Q to Quit
NEXT ACTION?  _                                            LLON1
```

7

Special Design Problems: Nonprint Materials and ISBD Punctuation

Most cataloging in most libraries is for books—printed, monographic, text materials. Most discussion of display and access deals with books, sometimes to the exclusion of other materials. Libraries with substantial nonprint collections frequently fail to integrate those materials into card catalogs, but we may hope for better treatment in online catalogs.

Examples used in earlier chapters deliberately include more nonbooks than books: three monographs, one score, one map, one sound recording, one videocassette and one serial. Statistical summaries in earlier chapters necessarily emphasize books, since roughly 85% of current cataloging activity in RLIN deals with books. That ratio probably holds for most general library collections. If anything, the volume of serials activity in RLIN may be disproportionate to relative collection concentrations. How many libraries have 10% as many serial titles as monographic titles?

This chapter provides more illustrations from several material formats, including archival and manuscript control, deliberately excluded from earlier statistics. We feel that the same display formats can be applied to all forms of material. However, music libraries will certainly find that their displays tend to be much longer than those for the library system as a whole. Archival displays will be long, a direct result of the new level of control available using the USMARC format for archival and manuscript control. All displays discussed or illustrated in this chapter are listed in Table 7.1.

Table 7.1: Displays Discussed in Chapter 7

Display	Name
CLON1	Cardlike long display
CMSX	Cardlike medium display, narrow lines, vertical spacing
CMTN	Cardlike medium display, narrow lines (60 columns)
CMTX	Cardlike display, like CMTN but with modified ISBD punctuation
LLON1	Labeled long display
LMGAT	Labeled medium display, gutter aligned, author/title split
LMGATX	Labeled display, like LMGAT but with modified ISBD punctuation

MATERIAL DIFFERENCES

Some Examples

Most of the figures in this chapter illustrate 12 more bibliographic records from RLIN, selected to show some different aspects of bibliographic displays. Every record appears using each of the following four displays:

1. CMSX, a cardlike medium display with spacing, appears in Figures 7.1 through 7.16. This display was first discussed in Chapter 2; other examples appear in Figures 2.9 through 2.11 and 3.9 through 3.14.
2. LMGAT, a labeled medium display, gutter-aligned and spaced, with title appearing first and with works separated from names, appears in Figures 7.17 through 7.36. This display also appears first in Chapter 2; other examples appear in Figures 2.21 through 2.23 and 4.34 through 4.41.
3. CLON1, a cardlike long display with spacing, appears in Figures 7.37 through 7.60. This display was discussed in Chapter 6, and other examples appear in Figures 6.25 through 6.41.
4. LLON1, a labeled long display, appears in Figures 7.61 through 7.88. This display was also discussed in Chapter 6; other examples appear in Figures 6.58 through 6.75.

The records used for these displays include

- a simple record for a poetry collection with a generic title and an untraced series (Figures 7.1, 7.17, 7.37, 7.61)
- an even simpler record for a very popular novel, typical of the simplest records for books (Figures 7.2, 7.18, 7.38, 7.62)

- a musical score (Figures 7.3, 7.19, 7.39, 7.63–7.64)
- a map with title main entry (Figures 7.4, 7.20–7.21, 7.40–7.41, 7.65–7.66)
- an early sound recording, with extensive notes (Figures 7.5–7.6, 7.22–7.23, 7.42–7.44, 7.67–7.70)
- a straightforward record for a popular sound recording (Figures 7.17, 7.24, 7.45, 7.71)
- a sound recording containing several works by several composers, fairly typical of cataloging for musical anthologies (Figures 7.8–7.10, 7.25–7.27, 7.46–7.49, 7.72–7.76)
- a serial (Figures 7.11, 7.28, 7.50, 7.77)
- two archival and manuscript control records, one for a single sheet of paper (Figures 7.12, 7.29–7.30, 7.51–7.54, 7.78–7.81) and one for a collection of papers (Figures 7.13–7.14, 7.31–7.33, 7.55–7.57, 7.82–7.85)
- a book with a uniform title main entry (Figures 7.15, 7.34, 7.58, 7.86)
- a machine-readable data file, in this case, microcomputer software and accompanying books (Figures 7.16, 7.35–7.36, 7.59–7.60, 7.87–7.88)

These additional illustrations should help show the problems of different material formats and how they work with various display options.

Field Profiles and Display Statistics

Librarians must use professional judgment when deciding what fields to include within a given display. That judgment should take into account the needs of all patrons; it should also include consideration of what is likely to be in the bibliographic items.

In most cases, decisions should be by category (e.g., notes, linking entries, subject headings) rather than by specific field (e.g., to include the 511 as opposed to the 515). Once a category is included, all fields within that category should be included unless there are good reasons not to.

The field occurrence tables in Appendix A provide a current picture of how often specific fields appear, and how long they are likely to be. Those profiles provide the following basic facts:

- Eighteen fields appear more than five times per hundred records measured: 100, 110, 245, 260, 300, 362, 440, 490, 500, 504, 600, 610, 650, 651, 700, 710, and 740.
- Edition statements appear roughly 15 times per hundred records, and average less than 14 characters (but can be over 600 characters).
- Physical descriptions average less than 24 characters.
- Contents notes appear less than five times per hundred records but average 215 characters each. General notes are much more common (64 fields per hundred records) and much shorter (45 characters), but can be more than 1000 characters long.

- Most subject entries are short—32 characters for the average topical heading, with the longest field just over 120 characters.

Many records aren't average, and online catalogs may not be for average collections. Libraries that specialize in maps, music or visual materials may have display problems different from those of libraries in which books predominate.

The brief notes that follow point out a few items taken from Appendix A. An explanation of the tables themselves appears in that appendix.

Books

Books records averaged about 1.7 subject entries, 0.7 added entries, 0.4 series statements and entries and roughly 1.2 notes each. Of fields other than notes, only conference entries, the title statement and corporate series normally require more than one 60-character line per field. The average contents note will require four lines, assuming that there is such a thing as an average contents note.

Archival and Manuscript Control (AMC)

The Research Libraries Group helped to develop the Archival and Manuscript Control (AMC) format and implemented it before it was published by the Library of Congress. By March 1986, RLIN's AMC file included more than 50,000 items; almost 4000 were added or updated during the test period.

AMC records can be quite brief or extremely long and complex. On average, RLIN AMC records have 9.12 subject and added entries, more than three times as many as the average book. AMC records also tend to have very short titles (35 characters) and very long and common summary notes (80 fields per hundred records, 356 characters: an average of six lines, with many requiring a full screen).

AMC records also have special note fields (fields 541 and 583) that provide many of the control facilities. These fields are not normal notes, and generally would not be displayed as part of notes (RLIN online users see them as "ARC segments," with a detailed set of mnemonics replacing subfield delimiters).

Machine-Readable Data File (MRDF)

Relatively little MRDF activity occurred during the six-week test period; only about 75 items were included in the overall tests. We felt that no sound conclusions could be drawn from such a small sample. We used the entire RLIN MRDF file—408 records in February 1986—for special tests.

These records are simpler than most others. We can't determine yet whether that simplicity is in the nature of MRDF cataloging or whether early cataloging reflects predominantly simple items. Fully half of the MRDF activity during the six-week period came from public libraries, compared with about 6% of overall activity. Most of the MRDF records we sampled were for microcomputer software. Except for the technical details access field (753) and note (538), material-specific fields were used lightly.

Maps

Maps included in the test runs show few subject entries, most of those geographic. One special field (the mathematical data area) appears frequently and is fairly long. Maps require about as much display space as books, with a few items requiring multiple screens.

Musical Scores

RLIN may have an unusually high concentration of musical scores—11,681 in the six-week test period, or almost 2% of the full test. One coded field, number of instruments or voices (048), would not be displayed directly but could be significant for retrieval or special purposes. It appears 77 times per hundred records, and is generally quite short. As expected, the records show a high concentration of uniform titles—66 per hundred records.

Serials

The second largest category of materials included 50,132 items during the test period. Serials include more fields and more complexity than any other form of material. Despite the complexity of serials field use, the items don't require unusually lengthy medium displays. Displays that include notes and linking entries may be quite long.

Sound Recordings

Most libraries, particularly public libraries, use the sound recordings part of the USMARC music format much more than they use scores. A significant percentage of sound recordings represents collections; these tend to have long contents notes and many added entries, resulting in an overall average of almost four added entries per item. Additionally, a full two thirds of the 4450 items included in the test have lengthy participant or performer notes, and uniform titles occur often here, as they do in scores.

Every medium display forces at least 30 items to four or more screens; in most cases, at least two or three items need more than 10 screens. The displays are also denser than average.

Visual Material

Films and other visual materials do not seem to pose any special display problems. In some ways, films make some choices easier: 94% of the visual material records in the six-week sample have title main entries, making the choice between main entry and title as the first display item largely irrelevant for films.

ISBD PUNCTUATION

This last section considers a curious issue, sometimes raised as one of the defects of recent cataloging: ISBD punctuation. Some self-styled defenders of the needs of the public denounce ISBD punctuation as a set of arcane markings that somehow reduces the usefulness or clarity of catalogs. A natural reaction to that argument may be amusement. While the space-mark-space pattern of ISBD punctuation is certainly not "normal," it's difficult to believe that patrons are in any way offended or disturbed by its presence.

As part of the Display Testbed design, the programmer attempted to build in the ability to "normalize" ISBD punctuation. The effort was not sophisticated, and did not go to the extreme of scanning all text strings. The algorithm used was quite straightforward, and was applied only at the ends of subfields and fields. If a space appeared followed by one of the ISBD punctuation marks, the space was removed. If the mark was a slash, it was changed to a comma. The two dashes that separate certain elements within some cardlike displays are also eliminated. No other conversions were attempted. In practice, other ISBD punctuation appears to be reasonably normal except for the leading space.

Display CMTX differs from CMTN only in that it uses the ISBD normalization. Figures 7.89 through 7.93 show four of the standard test items in that display; the same records displayed in CMTN appear in Figures 2.6 through 2.8, 3.3 and 3.7. In order to compare labeled displays, see display LMGATX, which differs from LMGAT only in that it uses the ISBD normalization. Figures 7.94 through 7.99 show the same four standard test items; those items displayed using LMGAT appear in Figures 2.21 through 2.23, 4.34, 4.39 and 4.40.

The first and most obvious question is: *If you had not known the difference, would you have noticed the difference?* That is, if figures from LMGATX and LMGAT were intermixed in a set of printed samples, or in an online catalog, would you even be aware of the difference? More significant, would any patron notice the difference, or care about it?

We will not argue the virtues of ISBD punctuation. While proponents may overstate the benefits, even the slightest benefit outweighs what we see as no damage at all. In fact, normalizing ISBD punctuation would require scanning all text strings, not just the ends of fields and subfields (as the d'Indy example shows). Even then, the results might not be consistent or useful. Those who prepare descriptive cataloging following current rules assume the presence of ISBD punctuation; other spacing decisions may depend on that assumption. Some observers prefer the displays with normalized ISBD punctuation; others find it no better and are disturbed by the lack of consistency.

We experimented with ISBD punctuation for quite a few tests. After considering those tests, and especially after showing examples to more typical library patrons, we came to two unanimous conclusions that prevented any attempt to refine the ISBD normalization routines. The first is that refined routines would be more difficult to design and more expensive to implement. The second and far more important conclusion is that we were looking for a solution to a problem that does not exist. ISBD punctuation only annoys those who are specifically looking for things to be annoyed about.

Figure 7.1

```
Your search: Winters, Yvor                         MEDIUM Display
     Finds: 1 record                               Screen  1 of  1
-------------------------------------------------------------------

        Winters, Yvor, 1900-
           Collected poems. [Rev. ed.] Chicago, Swallow Press [c1960]

           146 p. 19 cm.
            (A Swallow paperbook)




        -------------------------------------------------------------
NEXT ACTIONS      Key: ? for help            + to see the next screen
                       L to see a Longer display  - to see the previous screen
                       F to Find other items  Q to Quit
NEXT ACTION?   _                                          CMSX
```

Figure 7.2

```
Your search: Tyler, Anne#                          MEDIUM Display
     Finds: 1 record                               Screen  1 of  1
-------------------------------------------------------------------

        Tyler, Anne.
          The accidental tourist / Anne Tyler. -- 1st ed. -- New
        York : Knopf : Distributed by Random House, 1985.

           355 p. ; 22 cm.




        -------------------------------------------------------------
NEXT ACTIONS      Key: ? for help            + to see the next screen
                       L to see a Longer display  - to see the previous screen
                       F to Find other items  Q to Quit
NEXT ACTION?   _                                          CMSX
```

Figure 7.3

```
Your search: Lora, Antonio Joh#                    MEDIUM Display
     Finds: 1 record                               Screen  1 of  1
---------------------------------------------------------------------

        Lora, Antonio John, 1899-1965.
          In June : song for voice and piano / lyrics [by] Helen
        Field Watson ; music [by] Antonio Lora. -- New York :
        American Composers Alliance, [19--].

          1 score (5 p.)  ; 32 cm.

          1. Songs (Medium voice) with piano. 2. Watson, Helen
        Field--Musical settings. I. Watson, Helen Field.




---------------------------------------------------------------------
NEXT ACTIONS      Key: ? for help          + to see the next screen
                       L to see a Longer display  - to see the previous screen
                       F to Find other items  Q to Quit
NEXT ACTION?  _                                          CMSX
```

Figure 7.4

```
Your search: Plan of the Frenc#                    MEDIUM Display
     Finds: 1 record                               Screen  1 of  1
---------------------------------------------------------------------

        Plan of the French attacks upon the island of Grenada, with
          the engagement between the English fleet under the command
          of Admiral Byron and the French fleet under Count
          d'Estaing, drawn by an officer on board the fleet, July
          1779. J. Luffman, sc. London, J. Haris, 1779. [Chicago,
          Rand McNally and Co., 1974?]

          col. map 22 x 35 cm.

          1. Grenada, Battle of, 1779--Maps--To 1800. 2. Maps,
        Early--Facsimiles. I. Luffman, John, 1756-1846. II. Rand
        McNally and Company.



---------------------------------------------------------------------
NEXT ACTIONS      Key: ? for help          + to see the next screen
                       L to see a Longer display  - to see the previous screen
                       F to Find other items  Q to Quit
NEXT ACTION?  _                                          CMSX
```

Figure 7.5

```
Your search: Schoenberg, Arnol#                    MEDIUM Display
      Finds: 1 record                              Screen  1 of  2
-----------------------------------------------------------------------

        Schoenberg, Arnold, 1874-1951.
          Gurre-Lieder [sound recording] / Schonberg ; (words by
        Jacobsen). -- Camden, N.J. : RCA, 1932.

          14 sound discs : 78 rpm, mono. ; 12 in. + 1 pamphlet (11
        p. ; 24 cm.)

          1. Cantatas, Secular (Mixed voices) with orchestra. 2.
        Jacobsen, J. P. (Jens Peter), 1847-1885--Musical settings.
        I. Stokowski, Leopold. II. Philadelphia Orchestra. III.
        Vreeland, Jeanette. IV. Bampton, Rose. V. Betts, Robert. VI.
        Althouse, Paul. VII. Robofsky, Abrasha. VIII. De Loache,
        Benjamin. IX. Princeton Glee Club. X. Fortnightly Club. XI.
        Mendelssohn Club. XII. Schoenberg, Arnold, 1874-1951.

-----------------------------------------------------CONTINUED-------

NEXT ACTIONS    Key: ? for help            + to see the next screen
                     L to see a Longer display  - to see the previous screen
                     F to Find other items  Q to Quit

NEXT ACTION?  _                                            CMSX
```

Figure 7.6

```
Your search: Schoenberg, Arnol#                    MEDIUM Display
      Finds: 1 record                              Screen  2 of  2
-----------------------------------------------------------------------

        Gurre-Lieder. Libretto. English & German. XIII. Arnold,
        Robert Franz, 1872-1938.





-----------------------------------------------------------------------
NEXT ACTIONS    Key: ? for help            + to see the next screen
                     L to see a Longer display  - to see the previous screen
                     F to Find other items  Q to Quit
NEXT ACTION?  _                                            CMSX
```

Figure 7.7

```
Your search: X                                    MEDIUM Display
     Finds: 1 record                              Screen  1 of  1
-------------------------------------------------------------------

        X (Musical group)
          More fun in the new world [sound recording] / X. -- Los
        Angeles, CA : Elektra, c1983.

          1 sound disc : 33 1/3 rpm, stereo. ; 12 in.

          1. Rock music.




-------------------------------------------------------------------
NEXT ACTIONS      Key: ? for help           + to see the next screen
                       L to see a Longer display   - to see the previous screen
                       F to Find other items   Q to Quit
NEXT ACTION?  _                                            CMSX
```

Figure 7.8

```
Your search: Die Mannheimer Sc#                   MEDIUM Display
     Finds: 1 record                              Screen  1 of  3
-------------------------------------------------------------------

        Die Mannheimer Schule [sound recording] : Musik der
          Fruhklassik = music of the early classical era. -- [West
          Germany] : Archiv Produktion, p1980.

          3 sound discs : 33 1/3 rpm, stereo. ; 12 in.

          1. Orchestral music--18th century. 2. String orchestra
        music--18th century. 3. Music--Germany--18th century. 4.
        Concertos (Violin with string orchestra) 5. Symphonies
        (String orchestra) 6. Concertos (Violoncello with string
        orchestra) 7. Concertos (Oboe with string orchestra) 8.
        Concertos (Flute and string orchestra) I. Holliger, Heinz.
        II. Furi, Thomas. III. Demenga, Thomas. IV. Sax, Manfred. V.
        Schiller, Christoph. VI. Nicolet, Aurele. VII. Cannabich,

------------------------------------------------------CONTINUED-------
NEXT ACTIONS      Key: ? for help           + to see the next screen
                       L to see a Longer display   - to see the previous screen
                       F to Find other items   Q to Quit
NEXT ACTION?  _                                            CMSX
```

Figure 7.9

```
Your search: Die Mannheimer Sc#                    MEDIUM Display
       Finds: 1 record                             Screen  2 of  3
---------------------------------------------------------------------

        Christian, 1731-1798. Sinfonie concertanti, flute, oboe,
        bassoon, orchestra, C major. 1980. VIII. Cannabich,
        Christian, 1731-1798. Symphonies, Bb major. 1980. IX. Filtz,
        Johann Anton, ca. 1730-1760. Concertos, violoncello, string
        orchestra, G major. 1980. X. Holzbauer, Ignaz, 1711-1783.
        Sinfonie concertanti, violin, viola, violoncello, string
        orchestra, A major. 1980. XI. Holzbauer, Ignaz, 1711-1783.
        Symphonies, op. 4. No. 3. 1980. XII. Lebrun, Ludwig August,
        1752-1790. Concertos, oboe, orchestra, D minor. 1980. XIII.
        Richter, Franz Xaver, 1709-1789. Symphonies, string
        orchestra, Bb major. 1980. XIV. Richter, Franz Xaver,
        1709-1789. Concertos, flute, string orchestra, E minor.
        1980. XV. Stamitz, Johann, 1717-1757. Concertos, violin,
        string orchestra, C major. 1980. XVI. Stamitz, Johann,

---------------------------------------------------------CONTINUED-------

NEXT ACTIONS      Key: ? for help          + to see the next screen
                       L to see a Longer display  - to see the previous screen
                       F to Find other items      Q to Quit

NEXT ACTION?  _                                              CMSX
```

Figure 7.10

```
Your search: Die Mannheimer Sc#                    MEDIUM Display
       Finds: 1 record                             Screen  3 of  3
---------------------------------------------------------------------

        1717-1757. Trio sonatas, violins, continuo, op.1. No. 5.
        1980. XVII. Camerata Bern.




---------------------------------------------------------------------

NEXT ACTIONS      Key: ? for help          + to see the next screen
                       L to see a Longer display  - to see the previous screen
                       F to Find other items      Q to Quit

NEXT ACTION?  _                                              CMSX
```

Figure 7.11

```
Your search: U.S. Naval Observ#                    MEDIUM Display
     Finds: 1 record                               Screen  1 of  1
-----------------------------------------------------------------------

        U.S. Naval Observatory time signals. Bulletin A. --
           [Washington, D.C. : The Observatory, 1953-

        v. ; 36 cm.

        1. Time-signals--Periodicals. I. United States Naval
    Obsevatory.




    ------------------------------------------------------------------
NEXT ACTIONS      Key: ? for help          + to see the next screen
                       L to see a Longer display  - to see the previous screen
                       F to Find other items  Q to Quit
NEXT ACTION?   _                                          CMSX
```

Figure 7.12

```
Your search: Schoenberg, Arnol#                    MEDIUM Display
     Finds: 1 record                               Screen  1 of  1
-----------------------------------------------------------------------

        Schoenberg, Arnold, 1874-1951.
           Theater der Dichtung. 23.Mai 1931 / Arnold Schonberg.

        [1] leaf ; 30 cm.

        1. Essays. 2. Poetry. 3. Theater. 4. Kraus, Karl,
    1874-1936. 5. Performance art. 6. Oral interpretation. 7.
    Prospectuses. 8. Schoenberg, Arnold, 1874-1951--Marginalia.
    9. Manuscripts, German--California--Los Angeles. I.
    Schoenberg, Arnold, 1874-1951. ann. II. Kraus, Karl,
    1874-1936. Theater der Dichtung. III. Wedekind, Frank,
    1864-1918.



    ------------------------------------------------------------------
NEXT ACTIONS      Key: ? for help          + to see the next screen
                       L to see a Longer display  - to see the previous screen
                       F to Find other items  Q to Quit
NEXT ACTION?   _                                          CMSX
```

Figure 7.13

```
Your search: Douglass family#                        MEDIUM Display
     Finds: 1 record                                 Screen  1 of  2
--------------------------------------------------------------------------

        Douglass family.
          Papers, 1812-1911.

          8 linear ft., 3 v. [outsize] and 20 items [outsize].

          1. Photoprints. 2. Tintypes. 3. Daguerreotypes. 4. Detroit
       (Mich.). Board of Water Commissioners. 5. Flat River (Mich.)
       6. Grosse Ile (Mich.) 7. Houghton, Douglass, 1809-1845. 8.
       Lawyers. 9. Michigan Central Railroad. 10. Michigan,
       Northern Peninsula. 11. Welles family. I. Campbell, James V.
       (James Valentine), 1823-1890. II. Crapo, Henry Howland,
       1804-1869. III. Douglas, Silas Hamilton, 1816-1890. IV.
       Douglass, Benjamin. V. Douglass, Samuel Townsend, 1814-1898.
       VI. Duffield, George, 1794-1868. VII. Kearsley, Jonathan,

---------------------------------------------------------CONTINUED-------

NEXT ACTIONS      Key: ? for help           + to see the next screen
                       L to see a Longer display  - to see the previous screen
                       F to Find other items    Q to Quit

NEXT ACTION?  _                                                    CMSX
```

Figure 7.14

```
Your search: Douglass family#                        MEDIUM Display
     Finds: 1 record                                 Screen  2 of  2
--------------------------------------------------------------------------

          1786-1859. VIII. Pitcher, Zina, 1797-1872. IX. Sager, Abram,
       1810-1877. X. Sibley, Joseph. XI. Tappan, Henry Philip,
       1805-1881. XII. Walker, Edward Carey, 1820-1894. XIII.
       Walker, Henry Nelson, 1811-1886. XIV. Williams, George
       Palmer, 1802-1881.












------------------------------------------------------------------------

NEXT ACTIONS      Key: ? for help           + to see the next screen
                       L to see a Longer display  - to see the previous screen
                       F to Find other items    Q to Quit

NEXT ACTION?  _                                                    CMSX
```

Figure 7.15

```
Your search: Bible. English. A#                    MEDIUM Display
     Finds: 1 record                              Screen  1 of  1
---------------------------------------------------------------------

          Bible. English. Authorized. Selections. 1980.
            Meredith's book of Bible lists / J. L. Meredith. --
          Minneapolis, Minn. : Bethany Fellowship, c1980.

            287 p. : ill. ; 22 cm.

            1. Bible--Indexes. I. Meredith, J. L. (Joel L.), 1935-




---------------------------------------------------------------------
NEXT ACTIONS      Key: ? for help          + to see the next screen
                       L to see a Longer display  - to see the previous screen
                       F to Find other items   Q to Quit
NEXT ACTION?  _                                            CMSX
```

Figure 7.16

```
Your search: Spikell, Mark A#                     MEDIUM Display
     Finds: 1 record                              Screen  1 of  1
---------------------------------------------------------------------

          Spikell, Mark A.
            Brain ticklers, Apple II, IIe edition [machine-readable
          data file] : mathematical problem-solving with the
          microcomputer / Mark A. Spikell & Stephen L. Snover. --
          Englewood Cliffs, N.J. : Prentice-Hall, c1983.

            1 program file on 1 computer disk ; 5 1/4 in. +
          instructions (iv, 6 p.) + 2 books in loose-leaf binder.

            1. Mathematics--Problems, exercises, etc. 2. Mathematics--
          Computer programs. 3. Apple computer--Programming. 4.
          Problem solving--Data processing. I. Snover, Stephen L.


---------------------------------------------------------------------
NEXT ACTIONS      Key: ? for help          + to see the next screen
                       L to see a Longer display  - to see the previous screen
                       F to Find other items   Q to Quit
NEXT ACTION?  _                                            CMSX
```

Figure 7.17

```
Your search: Collected poems#                    MEDIUM Display
     Finds: 1 record                             Screen  1 of  1
---------------------------------------------------------------------


        TITLE: Collected poems.
      EDITION: [Rev. ed.]
    PUBLISHED: Chicago, Swallow Press [c1960]
     MATERIAL: 146 p. 19 cm.


        NAMES: Winters, Yvor, 1900-


       SERIES: A Swallow paperbook.






---------------------------------------------------------------------
NEXT ACTIONS      Key: ? for help          + to see the next screen
                       L to see a Longer display  - to see the previous screen
                       F to Find other items  Q to Quit

NEXT ACTION?  _                                            LMGAT
```

Figure 7.18

```
Your search: The accidental to#                  MEDIUM Display
     Finds: 1 record                             Screen  1 of  1
---------------------------------------------------------------------


        TITLE: The accidental tourist / Anne Tyler.
      EDITION: 1st ed.
    PUBLISHED: New York : Knopf : Distributed by Random House, 1985.
     MATERIAL: 355 p. ; 22 cm.


        NAMES: Tyler, Anne.







---------------------------------------------------------------------
NEXT ACTIONS      Key: ? for help          + to see the next screen
                       L to see a Longer display  - to see the previous screen
                       F to Find other items  Q to Quit

NEXT ACTION?  _                                            LMGAT
```

Figure 7.19

```
Your search: In June : song fo#                    MEDIUM Display
     Finds: 1 record                               Screen  1 of  1
------------------------------------------------------------------------


        TITLE: In June : song for voice and piano / lyrics [by] Helen Field
               Watson ; music [by] Antonio Lora.
    PUBLISHED: New York : American Composers Alliance, [19--].
     MATERIAL: 1 score (5 p.)  ; 32 cm.

        NAMES: Lora, Antonio John, 1899-1965.
               Watson, Helen Field.

     SUBJECTS: Songs (Medium voice) with piano.
               Watson, Helen Field--Musical settings.




------------------------------------------------------------------------
NEXT ACTIONS      Key: ? for help           + to see the next screen
                       L to see a Longer display  - to see the previous screen
                       F to Find other items  Q to Quit
NEXT ACTION?  _                                              LMGAT
```

Figure 7.20

```
Your search: Plan of the Frenc#                    MEDIUM Display
     Finds: 1 record                               Screen  1 of  2
------------------------------------------------------------------------


        TITLE: Plan of the French attacks upon the island of Grenada, with
               the engagement between the English fleet under the command
               of Admiral Byron and the French fleet under Count
               d'Estaing, drawn by an officer on board the fleet, July
               1779. J. Luffman, sc.
    PUBLISHED: London, J. Haris, 1779. [Chicago, Rand McNally and Co.,
               1974?]
     MATERIAL: col. map 22 x 35 cm.

        NAMES: Luffman, John, 1756-1846.
               Rand McNally and Company.

     SUBJECTS: Grenada, Battle of, 1779--Maps--To 1800.


------------------------------------------------------CONTINUED-------
NEXT ACTIONS      Key: ? for help           + to see the next screen
                       L to see a Longer display  - to see the previous screen
                       F to Find other items  Q to Quit
NEXT ACTION?  _                                              LMGAT
```

Figure 7.21

```
Your search: Plan of the Frenc#                      MEDIUM Display
     Finds: 1 record                                 Screen  2 of  2
------------------------------------------------------------------------

            Maps, Early--Facsimiles.









------------------------------------------------------------------------
NEXT ACTIONS       Key: ? for help              + to see the next screen
                        L to see a Longer display - to see the previous screen
                        F to Find other items    Q to Quit
NEXT ACTION?  _                                           LMGAT
```

Figure 7.22

```
Your search: Gurre-Lieder                            MEDIUM Display
     Finds: 1 record                                 Screen  1 of  2
------------------------------------------------------------------------
        TITLE: Gurre-Lieder [sound recording] / Schonberg ; (words by
               Jacobsen).
    PUBLISHED: Camden, N.J. : RCA, 1932.
     MATERIAL: 14 sound discs : 78 rpm, mono. ; 12 in. + 1 pamphlet (11 p.
               ; 24 cm.)

        NAMES: Schoenberg, Arnold, 1874-1951.
               Stokowski, Leopold.
               Philadelphia Orchestra.
               Vreeland, Jeanette.
               Bampton, Rose.
               Betts, Robert.
               Althouse, Paul.
               Robofsky, Abrasha.

-----------------------------------------------------------CONTINUED-------
NEXT ACTIONS       Key: ? for help              + to see the next screen
                        L to see a Longer display - to see the previous screen
                        F to Find other items    Q to Quit
NEXT ACTION?  _                                           LMGAT
```

Figure 7.23

```
Your search: Gurre-Lieder                          MEDIUM Display
     Finds: 1 record                               Screen  2 of  2
------------------------------------------------------------------------

                 De Loache, Benjamin.
                 Princeton Glee Club.
                 Fortnightly Club.
                 Mendelssohn Club.
                 Arnold, Robert Franz, 1872-1938.

     SUBJECTS: Cantatas, Secular (Mixed voices) with orchestra.
               Jacobsen, J. P. (Jens Peter), 1847-1885--Musical settings.

        WORKS: Schoenberg, Arnold, 1874-1951. Gurre-Lieder. Libretto.
               English & German.



------------------------------------------------------------------------
NEXT ACTIONS     Key: ? for help            + to see the next screen
                      L to see a Longer display  - to see the previous screen
                      F to Find other items  Q to Quit
NEXT ACTION?  _                                          LMGAT
```

Figure 7.24

```
Your search: More fun in the n#                    MEDIUM Display
     Finds: 1 record                               Screen  1 of  1
------------------------------------------------------------------------

         TITLE: More fun in the new world [sound recording] / X.
     PUBLISHED: Los Angeles, CA : Elektra, c1983.
      MATERIAL: 1 sound disc : 33 1/3 rpm, stereo. ; 12 in.

         NAMES: X (Musical group)

      SUBJECTS: Rock music.



------------------------------------------------------------------------
NEXT ACTIONS     Key: ? for help            + to see the next screen
                      L to see a Longer display  - to see the previous screen
                      F to Find other items  Q to Quit
NEXT ACTION?  _                                          LMGAT
```

Figure 7.25

```
Your search: Die Mannheimer Sc#                       MEDIUM Display
     Finds: 1 record                                  Screen  1 of  3
-----------------------------------------------------------------------

           TITLE: Die Mannheimer Schule [sound recording] : Musik der
                  Fruhklassik = music of the early classical era.
       PUBLISHED: [West Germany] : Archiv Produktion, p1980.
        MATERIAL: 3 sound discs : 33 1/3 rpm, stereo. ; 12 in.

           NAMES: Holliger, Heinz.
                  Furi, Thomas.
                  Demenga, Thomas.
                  Sax, Manfred.
                  Schiller, Christoph.
                  Nicolet, Aurele.
                  Camerata Bern.

        SUBJECTS: Orchestral music--18th century.

-------------------------------------------------------CONTINUED-------

NEXT ACTIONS       Key: ? for help           + to see the next screen
                        L to see a Longer display  - to see the previous screen
                        F to Find other items      Q to Quit
NEXT ACTION?  _                                               LMGAT
```

Figure 7.26

```
Your search: Die Mannheimer Sc#                       MEDIUM Display
     Finds: 1 record                                  Screen  2 of  3
-----------------------------------------------------------------------

               String orchestra music--18th century.
               Music--Germany--18th century.
               Concertos (Violin with string orchestra)
               Symphonies (String orchestra)
               Concertos (Violoncello with string orchestra)
               Concertos (Oboe with string orchestra)
               Concertos (Flute and string orchestra)

           WORKS: Cannabich, Christian, 1731-1798. Sinfonie concertanti,
                  flute, oboe, bassoon, orchestra, C major. 1980.
                  Cannabich, Christian, 1731-1798. Symphonies, Bb major. 1980.
                  Filtz, Johann Anton, ca. 1730-1760. Concertos, violoncello,
                  string orchestra, G major. 1980.

-------------------------------------------------------CONTINUED-------

NEXT ACTIONS       Key: ? for help           + to see the next screen
                        L to see a Longer display  - to see the previous screen
                        F to Find other items      Q to Quit
NEXT ACTION?  _                                               LMGAT
```

Figure 7.27

```
Your search: Die Mannheimer Sc#                    MEDIUM Display
      Finds: 1 record                              Screen  3 of  3
----------------------------------------------------------------------

             Holzbauer, Ignaz, 1711-1783. Sinfonie concertanti, violin,
                viola, violoncello, string orchestra, A major. 1980.
             Holzbauer, Ignaz, 1711-1783. Symphonies, op. 4. No. 3. 1980.
             Lebrun, Ludwig August, 1752-1790. Concertos, oboe,
                orchestra, D minor. 1980.
             Richter, Franz Xaver, 1709-1789. Symphonies, string
                orchestra, Bb major. 1980.
             Richter, Franz Xaver, 1709-1789. Concertos, flute, string
                orchestra, E minor. 1980.
             Stamitz, Johann, 1717-1757. Concertos, violin, string
                orchestra, C major. 1980.
             Stamitz, Johann, 1717-1757. Trio sonatas, violins, continuo,
                op.1. No. 5. 1980.


----------------------------------------------------------------------
NEXT ACTIONS     Key: ? for help          + to see the next screen
                   L to see a Longer display  - to see the previous screen
                   F to Find other items   Q to Quit
NEXT ACTION?  _                                           LMGAT
```

Figure 7.28

```
Your search: U.S. Naval Observ#                    MEDIUM Display
      Finds: 1 record                              Screen  1 of  1
----------------------------------------------------------------------

        TITLE: U.S. Naval Observatory time signals. Bulletin A.
    PUBLISHED: [Washington, D.C. : The Observatory, 1953-
     MATERIAL: v. ; 36 cm.

        NAMES: United States Naval Obsevatory.

     SUBJECTS: Time-signals--Periodicals.




----------------------------------------------------------------------
NEXT ACTIONS     Key: ? for help          + to see the next screen
                   L to see a Longer display  - to see the previous screen
                   F to Find other items   Q to Quit
NEXT ACTION?  _                                           LMGAT
```

Figure 7.29

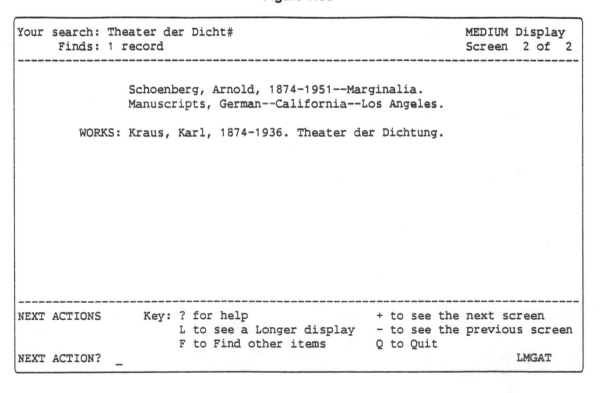

```
Your search: Theater der Dicht#                          MEDIUM Display
     Finds: 1 record                                     Screen  1 of  2
------------------------------------------------------------------------


        TITLE: Theater der Dichtung. 23.Mai 1931 / Arnold Schonberg.
     MATERIAL: [1] leaf ; 30 cm.

        NAMES: Schoenberg, Arnold, 1874-1951.
               Schoenberg, Arnold, 1874-1951. ann.
               Wedekind, Frank, 1864-1918.

     SUBJECTS: Essays.
               Poetry.
               Theater.
               Kraus, Karl, 1874-1936.
               Performance art.
               Oral interpretation.
               Prospectuses.


----------------------------------------------------------CONTINUED-------
NEXT ACTIONS      Key: ? for help              + to see the next screen
                       L to see a Longer display  - to see the previous screen
                       F to Find other items    Q to Quit
NEXT ACTION?  _                                             LMGAT
```

Figure 7.30

```
Your search: Theater der Dicht#                          MEDIUM Display
     Finds: 1 record                                     Screen  2 of  2
------------------------------------------------------------------------


           Schoenberg, Arnold, 1874-1951--Marginalia.
           Manuscripts, German--California--Los Angeles.

      WORKS: Kraus, Karl, 1874-1936. Theater der Dichtung.






--------------------------------------------------------------------
NEXT ACTIONS      Key: ? for help              + to see the next screen
                       L to see a Longer display  - to see the previous screen
                       F to Find other items    Q to Quit
NEXT ACTION?  _                                             LMGAT
```

Figure 7.31

```
Your search: Papers, 1812-1911#                    MEDIUM Display
     Finds: 1 record                               Screen  1 of  3
------------------------------------------------------------------------

        TITLE: Papers, 1812-1911.
     MATERIAL: 8 linear ft., 3 v. [outsize] and 20 items [outsize].

        NAMES: Douglass family.
               Campbell, James V. (James Valentine), 1823-1890.
               Crapo, Henry Howland, 1804-1869.
               Douglas, Silas Hamilton, 1816-1890.
               Douglass, Benjamin.
               Douglass, Samuel Townsend, 1814-1898.
               Duffield, George, 1794-1868.
               Kearsley, Jonathan, 1786-1859.
               Pitcher, Zina, 1797-1872.
               Sager, Abram, 1810-1877.
               Sibley, Joseph.

-----------------------------------------------------CONTINUED-------
NEXT ACTIONS      Key: ? for help              + to see the next screen
                       L to see a Longer display - to see the previous screen
                       F to Find other items   Q to Quit
NEXT ACTION?   _                                            LMGAT
```

Figure 7.32

```
Your search: Papers, 1812-1911#                    MEDIUM Display
     Finds: 1 record                               Screen  2 of  3
------------------------------------------------------------------------

               Tappan, Henry Philip, 1805-1881.
               Walker, Edward Carey, 1820-1894.
               Walker, Henry Nelson, 1811-1886.
               Williams, George Palmer, 1802-1881.

     SUBJECTS: Photoprints.
               Tintypes.
               Daguerreotypes.
               Detroit (Mich.). Board of Water Commissioners.
               Flat River (Mich.)
               Grosse Ile (Mich.)
               Houghton, Douglass, 1809-1845.
               Lawyers.
               Michigan Central Railroad.

-----------------------------------------------------CONTINUED-------
NEXT ACTIONS      Key: ? for help              + to see the next screen
                       L to see a Longer display - to see the previous screen
                       F to Find other items   Q to Quit
NEXT ACTION?   _                                            LMGAT
```

Figure 7.33

```
Your search: Papers, 1812-1911#                          MEDIUM Display
      Finds: 1 record                                    Screen  3 of  3
-----------------------------------------------------------------------

                    Michigan, Northern Peninsula.
                    Welles family.




















-----------------------------------------------------------------------
NEXT ACTIONS      Key: ? for help               + to see the next screen
                       L to see a Longer display - to see the previous screen
                       F to Find other items    Q to Quit
NEXT ACTION?   _                                               LMGAT
```

Figure 7.34

```
Your search: Meredith's book o#                          MEDIUM Display
      Finds: 1 record                                    Screen  1 of  1
-----------------------------------------------------------------------

         TITLE: Meredith's book of Bible lists / J. L. Meredith.
     PUBLISHED: Minneapolis, Minn. : Bethany Fellowship, c1980.
      MATERIAL: 287 p. : ill. ; 22 cm.

         NAMES: Meredith, J. L. (Joel L.), 1935-

      SUBJECTS: Bible--Indexes.

         WORKS: Bible. English. Authorized. Selections. 1980.




-----------------------------------------------------------------------
NEXT ACTIONS      Key: ? for help               + to see the next screen
                       L to see a Longer display - to see the previous screen
                       F to Find other items    Q to Quit
NEXT ACTION?   _                                               LMGAT
```

Figure 7.35

```
Your search: Brain ticklers, A#                       MEDIUM Display
       Finds: 1 record                                Screen  1 of  2
--------------------------------------------------------------------------

          TITLE: Brain ticklers, Apple II, IIe edition [machine-readable data
                 file] : mathematical problem-solving with the
                 microcomputer / Mark A. Spikell & Stephen L. Snover.
      PUBLISHED: Englewood Cliffs, N.J. : Prentice-Hall, c1983.
       MATERIAL: 1 program file on 1 computer disk ; 5 1/4 in. + instructions
                 (iv, 6 p.) + 2 books in loose-leaf binder.


          NAMES: Spikell, Mark A.
                 Snover, Stephen L.


       SUBJECTS: Mathematics--Problems, exercises, etc.
                 Mathematics--Computer programs.
                 Apple computer--Programming.



--------------------------------------------------------CONTINUED-------
NEXT ACTIONS     Key: ? for help            + to see the next screen
                      L to see a Longer display   - to see the previous screen
                      F to Find other items  Q to Quit
NEXT ACTION?  _                                                LMGAT
```

Figure 7.36

```
Your search: Brain ticklers, A#                       MEDIUM Display
       Finds: 1 record                                Screen  2 of  2
--------------------------------------------------------------------------
          Problem solving--Data processing.













--------------------------------------------------------------------------
NEXT ACTIONS     Key: ? for help            + to see the next screen
                      L to see a Longer display   - to see the previous screen
                      F to Find other items  Q to Quit
NEXT ACTION?  _                                                LMGAT
```

Figure 7.37

```
Your search: Winters, Yvor, 19#                    LONG Display
       Finds: 1 record                             Screen  1 of  1
------------------------------------------------------------------------

        Winters, Yvor, 1900-
          Collected poems. [Rev. ed.] Chicago, Swallow Press [c1960]

          146 p. 19 cm.




------------------------------------------------------------------------
NEXT ACTIONS      Key: ? for help            + to see the next screen
                       B to see a Brief display    - to see the previous screen
                       F to Find other items       Q to Quit
NEXT ACTION?   _                                            CLON1
```

Figure 7.38

```
Your search: Tyler, Anne#                          LONG Display
       Finds: 1 record                             Screen  1 of  1
------------------------------------------------------------------------

        Tyler, Anne.
          The accidental tourist / Anne Tyler. -- 1st ed. -- New
        York : Knopf : Distributed by Random House, 1985.

          355 p. ; 22 cm.




------------------------------------------------------------------------
NEXT ACTIONS      Key: ? for help            + to see the next screen
                       B to see a Brief display    - to see the previous screen
                       F to Find other items       Q to Quit
NEXT ACTION?   _                                            CLON1
```

Figure 7.39

```
Your search: Lora, Antonio Joh#                    LONG Display
      Finds: 1 record                               Screen  1 of  1
-----------------------------------------------------------------------

           Lora, Antonio John, 1899-1965.
             In June : song for voice and piano / lyrics [by] Helen
           Field Watson ; music [by] Antonio Lora. -- New York :
           American Composers Alliance, [19--].

             1 score (5 p.)  ; 32 cm.

           For medium voice and piano.
           Cover title.
           Reproduced from holograph.
           Duration: 2:45.

             1. Songs (Medium voice) with piano. 2. Watson, Helen
           Field--Musical settings. I. Watson, Helen Field.

-----------------------------------------------------------------------
NEXT ACTIONS      Key: ? for help           + to see the next screen
                       B to see a Brief display  - to see the previous screen
                       F to Find other items  Q to Quit
NEXT ACTION?  _                                         CLON1
```

Figure 7.40

```
Your search: Plan of the Frenc#                    LONG Display
      Finds: 1 record                               Screen  1 of  2
-----------------------------------------------------------------------

           Plan of the French attacks upon the island of Grenada, with
             the engagement between the English fleet under the command
             of Admiral Byron and the French fleet under Count
             d'Estaing, drawn by an officer on board the fleet, July
             1779. J. Luffman, sc. London, J. Haris, 1779. [Chicago,
             Rand McNally and Co., 1974?]

           col. map 22 x 35 cm.

           Scale ca. 1:14,700.
           Facsimile.
           Relief shown by hachures.
           Oriented with north to the left.
           Pictorial map.

--------------------------------------------------------CONTINUED-------
NEXT ACTIONS      Key: ? for help           + to see the next screen
                       B to see a Brief display  - to see the previous screen
                       F to Find other items  Q to Quit
NEXT ACTION?  _                                         CLON1
```

Figure 7.41

```
Your search: Plan of the Frenc#                       LONG Display
      Finds: 1 record                               Screen  2 of  2
-----------------------------------------------------------------------

         Includes descriptive notes.

         1. Grenada, Battle of, 1779--Maps--To 1800. 2. Maps,
      Early--Facsimiles. I. Luffman, John, 1756-1846. II. Rand
      McNally and Company.




-----------------------------------------------------------------------
NEXT ACTIONS      Key: ? for help            + to see the next screen
                       B to see a Brief display   - to see the previous screen
                       F to Find other items   Q to Quit
NEXT ACTION?   _                                           CLON1
```

Figure 7.42

```
Your search: Schoenberg, Arnol#                       LONG Display
      Finds: 1 record                               Screen  1 of  3
-----------------------------------------------------------------------

         Schoenberg, Arnold, 1874-1951.
           Gurre-Lieder [sound recording] / Schonberg ; (words by
         Jacobsen). -- Camden, N.J. : RCA, 1932.

         14 sound discs : 78 rpm, mono. ; 12 in. + 1 pamphlet (11
         p. ; 24 cm.)

           RCA Victor M127, 7524-7537 (side 1: Mx. d72621, side 2: Mx
         .b71674, side 5: Mx. a71677, side 6: Mx. a71678, side 7: Mx.
         71679, side 8: Mx. a71680, side 9: Mx. a71681, side 10: Mx.
         a71682, side 11: Mx. a71683, side 12: Mx. a71684, side 13:
         Mx. a71685, side 14: Mx. a71686, side 15: Mx. a71687, side
         16: Mx. a71688, side 17: Mx. a71689, side 18: Mx. a71690,
         side 19: Mx. a71691, side 20: Mx. a71692, side 21: Mx.

--------------------------------------------------------CONTINUED-------
NEXT ACTIONS      Key: ? for help            + to see the next screen
                       B to see a Brief display   - to see the previous screen
                       F to Find other items   Q to Quit
NEXT ACTION?   _                                           CLON1
```

Figure 7.43

```
Your search: Schoenberg, Arnol#                    LONG Display
       Finds: 1 record                             Screen  2 of  3
----------------------------------------------------------------------

        a71693, side 22: Mx. e71694. side 23: Mx. a71695, side 24:
     Mx. a71696, side 25: Mx. a71712, side 26: Mx. a71713)
        Cantata for speaker, solo voices (SATTB), one chorus
     (SSAATTBB), three choruses (TTBB), and large orchestra.
        Sung in German.
        Jeanette Vreeland (Tove) ; Rose Bampton (Waldtaube) ; Paul
     Althouse (Waldemar) ; Robert Betts (Klaus-Narr) ; Abrasha
     Robofsky (Bauer) ; Benjamin de Loache, narrator; Princeton
     Glee Club; Fortnightly Club; Mendelssohn Club; Philadelphia
     Orchestra; Leopold Stokowski, conductor.
        Recorded April 11, 1932 at the Metropolitan Opera House,
     Philadelphia.



-------------------------------------------------------CONTINUED-------

NEXT ACTIONS      Key: ? for help          + to see the next screen
                       B to see a Brief display  - to see the previous screen
                       F to Find other items   Q to Quit
NEXT ACTION?  _                                         CLON1
```

Figure 7.44

```
Your search: Schoenberg, Arnol#                    LONG Display
       Finds: 1 record                             Screen  3 of  3
----------------------------------------------------------------------

        1. Cantatas, Secular (Mixed voices) with orchestra. 2.
     Jacobsen, J. P. (Jens Peter), 1847-1885--Musical settings.
     I. Stokowski, Leopold. II. Philadelphia Orchestra. III.
     Vreeland, Jeanette. IV. Bampton, Rose. V. Betts, Robert. VI.
     Althouse, Paul. VII. Robofsky, Abrasha. VIII. De Loache,
     Benjamin. IX. Princeton Glee Club. X. Fortnightly Club. XI.
     Mendelssohn Club. XII. Schoenberg, Arnold, 1874-1951.
     Gurre-Lieder. Libretto. English & German. XIII. Arnold,
     Robert Franz, 1872-1938.






--------------------------------------------------------------------

NEXT ACTIONS      Key: ? for help          + to see the next screen
                       B to see a Brief display  - to see the previous screen
                       F to Find other items   Q to Quit
NEXT ACTION?  _                                         CLON1
```

Figure 7.45

```
Your search: X                                    LONG Display
     Finds: 1 record                              Screen  1 of  1
--------------------------------------------------------------------

        X (Musical group)
         More fun in the new world [sound recording] / X. -- Los
        Angeles, CA : Elektra, c1983.

          1 sound disc : 33 1/3 rpm, stereo. ; 12 in.

          1. Rock music.




--------------------------------------------------------------------
NEXT ACTIONS      Key: ? for help         + to see the next screen
                       B to see a Brief display  - to see the previous screen
                       F to Find other items     Q to Quit
NEXT ACTION?  _                                             CLON1
```

Figure 7.46

```
Your search: Die Mannheimer Sc#                   LONG Display
     Finds: 1 record                              Screen  1 of  4
--------------------------------------------------------------------

        Die Mannheimer Schule [sound recording] : Musik der
          Fruhklassik = music of the early classical era. -- [West
        Germany] : Archiv Produktion, p1980.

        3 sound discs : 33 1/3 rpm, stereo. ; 12 in.

        Title from container.
        Various soloists ; Camerata Bern ; Thomas Furi, conductor.
        Recorded in the Konservatorium Bern, Sept. 24-29, 1979
        (1st-4th, 7th-8th, 10th works) and DRS-Radio-Studio, Bern,
        Feb. 12-15, 1980 (the remainder)
         Program notes by Heinz Becker and notes on the ensemble by
        Urs Frauchinger in German with English and French
        translations (12 p. : ill.) laid in container.

-----------------------------------------------------CONTINUED-------
NEXT ACTIONS      Key: ? for help         + to see the next screen
                       B to see a Brief display  - to see the previous screen
                       F to Find other items     Q to Quit
NEXT ACTION?  _                                             CLON1
```

Figure 7.47

```
Your search: Die Mannheimer Sc#                    LONG Display
      Finds: 1 record                              Screen  2 of  4
----------------------------------------------------------------

      Contents: Sinfonia B-Dur (10:37) ; Konzert fur Flote und
   Streichorchester e-Moll (Aurele Nicolet, flute) (19:30) /
   Franz Xaver Richter -- Konzert fur Violine und
   Streichorchester C-Dur (Thomas Furi, violin) (15:47) ;
   Orchestertrio B-Dur op. 1, 5 (14:47) / Johann Stamitz --
   Konzert fur Violoncello und Streichorchester G-Dur / Anton
   Filtz (Thomas Demenga, violoncello) (21:19) -- Sinfonia
   concertante A-Dur, Vl. Solo, Vla. Solo, Vlc. Solo (Thomas
   Furi, violin ; Christoph Schiller, viola ; Thomas Demenga,
   violoncello) (15:16) ; Sinfonia Es-Dur op. 4, 3 (15:06) /
   Ignaz Holzbauer -- Sinfonia concertante C-Dur, Fl. Solo, Ob.
   Solo, Fag. Solo (Aurele Nicolet, flute ; Heinz Holliger,
   oboe ; Manfred Sax, bassoon) (8:40) ; Sinfonia B-dur (16:41)
   / Christian Cannabich -- Konzert fur Oboe und Orchester

-------------------------------------------------CONTINUED-------
NEXT ACTIONS     Key: ? for help          + to see the next screen
                      B to see a Brief display  - to see the previous screen
                      F to Find other items     Q to Quit
NEXT ACTION?  _                                          CLON1
```

Figure 7.48

```
Your search: Die Mannheimer Sc#                    LONG Display
      Finds: 1 record                              Screen  3 of  4
----------------------------------------------------------------

   d-Moll / Ludwig August Lebrun (Heinz Holliger, oboe) (19:32)

      1. Orchestral music--18th century. 2. String orchestra
   music--18th century. 3. Music--Germany--18th century. 4.
   Concertos (Violin with string orchestra) 5. Symphonies
   (String orchestra) 6. Concertos (Violoncello with string
   orchestra) 7. Concertos (Oboe with string orchestra) 8.
   Concertos (Flute and string orchestra) I. Holliger, Heinz.
   II. Furi, Thomas. III. Demenga, Thomas. IV. Sax, Manfred. V.
   Schiller, Christoph. VI. Nicolet, Aurele. VII. Cannabich,
   Christian, 1731-1798. Sinfonie concertanti, flute, oboe,
   bassoon, orchestra, C major. 1980. VIII. Cannabich,
   Christian, 1731-1798. Symphonies, Bb major. 1980. IX. Filtz,
   Johann Anton, ca. 1730-1760. Concertos, violoncello, string

-------------------------------------------------CONTINUED-------
NEXT ACTIONS     Key: ? for help          + to see the next screen
                      B to see a Brief display  - to see the previous screen
                      F to Find other items     Q to Quit
NEXT ACTION?  _                                          CLON1
```

Figure 7.49

```
Your search: Die Mannheimer Sc#                    LONG Display
      Finds: 1 record                              Screen   4 of   4
------------------------------------------------------------------------

         orchestra, G major. 1980. X. Holzbauer, Ignaz, 1711-1783.
         Sinfonie concertanti, violin, viola, violoncello, string
         orchestra, A major. 1980. XI. Holzbauer, Ignaz, 1711-1783.
         Symphonies, op. 4. No. 3. 1980. XII. Lebrun, Ludwig August,
         1752-1790. Concertos, oboe, orchestra, D minor. 1980. XIII.
         Richter, Franz Xaver, 1709-1789. Symphonies, string
         orchestra, Bb major. 1980. XIV. Richter, Franz Xaver,
         1709-1789. Concertos, flute, string orchestra, E minor.
         1980. XV. Stamitz, Johann, 1717-1757. Concertos, violin,
         string orchestra, C major. 1980. XVI. Stamitz, Johann,
         1717-1757. Trio sonatas, violins, continuo, op.1. No. 5.
         1980. XVII. Camerata Bern.



------------------------------------------------------------------------
NEXT ACTIONS      Key: ? for help          + to see the next screen
                       B to see a Brief display  - to see the previous screen
                       F to Find other items     Q to Quit
NEXT ACTION?   _                                          CLON1
```

Figure 7.50

```
Your search: U.S. Naval Observ#                    LONG Display
      Finds: 1 record                              Screen   1 of   1
------------------------------------------------------------------------

         U.S. Naval Observatory time signals. Bulletin A.
         -- 1 (2 June 1953)-
         -- [Washington, D.C. : The Observatory, 1953-

         v. ; 36 cm.

         Irregular.
         Title from caption.
         Merged with: U.S. Naval Observatory time signals. Bulletin
         B, to form: Time signals.

         1. Time-signals--Periodicals. I. United States Naval
         Obsevatory.


------------------------------------------------------------------------
NEXT ACTIONS      Key: ? for help          + to see the next screen
                       B to see a Brief display  - to see the previous screen
                       F to Find other items     Q to Quit
NEXT ACTION?   _                                          CLON1
```

Figure 7.51

```
Your search: Schoenberg, Arnol#                    LONG Display
     Finds: 1 record                              Screen  1 of  4
---------------------------------------------------------------------

        Schoenberg, Arnold, 1874-1951.
          Theater der Dichtung. 23.Mai 1931 / Arnold Schonberg.

        [1] leaf ; 30 cm.
        Holograph signed (black ink, blue and pink pencil),
      printed.

        Bears Schoenberg's classification: "Ku 321".
        In German fraktur.
        On a printed 2 page circular by Karl Kraus with the same
      title.  Edges of leaf reinforced with strips of music
      manuscript paper, left side punched with 2 holes.
        References: Rufer. Schriften IIE24.


-------------------------------------------------------CONTINUED-------
NEXT ACTIONS      Key: ? for help              + to see the next screen
                       B to see a Brief display - to see the previous screen
                       F to Find other items    Q to Quit

NEXT ACTION?  _                                          CLON1
```

Figure 7.52

```
Your search: Schoenberg, Arnol#                    LONG Display
     Finds: 1 record                              Screen  2 of  4
---------------------------------------------------------------------

        References: Christensen, Jean & Jesper. From Arnold
      Schoenberg's Literary Legacy: A Catalog of Neglected Items.
      Detroit: Detroit Information Coordinators, [1986]. Appendix
      II.
        Microfiche 56.
        Summary: The circular is a call for money for the founding
      of an ensemble "Theater der Dichtung" under the leadership
      of Karl Kraus.  Frank Wedekind comments on Kraus in the
      circular.  Schoenberg's lengthy annotations in the margins
      criticize the circular.  First he is offended that there is
      no personal salutation.  He says the ensemble is a hopeless
      venture even under the leadership of Kraus.  He discusses
      performing and concludes that rather than performing
      already-proven works, this "theater" should concentrate on

-------------------------------------------------------CONTINUED-------
NEXT ACTIONS      Key: ? for help              + to see the next screen
                       B to see a Brief display - to see the previous screen
                       F to Find other items    Q to Quit

NEXT ACTION?  _                                          CLON1
```

Figure 7.53

```
Your search: Schoenberg, Arnol#                    LONG Display
      Finds: 1 record                              Screen  3 of  4
--------------------------------------------------------------------
        new or unknown works.
           Opening words: "Es ist das 2te Mal, dass man mir so einen
        Zettel schickt [...]"
           Cite as: Arnold Schoenberg Institute, Text Mss. Aesthetik
        321, Box T1, Folder 21.
           In Schoenberg, Arnold, 1874-1951. Aesthetik, b). --
        1910-1932.

           1. Essays. 2. Poetry. 3. Theater. 4. Kraus, Karl,
        1874-1936. 5. Performance art. 6. Oral interpretation. 7.
        Prospectuses. 8. Schoenberg, Arnold, 1874-1951--Marginalia.
        9. Manuscripts, German--California--Los Angeles. I.
        Schoenberg, Arnold, 1874-1951. ann. II. Kraus, Karl,
        1874-1936. Theater der Dichtung. III. Wedekind, Frank,

--------------------------------------------------CONTINUED------
NEXT ACTIONS      Key: ? for help              + to see the next screen
                       B to see a Brief display - to see the previous screen
                       F to Find other items    Q to Quit
NEXT ACTION?  _                                          CLON1
```

Figure 7.54

```
Your search: Schoenberg, Arnol#                    LONG Display
      Finds: 1 record                              Screen  4 of  4
--------------------------------------------------------------------
        1864-1918.




--------------------------------------------------------------------
NEXT ACTIONS      Key: ? for help              + to see the next screen
                       B to see a Brief display - to see the previous screen
                       F to Find other items    Q to Quit
NEXT ACTION?  _                                          CLON1
```

Figure 7.55

```
Your search: Douglass family#                      LONG Display
      Finds: 1 record                              Screen  1 of  3
--------------------------------------------------------------------

        Douglass family.
          Papers, 1812-1911.

          8 linear ft., 3 v. [outsize] and 20 items [outsize].

          Papers of Benjamin Douglass and his sons, Samuel T.
        Douglass, Detroit attorney and jurist, and Silas H.
        Douglas(s), professor of chemistry at the University of
        Michigan, and member of Douglass Houghton's Northern
        Michigan survey.
          Summary: Correspondence, scrapbooks, letter books, and
        miscellanea concerning family affairs, business and
        University activities; papers of the Douglass and Walker and
        Campbell Law Firm; miscellaneous papers of the Douglass and

------------------------------------------------------CONTINUED-------

NEXT ACTIONS      Key: ? for help         + to see the next screen
                       B to see a Brief display  - to see the previous screen
                       F to Find other items     Q to Quit

NEXT ACTION?  _                                            CLON1
```

Figure 7.56

```
Your search: Douglass family#                      LONG Display
      Finds: 1 record                              Screen  2 of  3
--------------------------------------------------------------------

        Welles families; and photographs. Correspondents include:
        James V. Campbell, Henry H. Crapo, George Duffield, Douglass
        Houghton, Jonathan Kearsley, Zina Pitcher, Abram Sager,
        Joseph Sibley, Henry P. Tappan, Edward C. Walker, Henry N.
        Walker.
          Indexes: Finding aid in the library.
          Donor: 183, 1278, 2916.

          1. Photoprints. 2. Tintypes. 3. Daguerreotypes. 4. Detroit
        (Mich.). Board of Water Commissioners. 5. Flat River (Mich.)
        6. Grosse Ile (Mich.) 7. Houghton, Douglass, 1809-1845. 8.
        Lawyers. 9. Michigan Central Railroad. 10. Michigan,
        Northern Peninsula. 11. Welles family. I. Campbell, James V.
        (James Valentine), 1823-1890. II. Crapo, Henry Howland,

------------------------------------------------------CONTINUED-------

NEXT ACTIONS      Key: ? for help         + to see the next screen
                       B to see a Brief display  - to see the previous screen
                       F to Find other items     Q to Quit

NEXT ACTION?  _                                            CLON1
```

Figure 7.57

```
Your search: Douglass family#                    LONG Display
     Finds: 1 record                             Screen  3 of  3
---------------------------------------------------------------------

       1804-1869. III. Douglas, Silas Hamilton, 1816-1890. IV.
       Douglass, Benjamin. V. Douglass, Samuel Townsend, 1814-1898.
       VI. Duffield, George, 1794-1868. VII. Kearsley, Jonathan,
       1786-1859. VIII. Pitcher, Zina, 1797-1872. IX. Sager, Abram,
       1810-1877. X. Sibley, Joseph. XI. Tappan, Henry Philip,
       1805-1881. XII. Walker, Edward Carey, 1820-1894. XIII.
       Walker, Henry Nelson, 1811-1886. XIV. Williams, George
       Palmer, 1802-1881.




---------------------------------------------------------------------
NEXT ACTIONS      Key: ? for help          + to see the next screen
                       B to see a Brief display  - to see the previous screen
                       F to Find other items     Q to Quit
NEXT ACTION?  _                                            CLON1
```

Figure 7.58

```
Your search: Bible. English. A#                  LONG Display
     Finds: 1 record                             Screen  1 of  1
---------------------------------------------------------------------

       Bible. English. Authorized. Selections. 1980.
         Meredith's book of Bible lists / J. L. Meredith. --
       Minneapolis, Minn. : Bethany Fellowship, c1980.

       287 p. : ill. ; 22 cm.

       Consists to a large extent of Bible quotations.
       Includes bibliographical references.

       1. Bible--Indexes. I. Meredith, J. L. (Joel L.), 1935-



---------------------------------------------------------------------
NEXT ACTIONS      Key: ? for help          + to see the next screen
                       B to see a Brief display  - to see the previous screen
                       F to Find other items     Q to Quit
NEXT ACTION?  _                                            CLON1
```

Figure 7.59

```
Your search: Spikell, Mark A#                      LONG Display
      Finds: 1 record                              Screen  1 of  2
-----------------------------------------------------------------------

          Spikell, Mark A.
            Brain ticklers, Apple II, IIe edition [machine-readable
          data file] : mathematical problem-solving with the
          microcomputer / Mark A. Spikell & Stephen L. Snover. --
          Englewood Cliffs, N.J. : Prentice-Hall, c1983.

            1 program file on 1 computer disk ; 5 1/4 in. +
          instructions (iv, 6 p.) + 2 books in loose-leaf binder.

            Accompanying books titled: Brain ticklers : puzzles &
          pastimes for programmable calculators & personal computers;
          and Mathematical problem-solving with the microcomputer :
          projects to increase your BASIC programming skill.


---------------------------------------------------------CONTINUED-------
NEXT ACTIONS       Key: ? for help              + to see the next screen
                        B to see a Brief display  - to see the previous screen
                        F to Find other items    Q to Quit
NEXT ACTION?   _                                             CLON1
```

Figure 7.60

```
Your search: Spikell, Mark A#                      LONG Display
      Finds: 1 record                              Screen  2 of  2
-----------------------------------------------------------------------

          System requirements: 48K; single-disk drive; programs
        written in Applesoft BASIC; DOS 3.3.

          1. Mathematics--Problems, exercises, etc. 2. Mathematics--
        Computer programs. 3. Apple computer--Programming. 4.
        Problem solving--Data processing. I. Snover, Stephen L.




-----------------------------------------------------------------------
NEXT ACTIONS       Key: ? for help              + to see the next screen
                        B to see a Brief display  - to see the previous screen
                        F to Find other items    Q to Quit
NEXT ACTION?   _                                             CLON1
```

Figure 7.61

```
Your search: Collected poems#                         LONG Display
     Finds: 1 record                                  Screen  1 of  1
---------------------------------------------------------------------------

        TITLE: Collected poems.
      EDITION: [Rev. ed.]
    PUBLISHED: Chicago, Swallow Press [c1960]
     MATERIAL: 146 p. 19 cm.

        NAMES: Winters, Yvor, 1900-




---------------------------------------------------------------------------
NEXT ACTIONS     Key: ? for help              + to see the next screen
                      B to see a Brief display - to see the previous screen
                      F to Find other items    Q to Quit
NEXT ACTION?   _                                           LLON1
```

Figure 7.62

```
Your search: The accidental to#                       LONG Display
     Finds: 1 record                                  Screen  1 of  1
---------------------------------------------------------------------------

        TITLE: The accidental tourist / Anne Tyler.
      EDITION: 1st ed.
    PUBLISHED: New York : Knopf : Distributed by Random House, 1985.
     MATERIAL: 355 p. ; 22 cm.

        NAMES: Tyler, Anne.




---------------------------------------------------------------------------
NEXT ACTIONS     Key: ? for help              + to see the next screen
                      B to see a Brief display - to see the previous screen
                      F to Find other items    Q to Quit
NEXT ACTION?   _                                           LLON1
```

Figure 7.63

```
Your search: In June : song fo#                      LONG Display
      Finds: 1 record                                Screen  1 of  2
------------------------------------------------------------------------


          TITLE: In June : song for voice and piano / lyrics [by] Helen Field
                 Watson ; music [by] Antonio Lora.
      PUBLISHED: New York : American Composers Alliance, [19--].
       MATERIAL: 1 score (5 p.)  ; 32 cm.

          NAMES: Lora, Antonio John, 1899-1965.
                 Watson, Helen Field.

       SUBJECTS: Songs (Medium voice) with piano.
                 Watson, Helen Field--Musical settings.

          NOTES: For medium voice and piano.
                 Cover title.
                 Reproduced from holograph.

---------------------------------------------------------CONTINUED-------
NEXT ACTIONS      Key: ? for help              + to see the next screen
                       B to see a Brief display  - to see the previous screen
                       F to Find other items   Q to Quit
NEXT ACTION?   _                                              LLON1
```

Figure 7.64

```
Your search: In June : song fo#                      LONG Display
      Finds: 1 record                                Screen  2 of  2
------------------------------------------------------------------------
          Duration: 2:45.




















------------------------------------------------------------------------
NEXT ACTIONS      Key: ? for help              + to see the next screen
                       B to see a Brief display  - to see the previous screen
                       F to Find other items   Q to Quit
NEXT ACTION?   _                                              LLON1
```

Figure 7.65

```
Your search: Plan of the Frenc#                       LONG Display
       Finds: 1 record                                Screen  1 of  2
-----------------------------------------------------------------------


        TITLE: Plan of the French attacks upon the island of Grenada, with
                the engagement between the English fleet under the command
                of Admiral Byron and the French fleet under Count
                d'Estaing, drawn by an officer on board the fleet, July
                1779. J. Luffman, sc.
    PUBLISHED: London, J. Haris, 1779. [Chicago, Rand McNally and Co.,
                1974?]
     MATERIAL: col. map 22 x 35 cm.

        NAMES: Luffman, John, 1756-1846.
                Rand McNally and Company.

     SUBJECTS: Grenada, Battle of, 1779--Maps--To 1800.


-------------------------------------------------------CONTINUED-------
NEXT ACTIONS       Key: ? for help              + to see the next screen
                        B to see a Brief display  - to see the previous screen
                        F to Find other items     Q to Quit
NEXT ACTION?   _                                            LLON1
```

Figure 7.66

```
Your search: Plan of the Frenc#                       LONG Display
       Finds: 1 record                                Screen  2 of  2
-----------------------------------------------------------------------

                Maps, Early--Facsimiles.

        NOTES: Scale ca. 1:14,700.
                Facsimile.
                Relief shown by hachures.
                Oriented with north to the left.
                Pictorial map.
                Includes descriptive notes.






-----------------------------------------------------------------------
NEXT ACTIONS       Key: ? for help              + to see the next screen
                        B to see a Brief display  - to see the previous screen
                        F to Find other items     Q to Quit
NEXT ACTION?   _                                            LLON1
```

Figure 7.67

```
Your search: Gurre-Lieder                          LONG Display
     Finds: 1 record                               Screen  1 of  4
---------------------------------------------------------------------------

         TITLE: Gurre-Lieder [sound recording] / Schonberg ; (words by
                Jacobsen).
     PUBLISHED: Camden, N.J. : RCA, 1932.
      MATERIAL: 14 sound discs : 78 rpm, mono. ; 12 in. + 1 pamphlet (11 p.
                ; 24 cm.)

         NAMES: Schoenberg, Arnold, 1874-1951.
                Stokowski, Leopold.
                Philadelphia Orchestra.
                Vreeland, Jeanette.
                Bampton, Rose.
                Betts, Robert.
                Althouse, Paul.
                Robofsky, Abrasha.

---------------------------------------------------------CONTINUED-------
NEXT ACTIONS      Key: ? for help             + to see the next screen
                       B to see a Brief display  - to see the previous screen
                       F to Find other items   Q to Quit
NEXT ACTION?   _                                          LLON1
```

Figure 7.68

```
Your search: Gurre-Lieder                          LONG Display
     Finds: 1 record                               Screen  2 of  4
---------------------------------------------------------------------------

                De Loache, Benjamin.
                Princeton Glee Club.
                Fortnightly Club.
                Mendelssohn Club.
                Arnold, Robert Franz, 1872-1938.

      SUBJECTS: Cantatas, Secular (Mixed voices) with orchestra.
                Jacobsen, J. P. (Jens Peter), 1847-1885--Musical settings.

         WORKS: Schoenberg, Arnold, 1874-1951. Gurre-Lieder. Libretto.
                English & German.

---------------------------------------------------------CONTINUED-------
NEXT ACTIONS      Key: ? for help             + to see the next screen
                       B to see a Brief display  - to see the previous screen
                       F to Find other items   Q to Quit
NEXT ACTION?   _                                          LLON1
```

Figure 7.69

```
Your search: Gurre-Lieder                          LONG Display
       Finds: 1 record                             Screen  3 of  4
-----------------------------------------------------------------------

         NOTES: RCA Victor M127, 7524-7537 (side 1: Mx. d72621, side 2: Mx
                .b71674, side 5: Mx. a71677, side 6: Mx. a71678, side 7:
                Mx. 71679, side 8: Mx. a71680, side 9: Mx. a71681, side
                10: Mx. a71682, side 11: Mx. a71683, side 12: Mx. a71684,
                side 13: Mx. a71685, side 14: Mx. a71686, side 15: Mx.
                a71687, side 16: Mx. a71688, side 17: Mx. a71689, side 18:
                Mx. a71690, side 19: Mx. a71691, side 20: Mx. a71692, side
                21: Mx. a71693, side 22: Mx. e71694. side 23: Mx. a71695,
                side 24: Mx. a71696, side 25: Mx. a71712, side 26: Mx.
                a71713)
                Cantata for speaker, solo voices (SATTB), one chorus
                (SSAATTBB), three choruses (TTBB), and large orchestra.
                Sung in German.


-------------------------------------------------------CONTINUED-------
NEXT ACTIONS      Key: ? for help            + to see the next screen
                       B to see a Brief display  - to see the previous screen
                       F to Find other items     Q to Quit
NEXT ACTION?   _                                        LLON1
```

Figure 7.70

```
Your search: Gurre-Lieder                          LONG Display
       Finds: 1 record                             Screen  4 of  4
-----------------------------------------------------------------------

                Jeanette Vreeland (Tove) ; Rose Bampton (Waldtaube) ; Paul
                Althouse (Waldemar) ; Robert Betts (Klaus-Narr) ; Abrasha
                Robofsky (Bauer) ; Benjamin de Loache, narrator; Princeton
                Glee Club; Fortnightly Club; Mendelssohn Club;
                Philadelphia Orchestra; Leopold Stokowski, conductor.
                Recorded April 11, 1932 at the Metropolitan Opera House,
                Philadelphia.





-----------------------------------------------------------------------
NEXT ACTIONS      Key: ? for help            + to see the next screen
                       B to see a Brief display  - to see the previous screen
                       F to Find other items     Q to Quit
NEXT ACTION?   _                                        LLON1
```

Figure 7.71

```
Your search: More fun in the n#                      LONG Display
     Finds: 1 record                                 Screen  1 of  1
------------------------------------------------------------------------

        TITLE: More fun in the new world [sound recording] / X.
    PUBLISHED: Los Angeles, CA : Elektra, c1983.
     MATERIAL: 1 sound disc : 33 1/3 rpm, stereo. ; 12 in.

        NAMES: X (Musical group)

     SUBJECTS: Rock music.




------------------------------------------------------------------------
NEXT ACTIONS      Key: ? for help          + to see the next screen
                       B to see a Brief display   - to see the previous screen
                       F to Find other items  Q to Quit
NEXT ACTION?   _                                            LLON1
```

Figure 7.72

```
Your search: Die Mannheimer Sc#                      LONG Display
     Finds: 1 record                                 Screen  1 of  5
------------------------------------------------------------------------

        TITLE: Die Mannheimer Schule [sound recording] : Musik der
               Fruhklassik = music of the early classical era.
    PUBLISHED: [West Germany] : Archiv Produktion, p1980.
     MATERIAL: 3 sound discs : 33 1/3 rpm, stereo. ; 12 in.

        NAMES: Holliger, Heinz.
               Furi, Thomas.
               Demenga, Thomas.
               Sax, Manfred.
               Schiller, Christoph.
               Nicolet, Aurele.
               Camerata Bern.

     SUBJECTS: Orchestral music--18th century.

-------------------------------------------------CONTINUED-------
NEXT ACTIONS      Key: ? for help          + to see the next screen
                       B to see a Brief display   - to see the previous screen
                       F to Find other items  Q to Quit
NEXT ACTION?   _                                            LLON1
```

Figure 7.73

```
Your search: Die Mannheimer Sc#                    LONG Display
     Finds: 1 record                               Screen  2 of  5
------------------------------------------------------------------------

             String orchestra music--18th century.
             Music--Germany--18th century.
             Concertos (Violin with string orchestra)
             Symphonies (String orchestra)
             Concertos (Violoncello with string orchestra)
             Concertos (Oboe with string orchestra)
             Concertos (Flute and string orchestra)

      WORKS: Cannabich, Christian, 1731-1798. Sinfonie concertanti,
             flute, oboe, bassoon, orchestra, C major. 1980.
             Cannabich, Christian, 1731-1798. Symphonies, Bb major. 1980.
             Filtz, Johann Anton, ca. 1730-1760. Concertos, violoncello,
             string orchestra, G major. 1980.


------------------------------------------------------------CONTINUED-------

NEXT ACTIONS    Key: ? for help            + to see the next screen
                     B to see a Brief display  - to see the previous screen
                     F to Find other items  Q to Quit
NEXT ACTION?  _                                            LLON1
```

Figure 7.74

```
Your search: Die Mannheimer Sc#                    LONG Display
     Finds: 1 record                               Screen  3 of  5
------------------------------------------------------------------------

             Holzbauer, Ignaz, 1711-1783. Sinfonie concertanti, violin,
             viola, violoncello, string orchestra, A major. 1980.
             Holzbauer, Ignaz, 1711-1783. Symphonies, op. 4. No. 3. 1980.
             Lebrun, Ludwig August, 1752-1790. Concertos, oboe,
             orchestra, D minor. 1980.
             Richter, Franz Xaver, 1709-1789. Symphonies, string
             orchestra, Bb major. 1980.
             Richter, Franz Xaver, 1709-1789. Concertos, flute, string
             orchestra, E minor. 1980.
             Stamitz, Johann, 1717-1757. Concertos, violin, string
             orchestra, C major. 1980.
             Stamitz, Johann, 1717-1757. Trio sonatas, violins, continuo,
             op.1. No. 5. 1980.


------------------------------------------------------------CONTINUED-------

NEXT ACTIONS    Key: ? for help            + to see the next screen
                     B to see a Brief display  - to see the previous screen
                     F to Find other items  Q to Quit
NEXT ACTION?  _                                            LLON1
```

Figure 7.75

```
Your search: Die Mannheimer Sc#                    LONG Display
       Finds: 1 record                             Screen  4 of  5
---------------------------------------------------------------------

          NOTES: Title from container.
                 Various soloists ; Camerata Bern ; Thomas Furi, conductor.
                 Recorded in the Konservatorium Bern, Sept. 24-29, 1979
                     (1st-4th, 7th-8th, 10th works) and DRS-Radio-Studio, Bern,
                     Feb. 12-15, 1980 (the remainder)
                 Program notes by Heinz Becker and notes on the ensemble by
                     Urs Frauchinger in German with English and French
                     translations (12 p. : ill.) laid in container.
                 Contents: Sinfonia B-Dur (10:37) ; Konzert fur Flote und
                     Streichorchester e-Moll (Aurele Nicolet, flute) (19:30) /
                     Franz Xaver Richter -- Konzert fur Violine und
                     Streichorchester C-Dur (Thomas Furi, violin) (15:47) ;
                     Orchestertrio B-Dur op. 1, 5 (14:47) / Johann Stamitz --
                     Konzert fur Violoncello und Streichorchester G-Dur / Anton

-------------------------------------------------------CONTINUED-------
NEXT ACTIONS    Key: ? for help           + to see the next screen
                     B to see a Brief display   - to see the previous screen
                     F to Find other items      Q to Quit
NEXT ACTION?   _                                          LLON1
```

Figure 7.76

```
Your search: Die Mannheimer Sc#                    LONG Display
       Finds: 1 record                             Screen  5 of  5
---------------------------------------------------------------------

                 Filtz (Thomas Demenga, violoncello) (21:19) -- Sinfonia
                 concertante A-Dur, Vl. Solo, Vla. Solo, Vlc. Solo (Thomas
                 Furi, violin ; Christoph Schiller, viola ; Thomas Demenga,
                 violoncello) (15:16) ; Sinfonia Es-Dur op. 4, 3 (15:06) /
                 Ignaz Holzbauer -- Sinfonia concertante C-Dur, Fl. Solo,
                 Ob. Solo, Fag. Solo (Aurele Nicolet, flute ; Heinz
                 Holliger, oboe ; Manfred Sax, bassoon) (8:40) ; Sinfonia
                 B-dur (16:41) / Christian Cannabich -- Konzert fur Oboe
                 und Orchester d-Moll / Ludwig August Lebrun (Heinz
                 Holliger, oboe) (19:32)




---------------------------------------------------------------------
NEXT ACTIONS    Key: ? for help           + to see the next screen
                     B to see a Brief display   - to see the previous screen
                     F to Find other items      Q to Quit
NEXT ACTION?   _                                          LLON1
```

Figure 7.77

```
Your search: U.S. Naval Observ#                      LONG Display
     Finds: 1 record                                 Screen  1 of  1
------------------------------------------------------------------------

        TITLE: U.S. Naval Observatory time signals. Bulletin A.
      EDITION: 1 (2 June 1953)-
    PUBLISHED: [Washington, D.C. : The Observatory, 1953-
     MATERIAL: v. ; 36 cm.

        NAMES: United States Naval Obsevatory.

     SUBJECTS: Time-signals--Periodicals.

        NOTES: Irregular.
               Title from caption.
               Merged with: U.S. Naval Observatory time signals. Bulletin
                 B, to form: Time signals.


------------------------------------------------------------------------
NEXT ACTIONS      Key: ? for help            + to see the next screen
                       B to see a Brief display  - to see the previous screen
                       F to Find other items  Q to Quit
NEXT ACTION?   _                                           LLON1
```

Figure 7.78

```
Your search: Theater der Dicht#                      LONG Display
     Finds: 1 record                                 Screen  1 of  4
------------------------------------------------------------------------

        TITLE: Theater der Dichtung. 23.Mai 1931 / Arnold Schonberg.
     MATERIAL: [1] leaf ; 30 cm.

        NAMES: Schoenberg, Arnold, 1874-1951.
               Schoenberg, Arnold, 1874-1951. ann.
               Wedekind, Frank, 1864-1918.

     SUBJECTS: Essays.
               Poetry.
               Theater.
               Kraus, Karl, 1874-1936.
               Performance art.
               Oral interpretation.
               Prospectuses.

-----------------------------------------------------CONTINUED-------
NEXT ACTIONS      Key: ? for help            + to see the next screen
                       B to see a Brief display  - to see the previous screen
                       F to Find other items  Q to Quit
NEXT ACTION?   _                                           LLON1
```

Figure 7.79

```
Your search: Theater der Dicht#                    LONG Display
     Finds: 1 record                               Screen  2 of  4
-------------------------------------------------------------------

            Schoenberg, Arnold, 1874-1951--Marginalia.
            Manuscripts, German--California--Los Angeles.

     WORKS: Kraus, Karl, 1874-1936. Theater der Dichtung.

     NOTES: Holograph signed (black ink, blue and pink pencil), printed.
            Bears Schoenberg's classification: "Ku 321".
            In German fraktur.
            On a printed 2 page circular by Karl Kraus with the same
               title.  Edges of leaf reinforced with strips of music
               manuscript paper, left side punched with 2 holes.
            References: Rufer. Schriften IIE24.



     ------------------------------------------------------CONTINUED-------
NEXT ACTIONS      Key: ? for help              + to see the next screen
                       B to see a Brief display  - to see the previous screen
                       F to Find other items   Q to Quit
NEXT ACTION?  _                                            LLON1
```

Figure 7.80

```
Your search: Theater der Dicht#                    LONG Display
     Finds: 1 record                               Screen  3 of  4
-------------------------------------------------------------------

            References: Christensen, Jean & Jesper. From Arnold
               Schoenberg's Literary Legacy: A Catalog of Neglected
               Items. Detroit: Detroit Information Coordinators, [1986].
               Appendix II.
            Microfiche 56.
            Summary: The circular is a call for money for the founding
               of an ensemble "Theater der Dichtung" under the leadership
               of Karl Kraus.  Frank Wedekind comments on Kraus in the
               circular.  Schoenberg's lengthy annotations in the margins
               criticize the circular.  First he is offended that there
               is no personal salutation.  He says the ensemble is a
               hopeless venture even under the leadership of Kraus.  He
               discusses performing and concludes that rather than
               performing already-proven works, this "theater" should

     ------------------------------------------------------CONTINUED-------
NEXT ACTIONS      Key: ? for help              + to see the next screen
                       B to see a Brief display  - to see the previous screen
                       F to Find other items   Q to Quit
NEXT ACTION?  _                                            LLON1
```

Figure 7.81

```
Your search: Theater der Dicht#                      LONG Display
      Finds: 1 record                                Screen  4 of  4
----------------------------------------------------------------------
                  concentrate on new or unknown works.
              Opening words: "Es ist das 2te Mal, dass man mir so einen
                 Zettel schickt [...]"
              Cite as: Arnold Schoenberg Institute, Text Mss. Aesthetik
                 321, Box T1, Folder 21.
              In Schoenberg, Arnold, 1874-1951. Aesthetik, b). --
                 1910-1932.




          --------------------------------------------------------
NEXT ACTIONS       Key: ? for help              + to see the next screen
                        B to see a Brief display - to see the previous screen
                        F to Find other items    Q to Quit
NEXT ACTION?  _                                             LLON1
```

Figure 7.82

```
Your search: Papers, 1812-1911#                      LONG Display
      Finds: 1 record                                Screen  1 of  4
----------------------------------------------------------------------
         TITLE: Papers, 1812-1911.
      MATERIAL: 8 linear ft., 3 v. [outsize] and 20 items [outsize].

         NAMES: Douglass family.
                Campbell, James V. (James Valentine), 1823-1890.
                Crapo, Henry Howland, 1804-1869.
                Douglas, Silas Hamilton, 1816-1890.
                Douglass, Benjamin.
                Douglass, Samuel Townsend, 1814-1898.
                Duffield, George, 1794-1868.
                Kearsley, Jonathan, 1786-1859.
                Pitcher, Zina, 1797-1872.
                Sager, Abram, 1810-1877.
                Sibley, Joseph.
          ----------------------------------------------CONTINUED-------
NEXT ACTIONS       Key: ? for help              + to see the next screen
                        B to see a Brief display - to see the previous screen
                        F to Find other items    Q to Quit
NEXT ACTION?  _                                             LLON1
```

Figure 7.83

```
Your search: Papers, 1812-1911#                    LONG Display
      Finds: 1 record                              Screen  2 of  4
-----------------------------------------------------------------------
              Tappan, Henry Philip, 1805-1881.
              Walker, Edward Carey, 1820-1894.
              Walker, Henry Nelson, 1811-1886.
              Williams, George Palmer, 1802-1881.

    SUBJECTS: Photoprints.
              Tintypes.
              Daguerreotypes.
              Detroit (Mich.). Board of Water Commissioners.
              Flat River (Mich.)
              Grosse Ile (Mich.)
              Houghton, Douglass, 1809-1845.
              Lawyers.
              Michigan Central Railroad.

-----------------------------------------------------CONTINUED-------
NEXT ACTIONS      Key: ? for help            + to see the next screen
                       B to see a Brief display  - to see the previous screen
                       F to Find other items    Q to Quit
NEXT ACTION?  _                                           LLON1
```

Figure 7.84

```
Your search: Papers, 1812-1911#                    LONG Display
      Finds: 1 record                              Screen  3 of  4
-----------------------------------------------------------------------
            Michigan, Northern Peninsula.
            Welles family.

       NOTES: Papers of Benjamin Douglass and his sons, Samuel T.
              Douglass, Detroit attorney and jurist, and Silas H.
              Douglas(s), professor of chemistry at the University of
              Michigan, and member of Douglass Houghton's Northern
              Michigan survey.
              Summary: Correspondence, scrapbooks, letter books, and
              miscellanea concerning family affairs, business and
              University activities; papers of the Douglass and Walker
              and Campbell Law Firm; miscellaneous papers of the
              Douglass and Welles families; and photographs.
              Correspondents include: James V. Campbell, Henry H. Crapo,

-----------------------------------------------------CONTINUED-------
NEXT ACTIONS      Key: ? for help            + to see the next screen
                       B to see a Brief display  - to see the previous screen
                       F to Find other items    Q to Quit
NEXT ACTION?  _                                           LLON1
```

Figure 7.85

```
Your search: Papers, 1812-1911#                      LONG Display
     Finds: 1 record                                 Screen  4 of  4
-----------------------------------------------------------------------
              George Duffield, Douglass Houghton, Jonathan Kearsley,
              Zina Pitcher, Abram Sager, Joseph Sibley, Henry P. Tappan,
              Edward C. Walker, Henry N. Walker.
         Indexes: Finding aid in the library.
         Donor: 183, 1278, 2916.




-----------------------------------------------------------------------
NEXT ACTIONS      Key: ? for help            + to see the next screen
                       B to see a Brief display  - to see the previous screen
                       F to Find other items   Q to Quit
NEXT ACTION?  _                                            LLON1
```

Figure 7.86

```
Your search: Meredith's book o#                      LONG Display
     Finds: 1 record                                 Screen  1 of  1
-----------------------------------------------------------------------
        TITLE: Meredith's book of Bible lists / J. L. Meredith.
    PUBLISHED: Minneapolis, Minn. : Bethany Fellowship, c1980.
     MATERIAL: 287 p. : ill. ; 22 cm.

        NAMES: Meredith, J. L. (Joel L.), 1935-

     SUBJECTS: Bible--Indexes.

        WORKS: Bible. English. Authorized. Selections. 1980.

        NOTES: Consists to a large extent of Bible quotations.
               Includes bibliographical references.


-----------------------------------------------------------------------
NEXT ACTIONS      Key: ? for help            + to see the next screen
                       B to see a Brief display  - to see the previous screen
                       F to Find other items   Q to Quit
NEXT ACTION?  _                                            LLON1
```

Figure 7.87

```
Your search: Brain ticklers, A#                    LONG Display
     Finds: 1 record                               Screen  1 of  2
----------------------------------------------------------------------


        TITLE: Brain ticklers, Apple II, IIe edition [machine-readable data
               file] : mathematical problem-solving with the
               microcomputer / Mark A. Spikell & Stephen L. Snover.
    PUBLISHED: Englewood Cliffs, N.J. : Prentice-Hall, c1983.
     MATERIAL: 1 program file on 1 computer disk ; 5 1/4 in. + instructions
               (iv, 6 p.) + 2 books in loose-leaf binder.

        NAMES: Spikell, Mark A.
               Snover, Stephen L.

     SUBJECTS: Mathematics--Problems, exercises, etc.
               Mathematics--Computer programs.
               Apple computer--Programming.



-------------------------------------------------------CONTINUED-------
NEXT ACTIONS      Key: ? for help              + to see the next screen
                       B to see a Brief display  - to see the previous screen
                       F to Find other items   Q to Quit
NEXT ACTION?  _                                         LLON1
```

Figure 7.88

```
Your search: Brain ticklers, A#                    LONG Display
     Finds: 1 record                               Screen  2 of  2
----------------------------------------------------------------------


            Problem solving--Data processing.

      NOTES: Accompanying books titled: Brain ticklers : puzzles &
             pastimes for programmable calculators & personal
             computers; and Mathematical problem-solving with the
             microcomputer : projects to increase your BASIC
             programming skill.
             System requirements: 48K; single-disk drive; programs
             written in Applesoft BASIC; DOS 3.3.




-------------------------------------------------------------------
NEXT ACTIONS      Key: ? for help              + to see the next screen
                       B to see a Brief display  - to see the previous screen
                       F to Find other items   Q to Quit
NEXT ACTION?  _                                         LLON1
```

Figure 7.89

```
Your search: Anderson, Sparky#                      MEDIUM Display
     Finds: 1 record                                Screen  1 of  1
------------------------------------------------------------------------

        Anderson, Sparky, 1934-
          Bless you boys: diary of the Detroit Tigers' 1984 season,
        by Sparky Anderson, with Dan Ewald. Chicago: Contemporary
        Books, c1984.
          231 p.: ill.; 23 cm.
          1. Detroit Tigers (Baseball team) I. Ewald, Dan.





------------------------------------------------------------------------
NEXT ACTIONS      Key: ? for help            + to see the next screen
                       L to see a Longer display   - to see the previous screen
                       F to Find other items  Q to Quit
NEXT ACTION?    _                                        CMTX
```

Figure 7.90

```
Your search: Best American pla#                     MEDIUM Display
     Finds: 1 record                                Screen  1 of  1
------------------------------------------------------------------------

        Best American plays: sixth series, 1963-1967, edited by John
          Gassner and Clive Barnes, with an introduction and
          prefaces to the plays by Clive Barnes. New York: Crown,
          c1971.    .
          xii, 594 p.; 24 cm.
          1. American drama--20th century. 2. American drama--
        Collected works. I. Gassner, John, 1903-1967. II. Barnes,
        Clive, 1927-




------------------------------------------------------------------------
NEXT ACTIONS      Key: ? for help            + to see the next screen
                       L to see a Longer display   - to see the previous screen
                       F to Find other items  Q to Quit
NEXT ACTION?    _                                        CMTX
```

Figure 7.91

```
Your search: Indy, Vincent d'#                      MEDIUM Display
      Finds: 1 record                               Screen  1 of  2
----------------------------------------------------------------------

        Indy, Vincent d', 1851-1931.
          Suite en re dans le style ancien: op. 24 ; Karadec : op.
        34 ; Concert, op. 89 pour piano, flute, violoncello et
        orchestre a cordes [sound recording], Vincent d'Indy.
        France: Erato; Paris: Distribution en France RCA, p1982.
          1 sound disc: 33 1/3 rpm, stereo.; 12 in.
          1. Suites (Flutes (2), trumpet with string orchestra) 2.
        Music, Incidental. 3. Concertos (Piano, flute, violoncello
        with string orchestra) I. Rampal, Jean Pierre. II. Pierlot,
        Philippe. III. Andre, Maurice. IV. Duchable, Francois. V.
        Lodeon, Frederic. VI. Paillard, Jean Francois. VII. Indy,
        Vincent d', 1851-1931. Suite dans le style ancien. 1982.
        VIII. Indy, Vincent d', 1851-1931. Karadec. 1982. IX. Indy,
        Vincent d', 1851-1931. Concerto, piano, flute, violoncello,

----------------------------------------------------CONTINUED-------

NEXT ACTIONS       Key: ? for help            + to see the next screen
                        L to see a Longer display  - to see the previous screen
                        F to Find other items      Q to Quit
NEXT ACTION?  _                                             CMTX
```

Figure 7.92

```
Your search: Indy, Vincent d'#                      MEDIUM Display
      Finds: 1 record                               Screen  2 of  2
----------------------------------------------------------------------

        orchestra, op. 89. 1982. X. Orchestre de chambre
        Jean-Francois Paillard.








----------------------------------------------------------------------

NEXT ACTIONS       Key: ? for help            + to see the next screen
                        L to see a Longer display  - to see the previous screen
                        F to Find other items      Q to Quit
NEXT ACTION?  _                                             CMTX
```

Figure 7.93

```
Your search: Bureau of Mines T#                      MEDIUM Display
      Finds: 1 record                                Screen  1 of  1
-------------------------------------------------------------------------

        Bureau of Mines Technology Transfer Seminars (1982:
          Pittsburgh, Pa.)
          Postdisaster survival and rescue research: proceedings,
        Bureau of Mines Technology Transfer Seminar, Pittsburgh,
        Pa., November 16, 1982, compiled by staff, Bureau of Mines.
        [Avondale, Md.]: U.S. Dept. of the Interior, Bureau of
        Mines, 1982.
          iii, 91 p.: ill.; 28 cm. (Bureau of Mines information
        circular; 8907)
          1. Mine accidents--Congresses. 2. Mine rescue work--
        Congresses. I. United States. Bureau of Mines.




-------------------------------------------------------------------------
NEXT ACTIONS    Key: ? for help              + to see the next screen
                     L to see a Longer display  - to see the previous screen
                     F to Find other items   Q to Quit
NEXT ACTION?  _                                              CMTX
```

Figure 7.94

```
Your search: Bless you boys: d#                      MEDIUM Display
      Finds: 1 record                                Screen  1 of  1
-------------------------------------------------------------------------

        TITLE: Bless you boys: diary of the Detroit Tigers' 1984 season, by
               Sparky Anderson, with Dan Ewald.
    PUBLISHED: Chicago: Contemporary Books, c1984.
     MATERIAL: 231 p.: ill.; 23 cm.

        NAMES: Anderson, Sparky, 1934-
               Ewald, Dan.

     SUBJECTS: Detroit Tigers (Baseball team)




-------------------------------------------------------------------------
NEXT ACTIONS    Key: ? for help              + to see the next screen
                     L to see a Longer display  - to see the previous screen
                     F to Find other items   Q to Quit
NEXT ACTION?  _                                              LMGATX
```

Figure 7.95

```
Your search: Best American pla#                      MEDIUM Display
      Finds: 1 record                                Screen  1 of  1
-------------------------------------------------------------------

        TITLE: Best American plays: sixth series, 1963-1967, edited by John
               Gassner and Clive Barnes, with an introduction and
               prefaces to the plays by Clive Barnes.
    PUBLISHED: New York: Crown, c1971.
     MATERIAL: xii, 594 p.; 24 cm.

        NAMES: Gassner, John, 1903-1967.
               Barnes, Clive, 1927-

     SUBJECTS: American drama--20th century.
               American drama--Collected works.


-------------------------------------------------------------------
NEXT ACTIONS     Key: ? for help            + to see the next screen
                      L to see a Longer display  - to see the previous screen
                      F to Find other items  Q to Quit
NEXT ACTION?  _                                             LMGATX
```

Figure 7.96

```
Your search: Suite en re dans #                      MEDIUM Display
      Finds: 1 record                                Screen  1 of  2
-------------------------------------------------------------------

        TITLE: Suite en re dans le style ancien: op. 24 ; Karadec : op. 34
               ; Concert, op. 89 pour piano, flute, violoncello et
               orchestre a cordes [sound recording], Vincent d'Indy.
    PUBLISHED: France: Erato; Paris: Distribution en France RCA, p1982.
     MATERIAL: 1 sound disc: 33 1/3 rpm, stereo.; 12 in.

        NAMES: Indy, Vincent d', 1851-1931.
               Rampal, Jean Pierre.
               Pierlot, Philippe.
               Andre, Maurice.
               Duchable, Francois.
               Lodeon, Frederic.
               Paillard, Jean Francois.


----------------------------------------------------CONTINUED-------
NEXT ACTIONS     Key: ? for help            + to see the next screen
                      L to see a Longer display  - to see the previous screen
                      F to Find other items  Q to Quit
NEXT ACTION?  _                                             LMGATX
```

Figure 7.97

```
Your search: Suite en re dans #                    MEDIUM Display
      Finds: 1 record                              Screen  2 of  2
------------------------------------------------------------------------

            Orchestre de chambre Jean-Francois Paillard.

    SUBJECTS: Suites (Flutes (2), trumpet with string orchestra)
              Music, Incidental.
              Concertos (Piano, flute, violoncello with string orchestra)

       WORKS: Indy, Vincent d', 1851-1931. Suite dans le style ancien.
                 1982.
              Indy, Vincent d', 1851-1931. Karadec. 1982.
              Indy, Vincent d', 1851-1931. Concerto, piano, flute,
                 violoncello, orchestra, op. 89. 1982.




         --------------------------------------------------------------
NEXT ACTIONS     Key: ? for help              + to see the next screen
                      L to see a Longer display - to see the previous screen
                      F to Find other items   Q to Quit
NEXT ACTION?   _                                          LMGATX
```

Figure 7.98

```
Your search: Postdisaster surv#                    MEDIUM Display
      Finds: 1 record                              Screen  1 of  2
------------------------------------------------------------------------

       TITLE: Postdisaster survival and rescue research: proceedings,
              Bureau of Mines Technology Transfer Seminar, Pittsburgh,
              Pa., November 16, 1982, compiled by staff, Bureau of
              Mines.
   PUBLISHED: [Avondale, Md.]: U.S. Dept. of the Interior, Bureau of
              Mines, 1982.
    MATERIAL: iii, 91 p.: ill.; 28 cm.

       NAMES: Bureau of Mines Technology Transfer Seminars (1982:
              Pittsburgh, Pa.)
              United States. Bureau of Mines.

      SERIES: Bureau of Mines information circular; 8907.


         -------------------------------------------------CONTINUED-------
NEXT ACTIONS     Key: ? for help              + to see the next screen
                      L to see a Longer display - to see the previous screen
                      F to Find other items   Q to Quit
NEXT ACTION?   _                                          LMGATX
```

Figure 7.99

```
Your search: Postdisaster surv#                         MEDIUM Display
     Finds: 1 record                                    Screen  2 of  2
-------------------------------------------------------------------------

        SUBJECTS: Mine accidents--Congresses.
                  Mine rescue work--Congresses.







        -------------------------------------------------------------------------
NEXT ACTIONS    Key: ? for help            + to see the next screen
                     L to see a Longer display  - to see the previous screen
                     F to Find other items  Q to Quit
NEXT ACTION?  _                                         LMGATX
```

8

Design Possibilities

This book presents a range of possibilities, most of which show the effects of small changes or test distinct levels of displays. The 39 displays illustrated in Chapters 2 through 7 could easily be expanded to hundreds, possibly thousands of related possibilities.

Preliminary work on this project involved more than six dozen other displays, with variations such as different sets of fields, field order, top and bottom design and text width. We also experimented with different labels, particularly for the imprint, physical description and entries. Because we were able to test the designs against hundreds of thousands of real bibliographic records, we learned much about the real effects of variations in display design.

In this chapter each author discusses displays that he or she designed based on observations and individual preferences developed during the Testbed program. Although the designs presented here are not ideal, we think they offer interesting alternatives. And because these designs were included in the large-scale test run, statistics for each are also included.

Our notes on the designs are often critical because we are not completely satisfied with them. It was a learning experience, however, to see how our designs fared statistically. We hope this information and our comments will help future designers of bibliographic displays.

One author designed a brief and a long display using a different screen top and bottom; the other two authors designed new medium displays, though in one case the display is designed to function at all three levels—as a brief, medium and long display. Each of the four designs is illustrated with the usual eight records. Table 8.1 lists all displays discussed or illustrated in this chapter; Tables 8.2 through 8.4 show statistical results for these four designs.

Table 8.1: Displays Discussed in Chapter 8

Display	Name
CBCAP	Citation-style brief display with capitalized short title
KOBM	Kathleen Bales' medium display
LMCAP	Walt Crawford's medium display
LMCIT	Partially labeled medium display with citation-style description
LMG	Labeled medium display, gutter aligned with each group labeled
LMGSP	Labeled medium display, gutter aligned, vertical spacing
MDSBRF	Lennie Stovel's brief display
MDSLON	Lennie Stovel's long display

Table 8.2: Screen Summary Statistics

Display	Name	One Screen w/Holdings	One Screen: bib. only	Two Screens bib. only
MDSBRF	Designer's Brief	98.61%	99.89%	0.11%
	-- public libraries	99.78%	100.00%	<0.01%
KOBM	Designer's Medium	48.41%	88.90%	11.04%
	-- public libraries	60.44%	94.90%	5.09%
LMCAP	Designer's Medium	50.18%	87.94%	12.00%
MDSLON	Designer's Long	12.39%	49.06%	48.96%
	-- public libraries	23.71%	64.60%	35.05%

Table 8.3: Density Summary

Display	Name	Local Density	Global Density	L. Density to 30%
MDSBRF	Designer's Brief	17.74%	33.35%	95.26%
	-- public libraries	15.55%	32.08%	98.69%
KOBM	Designer's Medium	26.37%	35.99%	69.43%
	-- public libraries	23.15%	34.12%	82.10%
LMCAP	Designer's Medium	25.49%	35.48%	73.04%
MDSLON	Designer's Long	24.72%	37.38%	77.57%
	-- public libraries	22.32%	35.97%	86.13%

Table 8.4: Room for Holdings

Display	Name	Holdings Room on First Screen		
		4+ Lines	6+ Lines	8+ Lines
MDSBRF	Designer's Brief	97.31%	88.39%	35.80%
	-- public libraries	99.46%	95.63%	46.68%
KOBM	Designer's Medium	32.50%	10.08%	1.16%
	-- public libraries	43.99%	17.74%	0.59%
LMCAP	Designer's Medium	36.04%	12.78%	4.18%
MDSLON	Designer's Long	7.75%	2.75%	0.60%
	-- public libraries	16.76%	6.11%	0.19%

MDSBRF—A BRIEF DISPLAY

Figures 8.1 through 8.8 show a brief display designed by Lennie Stovel. Her notes on the display follow:

> My brief display contains only the main entry, the title statement, the publisher and date (but not the place of publication) and the physical description. I assume that this data will be followed by holdings information, and that this amount of information will be sufficient for the user to identify the item, determine if it's the one wanted and locate it within the library. In all other respects, this is a pared-down version of MDSLON (Figures 8.31 through 8.49), and the comments made with regard to that display also apply to this one.

KOBM—A MEDIUM DISPLAY

Figures 8.9 through 8.19 show a medium display designed by Kathleen Bales. Her notes on the display follow:

> I set up my display to reflect the order of importance of information to users. (The user is defined as a patron of a research library.) I feel that title information is the most common identification for a bibliographic item and should, therefore, be first. Access points for names, titles, subjects and series titles form the next logical group and should be visible to the searcher. Publishing information and physical description are last.

> Although there are some differences of opinion as to what information patrons actually use, this order seems sensible for printed materials. For nonbook materials, specifically recordings, placing the physical description near the bottom of the record might present problems. This arrangement is especially problematic with multiscreen records because the physical description may not be on the first screen. See Figures 8.14 and 8.15 for an example of this problem.

A labeled display can be very helpful to both patrons and library staff. However, choosing clear and concise labels proved to be quite difficult and I am not completely satisfied with this set. In retrospect, I would eliminate OTHER ENTRIES and use NAMES for all main and added name entries, since name/title entries will appear with the label RELATED WORKS. This leaves the problem of uniform titles, which could be solved by labeling them OTHER TITLES. Although this label is not ideal, it is better than FILING TITLE, a clear non sequitur in an online environment.

I chose TOPICS as a substitute for SUBJECTS, which seems to be satisfactory. I did have a problem, however, with labels for publishing information and physical description. MATERIAL may be vague enough to cover physical description of all kinds, but it may suggest yard goods rather than number of pages. PHYSICAL DESCRIPTION is lengthy and may not be meaningful to users. Although PUB-LISHED is a verb caught in an embarrassing position, it is my final choice because PUBLISHING INFORMATION consumes too much space.

The statistics for this display are somewhat discouraging. On average, less than half (48%) fit on a single screen with room for holdings; it is a real space hog. Statistics for individual formats range from 30% for sound recordings to 74% for serials.

The critical factor in KOBM is the use of spaces between groups, as pointed out in the comparison between LMG and LMGSP in Chapter 4. In order to improve the statistics next time, I would eliminate the blank lines between OTHER ENTRIES and TOPICS and between TOPICS and SERIES, which would reduce the rate of spillover to an additional screen.

LMCAP—A MEDIUM DISPLAY

A medium display designed by Walt Crawford is illustrated in Figures 8.20 through 8.30. His notes on the display follow:

I did not originally intend to provide a design for this chapter because experience has shown me that I am better at supporting, explaining, and commenting on displays than at designing them. But I am looking for a single format that can serve all three functions, and feel that LMCAP may fill that need.

LMCAP is not really a new design; it is display LMCIT (Figures 5.4–5.6) with the short title capitalized. I believe that a citation-style paragraph with capitalized short title makes a compact, recognizable, intelligible entry (as in CBCAP, Figures 6.17–6.24).

The illustrations do not represent LMCAP as I would see it being used, since holdings information was not displayed in this project. Holdings information should appear directly below the first paragraph, in a tabular form. If the first screen leaves room, LMCAP should appear as the combined brief and medium format; otherwise, the names, series, subjects and works should appear with an "L" or similar command. The long form of LMCAP would add notes, either as an extra screen from the medium display or by keying "L" again. I regard the label NOTES as silly, but harmless. An example of the display as it might be used with holdings appears in *Patron Access: Issues for Online Catalogs.*

I'm not entirely convinced that a citation form is better than either a traditional cardlike form or a fully labeled form. It is more compact than either, and avoids the labeling difficulties inherent in publication information and physical description. I do believe that a capitalized short title within an entry-first citation is preferable to either a title-first citation or an entry-first citation without capitalized title.

MDSLON—A LONG DISPLAY

Figures 8.31 through 8.49 show a long display designed by Lennie Stovel. Her notes on the display follow:

After looking at several hundred records on a variety of displays for this project, I developed a preference for labeled displays, with one label for a group of fields. I also used a display area that is narrower than the full width of a screen because it seems quicker to read. Although a narrower display area forces more records to continuation screens, I don't think that is a problem because the main goal of a long format is to show data, not to conserve screens. I used a four-character indention for continuation lines of a given field because it gives a more open, less dense appearance.

Many title fields used in serials cataloging, such as the variant access title and the augmented title, and numbers, such as ISBN and ISSN, do not appear in this display. Since an online patron access catalog's display options will always include a tagged display of the entire record with all fields and subfields, we can assume that this data is never completely unavailable. However, this format includes all the bibliographic notes, as it seems impossible to say of any given note that it is so useless that it should be excluded.

The title is displayed first in MDSLON because everything always has a title, at least in the RLIN system, and the title is often—though not always—the most recognizable and unique characteristic. The notes are last. Other fields (except for added entries) generally follow the same sequence as on a traditional catalog card, though I added some blank lines.

If the main entry is a personal name, it is labeled AUTHOR. Other types of main entry, including uniform titles, and all added entries except author/title added entries are labeled OTHER ENTRIES, and appear directly after the TITLE and the AUTHOR. This represents a couple of compromises in areas discussed in Chapter 4.

Although it can be confusing when the main entry is, for example, a congressional subcommittee, I decided to use AUTHOR because it is a familiar and comfortable concept. In order to alleviate any possible confusion, I grouped the other kinds of main entries with all the other access points and called them OTHER ENTRIES. However, since it also makes sense to differentiate author/title added entries from name-only added entries, I separated out the former and called them WORKS. It is hard to come up with a good label for author/title added entries, which can refer to related works or to works contained in the item represented by the bibliographic record.

The label MATERIAL for the physical description appeals to me for the nonbooks formats, and particularly for the visual materials format, whose scope includes many different kinds of materials.

CONCLUSIONS

We have experimented with scores of displays over the past few months. We did not set out to demonstrate that one display is superior to any other but to explore some of the consequences of display design. We were not working with a real online catalog, a real collection or a real library. Rather, we were looking at one subset of the many decisions that go into the development of an online catalog.

The illustrations and tables in this book should be taken into account in preparing new displays, but they do not offer proof of superiority for any particular display. We are not convinced that any single display will be ideal for all libraries. Good displays involve many factors, not the least of which are taste, preference, professional judgment and the environment surrounding the online catalog. We offer several hundred illustrations and several thousand statistics. Librarians and designers should draw their own conclusions.

Figure 8.1

```
┌────────────────────────────────────────────────────────────────────┐
│Your search: find title Bless you boys #            Brief Display     │
│     finds: 1 record                                Screen  1 of  1   │
│-----------------------------------------------------------------------│
│                                                                      │
│          TITLE: Bless you boys : diary of the Detroit Tigers' 1984   │
│                 season / by Sparky Anderson, with Dan Ewald.         │
│                                                                      │
│         AUTHOR: Anderson, Sparky, 1934-                              │
│      PUBLISHED: Contemporary Books, c1984.                          │
│       MATERIAL: 231 p. : ill. ; 23 cm.                              │
│                                                                      │
│                                                                      │
│                                                                      │
│                                                                      │
│                                                                      │
│-----------------------------------------------------------------------│
│NEXT ACTIONS:  To get help, type ?       To see the next screen, type +│
│               To find other items, type F  To see the previous screen, type -│
│               To quit, type Q           To see a longer display, type L│
│NEXT ACTION?  _                                              MDSBRF    │
└────────────────────────────────────────────────────────────────────┘
```

Figure 8.2

```
┌────────────────────────────────────────────────────────────────────┐
│Your search: find title Best American pla#          Brief Display     │
│     finds: 1 record                                Screen  1 of  1   │
│-----------------------------------------------------------------------│
│                                                                      │
│           TITLE: Best American plays : sixth series, 1963-1967 / edited│
│                  by John Gassner and Clive Barnes, with an introduction│
│                  and prefaces to the plays by Clive Barnes.          │
│                                                                      │
│       PUBLISHED: Crown, c1971.                                      │
│        MATERIAL: xii, 594 p. ; 24 cm.                               │
│                                                                      │
│                                                                      │
│                                                                      │
│                                                                      │
│                                                                      │
│-----------------------------------------------------------------------│
│NEXT ACTIONS:  To get help, type ?       To see the next screen, type +│
│               To find other items, type F  To see the previous screen, type -│
│               To quit, type Q           To see a longer display, type L│
│NEXT ACTION?  _                                              MDSBRF    │
└────────────────────────────────────────────────────────────────────┘
```

Figure 8.3

```
Your search: find title Bossa nova U.S.A#          Brief Display
     finds: 1 record                               Screen  1 of  1
-----------------------------------------------------------------

        TITLE: Bossa nova U.S.A. / [as performed by] the Dave Brubeck
               Quartet ; piano solo transcriptions by Howard Brubeck.

       AUTHOR: Brubeck, Dave.
    PUBLISHED: Derry Music Co. ; C. Hansen, distributor, c1963.
     MATERIAL: 49 p. of music ; 28 cm.




-----------------------------------------------------------------
NEXT ACTIONS:  To get help, type ?        To see the next screen, type +
               To find other items, type F  To see the previous screen, type -
               To quit, type Q             To see a longer display, type L
NEXT ACTION?  _                                               MDSBRF
```

Figure 8.4

```
Your search: find title The explorer's hi#        Brief Display
     finds: 1 record                               Screen  1 of  1
-----------------------------------------------------------------

        TITLE: The explorer's historical tourist map of Alaska, with
               maps of Anchorage, Fairbanks & Juneau : with notes on
               the Arctic, wildlife, hunting, fishing, camping,
               exploring & prospecting, festivals & events /
               cartography by William H. Stewart.

       AUTHOR: Stewart, William Herman, 1932-
    PUBLISHED: Economic Service Council, 1983.
     MATERIAL: 1 map : col. ; 65 x 71 cm., folded to 23 x 11 cm.




-----------------------------------------------------------------
NEXT ACTIONS:  To get help, type ?        To see the next screen, type +
               To find other items, type F  To see the previous screen, type -
               To quit, type Q             To see a longer display, type L
NEXT ACTION?  _                                               MDSBRF
```

Figure 8.5

```
Your search: find title Suite en re dans #                    Brief Display
     finds: 1 record                                          Screen  1 of  1
--------------------------------------------------------------------------------

            TITLE: Suite en re dans le style ancien : op. 24 ; Karadec :
                   op. 34 ; Concert, op. 89 pour piano, flute,
                   violoncello et orchestre a cordes [sound recording] /
                   Vincent d'Indy.

           AUTHOR: Indy, Vincent d', 1851-1931.
        PUBLISHED: Erato ; Distribution en France RCA, p1982.
         MATERIAL: 1 sound disc : 33 1/3 rpm, stereo. ; 12 in.




---------------------------------------------------------------------------

NEXT ACTIONS:   To get help, type ?        To see the next screen, type +
                To find other items, type F  To see the previous screen, type -
                To quit, type Q             To see a longer display, type L
NEXT ACTION?   _                                                    MDSBRF
```

Figure 8.6

```
Your search: find title Time                                  Brief Display
     finds: 1 record                                          Screen  1 of  1
--------------------------------------------------------------------------------

            TITLE: Time.

        PUBLISHED: Time Inc.]
         MATERIAL: v. ill. (incl. ports.) 28 cm.







---------------------------------------------------------------------------

NEXT ACTIONS:   To get help, type ?        To see the next screen, type +
                To find other items, type F  To see the previous screen, type -
                To quit, type Q             To see a longer display, type L
NEXT ACTION?   _                                                    MDSBRF
```

Figure 8.7

```
Your search: find title Postdisaster surv#                    Brief Display
      finds: 1 record                                        Screen  1 of  1
--------------------------------------------------------------------------------


          TITLE: Postdisaster survival and rescue research :
                 proceedings, Bureau of Mines Technology Transfer
                 Seminar, Pittsburgh, Pa., November 16, 1982 / compiled
                 by staff, Bureau of Mines.

   OTHER ENTRIES: Bureau of Mines Technology Transfer Seminars (1982 :
                 Pittsburgh, Pa.)
       PUBLISHED: U.S. Dept. of the Interior, Bureau of Mines, 1982.
        MATERIAL: iii, 91 p. : ill. ; 28 cm.




--------------------------------------------------------------------------------
NEXT ACTIONS:  To get help, type ?        To see the next screen, type +
               To find other items, type F  To see the previous screen, type -
               To quit, type Q             To see a longer display, type L
NEXT ACTION?  _                                                       MDSBRF
```

Figure 8.8

```
Your search: find title Citizen Kane                         Brief Display
      finds: 1 record                                        Screen  1 of  1
--------------------------------------------------------------------------------


          TITLE: Citizen Kane [videorecording] / an RKO Radio Picture ;
                 a Mercury production ; Orson Welles, direction,
                 production.

       PUBLISHED: VidAmerica, c1982.
        MATERIAL: 1 videocassette (119 min.) : sd., b&w ; 1/2 in.





--------------------------------------------------------------------------------
NEXT ACTIONS:  To get help, type ?        To see the next screen, type +
               To find other items, type F  To see the previous screen, type -
               To quit, type Q             To see a longer display, type L
NEXT ACTION?  _                                                       MDSBRF
```

Figure 8.9

```
Your search: Bless you boys #                          MEDIUM Display
     Finds: 1 record                                   Screen  1 of  1
---------------------------------------------------------------------

          TITLE: Bless you boys : diary of the Detroit Tigers' 1984 season /
                 by Sparky Anderson, with Dan Ewald.

          NAMES: Anderson, Sparky, 1934-
   OTHER ENTRIES: Ewald, Dan.

         TOPICS: Detroit Tigers (Baseball team)

      PUBLISHED: Chicago : Contemporary Books, c1984.
       MATERIAL: 231 p. : ill. ; 23 cm.



---------------------------------------------------------------------
NEXT ACTIONS      Type: ? for help            + to see the next screen
                        F to Find other items - to see the previous screen
                        Q to Quit             L to see a Longer display
NEXT ACTION?  _                                              KOBM
```

Figure 8.10

```
Your search: Best American pla#                        MEDIUM Display
     Finds: 1 record                                   Screen  1 of  1
---------------------------------------------------------------------

          TITLE: Best American plays : sixth series, 1963-1967 / edited by
                 John Gassner and Clive Barnes, with an introduction and
                 prefaces to the plays by Clive Barnes.

   OTHER ENTRIES: Gassner, John, 1903-1967.
                  Barnes, Clive, 1927-

         TOPICS: American drama--20th century.
                 American drama--Collected works.

      PUBLISHED: New York : Crown, c1971.
       MATERIAL: xii, 594 p. ; 24 cm.



---------------------------------------------------------------------
NEXT ACTIONS      Type: ? for help            + to see the next screen
                        F to Find other items - to see the previous screen
                        Q to Quit             L to see a Longer display
NEXT ACTION?  _                                              KOBM
```

Figure 8.11

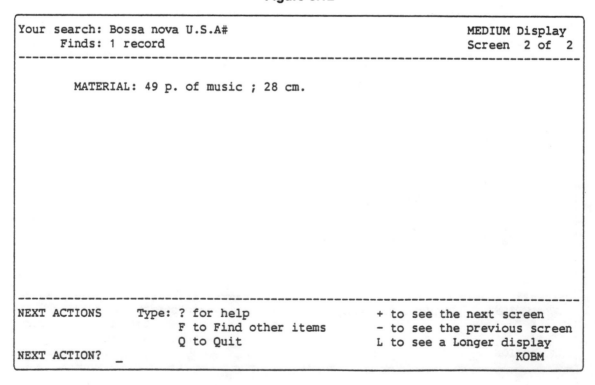

```
Your search: Bossa nova U.S.A#                    MEDIUM Display
      Finds: 1 record                             Screen  1 of  2
---------------------------------------------------------------------

            TITLE: Bossa nova U.S.A. / [as performed by] the Dave Brubeck
                   Quartet ; piano solo transcriptions by Howard Brubeck.

            NAMES: Brubeck, Dave.
    OTHER ENTRIES: Brubeck, Howard R.
                   Dave Brubeck Quartet.
    RELATED WORKS: Brubeck, Howard R. Theme for June; arr.
                   Macero, Teo, 1925- Coracao sensivel; arr.

           TOPICS: Piano music (Jazz), Arranged.
                   Jazz quartets--Piano scores.

        PUBLISHED: San Francisco, Calif. : Derry Music Co. ;  New York, N.Y. :
                   C. Hansen, distributor, c1963.

---------------------------------------------------CONTINUED-------
NEXT ACTIONS     Type: ? for help          + to see the next screen
                       F to Find other items  - to see the previous screen
                       Q to Quit           L to see a Longer display
NEXT ACTION?  _                                                  KOBM
```

Figure 8.12

```
Your search: Bossa nova U.S.A#                    MEDIUM Display
      Finds: 1 record                             Screen  2 of  2
---------------------------------------------------------------------

       MATERIAL: 49 p. of music ; 28 cm.




---------------------------------------------------------------------
NEXT ACTIONS     Type: ? for help          + to see the next screen
                       F to Find other items  - to see the previous screen
                       Q to Quit           L to see a Longer display
NEXT ACTION?  _                                                  KOBM
```

Figure 8.13

```
Your search: The explorer's hi#                        MEDIUM Display
       Finds: 1 record                                 Screen  1 of  1
---------------------------------------------------------------------
              TITLE: The explorer's historical tourist map of Alaska, with maps
                     of Anchorage, Fairbanks & Juneau : with notes on the
                     Arctic, wildlife, hunting, fishing, camping, exploring &
                     prospecting, festivals & events / cartography by William
                     H. Stewart.

              NAMES: Stewart, William Herman, 1932-
      OTHER ENTRIES: Economic Service Council.

             TOPICS: Alaska--Maps, Tourist.
                     Alaska--Maps, Pictorial.

          PUBLISHED: Charleston, W.Va. : Economic Service Council, 1983.
           MATERIAL: 1 map : col. ; 65 x 71 cm., folded to 23 x 11 cm.

---------------------------------------------------------------------
NEXT ACTIONS     Type: ? for help            + to see the next screen
                       F to Find other items - to see the previous screen
                       Q to Quit             L to see a Longer display
NEXT ACTION?     _                                              KOBM
```

Figure 8.14

```
Your search: Suite en re dans #                        MEDIUM Display
       Finds: 1 record                                 Screen  1 of  2
---------------------------------------------------------------------
              TITLE: Suite en re dans le style ancien : op. 24 ; Karadec : op. 34
                     ; Concert, op. 89 pour piano, flute, violoncello et
                     orchestre a cordes [sound recording] / Vincent d'Indy.

              NAMES: Indy, Vincent d', 1851-1931.
      OTHER ENTRIES: Rampal, Jean Pierre.
                     Pierlot, Philippe.
                     Andre, Maurice.
                     Duchable, Francois.
                     Lodeon, Frederic.
                     Paillard, Jean Francois.
                     Orchestre de chambre Jean-Francois Paillard.
      RELATED WORKS: Indy, Vincent d', 1851-1931. Suite dans le style ancien.
                     1982.

----------------------------------------------------CONTINUED-------
NEXT ACTIONS     Type: ? for help            + to see the next screen
                       F to Find other items - to see the previous screen
                       Q to Quit             L to see a Longer display
NEXT ACTION?     _                                              KOBM
```

Figure 8.15

```
Your search: Suite en re dans #                      MEDIUM Display
      Finds: 1 record                                Screen  2 of  2
--------------------------------------------------------------------

            Indy, Vincent d', 1851-1931. Karadec. 1982.
            Indy, Vincent d', 1851-1931. Concerto, piano, flute,
               violoncello, orchestra, op. 89. 1982.

         TOPICS: Suites (Flutes (2), trumpet with string orchestra)
                 Music, Incidental.
                 Concertos (Piano, flute, violoncello with string orchestra)

      PUBLISHED: France : Erato ; Paris : Distribution en France RCA, p1982.
       MATERIAL: 1 sound disc : 33 1/3 rpm, stereo. ; 12 in.




--------------------------------------------------------------------
NEXT ACTIONS     Type: ? for help            + to see the next screen
                       F to Find other items - to see the previous screen
                       Q to Quit             L to see a Longer display
NEXT ACTION?   _                                              KOBM
```

Figure 8.16

```
Your search: Time.                                   MEDIUM Display
      Finds: 1 record                                Screen  1 of  1
--------------------------------------------------------------------

          TITLE: Time.

   OTHER ENTRIES: Hadden, Briton, ed.
                  Luce, Henry Robinson, 1898- ed.

      PUBLISHED: [Chicago, etc., Time Inc.]
       MATERIAL: v. ill. (incl. ports.) 28 cm.




--------------------------------------------------------------------
NEXT ACTIONS     Type: ? for help            + to see the next screen
                       F to Find other items - to see the previous screen
                       Q to Quit             L to see a Longer display
NEXT ACTION?   _                                              KOBM
```

Figure 8.17

```
Your search: Postdisaster surv#                      MEDIUM Display
      Finds: 1 record                                Screen  1 of  2
-----------------------------------------------------------------------

            TITLE: Postdisaster survival and rescue research : proceedings,
                   Bureau of Mines Technology Transfer Seminar, Pittsburgh,
                   Pa., November 16, 1982 / compiled by staff, Bureau of
                   Mines.

            NAMES: Bureau of Mines Technology Transfer Seminars (1982 :
                   Pittsburgh, Pa.)
     OTHER ENTRIES: United States. Bureau of Mines.

           TOPICS: Mine accidents--Congresses.
                   Mine rescue work--Congresses.

           SERIES: Bureau of Mines information circular ; 8907.


-----------------------------------------------------CONTINUED-------
NEXT ACTIONS     Type: ? for help           + to see the next screen
                       F to Find other items  - to see the previous screen
                       Q to Quit              L to see a Longer display
NEXT ACTION?   _                                                KOBM
```

Figure 8.18

```
Your search: Postdisaster surv#                      MEDIUM Display
      Finds: 1 record                                Screen  2 of  2
-----------------------------------------------------------------------

        PUBLISHED: [Avondale, Md.] : U.S. Dept. of the Interior, Bureau of
                   Mines, 1982.
         MATERIAL: iii, 91 p. : ill. ; 28 cm.







-----------------------------------------------------------------------
NEXT ACTIONS     Type: ? for help           + to see the next screen
                       F to Find other items  - to see the previous screen
                       Q to Quit              L to see a Longer display
NEXT ACTION?   _                                                KOBM
```

Figure 8.19

```
Your search: Citizen Kane                         MEDIUM Display
      Finds: 1 record                             Screen  1 of  1
------------------------------------------------------------------------


            TITLE: Citizen Kane [videorecording] / an RKO Radio Picture ; a
                   Mercury production ; Orson Welles, direction, production.

     OTHER ENTRIES: Welles, Orson, 1915-
                    VidAmerica (Firm)
                    RKO Radio Pictures, inc.
                    Mercury Productions.

            TOPICS: Feature films.

            SERIES: Classic series.
         PUBLISHED: New York, N.Y. : VidAmerica, c1982.
          MATERIAL: 1 videocassette (119 min.) : sd., b&w ; 1/2 in.


------------------------------------------------------------------------
NEXT ACTIONS     Type: ? for help            + to see the next screen
                       F to Find other items - to see the previous screen
                       Q to Quit             L to see a Longer display
NEXT ACTION?  _                                                KOBM
```

Figure 8.20

```
Your search: Anderson, Sparky#                    MEDIUM Display
      Finds: 1 record                             Screen  1 of  1
------------------------------------------------------------------------

        Anderson, Sparky, 1934- BLESS YOU BOYS : diary of the
           Detroit Tigers' 1984 season / by Sparky Anderson, with
           Dan Ewald. Chicago : Contemporary Books, c1984. 231 p. :
           ill. ; .23 cm.

        NAMES: Anderson, Sparky, 1934-
               Ewald, Dan.

        SUBJECTS: Detroit Tigers (Baseball team)




------------------------------------------------------------------------
NEXT ACTIONS     Key: ? for help             + to see the next screen
                      L to see a Longer display - to see the previous screen
                      F to Find other items  Q to Quit
NEXT ACTION?  _                                                LMCAP
```

Figure 8.21

```
Your search: BEST AMERICAN PLA#                    MEDIUM Display
       Finds: 1 record                            Screen  1 of  1
-----------------------------------------------------------------------

         BEST AMERICAN PLAYS : sixth series, 1963-1967 / edited by
            John Gassner and Clive Barnes, with an introduction and
            prefaces to the plays by Clive Barnes. New York : Crown,
            c1971. xii, 594 p. ; 24 cm.

         NAMES: Gassner, John, 1903-1967.
                Barnes, Clive, 1927-

      SUBJECTS: American drama--20th century.
                American drama--Collected works.




-----------------------------------------------------------------------
NEXT ACTIONS      Key: ? for help          + to see the next screen
                       L to see a Longer display  - to see the previous screen
                       F to Find other items   Q to Quit
NEXT ACTION?    _                                          LMCAP
```

Figure 8.22

```
Your search: Brubeck, Dave.#                       MEDIUM Display
       Finds: 1 record                            Screen  1 of  2
-----------------------------------------------------------------------

         Brubeck, Dave. BOSSA NOVA U.S.A. / [as performed by] the
            Dave Brubeck Quartet ; piano solo transcriptions by
            Howard Brubeck. San Francisco, Calif. : Derry Music Co.
            ; New York, N.Y. : C. Hansen, distributor, c1963. 49 p.
            of music ; 28 cm.

         NAMES: Brubeck, Dave.
                Brubeck, Howard R.
                Dave Brubeck Quartet.

      SUBJECTS: Piano music (Jazz), Arranged.
                Jazz quartets--Piano scores.

         WORKS: Brubeck, Howard R. Theme for June; arr.

-----------------------------------------------------CONTINUED-------
NEXT ACTIONS      Key: ? for help          + to see the next screen
                       L to see a Longer display  - to see the previous screen
                       F to Find other items   Q to Quit
NEXT ACTION?    _                                          LMCAP
```

Figure 8.23

```
Your search: Brubeck, Dave.#                        MEDIUM Display
      Finds: 1 record                               Screen  2 of  2
--------------------------------------------------------------------------

            Macero, Teo, 1925- Coracao sensivel; arr.







--------------------------------------------------------------------------
NEXT ACTIONS      Key: ? for help               + to see the next screen
                       L to see a Longer display - to see the previous screen
                       F to Find other items    Q to Quit
NEXT ACTION?   _                                          LMCAP
```

Figure 8.24

```
Your search: Stewart, William #                     MEDIUM Display
      Finds: 1 record                               Screen  1 of  1
--------------------------------------------------------------------------

        Stewart, William Herman, 1932- THE EXPLORER'S HISTORICAL
            TOURIST MAP OF ALASKA, WITH MAPS OF ANCHORAGE, FAIRBANKS
            & JUNEAU : with notes on the Arctic, wildlife, hunting,
            fishing, camping, exploring & prospecting, festivals &
            events / cartography by William H. Stewart. Charleston,
            W.Va. : Economic Service Council, 1983. 1 map : col. ;
            65 x 71 cm., folded to 23 x 11 cm.

        NAMES: Stewart, William Herman, 1932-
               Economic Service Council.

     SUBJECTS: Alaska--Maps, Tourist.
               Alaska--Maps, Pictorial.


--------------------------------------------------------------------------
NEXT ACTIONS      Key: ? for help               + to see the next screen
                       L to see a Longer display - to see the previous screen
                       F to Find other items    Q to Quit
NEXT ACTION?   _                                          LMCAP
```

Figure 8.25

```
Your search: Indy, Vincent d'#                        MEDIUM Display
      Finds: 1 record                                 Screen  1 of  2
-----------------------------------------------------------------------

         Indy, Vincent d', 1851-1931. SUITE EN RE DANS LE STYLE
            ANCIEN : op. 24 ; Karadec : op. 34 ; Concert, op. 89
            pour piano, flute, violoncello et orchestre a cordes
            [sound recording] / Vincent d'Indy. France : Erato ;
            Paris : Distribution en France RCA, p1982. 1 sound disc
            : 33 1/3 rpm, stereo. ; 12 in.

         NAMES: Indy, Vincent d', 1851-1931.
                Rampal, Jean Pierre.
                Pierlot, Philippe.
                Andre, Maurice.
                Duchable, Francois.
                Lodeon, Frederic.
                Paillard, Jean Francois.

-----------------------------------------------------CONTINUED-------
NEXT ACTIONS      Key: ? for help            + to see the next screen
                       L to see a Longer display  - to see the previous screen
                       F to Find other items   Q to Quit
NEXT ACTION?   _                                          LMCAP
```

Figure 8.26

```
Your search: Indy, Vincent d'#                        MEDIUM Display
      Finds: 1 record                                 Screen  2 of  2
-----------------------------------------------------------------------

            Orchestre de chambre Jean-Francois Paillard.

      SUBJECTS: Suites (Flutes (2), trumpet with string orchestra)
                Music, Incidental.
                Concertos (Piano, flute, violoncello with string orchestra)

         WORKS: Indy, Vincent d', 1851-1931. Suite dans le style ancien.
                   1982.
                Indy, Vincent d', 1851-1931. Karadec. 1982.
                Indy, Vincent d', 1851-1931. Concerto, piano, flute,
                   violoncello, orchestra, op. 89. 1982.

-----------------------------------------------------------------------
NEXT ACTIONS      Key: ? for help            + to see the next screen
                       L to see a Longer display  - to see the previous screen
                       F to Find other items   Q to Quit
NEXT ACTION?   _                                          LMCAP
```

Figure 8.27

```
Your search: TIME.                              MEDIUM Display
      Finds: 1 record                           Screen  1 of  1
------------------------------------------------------------------

        TIME. [Chicago, etc., Time Inc.] v. ill. (incl. ports.) 28
          cm.

        NAMES: Hadden, Briton, ed.
               Luce, Henry Robinson, 1898- ed.






------------------------------------------------------------------
NEXT ACTIONS      Key: ? for help            + to see the next screen
                       L to see a Longer display  - to see the previous screen
                       F to Find other items  Q to Quit
NEXT ACTION?   _                                        LMCAP
```

Figure 8.28

```
Your search: Bureau of Mines T#                 MEDIUM Display
      Finds: 1 record                           Screen  1 of  2
------------------------------------------------------------------

      Bureau of Mines Technology Transfer Seminars (1982 :
          Pittsburgh, Pa.) POSTDISASTER SURVIVAL AND RESCUE
          RESEARCH : proceedings, Bureau of Mines Technology
          Transfer Seminar, Pittsburgh, Pa., November 16, 1982 ./
          compiled by staff, Bureau of Mines. [Avondale, Md.] :
          U.S. Dept. of the Interior, Bureau of Mines, 1982. iii,
          91 p. : ill. ; 28 cm.

        NAMES: Bureau of Mines Technology Transfer Seminars (1982 :
               Pittsburgh, Pa.)
               United States. Bureau of Mines.

        SERIES: Bureau of Mines information circular ; 8907.


-------------------------------------------------------CONTINUED-------
NEXT ACTIONS      Key: ? for help            + to see the next screen
                       L to see a Longer display  - to see the previous screen
                       F to Find other items  Q to Quit
NEXT ACTION?   _                                        LMCAP
```

Figure 8.29

```
Your search: Bureau of Mines T#                    MEDIUM Display
      Finds: 1 record                              Screen  2 of  2
------------------------------------------------------------------

      SUBJECTS: Mine accidents--Congresses.
                Mine rescue work--Congresses.







------------------------------------------------------------------
NEXT ACTIONS      Key: ? for help           + to see the next screen
                       L to see a Longer display   - to see the previous screen
                       F to Find other items   Q to Quit
NEXT ACTION?   _                                          LMCAP
```

Figure 8.30

```
Your search: CITIZEN KANE                          MEDIUM Display
      Finds: 1 record                              Screen  1 of  1
------------------------------------------------------------------

      CITIZEN KANE [videorecording] / an RKO Radio Picture ; a
          Mercury production ; Orson Welles, direction,
          production. New York, N.Y. : VidAmerica, c1982. 1
          videocassette (119 min.) : sd., b&w ; 1/2 in.

      NAMES: Welles, Orson, 1915-
             VidAmerica (Firm)
             RKO Radio Pictures, inc.
             Mercury Productions.

     SERIES: Classic series.

   SUBJECTS: Feature films.


------------------------------------------------------------------
NEXT ACTIONS      Key: ? for help           + to see the next screen
                       L to see a Longer display   - to see the previous screen
                       F to Find other items   Q to Quit
NEXT ACTION?   _                                          LMCAP
```

Figure 8.31

```
Your search: find title Bless you boys #                    LONG Display
     finds: 1 record                                        Screen  1 of  1
----------------------------------------------------------------------------

               TITLE: Bless you boys : diary of the Detroit Tigers' 1984
                      season / by Sparky Anderson, with Dan Ewald.

              AUTHOR: Anderson, Sparky, 1934-
        OTHER ENTRIES: Ewald, Dan.

           PUBLISHED: Chicago : Contemporary Books, c1984.
            MATERIAL: 231 p. : ill. ; 23 cm.

            SUBJECTS: Detroit Tigers (Baseball team)




----------------------------------------------------------------------------
NEXT ACTIONS:  To get help, type ?        To see the next screen, type +
               To find other items, type F  To see the previous screen, type -
               To quit, type Q             To see a longer display, type L
NEXT ACTION?   _                                                     MDSLON
```

Figure 8.32

```
Your search: find title Best American pla#                 LONG Display
     finds: 1 record                                        Screen  1 of  2
----------------------------------------------------------------------------

               TITLE: Best American plays : sixth series, 1963-1967 / edited
                      by John Gassner and Clive Barnes, with an
                      introduction and prefaces to the plays by Clive
                      Barnes.

       OTHER ENTRIES: Gassner, John, 1903-1967.
                      Barnes, Clive, 1927-

           PUBLISHED: New York : Crown, c1971.
            MATERIAL: xii, 594 p. ; 24 cm.

            SUBJECTS: American drama--20th century.
                      American drama--Collected works.

                                                            CONTINUED
----------------------------------------------------------------------------
NEXT ACTIONS:  To get help, type ?        To see the next screen, type +
               To find other items, type F  To see the previous screen, type -
               To quit, type Q             To see a longer display, type L
NEXT ACTION?   _                                                     MDSLON
```

Figure 8.33

```
Your search: find title Best American pla#           LONG Display
      finds: 1 record                                Screen  2 of  2
-----------------------------------------------------------------------

          NOTES: Contents: Tiny Alice / E. Albee -- Blues for Mister
                 Charlie / J. Baldwin -- The last analysis / S.
                 Bellow -- Hogan's goat / W. Alfred -- The
                 fantasticks / T. Jones -- The sign in Sidney
                 Brustein's window / L. Hansberry -- The lion in
                 winter / J. Goldman -- Hughie / E. O'Neill -- The
                 toilet / L. Jones -- You know I can't hear you
                 when the water is running / R. Anderson -- Benito
                 Cereno / R. Lowell -- Fiddler on the roof / J.
                 Stein -- Slow dance on the killing ground / W.
                 Hanley -- In white America / M.B. Duberman -- The
                 owl and the pussycat / B. Manhoff -- The odd
                 couple / W. Simon -- The subject was roses / F.D.
                 Gilroy.


-----------------------------------------------------------------------
NEXT ACTIONS:  To get help, type ?       To see the next screen, type +
               To find other items, type F  To see the previous screen, type -
               To quit, type Q          To see a longer display, type L
NEXT ACTION?   _                                             MDSLON
```

Figure 8.34

```
Your search: find title Bossa nova U.S.A#            LONG Display
      finds: 1 record                                Screen  1 of  3
-----------------------------------------------------------------------

          TITLE: Bossa nova U.S.A. / [as performed by] the Dave Brubeck
                 Quartet ; piano solo transcriptions by Howard
                 Brubeck.

         AUTHOR: Brubeck, Dave.
  OTHER ENTRIES: Bossa nova U.S.A. Selections; arr.
                 Brubeck, Howard R.
                 Dave Brubeck Quartet.

      PUBLISHED: San Francisco, Calif. : Derry Music Co. ;  New York,
                 N.Y. : C. Hansen, distributor, c1963.
       MATERIAL: 49 p. of music ; 28 cm.

       SUBJECTS: Piano music (Jazz), Arranged.

                                                     CONTINUED
-----------------------------------------------------------------------
NEXT ACTIONS:  To get help, type ?       To see the next screen, type +
               To find other items, type F  To see the previous screen, type -
               To quit, type Q          To see a longer display, type L
NEXT ACTION?   _                                             MDSLON
```

Figure 8.35

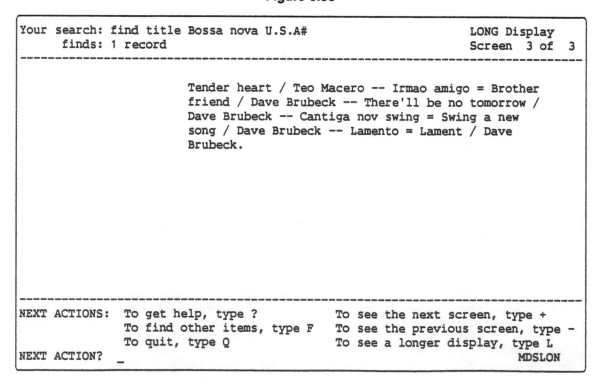

```
Your search: find title Bossa nova U.S.A#              LONG Display
       finds: 1 record                                 Screen  2 of  3
------------------------------------------------------------------------

                      Jazz quartets--Piano scores.

          WORKS: Brubeck, Howard R. Theme for June; arr.
                 Macero, Teo, 1925- Coracao sensivel; arr.

          NOTES: Jazz quartets arr. for piano solo; chord symbols and
                    fingerings included.
                 "Trolley song and This can't be love do not appear in
                    this collection due to copyright restrictions."
                 Notes on the music by Dave Brubeck, principal
                    composer, on covers.
                 Contents: Bossa nova U.S. A. / Dave Brubeck -- Vento
                    fresco = Cool wind / Dave Brubeck -- Theme for
                    June / Howard R. Brubeck -- Coracao sensivel =
                                                            CONTINUED
------------------------------------------------------------------------

NEXT ACTIONS:  To get help, type ?       To see the next screen, type +
               To find other items, type F  To see the previous screen, type -
               To quit, type Q            To see a longer display, type L
NEXT ACTION?  _                                             MDSLON
```

Figure 8.36

```
Your search: find title Bossa nova U.S.A#              LONG Display
       finds: 1 record                                 Screen  3 of  3
------------------------------------------------------------------------

                      Tender heart / Teo Macero -- Irmao amigo = Brother
                      friend / Dave Brubeck -- There'll be no tomorrow /
                      Dave Brubeck -- Cantiga nov swing = Swing a new
                      song / Dave Brubeck -- Lamento = Lament / Dave
                      Brubeck.








------------------------------------------------------------------------

NEXT ACTIONS:  To get help, type ?       To see the next screen, type +
               To find other items, type F  To see the previous screen, type -
               To quit, type Q            To see a longer display, type L
NEXT ACTION?  _                                             MDSLON
```

Figure 8.37

```
Your search: find title The explorer's hi#              LONG Display
      finds: 1 record                                  Screen  1 of  2
-----------------------------------------------------------------------

           TITLE: The explorer's historical tourist map of Alaska, with
                  maps of Anchorage, Fairbanks & Juneau : with notes
                  on the Arctic, wildlife, hunting, fishing,
                  camping, exploring & prospecting, festivals &
                  events / cartography by William H. Stewart.

          AUTHOR: Stewart, William Herman, 1932-
   OTHER ENTRIES: Economic Service Council.

         EDITION: Scale [ca. 1:3,200,000] (E 1720--W 1300/N 700--N 520).
       PUBLISHED: Charleston, W.Va. : Economic Service Council, 1983.
        MATERIAL: 1 map : col. ; 65 x 71 cm., folded to 23 x 11 cm.

        SUBJECTS: Alaska--Maps, Tourist.

                                                       CONTINUED
-----------------------------------------------------------------------
NEXT ACTIONS:   To get help, type ?         To see the next screen, type +
                To find other items, type F To see the previous screen, type -
                To quit, type Q             To see a longer display, type L
NEXT ACTION?  _                                                MDSLON
```

Figure 8.38

```
Your search: find title The explorer's hi#              LONG Display
      finds: 1 record                                  Screen  2 of  2
-----------------------------------------------------------------------

               Alaska--Maps, Pictorial.

           NOTES: Panel title.
                  Pictorial map.
                  Includes inset of the Aleutian Islands, notes, 3
                     diagrams, and ill.
                  Ancillary maps: Comparative size of Alaska -- Top of
                     the world -- Juneau -- Fairbanks -- Anchorage.




-----------------------------------------------------------------------
NEXT ACTIONS:   To get help, type ?         To see the next screen, type +
                To find other items, type F To see the previous screen, type -
                To quit, type Q             To see a longer display, type L
NEXT ACTION?  _                                                MDSLON
```

Figure 8.39

```
┌─────────────────────────────────────────────────────────────────────┐
│ Your search: find title Suite en re dans #          LONG Display     │
│       finds: 1 record                               Screen  1 of  3  │
│ --------------------------------------------------------------------- │
│                                                                       │
│            TITLE: Suite en re dans le style ancien : op. 24 ; Karadec :│
│                   op. 34 ; Concert, op. 89 pour piano, flute,         │
│                   violoncello et orchestre a cordes [sound            │
│                   recording] / Vincent d'Indy.                        │
│                                                                       │
│           AUTHOR: Indy, Vincent d', 1851-1931.                        │
│    OTHER ENTRIES: Instrumental music. Selections.                     │
│                   Rampal, Jean Pierre.                                │
│                   Pierlot, Philippe.                                  │
│                   Andre, Maurice.                                     │
│                   Duchable, Francois.                                 │
│                   Lodeon, Frederic.                                   │
│                   Paillard, Jean Francois.                            │
│                                                                       │
│                                                         CONTINUED     │
│ --------------------------------------------------------------------- │
│ NEXT ACTIONS:  To get help, type ?      To see the next screen, type +│
│                To find other items, type F  To see the previous screen, type -│
│                To quit, type Q          To see a longer display, type L│
│ NEXT ACTION?  _                                         MDSLON        │
└─────────────────────────────────────────────────────────────────────┘
```

Figure 8.40

```
┌─────────────────────────────────────────────────────────────────────┐
│ Your search: find title Suite en re dans #          LONG Display     │
│       finds: 1 record                               Screen  2 of  3  │
│ --------------------------------------------------------------------- │
│                                                                       │
│            Orchestre de chambre Jean-Francois Paillard.               │
│                                                                       │
│        PUBLISHED: France : Erato ; Paris : Distribution en France RCA,│
│                   p1982.                                              │
│         MATERIAL: 1 sound disc : 33 1/3 rpm, stereo. ; 12 in.         │
│                                                                       │
│         SUBJECTS: Suites (Flutes (2), trumpet with string orchestra)  │
│                   Music, Incidental.                                  │
│                   Concertos (Piano, flute, violoncello with string    │
│                   orchestra)                                          │
│                                                                       │
│            WORKS: Indy, Vincent d', 1851-1931. Suite dans le style    │
│                   ancien. 1982.                                       │
│                   Indy, Vincent d', 1851-1931. Karadec. 1982.         │
│                                                         CONTINUED     │
│ --------------------------------------------------------------------- │
│ NEXT ACTIONS:  To get help, type ?      To see the next screen, type +│
│                To find other items, type F  To see the previous screen, type -│
│                To quit, type Q          To see a longer display, type L│
│ NEXT ACTION?  _                                         MDSLON        │
└─────────────────────────────────────────────────────────────────────┘
```

Figure 8.41

```
Your search: find title Suite en re dans #            LONG Display
      finds: 1 record                                 Screen  3 of  3
-------------------------------------------------------------------
                Indy, Vincent d', 1851-1931. Concerto, piano, flute,
                   violoncello, orchestra, op. 89. 1982.

         NOTES: The 2nd work incidental music.
                Jean-Pierre Rampal, Philippe Pierlot, flutes, Maurice
                   Andre, trumpet (in the 1st work) ; Francois-Rene
                   Duchable, piano, Jean-Pierre Rampal, flute,
                   Frederic Lodeon, violoncello (in the 3rd) ;
                   Orchestre de chambre Jean-Francois Paillard ;
                   Jean-Francois Paillard, conductor.
                Recorded Jan. and Apr., 1981, l'IRCAM-Espace de
                   Projection, Paris.
                Eds. recorded: Heugel.
                Issued also as cassette: MCE 71423.

-------------------------------------------------------------------
NEXT ACTIONS:  To get help, type ?          To see the next screen, type +
               To find other items, type F  To see the previous screen, type -
               To quit, type Q              To see a longer display, type L
NEXT ACTION?  _                                                 MDSLON
```

Figure 8.42

```
Your search: find title Time.                        LONG Display
      finds: 1 record                                 Screen  1 of  3
-------------------------------------------------------------------
          TITLE: Time. v. 1-   Mar. 3, 1923-

  OTHER ENTRIES: Hadden, Briton, ed.
                 Luce, Henry Robinson, 1898- ed.

      PUBLISHED: [Chicago, etc., Time Inc.]
       MATERIAL: v. ill. (incl. ports.) 28 cm.

          NOTES: Weekly (except one week a year) <, Dec. 26, 1977->
                 Weekly <, April 15, 1985->
                 Indexed selectively by: ABI/INFORM March 1975-Jan.
                    1978.
                 Indexed in its entirety by: Abridged readers' guide to
                    periodical literature.
                                                        CONTINUED
-------------------------------------------------------------------
NEXT ACTIONS:  To get help, type ?          To see the next screen, type +
               To find other items, type F  To see the previous screen, type -
               To quit, type Q              To see a longer display, type L
NEXT ACTION?  _                                                 MDSLON
```

Figure 8.43

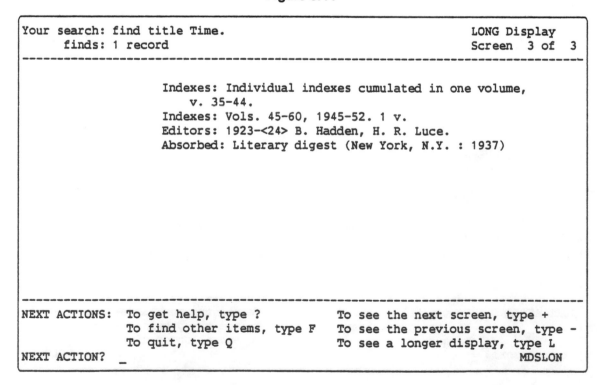

```
Your search: find title Time.                          LONG Display
       finds: 1 record                                 Screen  2 of  3
-------------------------------------------------------------------------

              Indexed selectively by: Book review index.
              Indexed selectively by: Cumulative index to nursing &
                 allied health literature.
              Indexed selectively by: Film literature index.
              Indexed selectively by: Hospital literature index.
              Indexed selectively by: Infobank Jan. 1969-
              Indexed selectively by: Popular magazine review 1984-
              Indexed selectively by: Predicasts.
              Indexed by: Biography index.
              Indexed in its entirety by: Readers' guide to
                 periodical literature.
              Indexed selectively by: Media review digest.
              Indexed selectively by: Energy information abstracts.
              Indexed selectively by: Environment abstracts.
                                                            CONTINUED
-------------------------------------------------------------------------
NEXT ACTIONS:  To get help, type ?        To see the next screen, type +
               To find other items, type F  To see the previous screen, type -
               To quit, type Q             To see a longer display, type L
NEXT ACTION?  _                                               MDSLON
```

Figure 8.44

```
Your search: find title Time.                          LONG Display
       finds: 1 record                                 Screen  3 of  3
-------------------------------------------------------------------------

              Indexes: Individual indexes cumulated in one volume,
                 v. 35-44.
              Indexes: Vols. 45-60, 1945-52. 1 v.
              Editors: 1923-<24> B. Hadden, H. R. Luce.
              Absorbed: Literary digest (New York, N.Y. : 1937)




-------------------------------------------------------------------------
NEXT ACTIONS:  To get help, type ?        To see the next screen, type +
               To find other items, type F  To see the previous screen, type -
               To quit, type Q             To see a longer display, type L
NEXT ACTION?  _                                               MDSLON
```

Figure 8.45

```
Your search: find title Postdisaster surv#              LONG Display
        finds: 1 record                                 Screen  1 of  2
---------------------------------------------------------------------------

          TITLE: Postdisaster survival and rescue research :
                 proceedings, Bureau of Mines Technology Transfer
                 Seminar, Pittsburgh, Pa., November 16, 1982 /
                 compiled by staff, Bureau of Mines.

   OTHER ENTRIES: Bureau of Mines Technology Transfer Seminars (1982 :
                 Pittsburgh, Pa.)
                 United States. Bureau of Mines.

       PUBLISHED: [Avondale, Md.] : U.S. Dept. of the Interior, Bureau
                 of Mines, 1982.
        MATERIAL: iii, 91 p. : ill. ; 28 cm.


                                                        CONTINUED
---------------------------------------------------------------------------
NEXT ACTIONS:  To get help, type ?        To see the next screen, type +
               To find other items, type F  To see the previous screen, type -
               To quit, type Q             To see a longer display, type L
NEXT ACTION?  _                                              MDSLON
```

Figure 8.46

```
Your search: find title Postdisaster surv#              LONG Display
        finds: 1 record                                 Screen  2 of  2
---------------------------------------------------------------------------

         SERIES: Bureau of Mines information circular ; 8907.

       SUBJECTS: Mine accidents--Congresses.
                 Mine rescue work--Congresses.

          NOTES: Includes bibliographies.






---------------------------------------------------------------------------
NEXT ACTIONS:  To get help, type ?        To see the next screen, type +
               To find other items, type F  To see the previous screen, type -
               To quit, type Q             To see a longer display, type L
NEXT ACTION?  _                                              MDSLON
```

Figure 8.47

```
Your search: find title Citizen Kane                    LONG Display
        finds: 1 record                                 Screen  1 of  3
----------------------------------------------------------------------

          TITLE: Citizen Kane [videorecording] / an RKO Radio Picture ;
                 a Mercury production ; Orson Welles, direction,
                 production.

  OTHER ENTRIES: Welles, Orson, 1915-
                 VidAmerica (Firm)
                 RKO Radio Pictures, inc.
                 Mercury Productions.

      PUBLISHED: New York, N.Y. : VidAmerica, c1982.
       MATERIAL: 1 videocassette (119 min.) : sd., b&w ; 1/2 in.

         SERIES: Classic series.

                                                       CONTINUED
----------------------------------------------------------------------
NEXT ACTIONS:  To get help, type ?        To see the next screen, type +
               To find other items, type F  To see the previous screen, type -
               To quit, type Q            To see a longer display, type L
NEXT ACTION?   _                                                MDSLON
```

Figure 8.48

```
Your search: find title Citizen Kane                    LONG Display
        finds: 1 record                                 Screen  2 of  3
----------------------------------------------------------------------

       SUBJECTS: Feature films.

          NOTES: Cast: Orson Welles, Joseph Cotton, Agnes Moorehead,
                 Everett Sloane.
                 Credits: Photography, Gregg Toland ; music, Bernard
                 Herrmann ; screenplay, Orson Welles, Herman J.
                 Mankiewicz.
                 Originally produced as motion picture in 1941.
                 VHS.
                 1941 Academy Award for best screenplay.
                 Summary: A story of the rise and fall of a great man
                 as the result of his accumulation of wealth and
                 subsequent isolation from the world. Based on the
                 life of newspaper tycoon William Randolph Hearst,
                                                       CONTINUED
----------------------------------------------------------------------
NEXT ACTIONS:  To get help, type ?        To see the next screen, type +
               To find other items, type F  To see the previous screen, type -
               To quit, type Q            To see a longer display, type L
NEXT ACTION?   _                                                MDSLON
```

Figure 8.49

```
Your search: find title Citizen Kane                     LONG Display
       finds: 1 record                                   Screen  3 of  3
-------------------------------------------------------------------------
                       this is classic American cinema.
                VidAmerica: #903.




-------------------------------------------------------------------------
NEXT ACTIONS:  To get help, type ?        To see the next screen, type +
               To find other items, type F  To see the previous screen, type -
               To quit, type Q            To see a longer display, type L
NEXT ACTION?  _                                              MDSLON
```

Appendix A: Field Occurrence
Tables and Display Summaries

The RLIN Monthly Process File contains all records added or updated in RLIN during the preceding 46 days. It serves as the basis for most Bibliographic Display Testbed test runs. Because very little cataloging was being done in the Machine-Readable Data File (MRDF) format, the complete RLIN MRDF file as of March 11, 1986, was used for format-specific test runs in order to provide a reasonably large sample. The Monthly Process File represents actual RLIN cataloging, acquisitions and retrospective conversion; batch-loaded items (such as LC MARC Distribution Service) are not included. Note that RLIN is not a master-record system; the same bibliographic item may appear in several RLIN MARC records if held by several libraries.

This appendix includes two types of tables: *field occurrence and average length*. These appear for all RLIN records (except AMC), public library records and each material format. *Display summaries* appear for the same categories, except that no such summary appears for books (since books represent 83% of all items in the study).

Table A.1 gives the names and descriptions for all displays that appear in the display summaries, in the same order as the summaries themselves.

Tables A.2 through A.5 give field occurrences and average field length for all records except Archival and Manuscript Control. The display summary for these records appears as Table A.6. Tables A.7 through A.9 give field occurrences and length for public library cataloging and the display summary for these records is in Table A.10.

Table A.11 compares two sets of field occurrences representing completely different sets of RLIN records (i.e., current cataloging from two periods separated by more than 46 days). This comparison of occurrences and average length for 35 common fields demonstrates the relatively high consistency of field occurrence within contemporary cataloging.

Tables A.12 and A.13 show field occurrence and length for records describing books. Tables A.14 and A.15 show field occurrence and length for Archival and

Manuscript Control records; Table A.16 gives display statistics for those records using 28 selected display options.

Table A.17 gives field occurrence and length for all Machine-Readable Data File records in RLIN as of March 11, 1986, and Table A.18 shows the results of display tests against those records. Tables A.19 and A.20 give field occurrence and length for maps records, with Table A.21 giving display results.

Tables A.22 and A.23 give field occurrence and length for musical scores records; Table A.24 shows display results. Tables A.25 through A.27 give field occurrences for serials records; display results appear in Table A.28. Tables A.29 and A.30 show field occurrences for sound recordings records, and Table A.31 shows display results. Finally, field occurrence and length for visual materials records appear in Tables A.32 and A.33 and Table A.34 shows display results.

NOTES ON FIELD OCCURRENCE TABLES

Field occurrence tables are based on all items in the Monthly Process File, including items for acquisitions (most of which contain full descriptive and subject cataloging) but excluding duplicate items. Fields 001, 005 and 008 do not appear. Each of these fields appears exactly once in each item, and fields 005 and 008 are fixed-length by definition. The average length of field 001 is peculiar to RLIN, and has no broader significance. Fields defined locally for RLIN that have neither bibliographic nor holdings information are also excluded.

The *average length* listed does not include minimum USMARC overhead (i.e., the indicators, initial subfield delimiter and field terminator). Thus, these averages have five fewer characters than the averages of lengths taken directly from the MARC directory.

Profiles are prepared from the directories, not by any examination of fields. Many fields have fewer textual characters than the averages listed because the fields include more than one subfield. Since a typical online display will replace the two-character subfield delimiter with a single space, the difference in space requirements is quite small.

Average lengths also reflect only what is in the MARC field, not what would appear in a display. Many notes and linking entries require display constants that would add to the number of characters displayed.

Averages should always be viewed cautiously, particularly when making any sweeping assumptions about display requirements. A good initial assumption is that fields appear for a reason; those items that have two or three times as much text as the average may require that much text to be fully useful.

Maximum field lengths do not appear, but the RLIN "Counter" program, used to prepare the statistics on which these profiles are based, reports the longest occurrence for each field. Any system that attempts to prevent fields from splitting over more than one screen should build in some overrides, given the realities of library bibliographic information. If a system allows 14 lines of 60 characters each, with a typical loss of 2.5 characters for line breaking, the system has room for roughly 805 text characters on a screen. In the overall sample, nine different fields exceed that limit at least once: 245, 500, 505, 515, 533, 550, 580, 590 and 700. Three of those (245, 505 and 700) can be displayed on a single screen only if all 80 columns and at least 20 lines are used, since each has a maximum length of more than 1500 characters. Even longer fields may appear in USMARC distribution. RLIN maintains a single-screen limit for any given occurrence of a field, but it uses a very large display area.

Occurrences per hundred represents a convenient way of stating a ratio. The number is the average number of fields per hundred records. If a sample of 1000 records contains 247 occurrences of a field, the field has 24.7 occurrences per hundred. A field may appear 10 times in one record and not at all in 19 other records; that represents 50 occurrences per hundred.

Some RLIN MARC fields appear in these tables: 090, 590, 690–699, 796–799, 896–899, 930, 936, 950 and 955. Those fields contain either local versions of notes or access points, or call number, location and holdings information.

Fields 066 and 880 appear only in those items with nonroman cataloging information. During these tests, nonroman cataloging in RLIN was limited to Chinese, Japanese or Korean (CJK). The fields are included to provide a more complete picture. One 066 field appears in each CJK item; each nonroman field is an 880. Thus, 2.7% of the records studied contain CJK data and each such record contains an average of 4.3 (11.93 divided by 2.74) nonroman fields.

The overall field occurrence table lists any field that appears at least once in 10,000 records (at least 62 times in the sample). Other tables are limited to 0.1, rounded: i.e., fields that appear at least once in 2000 records.

NOTES ON DISPLAY SUMMARIES

The overall display summary and the summary for public libraries (Tables A.6 and A.10, respectively) recapitulate the display statistics at the ends of Chapters 2 through 8, in a somewhat different form. These figures include the percentage of items requiring exactly three screens and the percentage requiring four or more screens. *One/Hold* means "one screen with room for minimal holdings"; *One* means "one screen without regard to holdings."

<0.1% means "at least one item, but less than one in 2000." "—" means "none." *100.0%* may represent rounding, but always means "greater than 99.95%."

The display statistics that follow each material format field occurrence show results of test runs done against that format. The number of items tested appears at the top of each figure.

USING THE TABLES

Field occurrence tables should be comparable to similar tables issued by other agencies. The tables should provide fairly reliable pictures of how fields are used in contemporary cataloging—how frequently fields appear and how long fields tend to be.

Format-specific display summaries should be particularly useful for libraries with high concentrations of certain formats. A music library must consider the generally greater display requirements of scores and sound recordings, as must a library specializing in AMC information.

Table A.1: Displays Represented in Appendix A

```
Display   Description
-------   -------------------------------------------------------------------
CMTW      Cardlike medium display, wide lines  (80 columns)
CMTN      Cardlike medium display, narrow lines (60 columns)
CMSX      Cardlike medium display, narrow lines, vertical spacing
CMSL      Cardlike medium display, narrow lines, new line for each entry

CMCIT     Cardlike medium display with citation-style description
CMTCIT    Cardlike medium display with title-citation description

LMLFT     Labeled medium display with flush-left labels and text
LMRI      Labeled medium display, gutter aligned with each field labeled
LMG       Labeled medium display, gutter aligned with each group labeled
LMGCON    Labeled medium display, gutter aligned, concatenated entries

LMGSP     Labeled medium display, gutter aligned, vertical spacing
LMGAT     Labeled medium display, gutter aligned, author/title split
LMGWI     Labeled medium display, like LMGAT but with wide indentation
LMGAT17   Labeled medium display, like LMGAT but with seventeen display lines
LMGAT50   Labeled medium display, like LMGAT but with 50-column lines

LMTCIT    Partially labeled medium display with title-citation description
CXSIMPL   Simple cardlike display
LXSIMPL   Simple labeled display

CXMATT    Cardlike display based on Joseph Matthews' list of fields
LXMATT    Labeled display based on Joseph Matthews' list of fields

CXPLM1    Cardlike display based on Richard Palmer's short list of fields
LXPLM1    Labeled display based on Richard Palmer's short list of fields

CXPLM2    Cardlike display based on Richard Palmer's long list of fields
LXPLM2    Labeled display based on Richard Palmer's long list of fields

CBRF1     Cardlike brief display
LBRF1     Labeled brief display
CBCAP     Citation-style brief display with capitalized short title

CLON1     Cardlike long display
CLCIT1    Cardlike long display with citation-style description
LLON1     Labeled long display

MDSBRF    Lennie Stovel's brief display
KOBM      Kathleen Bales' medium display
LMCAP     Walt Crawford's medium display
MDSLON    Lennie Stovel's long display
```

Table A.2: Field Occurrence, All but AMC (Part 1)

Tag	ALL RECORDS EXCEPT AMC Description [628,142 records]	Occurrences per hundred	Average Length
007	Physical Description Fixed Field	3.18	13.4
010	LC Control Number (LCCN)	58.96	11.8
011	Linking LC Control Number	0.02	8.5
015	National Bibliography Number	3.26	7.3
017	Copyright Registration Number	0.01	22.0
020	ISBN	55.64	18.7
022	ISSN	3.64	9.5
024	Standard Recording Number	0.04	10.1
025	Overseas Acquisition Number	0.34	10.6
027	Standard Technical Report Number (STRN)	0.03	12.0
028	Publisher Number for Music	1.85	22.0
030	CODEN Designation	0.60	6.0
033	Capture Date and Place	0.14	17.2
034	Coded Mathematical Data	0.11	25.4
035	System Control Number	7.61	11.8
037	Stock Number	0.05	18.6
040	Cataloging Source	79.43	12.5
041	Language Code	6.93	7.6
042	Authentication Agency Code	3.25	5.6
043	Geographic Area Code	31.33	8.2
045	Chronological Code or Date/Time	1.55	6.2
047	Form of Composition Code	0.16	10.2
048	Number of Instruments or Voices Code	1.93	9.9
050	Library of Congress Class/Call Number	53.18	16.5
051	LC Copy, Issue, Offprint Statement	0.13	28.7
052	Geographic Classification Code	0.11	6.6
055	Call Numbers/Class Numbers Assigned in Canada	0.07	7.4
060	National Library of Medicine Call Number	2.29	14.3
066	Character Sets Present	2.74	2.0
070	National Agricultural Library Call Number	0.16	11.0
072	Subject Category Code	0.03	4.1
074	GPO Item Number	0.29	9.1
082	Dewey Decimal Classification Number	43.26	11.8
086	Government Document Classification No.	0.68	17.8
088	Report Number	0.04	18.7
090	Local call number (& other local inf.)	100.00	19.6

Table A.3: Field Occurrence, All but AMC (Part 2)

```
      ALL RECORDS EXCEPT AMC   [Continued]      Occurrences        Average
 Tag  Description        [628,142 records]      per hundred        Length
 ---  ------------------------------------      -----------        -------
 100  Main Entry - Personal Name                   67.43             22.6
 110  Main Entry - Corporate Name                   6.03             45.5
 111  Main Entry - Conference or Meeting            1.64             78.5
 130  Main Entry - Uniform Title Heading            0.85             40.5

 210  Abbreviated Title                             1.30             20.8
 212  Variant Access Title                          0.41             44.1
 222  Key Title                                     2.55             32.8
 240  Uniform Title                                 4.91             30.7

 241  Romanized Title                               0.06             39.1
 245  Title Statement                             100.00             86.6
 246  Varying Form of Title                         2.41             32.9
 247  Former Title or Title Variations              0.57             52.3

 250  Edition Statement                            14.81             13.8
 254  Musical Presentation Area                     0.10             13.4
 255  Mathematical Data Area                        0.16             35.8
 260  Publication, Distribution, etc. (Imprint)    99.05             46.8

 262  Imprint Statement for Sound Recordings        0.12             33.7
 263  Projected Publication Date                    4.95              4.0
 265  Source for Acquisition/Subscription Address   1.95             64.7
 300  Physical Description                         93.52             23.8
 305  Physical Description for Sound Recordings     0.13             37.8

 306  Duration                                      0.25             13.0
 310  Current Frequency                             2.06             13.9
 321  Former Frequency                              0.53             23.4
 350  Price                                         1.42             17.9

 362  Dates of Publication and Volume Designation   6.12             20.4
 400  Series Statement - Personal Name/Title        0.08             39.5
 410  Series Statement - Corporate Name/Title       0.36             65.6
 440  Series Statement - Title (Traced)            13.80             42.0

 490  Series Untraced or Traced Differently        15.62             41.7
 500  General Note                                 64.40             45.4
 501  "With" Note                                   0.08            104.2
 502  Dissertation Note                             1.60             49.6

 503  Bibliographic History Note                    0.11             87.2
 504  Bibliography/Discography Note                42.99             30.2
 505  Contents Note (Formatted)                     4.37            215.0
 506  Restrictions on Access                        0.04             26.9
```

Table A.4: Field Occurrence, All but AMC (Part 3)

Tag	ALL RECORDS EXCEPT AMC [Continued] Description [628,142 records]	Occurrences per hundred	Average Length
507	Scale Note	0.01	24.9
508	Credits Note	0.05	61.1
510	Citation Note (Brief Form)/References	3.71	36.7
511	Participant or Performer Note	0.51	89.8
515	Numbering Peculiarities Note	1.11	54.4
518	Data on Capture Session Note	0.17	66.9
520	Summary, Abstract, Annotation, etc.	1.41	133.4
521	Users/Intended Audience Note	0.04	11.7
525	Supplement Note	0.24	53.9
530	Additional Physical Form Available Note	0.13	53.3
533	Reproduction Note	1.80	119.2
534	Original Version Note	0.27	77.5
538	Technical Details Note	0.01	68.3
541	Immediate Source of Acquisition	0.01	50.4
546	Language Note	0.67	37.5
547	Former Title Complexity note	0.01	156.1
550	Issuing Body Note	1.36	110.0
555	Cumulative Index/Finding Aids Note	0.38	72.9
570	Editor Note	0.40	51.2
580	Linking Entry Complexity Note	0.72	110.9
590	Local Note	1.62	51.8
600	Subject Added Entry - Personal Name	14.42	39.3
610	Subject Added Entry - Corporate Name	5.01	42.0
611	Subject Added Entry - Conference or Meeting	0.11	53.6
630	Subject Added Entry - Uniform Title	0.93	37.5
650	Subject Added Entry - Topical Heading	123.97	32.0
651	Subject Added Entry - Geographic Name	21.09	39.1
653	Subject Added Entry - Uncontrolled Term	0.02	9.1
655	Genre / Form Heading	0.24	30.6
690	Local Subject A.E. - Topical Heading	2.16	28.4
691	Local Subject A.E. - Geographic Name	0.18	34.4
696	Local Subject A.E. - Personal Name	0.33	47.8
697	Local Subject A.E. - Corporate Name	0.04	39.3
699	Local Subject A.E. - Uniform Title	0.04	28.7
700	Added Entry - Personal Name	44.79	24.4
710	Added Entry - Corporate Name	19.51	44.9

Table A.5: Field Occurrence, All but AMC (Part 4)

Tag	ALL RECORDS EXCEPT AMC [Continued] Description [628,142 records]	Occurrences per hundred	Average Length
711	Added Entry - Conference or Meeting	0.71	79.7
730	Added Entry - Uniform Title Heading	1.15	31.8
740	Added Entry - Title Traced Differently	8.62	32.8
752	Added Entry - Place of Publication/Prod.	0.35	42.5
753	Technical Details Access to MRDF	0.01	12.4
760	Main Series Entry	0.45	41.4
762	Subseries Entry	0.01	42.0
765	Original Language Entry	0.03	41.7
770	Supplement / Special Issue Entry	0.12	53.3
772	Parent Record Entry	0.12	43.4
773	Host Item Entry	0.06	85.7
775	Other Edition Available Entry	0.07	42.8
776	Additional Physical Form Available Entry	0.03	38.7
777	Issued With Entry	0.05	45.8
780	Preceding Entry	2.29	54.4
785	Succeeding Entry	1.12	55.1
787	Nonspecific Relationship Entry	0.18	46.9
796	Local A.E. - Personal Name	0.44	33.0
797	Local A.E. - Corporate Name	0.92	31.2
798	Local A.E. - Conference/Meeting Name	0.07	42.0
799	Local A.E. - Uniform Title Heading	0.26	34.1
800	Series Added Entry - Personal Name/Title	0.32	58.0
810	Series Added Entry - Corporate Name/Title	1.16	80.0
811	Series Added Entry - Conference or Mtg/Title	0.02	136.0
830	Series Added Entry - Uniform Title Heading	4.29	55.1
840	Series Added Entry - Title	0.26	47.8
850	Holdings	0.02	4.1
870	Variant Personal Name	0.02	47.5
871	Variant Corporate Name	0.12	56.1
872	Variant Conference or Meeting Name	0.01	81.8
880	Alternate Graphic Representation	11.93	69.7
899	Local Series A.E. - Uniform Title	0.10	39.1
930	Summary Holdings Statement	1.14	53.2
936	Piece Used for Cataloging	0.22	10.8
950	Location-level Holdings, Call Numbers, etc.	86.80	27.1
955	Copy-level Holdings, Call Numbers, etc.	76.90	29.8

Table A.6: Overall Display Summary

```
┌──────────────────────────────────────────────────────────────────────────┐
│        All Materials Except AMC (395,000-405,000 items tested)            │
│                                                                            │
│              NUMBER OF SCREENS REQUIRED FOR DISPLAY          Local         │
│  Display  One/Hold    One       Two       Three     Four +   Density       │
│  -------  --------  --------  --------  --------  --------  --------        │
│  CMTW      98.5%     99.9%     0.1%     <0.1%     <0.1%     26.0%          │
│  CMTN      92.5%     99.1%     0.8%     <0.1%     <0.1%     26.1%          │
│  CMSX      76.2%     97.1%     2.9%     <0.1%     <0.1%     25.5%          │
│  CMSL      60.8%     91.7%     8.3%     <0.1%     <0.1%     23.6%          │
│                                                                            │
│  CMCIT     84.5%     97.1%     2.9%     <0.1%     <0.1%     24.5%          │
│  CMTCIT    81.9%     96.7%     3.3%     <0.1%     <0.1%     24.4%          │
│                                                                            │
│  LMLFT     87.1%     98.3%     1.6%     <0.1%     <0.1%     29.8%          │
│  LMRI      81.4%     96.7%     3.3%     <0.1%     <0.1%     29.9%          │
│  LMG       81.4%     96.7%     3.3%     <0.1%     <0.1%     29.0%          │
│  LMGCON    88.3%     98.6%     1.4%     <0.1%     <0.1%     29.8%          │
│                                                                            │
│  LMGSP     55.3%     90.1%     9.8%     <0.1%     <0.1%     27.2%          │
│  LMGAT     41.2%     85.1%    14.9%      0.1%     <0.1%     25.6%          │
│  LMGWI     41.1%     84.8%    15.2%      0.1%     <0.1%     25.5%          │
│  LMGAT17   85.1%     97.3%     2.7%     <0.1%     <0.1%     22.3%          │
│  LMGAT50   33.9%     77.8%    22.0%      0.2%     <0.1%     24.1%          │
│                                                                            │
│  LMTCIT    60.3%     91.8%     8.2%     <0.1%     <0.1%     24.8%          │
│  CXSIMPL   95.8%     99.6%     0.4%     <0.1%     <0.1%     17.5%          │
│  LXSIMPL   89.7%     98.6%     1.4%     <0.1%     <0.1%     19.1%          │
│                                                                            │
│  CXMATT    92.2%     99.3%     0.6%     <0.1%     <0.1%     19.0%          │
│  LXMATT    50.6%     90.5%     9.5%     <0.1%     <0.1%     19.1%          │
│                                                                            │
│  CXPLM1    94.9%     98.9%     1.0%     <0.1%     <0.1%     21.0%          │
│  LXPLM1    79.3%     97.0%     2.9%      0.1%     <0.1%     22.8%          │
│                                                                            │
│  CXPLM2    91.7%     98.2%     1.7%      0.1%     <0.1%     23.3%          │
│  LXPLM2    75.3%     94.8%     5.0%      0.1%     <0.1%     24.8%          │
│                                                                            │
│  CBRF1     99.7%    <100.0%   <0.1%     <0.1%      --       14.8%          │
│  LBRF1     99.5%    <100.0%   <0.1%     <0.1%      --       17.5%          │
│  CBCAP     99.7%    <100.0%   <0.1%     <0.1%      --       16.2%          │
│                                                                            │
│  CLON1     33.8%     77.9%    21.5%      0.5%     <0.1%     27.2%          │
│  CLCIT1    54.3%     84.4%    15.1%      0.5%     <0.1%     27.7%          │
│  LLON1     21.5%     63.6%    35.3%      1.0%      0.1%     27.0%          │
│                                                                            │
│  MDSBRF    98.6%     99.9%     0.1%     <0.1%      --       17.7%          │
│  KOBM      48.4%     88.9%    11.0%      0.1%     <0.1%     26.4%          │
│  LMCAP     50.2%     87.9%    12.0%      0.1%     <0.1%     25.5%          │
│  MDSLON    12.4%     49.1%    49.0%      1.8%      0.2%     24.7%          │
└──────────────────────────────────────────────────────────────────────────┘
```

Table A.7: Field Occurrence, Public Library Records (Part 1)

```
      PUBLIC LIBRARY CATALOGING                    Occurrences      Average
  Tag   Description      [34,941 records]          per hundred      Length
  ---   -----------------------------------        -----------      -------
```

Tag	Description	Occurrences per hundred	Average Length
007	Physical Description Fixed Field	1.7	10.9
010	LC Control Number (LCCN)	76.7	11.8
015	National Bibliography Number	0.5	6.7
020	ISBN	94.0	21.3
022	ISSN	1.2	9.6
028	Publisher Number for Music	0.8	21.3
035	System Control Number	7.6	5.8
037	Stock Number	0.1	19.3
040	Cataloging Source	90.6	11.1
041	Language Code	5.8	6.9
042	Authentication Agency Code	1.1	6.8
043	Geographic Area Code	24.0	8.2
045	Chronological Code or Date/Time	0.2	7.3
048	Number of Instruments or Voices Code	0.3	7.6
050	Library of Congress Class/Call Number	66.3	17.6
051	LC Copy, Issue, Offprint Statement	0.1	53.9
060	National Library of Medicine Call Number	1.1	11.9
074	GPO Item Number	0.4	7.2
082	Dewey Decimal Classification Number	67.3	11.7
086	Government Document Classification No.	0.9	18.6
088	Report Number	0.1	17.3
090	Local call number (& other local inf.)	100.0	33.2
100	Main Entry - Personal Name	03.4	19.3
110	Main Entry - Corporate Name	1.7	40.9
111	Main Entry - Conference or Meeting	0.1	63.8
130	Main Entry - Uniform Title Heading	0.4	33.0
210	Abbreviated Title	0.3	23.5
212	Variant Access Title	0.1	50.8
222	Key Title	1.0	32.3
240	Uniform Title	4.3	27.8
245	Title Statement	100.0	72.2
246	Varying Form of Title	1.3	29.9
247	Former Title or Title Variations	0.1	45.3
250	Edition Statement	32.3	10.6
260	Publication, Distribution, etc. (Imprint)	99.8	42.0
263	Projected Publication Date	4.8	4.0

Table A.8: Field Occurrence, Public Library Records (Part 2)

Tag	PUBLIC LIBRARY CATALOGING [Continued] Description [34,941 records]	Occurrences per hundred	Average Length
265	Source for Acquisition/Subscription Address	0.7	61.7
300	Physical Description	99.0	23.8
310	Current Frequency	0.7	8.6
350	Price	0.6	7.4
362	Dates of Publication and Volume Designation	1.5	11.1
440	Series Statement - Title (Traced)	4.2	28.8
490	Series Untraced or Traced Differently	14.3	26.8
500	General Note	57.9	29.9
503	Bibliographic History Note	0.1	69.1
504	Bibliography/Discography Note	25.5	27.7
505	Contents Note (Formatted)	1.8	177.4
506	Restrictions on Access	0.6	26.0
508	Credits Note	0.3	48.2
510	Citation Note (Brief Form)/References	0.1	45.0
511	Participant or Performer Note	1.0	50.8
515	Numbering Peculiarities Note	0.1	51.1
520	Summary, Abstract, Annotation, etc.	13.1	137.4
521	Users/Intended Audience Note	0.9	11.1
538	Technical Details Note	0.1	76.5
550	Issuing Body Note	0.2	108.9
570	Editor Note	0.4	39.0
580	Linking Entry Complexity Note	0.1	93.4
590	Local Note	1.9	25.9
600	Subject Added Entry - Personal Name	12.7	31.9
610	Subject Added Entry - Corporate Name	3.4	37.0
611	Subject Added Entry - Conference or Meeting	0.2	51.8
630	Subject Added Entry - Uniform Title	0.6	33.9
650	Subject Added Entry - Topical Heading	140.3	27.3
651	Subject Added Entry - Geographic Name	18.8	38.9
690	Local Subject A.E. - Topical Heading	6.4	30.1
691	Local Subject A.E. - Geographic Name	0.6	38.5
696	Local Subject A.E. - Personal Name	0.2	34.3
697	Local Subject A.E. - Corporate Name	0.1	31.6
700	Added Entry - Personal Name	36.4	21.6
710	Added Entry - Corporate Name	9.9	36.2
711	Added Entry - Conference or Meeting	0.1	73.5

Table A.9: Field Occurrence, Public Library Records (Part 3)

Tag	PUBLIC LIBRARY CATALOGING [Continued] Description [34,941 records]	Occurrences per hundred	Average Length
730	Added Entry - Uniform Title Heading	1.8	24.2
740	Added Entry - Title Traced Differently	11.2	28.8
753	Technical Details Access to MRDF	0.2	14.2
760	Main Series Entry	0.2	30.2
780	Preceding Entry	0.7	50.3
796	Local A.E. - Personal Name	0.1	50.6
797	Local A.E. - Corporate Name	0.2	30.1
800	Series Added Entry - Personal Name/Title	0.5	48.3
810	Series Added Entry - Corporate Name/Title	0.2	75.1
830	Series Added Entry - Uniform Title Heading	0.9	44.3
840	Series Added Entry - Title	0.1	35.8
950	Location-level Holdings, Call Numbers, etc.	288.1	17.9
955	Copy-level Holdings, Call Numbers, etc.	96.7	32.3

Table A.10: Public Library Display Summary

```
          Public Library Cataloging (34,941 items tested)

          NUMBER OF SCREENS REQUIRED FOR DISPLAY        Local
Display   One/Hold   One       Two       Three     Four +    Density
-------   --------   --------  --------  --------  --------  --------
CMTW      99.7%     <100.0%    <0.1%      --        --       21.3%
CMTN      97.5%      99.8%      0.2%      --        --       21.5%
CMSX      88.8%      99.2%      0.8%      --        --       21.4%
CMSL      74.1%      96.7%      3.3%     <0.1%      --       20.2%

CMCIT     92.3%      99.1%      0.9%     <0.1%      --       20.4%
CMTCIT    90.3%      98.9%      1.0%     <0.1%      --       20.3%

LMLFT     92.2%      99.4%      0.6%     <0.1%      --       25.2%
LMRI      89.1%      98.8%      1.2%     <0.1%      --       25.7%
LMG       89.1%      98.8%      1.2%     <0.1%      --       24.9%
LMGCON    95.1%      99.7%      0.3%      --        --       25.3%

LMGSP     67.1%      95.5%      4.5%     <0.1%      --       24.1%
LMGAT     51.7%      92.4%      7.6%     <0.1%      --       23.0%
LMGWI     51.6%      92.3%      7.7%     <0.1%      --       23.0%
LMGAT17   92.4%      99.2%      0.8%     <0.1%      --       19.1%
LMGAT50   45.3%      88.3%     11.7%     <0.1%     <0.1%     22.1%

LMTCIT    71.9%      96.5%      3.5%     <0.1%      --       21.2%
CXSIMPL   99.0%      99.9%      0.1%      --        --       13.1%
LXSIMPL   95.4%      99.6%      0.4%     <0.1%      --       14.9%

CXMATT    96.9%      99.8%      0.2%      --        --       15.6%
LXMATT    49.3%      93.7%      6.3%     <0.1%      --       16.5%

CXPLM1    98.2%      99.8%      0.2%     <0.1%     <0.1%     17.5%
LXPLM1    85.3%      98.8%      1.2%     <0.1%     <0.1%     19.5%

CXPLM2    97.1%      99.6%      0.4%     <0.1%     <0.1%     19.1%
LXPLM2    82.8%      98.0%      2.0%     <0.1%     <0.1%     21.2%

CBRF1    100.0%     100.0%      --        --        --       12.7%
LBRF1    100.0%     100.0%      --        --        --       15.4%
CBCAP    100.0%     100.0%      --        --        --       14.0%

CLON1     51.8%      90.8%      9.1%      0.1%     <0.1%     23.8%
CLCIT1    69.6%      93.3%      6.7%      0.1%     <0.1%     23.3%
LLON1     34.7%      77.6%     22.3%      0.1%     <0.1%     24.2%

MDSBRF    99.8%     <100.0%    <0.1%      --        --       15.6%
KOBM      60.4%      94.9%      5.1%     <0.1%      --       23.1%
MDSLON    23.7%      64.6%     35.0%      0.3%     <0.1%     22.3%
```

Table A.11: Selected Fields, Comparison of Two Large Samples

TAG	March 1986 (n=628,142) Occurrences per Hundred	Average Length	December 1985 (n=602,686) Occurrences per Hundred	Average Length
100	67.4	22.6	68.0	22.6
110	6.0	45.5	5.9	46.2
111	1.6	78.5	1.7	78.9
130	0.9	40.5	0.8	39.7
240	4.9	30.7	5.2	31.0
245	100.0	86.6	100.0	87.5
250	14.8	13.8	14.4	13.4
260	99.1	46.8	99.3	46.8
300	93.5	23.8	93.9	23.9
440	13.8	42.0	13.9	41.4
490	15.6	41.7	15.9	41.5
500	64.4	45.4	64.0	45.5
504	43.0	30.2	42.8	30.3
505	4.4	215.0	4.3	217.5
510	3.7	36.7	3.3	36.8
515	1.1	54.4	1.1	54.7
520	1.4	133.4	1.4	135.1
533	1.8	119.2	1.7	115.9
550	1.4	110.0	1.3	110.0
590	1.6	51.8	1.8	55.7
600	14.4	39.3	13.8	38.6
610	5.0	42.0	5.1	41.3
650	124.0	32.0	124.7	31.9
651	21.1	39.1	21.9	38.8
690	2.2	28.4	2.4	28.7
700	44.8	24.4	45.0	24.5
710	19.5	44.9	19.7	44.3
730	1.1	31.8	1.2	32.4
740	8.6	32.8	8.5	33.0
780	2.3	54.4	2.2	52.9
810	1.2	80.0	1.3	79.8
830	4.3	55.1	4.0	54.9
880	11.9	69.7	11.8	69.4
950	86.8	27.1	86.5	27.7
955	76.9	29.8	73.6	29.9

Table A.12: Field Occurrence, Books (Part 1)

Tag	BOOKS Description [522,956 records]	Occurrences per hundred	Average Length
007	Physical Description Fixed Field	2.2	14.0
010	LC Control Number (LCCN)	61.4	11.7
015	National Bibliography Number	3.7	7.3
020	ISBN	63.3	18.7
035	System Control Number	7.2	11.7
040	Cataloging Source	78.8	11.1
041	Language Code	6.3	7.1
043	Geographic Area Code	32.4	8.2
050	Library of Congress Class/Call Number	56.2	16.9
051	LC Copy, Issue, Offprint Statement	0.1	30.0
060	National Library of Medicine Call Number	2.0	15.5
066	Character Sets Present	3.1	2.0
074	GPO Item Number	0.1	9.5
082	Dewey Decimal Classification Number	46.6	12.0
086	Government Document Classification No.	0.5	19.9
090	Local call number (& other local inf.)	100.0	19.1
100	Main Entry - Personal Name	73.7	22.4
110	Main Entry - Corporate Name	4.8	47.3
111	Main Entry - Conference or Meeting	1.8	81.1
130	Main Entry - Uniform Title Heading	0.4	34.0
240	Uniform Title	3.6	30.8
245	Title Statement	100.0	91.4
250	Edition Statement	16.4	13.5
260	Publication, Distribution, etc. (Imprint)	99.6	47.1
263	Projected Publication Date	5.6	4.0
300	Physical Description	95.3	24.0
350	Price	0.5	6.5
410	Series Statement - Corporate Name/Title	0.4	65.7
440	Series Statement - Title (Traced)	15.2	42.0
490	Series Untraced or Traced Differently	16.7	41.9
500	General Note	62.7	42.5
502	Dissertation Note	1.9	49.4

Table A.13: Field Occurrence, Books (Part 2)

Tag	BOOKS [Continued] Description [522,956 records]	Occurrences per hundred	Average Length
504	Bibliography/Discography Note	48.7	30.2
505	Contents Note (Formatted)	4.3	213.7
510	Citation Note (Brief Form)/References	0.8	26.4
520	Summary, Abstract, Annotation, etc.	1.1	131.6
533	Reproduction Note	1.7	118.6
534	Original Version Note	0.3	76.3
590	Local Note	1.7	50.9
600	Subject Added Entry - Personal Name	15.7	39.1
610	Subject Added Entry - Corporate Name	5.2	40.9
611	Subject Added Entry - Conference or Meeting	0.1	52.4
630	Subject Added Entry - Uniform Title	1.0	37.7
650	Subject Added Entry - Topical Heading	126.7	31.8
651	Subject Added Entry - Geographic Name	21.6	39.1
690	Local Subject A.E. - Topical Heading	2.1	29.2
691	Local Subject A.E. - Geographic Name	0.2	34.2
696	Local Subject A.E. - Personal Name	0.4	47.8
700	Added Entry - Personal Name	46.3	23.4
710	Added Entry - Corporate Name	15.5	44.8
711	Added Entry - Conference or Meeting	0.8	81.2
730	Added Entry - Uniform Title Heading	1.0	32.0
740	Added Entry - Title Traced Differently	8.8	33.6
752	Added Entry - Place of Publication/Prod.	0.3	44.0
796	Local A.E. - Personal Name	0.6	31.9
797	Local A.E. - Corporate Name	0.7	35.2
799	Local A.E. - Uniform Title Heading	0.2	34.9
800	Series Added Entry - Personal Name/Title	0.3	56.9
810	Series Added Entry - Corporate Name/Title	1.2	81.1
830	Series Added Entry - Uniform Title Heading	4.5	56.0
840	Series Added Entry - Title	0.3	48.2
880	Alternate Graphic Representation	13.7	69.2
899	Local Series A.E. - Uniform Title	0.1	39.0
950	Location-level Holdings, Call Numbers, etc.	87.1	23.8
955	Copy-level Holdings, Call Numbers, etc.	75.5	29.0

Table A.14: Field Occurrence, Archival and Manuscript Control (Part 1)

Tag	ARCHIVAL AND MANUSCRIPT CONTROL Description [3,975 records]	Occurrences per hundred	Average Length
007	Physical Description Fixed Field	2.7	14.0
010	LC Control Number (LCCN)	3.1	12.1
035	System Control Number	36.2	14.9
040	Cataloging Source	96.2	17.1
041	Language Code	8.0	4.7
052	Geographic Classification Code	11.3	5.9
072	Subject Category Code	10.4	10.7
090	Local call number (& other local inf.)	100.0	12.1
100	Main Entry - Personal Name	68.4	27.4
110	Main Entry - Corporate Name	26.8	42.5
111	Main Entry - Conference or Meeting	0.4	48.0
130	Main Entry - Uniform Title Heading	0.1	18.5
240	Uniform Title	0.1	90.3
245	Title Statement	100.0	35.2
260	Publication, Distribution, etc. (Imprint)	1.0	37.2
300	Physical Description	100.2	16.1
340	Medium	1.8	24.1
351	Organization and Arrangement	11.0	77.4
500	General Note	60.2	49.1
505	Contents Note (Formatted)	0.1	369.0
506	Restrictions on Access	18.5	51.0
510	Citation Note (Brief Form)/References	5.1	69.6
520	Summary, Abstract, Annotation, etc.	79.6	355.7
524	Preferred Citation of Described Materials	18.8	95.2
530	Additional Physical Form Available Note	3.2	119.3
533	Reproduction Note	5.4	46.7
535	Locations of Originals / Duplicates	2.6	64.7
540	Terms Governing Use and Reproduction	1.1	89.8
541	Immediate Source of Acquisition	136.3	63.1
544	Location of Associated Materials	1.7	117.5
545	Biographical or Historical Note	57.0	189.8
546	Language Note	4.1	27.8

Table A.15: Field Occurrence, Archival and Manuscript Control (Part 2)

```
     ARCHIVAL AND MANUSCRIPT CONTROL [Continued]  Occurrences      Average
 Tag  Description         [3,975 records]         per hundred      Length
 ---  --------------------------------------      -----------      -------
 555  Cumulative Index / Finding Aids Note           22.5           61.0
 561  Provenance                                     18.8           41.8
 562  Copy and Version Identification                 0.1           74.6
 580  Linking Entry Complexity Note                   9.9           82.8

 583  Actions                                       159.5           67.9
 590  Local Note                                      9.9           51.9
 600  Subject Added Entry - Personal Name           198.3           26.8
 610  Subject Added Entry - Corporate Name          102.5           37.7

 611  Subject Added Entry - Conference or Meeting     2.0           51.7
 630  Subject Added Entry - Uniform Title             3.5           20.3
 650  Subject Added Entry - Topical Heading         166.3           24.6
 651  Subject Added Entry - Geographic Name         107.1           30.0

 655  Genre / Form Heading                           75.4           19.0
 656  Index Term -- Occupation                       19.3           19.4
 657  Index Term -- Function                          0.1           57.7
 690  Local Subject A.E. - Topical Heading          117.9           20.4

 691  Local Subject A.E. - Geographic Name            6.2           43.8
 696  Local Subject A.E. - Personal Name              2.2           20.7
 697  Local Subject A.E. - Corporate Name            11.1           42.2
 699  Local Subject A.E. - Uniform Title              1.8           25.5

 700  Added Entry - Personal Name                    88.0           29.5
 710  Added Entry - Corporate Name                    6.4           35.4
 711  Added Entry - Conference or Meeting             0.1           53.4
 730  Added Entry - Uniform Title Heading             0.3           38.9

 740  Added Entry - Title Traced Differently          2.2           37.0
 773  Host Item Entry                                24.2           79.9
 796  Local A.E. - Personal Name                      0.1           25.2
 797  Local A.E. - Corporate Name                     1.4           48.0

 851  Location                                       68.5           79.7
 950  Location-level Information                     99.9           16.0
 960  Physical Location                              45.0           86.6
```

Table A.16: Archival and Manuscript Control Display Summary

Archival and Manuscript Control (3,972 items tested)

Display	One/Hold	NUMBER OF SCREENS REQUIRED FOR DISPLAY One	Two	Three	Four +	Local Density
CMTN	82.5%	90.8%	6.1%	1.6%	0.5%	27.6%
CMSX	72.4%	87.3%	9.1%	1.9%	1.6%	26.7%
CMSL	53.2%	72.5%	18.7%	4.6%	4.3%	19.5%
CMCIT	65.4%	78.1%	14.1%	3.7%	4.0%	20.5%
CMTCIT	63.3%	77.3%	14.9%	3.8%	4.1%	20.4%
LMG	64.3%	77.7%	14.6%	3.7%	4.0%	22.7%
LMGCON	82.6%	90.8%	6.2%	1.6%	1.4%	29.2%
LMGSP	53.2%	72.4%	18.8%	4.5%	4.3%	21.6%
LMGAT	47.8%	68.6%	22.1%	4.9%	4.5%	20.7%
LMTCIT	52.3%	72.0%	19.2%	4.6%	4.3%	20.3%
CXSIMPL	84.7%	91.6%	5.4%	1.5%	1.5%	25.1%
LXSIMPL	70.0%	80.3%	12.5%	3.4%	3.8%	19.9%
CXMATT	84.7%	91.6%	5.4%	1.5%	1.5%	25.1%
LXMATT	60.1%	76.6%	15.5%	3.8%	4.1%	19.1%
CXPLM1	84.2%	91.9%	5.6%	1.4%	1.0%	24.4%
LXPLM1	55.9%	73.9%	18.4%	4.3%	3.4%	18.9%
CXPLM2	82.5%	90.8%	6.1%	1.6%	1.5%	26.3%
LXPLM2	59.3%	75.2%	16.7%	4.0%	4.2%	20.4%
CBRF1	100.0%	100.0%	--	--	--	7.4%
LBRF1	100.0%	100.0%	--	--	--	9.4%
CBCAP	100.0%	100.0%	--	--	--	7.4%
CLON1	20.3%	35.5%	45.3%	10.9%	8.3%	37.3%
LLON1	19.9%	31.2%	43.2%	14.1%	11.5%	33.6%
CLCIT1	24.7%	40.1%	38.0%	11.5%	10.4%	34.8%
MDSBRF	100.0%	100.0%	--	--	--	9.8%
LMCAP	48.7%	69.7%	21.1%	4.7%	4.4%	21.7%
KOBM	54.3%	73.4%	18.1%	4.2%	4.3%	20.4%
MDSLON	17.2%	23.5%	42.7%	17.7%	16.1%	31.7%

Table A.17: Field Occurrence, Machine-Readable Data Files

	MACHINE READABLE DATA FILES	Occurrences	Average
Tag	Description [408 records]	per hundred	Length
010	LC Control Number (LCCN)	1.0	11.0
020	ISBN	20.1	17.7
035	System Control Number	32.8	17.9
040	Cataloging Source	84.3	11.3
041	Language Code	1.0	6.5
090	Local call number (& other local inf.)	100.0	25.3
100	Main Entry - Personal Name	28.7	16.6
110	Main Entry - Corporate Name	0.5	33.5
245	Title Statement	100.0	71.0
250	Edition Statement	27.7	13.1
260	Publication, Distribution, etc. (Imprint)	99.8	52.2
265	Source for Acquisition	0.2	74.0
300	Physical Description	96.6	68.8
315	Frequency	0.2	6.0
440	Series Statement - Title (Traced)	9.1	31.1
490	Series Untraced or Traced Differently	1.7	14.2
500	General Note	79.9	49.9
505	Contents Note (Formatted)	5.1	100.1
520	Summary, Abstract, Annotation, etc.	47.8	128.3
521	Users / Intended Audience Note	4.9	32.0
536	Funding Information Note	0.2	29.0
537	Source of Data Note	0.2	130.0
538	Technical Details Note	67.9	67.0
556	Information About Documentation Note	1.7	112.0
565	Case File Characteristics Note	2.7	47.8
581	Publications Note	0.2	57.0
582	Related Machine-Readable Files Note	0.2	48.0
590	Local Note	3.9	50.5
600	Subject Added Entry - Personal Name	0.2	86.0
650	Subject Added Entry - Topical Heading	183.8	28.4
651	Subject Added Entry - Geographic Name	2.2	32.1
690	Local Subject A.E. - Topical Heading	41.4	34.5
700	Added Entry - Personal Name	29.4	17.7
710	Added Entry - Corporate Name	30.9	31.3
730	Added Entry - Uniform Title Heading	0.7	9.0
740	Added Entry - Title Traced Differently	20.8	24.4
753	Technical Details Access to MRDF	75.7	12.5
950	Location-level Information	104.7	24.3
955	Copy-level Information	75.0	37.4

Table A.18: Machine-Readable Data Files Display Summary

	Machine Readable Data Files (408 items tested)					
	NUMBER OF SCREENS REQUIRED FOR DISPLAY					Local
Display	One/Hold	One	Two	Three	Four +	Density
--------	---------	---------	--------	---------	---------	---------
CMTN	94.4%	100.0%	--	--	--	26.6%
CMSX	76.2%	99.3%	0.7%	--	--	26.4%
CMSL	56.4%	94.4%	5.6%	--	--	24.4%
CMCIT	82.4%	98.8%	1.2%	--	--	25.2%
CMTCIT	77.9%	98.3%	1.7%	--	--	25.0%
LMG	79.7%	98.3%	1.7%	--	--	29.3%
LMGCON	90.9%	100.0%	--	--	--	30.1%
LMGSP	52.7%	93.1%	6.9%	--	--	27.9%
LMGAT	44.1%	85.8%	14.2%	--	--	25.7%
LMTCIT	55.1%	94.4%	5.6%	--	--	25.3%
CXSIMPL	99.3%	100.0%	--	--	--	14.9%
LXSIMPL	94.6%	99.5%	0.5%	--	--	16.3%
CXMATT	97.5%	100.0%	--	--	--	15.8%
LXMATT	66.2%	94.6%	5.4%	--	--	16.4%
CXPLM1	97.5%	99.8%	0.2%	--	--	18.8%
LXPLM1	83.1%	98.5%	1.5%	--	--	20.3%
CXPLM2	95.1%	99.5%	0.5%	--	--	20.7%
LXPLM2	76.5%	97.1%	2.9%	--	--	22.2%
CBRF1	100.0%	100.0%	--	--	--	15.7%
LBRF1	100.0%	100.0%	--	--	--	18.1%
CBCAP	100.0%	100.0%	--	--	--	17.5%
CLON1	23.8%	63.2%	36.8%	--	--	29.1%
CLCIT1	32.6%	67.9%	31.9%	0.2%	--	29.4%
LLON1	25.7%	52.9%	46.8%	0.2%	--	29.4%
MDSBRF	99.5%	100.0%	--	--	--	18.1%
KOBM	49.3%	91.2%	8.8%	--	--	26.7%
LMCAP	52.5%	90.9%	9.1%	--	--	24.9%
MDSLON	18.6%	34.8%	61.5%	3.7%	--	26.8%

Table A.19: Field Occurrence, Maps (Part 1)

Tag	MAPS Description [1,002 records]	Occurrences per hundred	Average Length
007	Physical Description Fixed Field	7.6	9.0
010	LC Control Number (LCCN)	23.6	15.8
017	Copyright Registration Number	0.6	25.5
020	ISBN	8.2	8.4
034	Coded Mathematical Data	48.1	34.6
035	System Control Number	2.6	9.4
037	Stock Number	1.0	19.9
040	Cataloging Source	55.2	8.9
041	Language Code	9.0	8.3
045	Chronological Code or Date/Time	12.4	4.2
050	Library of Congress Class/Call Number	23.2	19.0
052	Geographical Classification Code	64.6	6.2
074	GPO Item Number	3.0	5.5
086	Government Document Classification No.	3.6	20.8
090	Local call number (& other local inf.)	100.0	8.3
100	Main Entry - Personal Name	17.7	19.2
110	Main Entry - Corporate Name	63.4	34.1
245	Title Statement	100.0	94.0
250	Edition Statement	14.8	13.8
255	Mathematical Data Area	68.3	45.5
260	Publication, Distribution, etc. (Imprint)	99.5	47.5
265	Source for Acquisition/Subscription Address	6.5	65.4
300	Physical Description	91.7	36.4
315	Frequency	0.2	8.5
362	Dates of Publication and Volume Designation	0.2	43.5
400	Series Statement - Personal Name/Title	0.1	25.0
410	Series Statement - Corporate Name/Title	0.4	34.0
440	Series Statement - Title (Traced)	4.6	31.5
490	Series Untraced or Traced Differently	14.4	44.9
500	General Note	200.3	53.0
504	Bibliography/Discography Note	3.9	32.6
505	Contents Note (Formatted)	3.7	151.7

Table A.20: Field Occurrence, Maps (Part 2)

Tag	MAPS [Continued] Description [1,002 records]	Occurrences per hundred	Average Length
507	Scale Note	9.0	27.3
510	Citation Note (Brief Form)/References	0.1	28.0
520	Summary, Abstract, Annotation, etc.	0.1	192.0
533	Reproduction Note	0.2	62.0
534	Original Version Note	0.3	57.0
590	Local Note	1.2	50.0
610	Subject Added Entry - Corporate Name	0.9	47.3
650	Subject Added Entry - Topical Heading	46.2	32.4
651	Subject Added Entry - Geographic Name	63.3	29.7
652	Subject Added Entry - Reversed Geographic	0.1	24.0
691	Local Subject A.E. - Geographic Name	7.9	33.4
696	Local Subject A.E. - Personal Name	0.2	28.5
699	Local Subject A.E. - Uniform Title	0.1	29.0
700	Added Entry - Personal Name	20.5	20.4
710	Added Entry - Corporate Name	31.8	37.9
730	Added Entry - Uniform Title Heading	0.1	65.0
740	Added Entry - Title Traced Differently	18.7	41.0
796	Local A.E. - Personal Name	0.1	26.0
797	Local A.E. - Corporate Name	3.3	13.3
810	Series Added Entry - Corporate Name/Title	0.5	68.2
830	Series Added Entry - Uniform Title Heading	6.0	61.6
930	Summary Holdings Statement	0.1	51.0
950	Location-level Holdings, Call Numbers, etc.	54.1	46.9
955	Copy-level Holdings, Call Numbers, etc.	47.8	26.4

Table A.21: Maps Display Summary

```
                    Maps (526 items tested)

            NUMBER OF SCREENS REQUIRED FOR DISPLAY          Local
Display   One/Hold      One       Two     Three    Four +   Density
-------   --------   --------  --------  --------  --------  --------
CMTN       85.0%      97.5%      2.5%      --        --       31.5%
CMSX       62.2%      90.9%      8.7%      0.4%      --       29.5%
CMSL       51.0%      84.6%     15.0%      0.4%      --       27.2%

CMCIT      76.0%      92.0%      7.6%      0.4%      --       28.8%
CMTCIT     73.4%      91.3%      8.4%      0.4%      --       28.6%

LMG        73.4%      92.0%      7.6%      0.4%      --       33.3%
LMGCON     79.7%      95.1%      4.6%      0.4%      --       34.5%

LMGSP      43.9%      82.9%     16.7%      0.4%      --       30.8%
LMGAT      29.8%      76.8%     22.8%      0.4%      --       28.8%

LMTCIT     47.1%      83.3%     16.3%      0.4%      --       28.1%
CXSIMPL    93.3%     100.0%      --        --        --       18.7%
LXSIMPL    87.1%      98.7%      1.3%      --        --       20.4%

CXMATT     93.3%     100.0%      --        --        --       19.0%
LXMATT     62.7%      93.0%      7.0%      --        --       19.6%

CXPLM1     91.8%      98.7%      1.1%      0.2%      --       24.7%
LXPLM1     69.4%      95.4%      4.0%      0.6%      --       26.2%

CXPLM2     86.7%      97.7%      2.1%      0.2%      --       27.1%
LXPLM2     67.3%      91.4%      8.0%      0.4%      0.2%     27.6%

CBRF1      98.5%      99.4%      0.6%      --        --       20.7%
LBRF1      98.1%      99.4%      0.6%      --        --       23.5%
CBCAP      98.9%      99.4%      0.6%      --        --       22.2%

CLON1       2.7%      32.9%     64.8%      1.9%      0.4%     31.5%
CLCIT1     16.9%      54.6%     43.7%      1.3%      0.4%     32.3%
LLON1       1.5%      17.7%     77.6%      4.4%      0.4%     30.7%

MDSBRF     95.1%      99.4%      0.6%      --        --       24.0%
KOBM       37.3%      80.4%     19.0%      0.6%      --       29.5%
LMCAP      35.6%      76.6%     23.0%      0.4%      --       28.7%
MDSLON      0.2%       8.9%     82.3%      8.0%      0.8%     29.4%
```

Table A.22: Field Occurrence, Musical Scores (Part 1)

Tag	MUSICAL SCORES Description [11,681 records]	Occurrences per hundred	Average Length
007	Physical Description Fixed Field	0.7	14.0
010	LC Control Number (LCCN)	27.9	12.5
020	ISBN	10.6	15.5
028	Publisher Number for Music	55.6	22.5
035	System Control Number	3.9	10.9
040	Cataloging Source	82.4	13.6
041	Language Code	21.4	8.7
043	Geographic Area Code	2.8	7.2
045	Chronological Code or Date/Time	60.1	5.8
047	Form of Composition Code	4.4	11.1
048	Number of Instruments or Voices Code	77.1	9.7
050	Library of Congress Class/Call Number	26.4	16.1
082	Dewey Decimal Classification Number	0.6	8.6
090	Local call number (& other local inf.)	100.0	20.5
100	Main Entry - Personal Name	89.1	27.6
110	Main Entry - Corporate Name	2.0	36.3
130	Main Entry - Uniform Title Heading	0.4	25.6
240	Uniform Title	66.0	30.0
243	Uniform Title, Collective	0.1	16.5
245	Title Statement	100.0	91.3
250	Edition Statement	7.4	26.0
254	Musical Presentation Area	4.6	13.9
260	Publication, Distribution, etc. (Imprint)	98.0	40.8
263	Projected Publication Date	0.7	4.0
300	Physical Description	95.5	26.6
306	Duration	3.7	6.2
440	Series Statement - Title (Traced)	13.8	39.5
490	Series Untraced or Traced Differently	18.8	38.0
500	General Note	141.9	49.4
502	Dissertation Note	0.1	53.0
503	Bibliographic History Note	0.6	87.3
504	Bibliography/Discography Note	3.2	33.1

Table A.23: Field Occurrence, Musical Scores (Part 2)

Tag	MUSICAL SCORES [Continued] Description [11,681 records]	Occurrences per hundred	Average Length
505	Contents Note (Formatted)	17.4	183.5
510	Citation Note (Brief Form)/References	0.5	19.7
533	Reproduction Note	1.2	78.3
534	Original Version Note	1.4	76.8
590	Local Note	4.2	49.7
600	Subject Added Entry - Personal Name	6.3	48.5
610	Subject Added Entry - Corporate Name	0.2	32.6
650	Subject Added Entry - Topical Heading	116.4	30.4
651	Subject Added Entry - Geographic Name	0.1	33.5
690	Local Subject A.E. - Topical Heading	4.9	26.3
696	Local Subject A.E. - Personal Name	0.2	37.8
700	Added Entry - Personal Name	63.1	31.4
710	Added Entry - Corporate Name	4.3	51.4
730	Added Entry - Uniform Title Heading	1.0	22.2
740	Added Entry - Title Traced Differently	18.9	22.1
796	Local A.E. - Personal Name	1.3	26.0
797	Local A.E. - Corporate Name	1.2	41.9
799	Local A.E. - Uniform Title Heading	2.4	32.8
800	Series Added Entry - Personal Name/Title	1.0	63.2
810	Series Added Entry - Corporate Name/Title	0.2	124.6
830	Series Added Entry - Uniform Title Heading	3.8	41.1
840	Series Added Entry - Title	0.1	35.7
870	Variant Personal Name	0.1	46.5
950	Location-level Holdings, Call Numbers, etc.	76.3	35.2
955	Copy-level Holdings, Call Numbers, etc.	87.6	28.1

Table A.24: Musical Scores Display Summary

```
                Musical Scores (8,701 items tested)

              NUMBER OF SCREENS REQUIRED FOR DISPLAY      Local
Display   One/Hold    One       Two       Three     Four +    Density
-------   --------  --------  --------  --------  --------  --------
CMTN       95.0%     99.5%     0.4%      0.1%       --        25.9%
CMSX       79.0%     98.4%     1.4%      0.1%      <0.1%      25.6%
CMSL       62.8%     93.6%     6.2%     <0.1%       0.1%      23.9%

CMCIT      87.9%     98.1%     1.7%      0.1%       0.1%      24.7%
CMTCIT     85.4%     97.7%     2.1%     <0.1%       0.1%      24.6%

LMG        85.4%     97.8%     2.1%      0.1%       0.1%      29.5%
LMGCON     90.4%     99.2%     0.7%      0.1%       --        30.1%

LMGSP      56.6%     92.2%     7.6%     <0.1%       0.1%      28.0%
LMGAT      42.4%     87.9%    12.0%      0.1%       0.1%      26.3%

LMTCIT     61.5%     93.3%     6.5%      0.1%       0.1%      25.3%
CXSIMPL    97.4%     99.7%     0.2%      0.1%       --        17.0%
LXSIMPL    93.0%     99.1%     0.8%      0.1%       0.1%      19.0%

CXMATT     90.3%     99.3%     0.6%      0.1%       --        20.9%
LXMATT     37.5%     89.8%     9.9%      0.1%       0.1%      21.3%

CXPLM1     91.2%     97.8%     2.0%      0.1%      <0.1%      22.4%
LXPLM1     77.5%     96.1%     3.6%      0.2%      <0.1%      24.5%

CXPLM2     87.8%     96.8%     2.8%      0.2%       0.2%      24.7%
LXPLM2     74.4%     94.1%     5.4%      0.3%       0.2%      26.4%

CBRF1      99.9%    <100.0%   <0.1%      --         --        16.0%
LBRF1      99.8%    <100.0%   <0.1%      --         --        18.9%
CBCAP      99.9%    <100.0%   <0.1%      --         --        17.2%

CLON1      19.5%     65.2%    33.5%      0.9%       0.4%      28.7%
CLCIT1     48.6%     80.0%    18.9%      0.7%       0.4%      29.9%
LLON1       6.2%     44.1%    53.5%      1.9%       0.5%      27.5%

MDSBRF     99.2%    <100.0%   <0.1%      --         --        19.0%
KOBM       48.6%     91.5%     8.4%     <0.1%       0.1%      27.3%
LMCAP      47.6%     89.4%    10.5%     <0.1%       0.1%      26.5%
MDSLON      3.5%     36.0%    59.4%      3.9%       0.7%      26.4%
```

Table A.25: Field Occurrence, Serials (Part 1)

```
              SERIALS                    Occurrences      Average
  Tag   Description        [50,132 records]  per hundred    Length
  ---   ------------------------------------  -----------    -------
  007   Physical Description Fixed Field         2.8          14.0
  010   LC Control Number (LCCN)                45.1          13.7
  015   National Bibliography Number             0.1          11.6
  022   ISSN                                    41.7           9.5

  025   Overseas Acquisition Number              0.3          14.6
  030   CODEN Designation                        6.4           6.0
  032   Postal Registration Number               0.1          11.8
  035   System Control Number                   11.8          13.0

  037   Stock Number                             0.2          15.5
  040   Cataloging Source                       83.3          24.6
  041   Language Code                            7.7           8.4
  042   Authentication Agency Code              37.1           5.6

  043   Geographic Area Code                    31.5           7.7
  045   Chronological Code or Date/Time          0.1           3.9
  050   Library of Congress Class/Call Number   31.2          11.1
  051   LC Copy, Issue, Offprint Statement       0.1          19.9

  055   Call/Class Numbers Assigned in Canada    0.8           5.6
  060   National Library of Medicine Call Number 4.9           9.6
  066   Character Sets Present                   0.6           2.0
  070   National Agricultural Library Call Number 0.8          9.7

  072   Subject Category Code                    0.4           4.1
  074   GPO Item Number                          1.7           8.4
  082   Dewey Decimal Classification Number     23.6           9.7
  086   Government Document Classification No.    2.5          13.5

  090   Local call number (& other local inf.) 100.0          24.4
  100   Main Entry - Personal Name               0.4          24.3
  110   Main Entry - Corporate Name             18.7          42.4
  111   Main Entry - Conference or Meeting       1.4          45.4

  130   Main Entry - Uniform Title Heading       5.3          46.8
  210   Abbreviated Title                       14.6          20.7
  212   Variant Access Title                     4.7          44.0
  222   Key Title                               29.1          32.9

  240   Uniform Title                            0.6          28.1
  245   Title Statement                        100.0          40.7
  246   Varying Form of Title                   26.8          32.8
  247   Former Title or Title Variations         6.8          52.9
```

Table A.26: Field Occurrence, Serials (Part 2)

Tag	SERIALS [Continued] Description [50,132 records]	Occurrences per hundred	Average Length
250	Edition Statement	0.6	17.3
260	Publication, Distribution, etc. (Imprint)	95.1	45.8
263	Projected Publication Date	0.6	4.0
265	Source for Acquisition/Subscription Address	21.8	64.7
300	Physical Description	73.7	16.5
310	Current Frequency	23.2	13.9
321	Former Frequency	6.2	23.6
350	Price	10.9	24.0
362	Dates of Publication and Volume Designation	69.9	20.1
410	Series Statement - Corporate Name/Title	0.1	50.2
440	Series Statement - Title (Traced)	1.9	33.1
490	Series Untraced or Traced Differently	4.1	37.4
500	General Note	48.4	50.8
504	Bibliography/Discography Note	1.1	32.9
510	Citation Note (Brief Form)/References	31.6	39.9
515	Numbering Peculiarities Note	12.4	54.9
520	Summary, Abstract, Annotation, etc.	1.9	94.8
525	Supplement Note	2.7	52.2
530	Additional Physical Form Available Note	1.6	53.3
533	Reproduction Note	2.7	96.0
534	Original Version Note	0.1	99.0
546	Language Note	7.4	37.6
547	Former Title Complexity Note	0.2	162.3
550	Issuing Body Note	15.2	108.8
555	Cumulative Index/Finding Aids Note	4.1	69.9
570	Editor Note	4.4	51.2
580	Linking Entry Complexity Note	8.2	110.6
590	Local Note	2.3	52.1
600	Subject Added Entry - Personal Name	0.8	51.3
610	Subject Added Entry - Corporate Name	6.3	50.7
630	Subject Added Entry - Uniform Title	0.2	42.4
650	Subject Added Entry - Topical Heading	107.7	36.4
651	Subject Added Entry - Geographic Name	17.7	39.3
690	Local Subject A.E. - Topical Heading	1.6	26.8
691	Local Subject A.E. - Geographic Name	0.2	33.5
700	Added Entry - Personal Name	7.3	26.6

Table A.27: Field Occurrence, Serials (Part 3)

Tag	SERIALS [Continued] Description [50,132 records]	Occurrences per hundred	Average Length
710	Added Entry - Corporate Name	60.0	46.1
711	Added Entry - Conference or Meeting	0.5	55.9
730	Added Entry - Uniform Title Heading	2.8	32.6
752	Added Entry - Place of Publication/Prod.	0.3	33.6
760	Main Series Entry	5.1	40.5
762	Subseries Entry	0.1	37.8
765	Original Language Entry	0.4	38.3
770	Supplement / Special Issue Entry	1.4	50.4
772	Parent Record Entry	1.6	43.7
775	Other Edition Available Entry	0.9	45.7
776	Additional Physical Form Available Entry	0.4	35.5
777	Issued With Entry	0.6	42.2
780	Preceding Entry	26.3	54.2
785	Succeeding Entry	12.7	55.1
787	Nonspecific Relationship Entry	2.0	47.6
797	Local A.E. - Corporate Name	3.4	24.4
799	Local A.E. - Uniform Title Heading	0.1	28.7
810	Series Added Entry - Corporate Name/Title	0.7	69.4
830	Series Added Entry - Uniform Title Heading	1.7	44.1
840	Series Added Entry - Title	0.1	36.7
850	Holdings	0.3	4.1
871	Variant Corporate Name	1.2	54.6
880	Alternate Graphic Representation	2.4	75.9
899	Local Series A.E. - Uniform Title	0.2	37.4
930	Summary Holdings Statement	13.1	52.7
936	Piece Used for Cataloging	2.9	11.6
950	Location-level Holdings, Call Numbers, etc.	86.5	58.9
955	Copy-level Holdings, Call Numbers, etc.	80.7	37.6

Table A.28: Serials Display Summary

```
+-------------------------------------------------------------------------+
|                    Serials (35,765 items tested)                        |
|                                                                         |
|              NUMBER OF SCREENS REQUIRED FOR DISPLAY        Local         |
|   Display  One/Hold     One      Two      Three    Four +  Density       |
|   -------  ---------  --------- -------- --------- -------- ---------     |
|   CMTN       97.2%      99.7%     0.3%    <0.1%      --      20.1%        |
|   CMSX       90.6%      99.0%     1.0%    <0.1%      --      20.0%        |
|   CMSL       84.4%      97.7%     2.2%    <0.1%    <0.1%     19.0%        |
|                                                                         |
|   CMCIT      94.2%      99.2%     0.8%    <0.1%    <0.1%     19.2%        |
|   CMTCIT     93.9%      99.1%     0.8%    <0.1%    <0.1%     19.2%        |
|                                                                         |
|   LMG        93.5%      99.1%     0.9%    <0.1%    <0.1%     23.2%        |
|   LMGCON     95.7%      99.5%     0.5%    <0.1%      --      23.6%        |
|                                                                         |
|   LMGSP      81.6%      97.3%     2.7%    <0.1%    <0.1%     22.8%        |
|   LMGAT      71.6%      95.7%     4.3%    <0.1%    <0.1%     22.0%        |
|                                                                         |
|   LMTCIT     83.3%      97.6%     2.4%    <0.1%    <0.1%     20.1%        |
|   CXSIMPL    98.6%      99.9%     0.1%    <0.1%      --      14.5%        |
|   LXSIMPL    96.8%      99.6%     0.4%    <0.1%      --      15.9%        |
|                                                                         |
|   CXMATT     97.6%      99.8%     0.2%    <0.1%      --      15.2%        |
|   LXMATT     81.1%      97.8%     2.2%    <0.1%    <0.1%     16.3%        |
|                                                                         |
|   CXPLM1     99.4%    <100.0%    <0.1%      --        --     15.1%        |
|   LXPLM1     95.7%      99.7%     0.3%    <0.1%      --      17.0%        |
|                                                                         |
|   CXPLM2     97.4%      99.8%     0.2%    <0.1%      --      18.5%        |
|   LXPLM2     90.5%      98.7%     1.2%    <0.1%    <0.1%     20.4%        |
|                                                                         |
|   CBRF1    <100.0%    <100.0%    <0.1%      --        --      9.0%        |
|   LBRF1    <100.0%    <100.0%    <0.1%      --        --     11.2%        |
|   CBCAP    <100.0%    <100.0%    <0.1%      --        --     10.1%        |
|                                                                         |
|   CLON1      23.6%      62.4%    35.6%     1.8%      0.2%     25.1%        |
|   CLCIT1     48.8%      78.9%    19.8%     1.2%      0.1%     26.8%        |
|   LLON1      23.4%      58.1%    39.3%     2.3%      0.2%     27.0%        |
|                                                                         |
|   MDSBRF     99.9%    <100.0%    <0.1%      --        --     11.4%        |
|   KOBM       73.5%      96.3%     3.6%    <0.1%    <0.1%     22.4%        |
|   MDSLON     18.6%      49.7%    46.5%     3.4%      0.5%     25.3%        |
+-------------------------------------------------------------------------+
```

Table A.29: Field Occurrence, Sound Recordings (Part 1)

Tag	SOUND RECORDINGS Description [4,450 records]	Occurrences per hundred	Average Length
007	Physical Description Fixed Field	68.3	14.0
010	LC Control Number (LCCN)	30.9	12.2
020	ISBN	4.4	7.0
024	Standard Recording Number	4.7	10.2
028	Publisher Number for Music	93.6	21.3
033	Capture Date and Place	18.9	17.2
035	System Control Number	16.7	9.8
040	Cataloging Source	75.9	14.3
041	Language Code	35.8	11.5
043	Geographic Area Code	8.7	7.1
045	Chronological Code or Date/Time	39.2	7.9
047	Form of Composition Code	11.8	9.3
048	Number of Instruments or Voices Code	46.6	11.0
050	Library of Congress Class/Call Number	22.5	7.8
082	Dewey Decimal Classification Number	0.1	5.7
090	Local call number (& other local inf.)	100.0	18.3
100	Main Entry - Personal Name	76.3	27.2
110	Main Entry - Corporate Name	3.0	23.3
111	Main Entry - Conference or Meeting	0.9	81.3
130	Main Entry - Uniform Title	0.1	27.3
240	Uniform Title	46.7	31.7
245	Title Statement	100.0	70.8
260	Publication, Distribution, etc. (Imprint)	75.8	37.7
262	Imprint Statement for Sound Recordings	18.5	33.2
300	Physical Description	77.1	42.3
305	Physical Description for Sound Recordings	18.9	38.1
306	Duration	23.8	15.8
410	Series Statement - Corporate Name/Title	0.4	82.7
440	Series Statement - Title (Traced)	6.3	31.5
490	Series Untraced or Traced Differently	14.2	27.0
500	General Note	157.9	55.7
501	"With" Note	4.6	69.1
503	Bibliographic History Note	0.4	79.1
504	Bibliography/Discography Note	0.4	32.8
505	Contents Note (Formatted)	28.8	302.5
506	Restrictions on Access	0.1	61.0

Table A.30: Field Occurrence, Sound Recordings (Part 2)

Tag	SOUND RECORDINGS [Continued] Description [4,450 records]	Occurrences per hundred	Average Length
510	Citation Note (Brief Form)/References	0.4	42.3
511	Participant or Performer Note	65.5	95.4
518	Data on Capture Session Note	23.5	64.1
520	Summary, Abstract, Annotation, etc.	1.2	174.6
533	Reproduction Note	2.4	60.3
534	Original Version Note	0.5	115.6
541	Immediate Source of Acquisition	1.6	36.8
590	Local Note	0.5	53.0
600	Subject Added Entry - Personal Name	2.7	39.9
610	Subject Added Entry - Corporate Name	0.3	34.8
630	Subject Added Entry - Uniform Title	0.1	29.2
650	Subject Added Entry - Topical Heading	127.4	22.4
651	Subject Added Entry - Geographic Name	1.3	37.6
690	Local Subject A.E. - Topical Heading	6.7	23.5
700	Added Entry - Personal Name	284.2	40.5
710	Added Entry - Corporate Name	58.3	33.0
711	Added Entry - Conference or Meeting	0.2	69.7
730	Added Entry - Uniform Title Heading	2.7	30.0
740	Added Entry - Title Traced Differently	35.7	22.0
773	Host Item Entry	1.9	57.2
796	Local A.E. - Personal Name	3.5	46.2
797	Local A.E. - Corporate Name	0.1	42.0
799	Local A.E. - Uniform Title Heading	1.4	32.6
800	Series Added Entry - Personal Name/Title	0.8	65.7
830	Series Added Entry - Uniform Title Heading	1.4	47.9
840	Series Added Entry - Title	1.0	43.2
870	Variant Personal Name	4.0	66.4
871	Variant Corporate Name	0.1	51.0
873	Variant Uniform Title	0.4	60.3
950	Location-level Holdings, Call Numbers, etc.	70.8	25.9
955	Copy-level Holdings, Call Numbers, etc.	65.6	31.0

Table A.31: Sound Recordings Display Summary

		NUMBER OF SCREENS REQUIRED FOR DISPLAY				Local
Display	One/Hold	One	Two	Three	Four +	Density
CMTN	76.3%	91.0%	8.1%	0.8%	0.1%	32.6%
CMSX	58.7%	85.7%	13.2%	1.1%	0.1%	30.9%
CMSL	37.9%	67.9%	28.4%	3.0%	0.7%	24.8%
CMCIT	56.1%	77.1%	19.9%	2.4%	0.6%	26.6%
CMTCIT	53.3%	75.1%	21.7%	2.5%	0.6%	26.1%
LMG	55.1%	76.4%	20.5%	2.6%	0.5%	30.4%
LMGCON	70.9%	89.9%	9.2%	0.8%	0.1%	35.5%
LMGSP	35.9%	65.9%	30.5%	3.0%	0.7%	28.0%
LMGAT	26.8%	59.4%	36.6%	3.3%	0.7%	26.1%
LMTCIT	35.8%	61.7%	34.1%	3.3%	0.8%	24.7%
CXSIMPL	81.4%	93.2%	6.0%	0.7%	0.1%	25.5%
LXSIMPL	59.3%	79.6%	18.2%	1.7%	0.5%	22.8%
CXMATT	68.4%	89.1%	9.9%	0.9%	0.1%	27.1%
LXMATT	23.2%	55.1%	40.5%	3.6%	0.8%	21.7%
CXPLM1	79.0%	92.1%	7.3%	0.6%	0.1%	24.0%
LXPLM1	67.6%	88.4%	10.8%	0.7%	0.1%	25.3%
CXPLM2	63.7%	80.2%	16.6%	2.5%	0.7%	32.9%
LXPLM2	38.5%	65.5%	28.1%	4.6%	1.8%	29.2%
CBRF1	100.0%	100.0%	--	--	--	14.8%
LBRF1	99.9%	100.0%	--	--	--	16.5%
CBCAP	100.0%	100.0%	--	--	--	15.9%
CLON1	13.1%	30.9%	55.9%	10.1%	3.0%	35.4%
CLCIT1	19.1%	36.9%	46.1%	12.6%	4.4%	33.3%
LLON1	9.9%	21.1%	53.2%	20.0%	5.7%	32.2%
MDSBRF	99.8%	100.0%	--	--	--	17.7%
KOBM	29.9%	61.1%	34.8%	3.4%	0.7%	27.1%
LMCAP	28.3%	60.0%	36.1%	3.2%	0.7%	25.9%
MDSLON	6.5%	16.6%	50.2%	24.7%	8.5%	30.4%

Sound Recordings (3,034 items tested)

Table A.32: Field Occurrence, Visual Materials (Part 1)

Tag	VISUAL MATERIAL Description [1,673 records]	Occurrences per hundred	Average Length
007	Physical Description Fixed Field	81.0	8.4
010	LC Control Number (LCCN)	9.1	12.5
020	ISBN	3.2	21.8
033	Capture Date and Place	0.4	16.5
035	System Control Number	32.8	9.4
040	Cataloging Source	72.6	13.1
041	Language Code	2.5	7.9
043	Geographic Area Code	17.5	7.7
044	Country of Producer Code	0.1	8.0
045	Chronological Code or Date/Time	1.2	5.0
050	Library of Congress Class/Call Number	5.8	6.2
052	Geographic Classification Code	0.1	9.0
060	National Library of Medicine Call Number	0.1	21.0
082	Dewey Decimal Classification Number	7.6	6.2
090	Local call number (& other local inf.)	100.0	15.2
100	Main Entry - Personal Name	4.7	18.7
110	Main Entry - Corporate Name	0.7	32.2
130	Main Entry - Uniform Title Heading	1.1	30.6
240	Uniform Title	0.3	12.1
245	Title Statement	100.0	77.8
250	Edition Statement	0.3	8.4
260	Publication, Distribution, etc. (Imprint)	95.6	46.1
261	Imprint Statement for Films	2.6	43.6
265	Source for Acquisition/Subscription Address	0.3	63.2
300	Physical Description	108.7	46.9
400	Series Statement - Personal Name/Title	0.1	41.0
440	Series Statement - Title (Traced)	10.3	23.8
490	Series Untraced or Traced Differently	13.6	29.3
500	General Note	129.0	45.7
501	"With" Note	0.8	87.5
505	Contents Note (Formatted)	4.0	240.1
506	Restrictions on Access	19.2	26.0

Table A.33: Field Occurrence, Visual Materials (Part 2)

Tag	VISUAL MATERIAL [Continued] Description [1,673 records]	Occurrences per hundred	Average Length
508	Credits Note	25.2	61.8
511	Participant or Performer Note	28.6	51.9
517	Categories of Films Note (Archival)	0.1	8.0
518	Data on Capture Session Note	0.7	65.8
520	Summary, Abstract, Annotation, etc.	69.6	180.2
521	Users/Intended Audience Note	22.0	10.1
561	Provenance	0.1	49.0
590	Local Note	0.8	39.6
600	Subject Added Entry - Personal Name	41.5	36.9
610	Subject Added Entry - Corporate Name	2.5	33.5
611	Subject Added Entry - Conference or Meeting	0.1	19.0
650	Subject Added Entry - Topical Heading	147.5	20.8
651	Subject Added Entry - Geographic Name	18.0	42.5
655	Genre/Form Heading	25.6	20.5
690	Local Subject A.E. - Topical Heading	4.1	25.5
691	Local Subject A.E. - Geographic Name	0.1	14.0
696	Local Subject A.E. - Personal Name	0.1	40.0
700	Added Entry - Personal Name	83.3	23.4
710	Added Entry - Corporate Name	46.2	29.9
730	Added Entry - Uniform Title Heading	1.7	35.6
740	Added Entry - Title Traced Differently	14.9	32.5
797	Local A.E. - Corporate Name	0.1	17.5
800	Series Added Entry - Personal Name/Title	0.1	75.0
830	Series Added Entry - Uniform Title Heading	3.6	49.0
840	Series Added Entry - Title	2.5	51.9
950	Location-level Holdings, Call Numbers, etc.	84.3	24.4
955	Copy-level Holdings, Call Numbers, etc.	38.4	38.8

Table A.34: Visual Materials Display Summary

```
Visual Material (1,114 items tested)

          NUMBER OF SCREENS REQUIRED FOR DISPLAY        Local
Display   One/Hold    One       Two     Three   Four +   Density
-------   --------  --------  --------  --------  --------  --------
CMTN       92.7%     99.3%     0.7%      --        --       29.9%
CMSX       75.2%     97.5%     2.5%      --        --       29.4%
CMSL       44.2%     81.7%    18.3%      --        --       24.4%

CMCIT      64.2%     89.9%    10.1%      --        --       25.9%
CMTCIT     63.9%     89.9%    10.1%      --        --       25.9%

LMG        67.4%     89.9%    10.1%      --        --       29.8%
LMGCON     88.2%     98.9%     1.1%      --        --       33.0%

LMGSP      40.6%     78.9%    21.1%      --        --       27.1%
LMGAT      32.0%     75.2%    24.8%      --        --       26.0%

LMTCIT     39.7%     82.7%    17.3%      --        --       25.5%
CXSIMPL    97.8%    100.0%      --       --        --       18.6%
LXSIMPL    76.0%     94.7%     5.3%      --        --       18.8%

CXMATT     97.8%    100.0%      --       --        --       18.6%
LXMATT     59.0%     88.9%    11.1%      --        --       17.7%

CXPLM1     97.4%     99.5%     0.4%     0.1%      0.1%      21.5%
LXPLM1     75.9%     92.2%     7.6%     0.1%      0.1%      21.3%

CXPLM2     94.8%     98.7%     1.1%     0.1%      0.1%      24.7%
LXPLM2     62.6%     88.8%    11.0%     0.1%      0.2%      23.8%

CBRF1     100.0%    100.0%      --       --        --       16.3%
LBRF1     100.0%    100.0%      --       --        --       18.6%
CBCAP     100.0%    100.0%      --       --        --       17.3%

CLON1       6.6%     25.6%    72.6%     1.6%      0.2%      31.7%
CLCIT1      9.1%     25.5%    72.1%     2.2%      0.2%      30.7%
LLON1       6.6%     16.3%    79.2%     4.2%      0.3%      31.2%

MDSBRF     99.9%    100.0%      --       --        --       18.6%
KOBM       35.8%     77.6%    22.4%      --        --       26.7%
LMCAP      35.6%     80.4%    19.6%      --        --       25.1%
MDSLON      3.4%     11.7%    79.7%     8.1%      0.5%      30.1%
```

Appendix B: MARC Tagged Listings for Sample Records

Figure B.1

```
010     ‡a    84023303↵
020     ‡a0-8092-5307-0 (pbk.) :‡c$7.95↵
050 0   ‡aGV875.D6‡bA53 1984↵
082 0   ‡a796.357/64/0977434‡219↵
100 10  ‡aAnderson, Sparky,‡d1934-↵
245 10  ‡aBless you boys :‡bdiary of the Detroit Tigers' 1984 season /‡cby Sparky
         Anderson, with Dan Ewald.↵
260 0   ‡aChicago :‡bContemporary Books,‡cc1984.↵
300     ‡a231 p. :‡bill. ;‡c23 cm.↵
610 20  ‡aDetroit Tigers (Baseball team)↵
700 10  ‡aEwald, Dan.↵
```

Figure B.2

```
020     ‡a0-517-50951-2 :‡c$14.95↵
245 00  ‡aBest American plays :‡bsixth series, 1963-1967 /‡cedited by John Gassne
         r and Clive Barnes, with an introduction and prefaces to the plays by Cli
         ve Barnes.↵
260 0   ‡aNew York :‡bCrown,‡cc1971.↵
300     ‡axii, 594 p. ;‡c24 cm.↵
505 0   ‡aTiny Alice / E. Albee -- Blues for Mister Charlie / J. Baldwin -- The l
         ast analysis / S. Bellow -- Hogan's goat / W. Alfred -- The fantasticks /
          T. Jones -- The sign in Sidney Brustein's window / L. Hansberry -- The l
         ion in winter / J. Goldman -- Hughie / E. O'Neill -- The toilet / L. Jone
         s -- You know I can't hear you when the water is running / R. Anderson --
          Benito Cereno / R. Lowell -- Fiddler on the roof / J. Stein -- Slow danc
         e on the killing ground / W. Hanley -- In white America / M.B. Duberman -
         - The owl and the pussycat / B. Manhoff -- The odd couple / W. Simon -- T
         he subject was roses / F.D. Gilroy.↵
650 0   ‡aAmerican drama‡y20th century.↵
650 0   ‡aAmerican drama‡xCollected works.↵
700 10  ‡aGassner, John,‡d1903-1967.↵
700 10  ‡aBarnes, Clive,‡d1927-↵
740 00  ‡aTiny Alice.↵
740 00  ‡aBlues for Mister Charlie.↵
740 40  ‡aThe last analysis.↵
740 00  ‡aHogan's goat.↵
740 40  ‡aThe fantasticks.↵
740 40  ‡aThe sign in Sidney Brustein's window.↵
740 40  ‡aThe lion in winter.↵
740 00  ‡aHughie.↵
740 40  ‡aThe toilet.↵
740 00  ‡aYou know I can't hear you when the water's running.↵
740 00  ‡aBenito Cereno.↵
740 00  ‡aFiddler on the roof.↵
740 00  ‡aSlow dance on the killing ground.↵
740 00  ‡aIn white America.↵
740 40  ‡aThe owl and the pussycat.↵
740 40  ‡aThe odd couple.↵
740 40  ‡aThe subject was roses.↵
```

Figure B.3

```
010      ‡a    80014486//r854↵
020      ‡a0-87123-023-2 (pbk.) :‡c$4.95↵
050  0   ‡aBS391.2‡b.M47↵
082  0   ‡a220/.0216‡219↵
130  00  ‡aBible.‡lEnglish.‡sAuthorized.‡kSelections.‡f1980.↵
245  10  ‡aMeredith's book of Bible lists /‡cJ. L. Meredith.↵
260  0   ‡aMinneapolis, Minn. :‡bBethany Fellowship,‡cc1980.↵
300      ‡a287 p. :‡bill. ;‡c22 cm.↵
500      ‡aConsists to a large extent of Bible quotations.↵
504      ‡aIncludes bibliographical references.↵
630  00  ‡aBible‡xIndexes.↵
700  10  ‡aMeredith, J. L.‡q(Joel L.),‡d1935–↵
740  01  ‡aBook of Bible lists.↵
```

Figure B.4

```
028  32  ‡bDerry Music Co.‡aD233.↵
100  10  ‡aBrubeck, Dave.↵
240  10  ‡aBossa nova U.S.A.‡kSelections;‡oarr.↵
245  10  ‡aBossa nova U.S.A. /‡c[as performed by] the Dave Brubeck Quartet ; piano
         solo transcriptions by Howard Brubeck.↵
260  0   ‡aSan Francisco, Calif. :‡bDerry Music Co. ;‡a New York, N.Y. :‡bC. Hanse
         n, distributor,‡cc1963.↵
300      ‡a49 p. of music ;‡c28 cm.↵
500      ‡aJazz quartets arr. for piano solo; chord symbols and fingerings include
         d.↵
500      ‡a"Trolley song and This can't be love do not appear in this collection d
         ue to copyright restrictions."↵
500      ‡aNotes on the music by Dave Brubeck, principal composer, on covers.↵
505  0   ‡aBossa nova U.S.A. / Dave Brubeck -- Vento fresco = Cool wind / Dave Br
         ubeck -- Theme for June / Howard R. Brubeck -- Cora͵c~ao sensivel = Tende
         r heart / Teo Macero -- Irm~ao amigo = Brother friend / Dave Brubeck -- T
         here'll be no tomorrow / Dave Brubeck -- Cantiga nov swing = Swing a new
         song / Dave Brubeck -- Lamento = Lament / Dave Brubeck.↵
650  0   ‡aPiano music (Jazz), Arranged.↵
650  0   ‡aJazz quartets‡zPiano scores.↵
700  11  ‡aBrubeck, Howard R.↵
700  12  ‡aBrubeck, Howard R.‡tTheme for June;‡oarr.↵
700  12  ‡aMacero, Teo,‡d1925–‡tCora͵c~ao sensivel;‡oarr.↵
710  21  ‡aDave Brubeck Quartet.↵
740  01  ‡aBossa nova USA.↵
```

Figure B.5

```
010     ‡a    82600311⤶
050  0  ‡aTN295‡b.U4 no. 8907‡aTN311⤶
082  0  ‡a622 s‡a622/.8‡219⤶
086     ‡aI 19.4/2:8907⤶
111  20 ‡aBureau of Mines Technology Transfer Seminars‡d(1982 :‡cPittsburgh, Pa.)
        ⤶
245  10 ‡aPostdisaster survival and rescue research :‡bproceedings, Bureau of Min
        es Technology Transfer Seminar, Pittsburgh, Pa., November 16, 1982 /‡ccom
        piled by staff, Bureau of Mines.⤶
260  0  ‡a[Avondale, Md.] :‡bU.S. Dept. of the Interior, Bureau of Mines,‡c1982.⤶
300     ‡aiii, 91 p. :‡bill. ;‡c28 cm.⤶
490  1  ‡aBureau of Mines information circular ;‡v8907⤶
504     ‡aIncludes bibliographies.⤶
650  0  ‡aMine accidents‡xCongresses.⤶
650  0  ‡aMine rescue work‡xCongresses.⤶
710  10 ‡aUnited States.‡bBureau of Mines.⤶
830  0  ‡aInformation circular (United States. Bureau of Mines) ;‡v8907.⤶
```

Figure B.6

```
245  00 ‡aCitizen Kane‡h[videorecording] /‡can RKO Radio Picture ; a Mercury prod
        uction ; Orson Welles, direction, production.⤶
260     ‡aNew York, N.Y. :‡bVidAmerica,‡cc1982.⤶
300     ‡a1 videocassette (119 min.) :‡bsd., b&w ;‡c1/2 in.⤶
490  0  ‡aClassic series⤶
511  1  ‡aOrson Welles, Joseph Cotton, Agnes Moorehead, Everett Sloane.⤶
508     ‡aPhotography, Gregg Toland ; music, Bernard Herrmann ; screenplay, Orson
         Welles, Herman J. Mankiewicz.⤶
500     ‡aOriginally produced as motion picture in 1941.⤶
500     ‡aVHS.⤶
500     ‡a1941 Academy Award for best screenplay.⤶
520     ‡aA story of the rise and fall of a great man as the result of his accumu
        lation of wealth and subsequent isolation from the world. Based on the li
        fe of newspaper tycoon William Randolph Hearst, this is classic American
        cinema.⤶
500     ‡aVidAmerica: #903.⤶
650  0  ‡aFeature films.⤶
700  11 ‡aWelles, Orson,‡d1915-⤶
700  21 ‡aVidAmerica (Firm)⤶
710  21 ‡aRKO Radio Pictures, inc.⤶
710  21 ‡aMercury Productions.⤶
```

Figure B.7

```
100  3    ‡aDouglass family.←
245 00    ‡kPapers,‡f1812-1911.←
300       ‡a8 linear ft., 3 v. [outsize] and 20 items [outsize].←
545       ‡aPapers of Benjamin Douglass and his sons, Samuel T. Douglass, Detroit a
          ttorney and jurist, and Silas H. Douglas(s), professor of .chemistry at th
          e University of Michigan, and member of Douglass Houghton's Northern Mich
          igan survey.←
520       ‡aCorrespondence, scrapbooks, letter books, and miscellanea concerning fa
          mily affairs, business and University activities; papers of the Douglass
          and Walker and Campbell Law Firm; miscellaneous papers of the Douglass an
          d Welles families; and photographs. Correspondents include: James V. Camp
          bell, Henry H. Crapo, George Duffield, Douglass Houghton, Jonathan Kearsl
          ey, Zina Pitcher, Abram Sager, Joseph Sibley, Henry P. Tappan, Edward C.
          Walker, Henry N. Walker.←
555       ‡aFinding aid in the library.←
500       ‡aDonor: 183, 1278, 2916←
541       ‡*Y‡31←
583       ‡31‡*Y‡an‡c1901←
655       ‡aPhotoprints.←
655       ‡aTintypes.←
655       ‡aDaguerreotypes.←
610 10    ‡aDetroit (Mich.).‡bBoard of Water Commissioners.←
651  0    ‡aFlat River (Mich.)←
651  0    ‡aGrosse Ile (Mich.)←
600 10    ‡aHoughton, Douglass,‡d1809-1845.←
656  7    ‡aLawyers.‡2lcsh←
610 20    ‡aMichigan Central Railroad.←
651  0    ‡aMichigan, Northern Peninsula.←
600 30    ‡aWelles family.←
700 11    ‡aCampbell, James V.‡q(James Valentine),‡d1823-1890.←
700 11    ‡aCrapo, Henry Howland,‡d1804-1869.←
700 11    ‡aDouglas, Silas Hamilton,‡d1816-1890.←
700 11    ‡aDouglass, Benjamin.←
700 11    ‡aDouglass, Samuel Townsend,‡d1814-1898.←
700 11    ‡aDuffield, George,‡d1794-1868.←
700 11    ‡aKearsley, Jonathan,‡d1786-1859.←
700 11    ‡aPitcher, Zina,‡d1797-1872.←
700 11    ‡aSager, Abram,‡d1810-1877.←
700 11    ‡aSibley, Joseph.←
700 11    ‡aTappan, Henry Philip,‡d1805-1881.←
700 11    ‡aWalker, Edward Carey,‡d1820-1894.←
700 11    ‡aWalker, Henry Nelson,‡d1811-1886.←
700 11    ‡aWilliams, George Palmer,‡d1802-1881.←
851       ‡aBentley Historical Library,‡bUniversity of Michigan,‡cAnn Arbor, Michig
          an 48109-2113←
```

Figure B.8

```
010    ‡a    84760155/R←
028 00 ‡aMCE 71423‡bErato←
028 02 ‡aSTU 71423‡bErato←
050 0  ‡aErato STU 71423←
100 10 ‡aIndy, Vincent d',‡d1851-1931.←
240 10 ‡aInstrumental music.‡kSelections←
245 10 ‡aSuite en r′e dans le style ancien :‡bop. 24 ; Karadec : op. 34 ; Concer
       t, op. 89 pour piano, fl^ute, violoncello et orchestre ^a cordes‡h[sound
       recording] /‡cVincent d'Indy.←
260 0  ‡aFrance :‡bErato ;‡aParis :‡bDistribution en France RCA,‡cp1982.←
300    ‡a1 sound disc :‡b33 1/3 rpm, stereo. ;‡c12 in.←
500    ‡aThe 2nd work incidental music.←
511 0  ‡aJean-Pierre Rampal, Philippe Pierlot, flutes, Maurice Andr′e, trumpet (
       in the 1st work) ; Francois-Ren′e Duch^able, piano, Jean-Pierre Rampal, f
       lute, Fr′ed′eric Lod′eon, violoncello (in the 3rd) ; Orchestre de chambre
        Jean-Fran͵cois Paillard ; Jean-Fran͵cois Paillard, conductor.←
518    ‡aRecorded Jan. and Apr., 1981, l'IRCAM-Espace de Projection, Paris.←
500    ‡aEds. recorded: Heugel.←
500    ‡aIssued also as cassette: MCE 71423.←
650 0  ‡aSuites (Flutes (2), trumpet with string orchestra)←
650 0  ‡aMusic, Incidental.←
650 0  ‡aConcertos (Piano, flute, violoncello with string orchestra)←
700 10 ‡aRampal, Jean Pierre.‡4prf←
700 10 ‡aPierlot, Philippe.‡4prf←
700 10 ‡aAndr′e, Maurice.‡4prf←
700 10 ‡aDuch^able, Fran͵cois.‡4prf←
700 10 ‡aLod′eon, Fr′ed′eric.‡4prf←
700 10 ‡aPaillard, Jean Fran͵cois.‡4cnd←
700 12 ‡aIndy, Vincent d',‡d1851-1931.‡tSuite dans le style ancien.‡f1982.←
700 12 ‡aIndy, Vincent d',‡d1851-1931.‡tKaradec.‡f1982.←
700 12 ‡aIndy, Vincent d',‡d1851-1931.‡tConcerto,‡mpiano, flute, violoncello, or
       chestra,‡nop. 89.‡f1982.←
710 20 ‡aOrchestre de chambre Jean-Fran͵cois Paillard.‡4prf←
740 01 ‡aKaradec.←
```

Figure B.9

```
100 10 ‡aLora, Antonio John,‡d1899-1965.←
245 10 ‡aIn June :‡bsong for voice and piano /‡clyrics [by] Helen Field Watson ;
       music [by] Antonio Lora.←
260 0  ‡aNew York :‡bAmerican Composers Alliance,‡c[19--].←
300    ‡a1 score (5 p.)  ;‡c32 cm.←
500    ‡aFor medium voice and piano.←
500    ‡aCover title.←
500    ‡aReproduced from holograph.←
500    ‡aDuration: 2:45.←
650 0  ‡aSongs (Medium voice) with piano.←
600 10 ‡9x‡aWatson, Helen Field‡xMusical settings.←
700 10 ‡9x‡aWatson, Helen Field.←
```

Figure B.10

```
010      ‡a    83750689/R⤸
028 02 ‡bArchiv Produktion‡a2723 068 (2565 127--2565 129).⤸
050 0  ‡aM5⤸
245 04 ‡aDie Mannheimer Schule‡h[sound recording] :‡bMusik der Fr¨uhklassik = mu
         sic of the early classical era.⤸
260 0  ‡a[West Germany] :‡bArchiv Produktion,‡cp1980.⤸
300      ‡a3 sound discs :‡b33 1/3 rpm, stereo. ;‡c12 in.⤸
500      ‡aTitle from container.⤸
511 0  ‡aVarious soloists ; Camerata Bern ; Thomas F¨uri, conductor.⤸
518      ‡aRecorded in the Konservatorium Bern, Sept. 24-29, 1979 (1st-4th, 7th-8t
         h, 10th works) and DRS-Radio-Studio, Bern, Feb. 12-15, 1980 (the remainde
         r)⤸
500      ‡aProgram notes by Heinz Becker and notes on the ensemble by Urs Frauchin
         ger in German with English and French translations (12 p. : ill.) laid in
          container.⤸
505 0  ‡aSinfonia B-Dur (10:37) ; Konzert f¨ur Fl¨ote und Streichorchester e-Mol
         l (Aur^ele Nicolet, flute)  (19:30) / Franz Xaver Richter -- Konzert f¨ur
          Violine und Streichorchester C-Dur (Thomas F¨uri, violin) (15:47) ; Orch
         estertrio B-Dur op. 1, 5 (14:47) / Johann Stamitz -- Konzert f¨ur Violonc
         ello und Streichorchester G-Dur / Anton Filtz (Thomas Demenga, violoncell
         o) (21:19) -- Sinfonia concertante A-Dur, Vl. Solo, Vla. Solo, Vlc. Solo
         (Thomas F¨uri, violin ; Christoph Schiller, viola ; Thomas Demenga, violo
         ncello) (15:16) ; Sinfonia Es-Dur op. 4, 3 (15:06) / Ignaz Holzbauer -- S
         infonia concertante C-Dur, Fl. Solo, Ob. Solo, Fag. Solo (Aur^ele Nicolet
         , flute ; Heinz Holliger, oboe ; Manfred Sax, bassoon) (8:40) ; Sinfonia
         B-dur (16:41) / Christian Cannabich -- Konzert f¨ur Oboe und Orchester d-
         Moll / Ludwig August Lebrun (Heinz Holliger, oboe) (19:32)⤸
650 0  ‡aOrchestral music‡y18th century.⤸
650 0  ‡aString orchestra music‡y18th century.⤸
650 0  ‡aMusic‡zGermany‡y18th century.⤸
650 0  ‡aConcertos (Violin with string orchestra)⤸
650 0  ‡aSymphonies (String orchestra)⤸
650 0  ‡aConcertos (Violoncello with string orchestra)⤸
650 0  ‡aConcertos (Oboe with string orchestra)⤸
650 0  ‡aConcertos (Flute and string orchestra)⤸
```

Figure B.11

```
  Die Mannheimer Schule (CONTINUED)
700 10 ‡aHolliger, Heinz.‡4prf←
700 10 ‡aF¨uri, Thomas.‡4prf←
700 10 ‡aDemenga, Thomas.‡4prf←
700 10 ‡aSax, Manfred.‡4prf←
700 10 ‡aSchiller, Christoph.‡4prf←
700 10 ‡aNicolet, Aur^ele.‡4prf←
700 12 ‡aCannabich, Christian,‡d1731-1798.‡tSinfonie concertanti,‡mflute, oboe,
        bassoon, orchestra,‡rC major.‡f1980.←
700 12 ‡aCannabich, Christian,‡d1731-1798.‡tSymphonies,‡rBb major.‡f1980.←
700 12 ‡aFiltz, Johann Anton,‡dca. 1730-1760.‡tConcertos,‡mvioloncello, string o
        rchestra,‡rG major.‡f1980.←
700 12 ‡aHolzbauer, Ignaz,‡d1711-1783.‡tSinfonie concertanti,‡mviolin, viola, vi
        oloncello, string orchestra,‡rA major.‡f1980.←
700 12 ‡aHolzbauer, Ignaz,‡d1711-1783.‡tSymphonies,‡nop. 4.‡nNo. 3.‡f1980.←
700 12 ‡aLebrun, Ludwig August,‡d1752-1790.‡tConcertos,‡moboe, orchestra,‡rD min
        or.‡f1980.←
700 12 ‡aRichter, Franz Xaver,‡d1709-1789.‡tSymphonies,‡mstring orchestra,‡rBb m
        ajor.‡f1980.←
700 12 ‡aRichter, Franz Xaver,‡d1709-1789.‡tConcertos,‡mflute, string orchestra,
        ‡rE minor.‡f1980.←
700 12 ‡aStamitz, Johann,‡d1717-1757.‡tConcertos,‡mviolin, string orchestra,‡rC
        major.‡f1980.←
700 12 ‡aStamitz, Johann,‡d1717-1757.‡tTrio sonatas,‡mviolins, continuo,‡nop.1.‡
        nNo. 5.‡f1980.←
710 20 ‡aCamerata Bern.‡4prf←
```

Figure B.12

```
010     ‡a   74695811/MAPS/r75←
050 0   ‡aG5131.S3 1779‡b.P5 1974←
052     ‡a5131←
245 00  ‡aPlan of the French attacks upon the island of Grenada,‡bwith the engage
        ment between the English fleet under the command of Admiral Byron and the
         French fleet under Count d'Estaing,‡cdrawn by an officer on board the fl
        eet, July 1779. J. Luffman, sc.←
260 0   ‡aLondon,‡bJ. Haris,‡c1779.‡a[Chicago,‡bRand McNally and Co.,‡c1974?]←
300     ‡acol. map‡c22 x 35 cm.←
507     ‡aScale ca. 1:14,700.←
500     ‡aFacsimile.←
500     ‡aRelief shown by hachures.←
500     ‡aOriented with north to the left.←
500     ‡aPictorial map.←
500     ‡aIncludes descriptive notes.←
650 0   ‡aGrenada, Battle of, 1779‡xMaps‡yTo 1800.←
650 0   ‡aMaps, Early‡xFacsimiles.←
700 10  ‡aLuffman, John,‡d1756-1846.←
710 20  ‡aRand McNally and Company.←
```

Figure B.13

```
028 03 ‡bRCA Victor‡aM127.←
100 10 ‡aSchoenberg, Arnold,‡d1874-1951.←
245 10 ‡aGurre-Lieder‡h[sound recording] /‡cSch"onberg ; (words by Jacobsen).←
260 0  ‡aCamden, N.J. :‡bRCA,‡c1932.←
300    ‡a14 sound discs :‡b78 rpm, mono. ;‡c12 in. +‡e1 pamphlet‡a(11 p. ;‡c24 c
       m.)←
500    ‡aRCA Victor M127, 7524-7537 (side 1: Mx. d72621, side 2: Mx .b71674, sid
       e 5: Mx. a71677, side 6: Mx. a71678, side 7: Mx. 71679, side 8: Mx. a7168
       0, side 9: Mx. a71681, side 10: Mx. a71682, side 11: Mx. a71683, side 12:
        Mx. a71684, side 13: Mx. a71685, side 14: Mx. a71686, side 15: Mx. a7168
       7, side 16: Mx. a71688, side 17: Mx. a71689, side 18: Mx. a71690, side 19
       : Mx. a71691, side 20: Mx. a71692, side 21: Mx. a71693, side 22: Mx. e716
       94. side 23: Mx. a71695, side 24: Mx. a71696, side 25: Mx. a71712, side 2
       6: Mx. a71713)←
500    ‡aCantata for speaker, solo voices (SATTB), one chorus (SSAATTBB), three
       choruses (TTBB), and large orchestra.←
500    ‡aSung in German.←
511 0  ‡aJeanette Vreeland (Tove) ; Rose Bampton (Waldtaube) ; Paul Althouse (Wa
       ldemar) ; Robert Betts (Klaus-Narr) ; Abrasha Robofsky (Bauer) ; Benjamin
        de Loache, narrator; Princeton Glee Club; Fortnightly Club; Mendelssohn
       Club; Philadelphia Orchestra; Leopold Stokowski, conductor.←
518    ‡aRecorded April 11, 1932 at the Metropolitan Opera House, Philadelphia.←
650 0  ‡aCantatas, Secular (Mixed voices) with orchestra.←
600 10 ‡aJacobsen, J. P.‡q(Jens Peter),‡d1847-1885‡xMusical settings.←
700 11 ‡aStokowski, Leopold.‡4prf←
710 21 ‡aPhiladelphia Orchestra.‡4prf←
700 11 ‡aVreeland, Jeanette.‡4prf←
700 11 ‡aBampton, Rose.‡4prf←
700 11 ‡aBetts, Robert.‡4prf←
700 11 ‡aAlthouse, Paul.‡4prf←
700 11 ‡aRobofsky, Abrasha.‡4prf←
700 11 ‡aDe Loache, Benjamin.‡4prf←
710 20 ‡aPrinceton Glee Club.‡4prf←
710 20 ‡aFortnightly Club.‡4prf←
710 20 ‡aMendelssohn Club.‡4prf←
700 12 ‡aSchoenberg, Arnold,‡d1874-1951.‡tGurre-Lieder.‡kLibretto.‡lEnglish & Ge
       rman.←
700 10 ‡aArnold, Robert Franz,‡d1872-1938.←
```

Figure B.14

```
100 1   ‡aSchoenberg, Arnold,‡d1874-1951.↵
245 10  ‡aTheater der Dichtung.‡f23.Mai 1931 /‡cArnold Sch¨onberg.↵
300     ‡a[1]‡fleaf ;‡c30 cm.↵
340     ‡dHolograph signed‡c(black ink, blue and pink pencil),‡dprinted.↵
580     ‡aBears Schoenberg's classification: "K¨u 321".↵
546     ‡aIn German fraktur.↵
500     ‡aOn a printed 2 page circular by Karl Kraus with the same title.  Edges
        of leaf reinforced with strips of music manuscript paper, left side punch
        ed with 2 holes.↵
510 4   ‡aRufer.‡cSchriften IIE24.↵
510 4   ‡aChristensen, Jean & Jesper. From Arnold Schoenberg's Literary Legacy: A
         Catalog of Neglected Items. Detroit: Detroit Information Coordinators, [
        1986].‡cAppendix II.↵
530     ‡aMicrofiche‡d56.↵
520     ‡aThe circular is a call for money for the founding of an ensemble "Theat
        er der Dichtung" under the leadership of Karl Kraus.  Frank Wedekind comm
        ents on Kraus in the circular.  Schoenberg's lengthy annotations in the m
        argins criticize the circular.  First he is offended that there is no per
        sonal salutation.  He says the ensemble is a hopeless venture even under
        the leadership of Kraus.  He discusses performing and concludes that rath
        er than performing already-proven works, this "theater" should concentrat
        e on new or unknown works.↵
500     ‡aOpening words: "Es ist das 2te Mal, dass man mir so einen Zettel schick
        t [...]"↵
524     ‡aArnold Schoenberg Institute, Text Mss. Aesthetik 321, Box T1, Folder 21
        .↵
541     ‡*Y‡31↵
583     ‡31‡*Y‡an‡c1901↵
655 7   ‡aEssays.‡2rbgenr↵
650 0   ‡aPoetry.↵
650 0   ‡aTheater.↵
600 10  ‡aKraus, Karl,‡d1874-1936.↵
650 0   ‡aPerformance art.↵
650 0   ‡aOral interpretation.↵
655 7   ‡aProspectuses.‡2ftamc↵
600 0   ‡aSchoenberg, Arnold,‡d1874-1951‡xMarginalia.↵
650 0   ‡aManuscripts, German‡zCalifornia‡zLos Angeles.↵
700 10  ‡aSchoenberg, Arnold,‡d1874-1951.‡eann↵
700 12  ‡aKraus, Karl,‡d1874-1936.‡tTheater der Dichtung.↵
700 12  ‡aWedekind, Frank,‡d1864-1918.↵
740 00  ‡aK¨unste,‡n321.↵
740 00  ‡aAesthetik,‡n321.↵
740 00  ‡aEs ist das 2te Mal, dass man mir so einen Zettel schickt.↵
740 00  ‡aMit diesem Aufruf appellieren wir an alle.↵
773 0   ‡7p1bc‡aSchoenberg, Arnold, 1874-1951.‡tAesthetik, b).‡d1910-1932.‡w(CLAS
        )CASG86-A13↵
```

Figure B.15

```
020     ‡a0-13-081026-6 (set)⤺
100 1   ‡aSpikell, Mark A.⤺
245 10  ‡aBrain ticklers, Apple II, IIe edition‡h[machine-readable data file] :‡b
        mathematical problem-solving with the microcomputer /‡cMark A. Spikell &
        Stephen L. Snover.⤺
260     ‡aEnglewood Cliffs, N.J. :‡bPrentice-Hall,‡cc1983.⤺
300     ‡a1 program file on 1 computer disk ;‡c5 1/4 in. +‡einstructions (iv, 6 p
        .) + 2 books in loose-leaf binder.⤺
500     ‡aAccompanying books titled: Brain ticklers : puzzles & pastimes for prog
        rammable calculators & personal computers; and Mathematical problem-solvi
        ng with the microcomputer : projects to increase your BASIC programming s
        kill.⤺
538     ‡aSystem requirements: 48K; single-disk drive; programs written in Apples
        oft BASIC; DOS 3.3.⤺
650  0  ‡aMathematics‡xProblems, exercises, etc.⤺
650  0  ‡aMathematics‡xComputer programs.⤺
650  0  ‡aApple computer‡xProgramming.⤺
650  0  ‡aProblem solving‡xData processing.⤺
700 10  ‡aSnover, Stephen L.⤺
740 01  ‡aMathematical problem-solving with the microcomputer.⤺
753     ‡aApple II‡bApplesoft Basic‡cDOS 3.3⤺
753     ‡aApple IIe‡bApplesoft Basic‡cDOS 3.3⤺
```

Figure B.16

```
010     ‡a    84692964/MAPS⤺
017     ‡aVA 127-611‡bU.S. Copyright Office⤺
050 0   ‡aG4371.E635 1983 ‡b.S7⤺
052     ‡a4371⤺
100 1   ‡aStewart, William Herman,‡d1932--⤺
245 14  ‡aThe explorer's historical tourist map of Alaska, with maps of Anchorage
        , Fairbanks & Juneau :‡bwith notes on the Arctic, wildlife, hunting, fish
        ing, camping, exploring & prospecting, festivals & events /‡ccartography
        by William H. Stewart.⤺
255     ‡aScale [ca. 1:3,200,000]‡c(E 172°--W 130°/N 70°--N 52°).⤺
260 0   ‡aCharleston, W.Va. :‡bEconomic Service Council,‡c1983.⤺
300     ‡a1 map :‡bcol. ;‡c65 x 71 cm., folded to 23 x 11 cm.⤺
500     ‡aPanel title.⤺
500     ‡aPictorial map.⤺
500     ‡aIncludes inset of the Aleutian Islands, notes, 3 diagrams, and ill.⤺
500     ‡aAncillary maps: Comparative size of Alaska -- Top of the world -- Junea
        u -- Fairbanks -- Anchorage.⤺
651  0  ‡aAlaska‡xMaps, Tourist.⤺
651  0  ‡aAlaska‡xMaps, Pictorial.⤺
```

Figure B.17

```
010      ‡a    25011669↵
022 0  ‡a0040-781X↵
050 0  ‡aAP2‡b.T37↵
082      ‡a051↵
210 0  ‡aTime‡b(Chicago)↵
222 10 ‡aTime‡b(Chicago)↵
245 00 ‡aTime.↵
260 00 ‡a[Chicago, etc.,‡bTime Inc.]↵
265      ‡aTime Inc., 10880 Wilshire Blvd., Los Angeles, CA 90024-4193↵
300      ‡av.‡bill. (incl. ports.)‡c28 cm.↵
310      ‡aWeekly‡b<, April 15, 1985->↵
321      ‡aWeekly (except one week a year)‡b<, Dec. 26, 1977->↵
350      ‡a$51.50↵
362 0  ‡av. 1-    Mar. 3, 1923-↵
510 2  ‡aABI/INFORM‡bMarch 1975-Jan. 1978↵
510 1  ‡aAbridged readers' guide to periodical literature‡x0001-334X↵
510 2  ‡aBook review index‡x0524-0581↵
510 2  ‡aCumulative index to nursing & allied health literature‡x0146-5554↵
510 2  ‡aFilm literature index‡x0093-6758↵
510 2  ‡aHospital literature index‡x0018-5736↵
510 2  ‡aInfobank‡bJan. 1969-↵
510 2  ‡aPopular magazine review‡x0740-3763‡b1984-↵
510 2  ‡aPredicasts↵
510 0  ‡aBiography index‡x0006-3053↵
510 1  ‡aReaders' guide to periodical literature‡x0034-0464↵
510 2  ‡aMedia review digest‡x0363-7778↵
510 2  ‡aEnergy information abstracts‡x0147-6521↵
510 2  ‡aEnvironment abstracts‡x0093-3287↵
555      ‡aIndividual indexes cumulated in one volume, v. 35-44.↵
555      ‡aVols. 45-60, 1945-52. 1 v.↵
570      ‡aEditors: 1923-<24> B. Hadden, H. R. Luce.↵
700 11 ‡aHadden, Briton,‡eed.↵
700 11 ‡aLuce, Henry Robinson,‡d1898-‡eed.↵
780 05 ‡tLiterary digest (New York, N.Y. : 1937)↵
```

Figure B.18

```
010      ‡a    85040161↵
020      ‡a0-394-54689-X↵
050 0  ‡aPS3570.Y45‡bA64 1985↵
082 0  ‡a813/.54‡219↵
100 10 ‡aTyler, Anne.↵
245 14 ‡aThe accidental tourist /‡cAnne Tyler.↵
250      ‡a1st ed.↵
260 0  ‡aNew York :‡bKnopf :‡bDistributed by Random House,‡c1985.↵
300      ‡a355 p. ;‡c22 cm.↵
```

Figure B.19

```
245 00  ‡aU.S. Naval Observatory time signals.‡nBulletin A.←
246 10  ‡aTime signals.‡nBulletin A←
260 01  ‡a[Washington, D.C. :‡bThe Observatory,‡c1953--←
300     ‡av. ;‡c36 cm.←
362 0   ‡a1 (2 June 1953)--←
500     ‡aTitle from caption.←
580     ‡aMerged with: U.S. Naval Observatory time signals. Bulletin B, to form:
        Time signals.←
650  0  ‡aTime-signals‡xPeriodicals.←
710 20  ‡aUnited States Naval Obsevatory.←
785 17  ‡tU.S. Naval Observatory time signals. Bulletin B←
785 17  ‡tTime signals←
```

Figure B.20

```
050     ‡aPS3545 .I765 A17 1960A←
100     ‡aWinters, Yvor,‡d1900--←
245 00  ‡aCollected poems.←
250     ‡a[Rev. ed.]←
260     ‡aChicago,‡bSwallow Press‡c[c1960]←
300     ‡a146 p.‡c19 cm.←
490     ‡aA Swallow paperbook←
```

Figure B.21

```
028 02  ‡bElektra‡a60283←
110 20  ‡aX (Musical group)←
245 10  ‡aMore fun in the new world‡h[sound recording] /‡cX.←
260 0   ‡aLos Angeles, CA :‡bElektra,‡cc1983.←
300     ‡a1 sound disc :‡b33 1/3 rpm, stereo. ;‡c12 in.←
650  0  ‡aRock music.←
```

References

This reference section includes only those items cited within the text.

Crawford, Walt. *Patron Access: Issues for Online Catalogs.* Forthcoming.

Crawford, Walt. *Patron Access Project: Phase I; Report to Phase II: Development Issues.* Stanford, CA: The Research Libraries Group, Inc.; 1985. (RLG Document Code 85-52.)

Matthews, Joseph S. "Screen Layouts and Displays." In *Online Catalog Design Issues: A Series of Discussions,* edited by Brian Aveney. Washington, DC: Council on Library Resources; 1984 July.

Palmer, Richard P. *Computerizing the Card Catalog in the University Library.* Littleton, CO: Libraries Unlimited; 1972.

Peters, Paul Evan, ed. *Command Language and Screen Displays for Public Online Systems: Report of a Meeting Sponsored by the Council on Library Resources, March 29–30, 1984, Dublin. OH.* Washington, DC: Council on Library Resources; 1985.

Index to Figures

This index includes the main entry, title, and display name for each figure in Chapters 1-8 and Appendix B.

General Index

About the Authors

Walt Crawford is the assistant director for Special Services at the Research Libraries Group (RLG). He was manager of the Product Batch Group at RLG from 1980 through August 1986. His previous experience in library automation is from the University of California, Berkeley. Mr. Crawford is currently a member of MARBI and editor of the *LITA Newsletter*. Mr. Crawford also wrote *MARC for Library Use: Understanding the USMARC Formats* and *Technical Standards: An Introduction for Librarians* (both published by Knowledge Industry Publications, Inc.), and *Common Sense Personal Computing* (Picrian Press). His next book, *Patron Access: Issues for Online Catalogs,* will be published by Knowledge Industry Publications, Inc. in early 1987.

Lennie Stovel is a library systems analyst in the Library Systems Division of the Research Libraries Group. She came to Stanford University in 1970 as an analyst for the BALLOTS Project. From 1983 to 1985, she was assistant municipal librarian for automation at the Anchorage Municipal Libraries, where she managed the installation of an integrated system that included an online catalog module.

Kathleen Bales has held a variety of positions at RLG, where she has worked since 1978; she is currently manager, Systems Analysis and Design. Her library experience includes technical services, circulation, public services and teaching Cataloging and Classification at the School of Library and Information Science, University of California, Berkeley. Ms. Bales is currently a member of MARBI and of the LITA Bylaws Committee; her professional participation in the past includes CCS committees in ALA, as well as ALA regional groups.

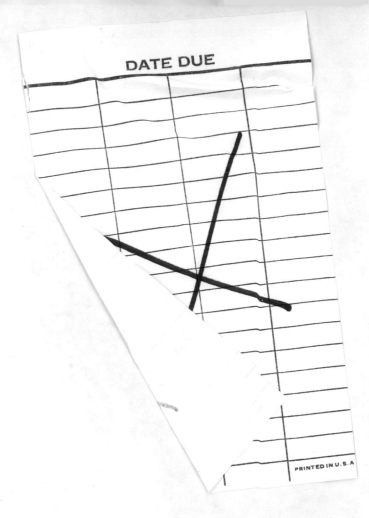

DATE DUE

PRINTED IN U.S.A

138 1109